"Don Scott, Sr. has written an epi[c that will] become a classic as a work of histor[y] of the Montier family from the 17th century to the 21st. Scott's writing is sharp, authoritative, and fluid …. *The Montiers* demonstrates the incredible human story of an African American family, intertwined with the various tributaries that enter from other cultures. *The Montiers* is a magisterial work with social and cultural implications … [commencing] when Richard Morrey, the son of Philadelphia's first mayor, the Quaker Humphrey Morrey, had five children by Cremona, a former enslaved woman who had worked for the Morrey family. The family would give us the Bustills, the Pickenses, the Robesons, the Bowsers, and even more, a picture of our evolving American nation. Scott's handling of this multifaceted narrative shows his fascinating talent at weaving a very believable account of our story. … It is the long-awaited epic story of one of the earliest Philadelphia families told by a master storyteller."
—Molefi Kete Asante, PhD, preeminent Afrocentricity scholar and Africology professor, author of *The African American People: A Global History* and many other titles

"Don Scott, Sr. gained recognition for his epic history on Camp William Penn and the United States Colored Troops during the Civil War. *The Montiers* puts this historian's deep knowledge of the black experience in Pennsylvania fighting for power and civil rights on a sweeping stage spanning the 18th century until today. It all starts with the incredible courage and valiant tenacity of enslaved house servant Cremona Morrey, who navigated 'landmines' to make a legacy for her interracial children, then tells the history of the settlement of Guineatown on her land, and continues with her descendants' activism through the lives of William Pickens, Sr., a co-founder of the NAACP, and the great singer and activist Paul Robeson, who devoted his life to the international cause of humanity for freedom and unity. Thank you, Don Scott, Sr., for your commitment to researching and honoring the lives of Cremona Morrey and so many other black Pennsylvanians who fought for their freedom and liberation and continue to inspire and change history through their example."
—Laurie Zierer, Executive Director of PA Humanities

"Don Scott, Sr. continues his mission of documenting the lives of people whose role in American history has been forgotten, disregarded or marginalized. As a result, he has illuminated vital parts of the American story. By focusing his latest work on the lives of Hiram Charles and Elizabeth Brown Montier, their ancestors and descendants, Scott has taken two people painted in historic portraits and placed them in the context of the times, shining a light not only on their lives, but also on American history."
—Kristin Holmes, deputy editor of the *Chestnut Hill Local* and retired staff reporter with *The Philadelphia Inquirer*

"In his new work, Don Scott Sr. reveals how family histories constitute national narratives. In *The Montiers*, Scott Sr. charts the legacy of an unlikely [common-law] marriage between the son of Philadelphia's first mayor, Richard Morrey, and an enslaved woman, Cremona, to whom he gave 200 acres of land, thus becoming an independent woman of some means, rare for the 18th century. Their union and their legacy speak to the successes, contradictions, and unresolved challenges in creating a democratic United States. The author's relentless and expansive research into Morrey and Cremona's descendants identified patriots in our country's wars, the polymath artist Paul Robeson, and a co-founder of the NAACP. Scott deftly circumscribes a family history with rich social, political, and economic contexts and abundantly demonstrates an American truth: that the boundaries we are told separate us are indeed permeable. People have a knack for inventing their own pathways."

—Robert D. Hicks, PhD, author and former director,
Mütter Museum and Historical Medical Library,
College of Physicians of Philadelphia

"*The Montiers* reads like a historical novel, connecting contemporary African American iconic figures with its mixed-race ancestors, whose 'Guineatown' Georgian style colonial home of 1771 ... [still stands] in today's Cheltenham, PA. Drawing from major historians, Benjamin Quarles and the late Charles Blockson, noted historian and author, Donald Scott, Sr., presents a cautionary narrative of the lives and loves of black self-sufficiency in America's primal evolution. Beyond its opening with a genealogical genesis of 'begets' the story is revealed in its investigation of 'Protecting the Interest of the Property Class,' among Quakers, the Lenni Lenape [natives] of the Delaware Valley, the titled immigrant class, the invading British Army, and free and enslaved Africans. The more you delve into the Montiers family line[s], the more enriched and aware you understand about the backstory of General George Washington and his starving troops on the Delaware, and the faces of [the family's] humanity who saved him from a frozen grave. Fast forward to the era of the humanitarian-patriot, Paul Robeson, a [family] descendant ..., makes it clear that the struggle to be free is made of flesh and bone, is passed from one generation to the next, and is found in recordings of the basso profundo of Robeson singing 'Ballad for Americans'!"

—Ty Collins, public history interpreter

THE MONTIERS

From Enslavement to Paul Robeson and Beyond

BY DONALD SCOTT SR.

BROOKLINE
books
Havertown, Pennsylvania

Brookline Books is an imprint of Casemate Publishers

Published in the United States of America and Great Britain in 2025 by
BROOKLINE BOOKS
1950 Lawrence Road, Havertown, PA 19083
and
47 Church Street, Barnsley, S70 2AS, UK

Copyright 2025 © Donald Scott Sr.

Paperback Edition: ISBN 978-1-955041-04-1
Digital Edition: ISBN 978-1-955041-05-8

A CIP record for this book is available from the British Library

All rights reserved. No part of this book may be reproduced or transmitted in any form or by any means, electronic or mechanical including photocopying, recording or by any information storage and retrieval system, without permission from the publisher in writing.

Printed and bound in the United Kingdom by CPI Group (UK) Ltd, Croydon, CR0 4YY

Typeset in India by Lapiz Digital Services, Chennai.

For a complete list of Brookline Books titles, please contact:

CASEMATE PUBLISHERS (US)
Telephone (610) 853-9131
Fax (610) 853-9146
Email: casemate@casematepublishers.com
www.casematepublishers.com

CASEMATE PUBLISHERS (UK)
Telephone (0)1226 734350
Email: casemate@casemateuk.com
www.casemateuk.com

Cover images: (front, left) Portrait of Hiram Charles Montier. (Philadelphia Museum of Art: On loan from the Collection of Mr. and Mrs. William Pickens III, 192-2022-1) and (front, right) Portrait of Elizabeth Brown Montier. (Philadelphia Museum of Art: On loan from the Collection of Mr. and Mrs. William Pickens III, 192-2022-2)
(back, left) Mossell family portrait. (University of Pennsylvania) and (back, right) Paul Robeson leading Moore Shipyard workers in singing "The Star Spangled Banner." (Wikimedia Commons)

To Cremona Morrey Fry—For your guiding wisdom, tremendous courage, and unparalleled foresight that helped shape destinies, build dynasties, and change the course of history.

Contents

Acknowledgments   ix
About the Author   xiii
Family Tree   xv
Preface   xvii

Introduction   1
1   The Early Life of Cremona Morrey: Navigating Momentous "Landmines"   5
2   The Privileged English, New York, and Philadelphia Quakers: Humphrey and Richard Morrey   35
3   A Forbidden Relationship Develops during Racially Explosive Times   63
4   Richard and Cremona's Visible, Child-Producing Union   91
5   Richard Passes to Cremona Nearly Two Hundred Acres before His Death   105
6   Brave New Horizons: Challenges as a Land-Owning Black Woman Moving Forward   115
7   Cremona Jr., Her Marriage to John Montier, and the Genesis of the Bustills   123
8   The Development of Guineatown and Early Flourishing of the Montiers and Other Residents   135
9   Hiram and Elizabeth Brown Montier and the Family Dynasties that Followed: Surviving "Through Sunny and Stormy Weather"   153
10   Honoring the Ancestors and Legacy of the Historic Interracial Relationship   193

Epilogue: Carrying the Torch Forward   215
Endnotes   223
Index   281

Acknowledgments

This book would not have been possible without the information obtained from numerous descendants and their personal collections, historical organizations, universities, museums, libraries, government agencies, and other institutions. I am privileged to have received assistance in bringing this project to fruition from these multiple resources and a range of individuals.

I give my heartfelt thanks to Reginald H. Pitts, J.D., historical researcher and genealogist, for his early research and writing on the Montiers and related family lines. And especially helpful was Erika Piola, associate curator of the Prints & Photographs Department and director of Visual Culture Programs at The Library Company of Philadelphia. I'm also especially thankful for the early assistance of the late Charles Blockson, distinguished black-history scholar, and Diane D. Turner, PhD, curator of the Charles L. Blockson Afro-American Collection in conjunction with the Africology and African American Studies Department at Temple University and its preeminent Afrocentricity scholar, Molefi Kete Asante, PhD.

And I deeply appreciate the assistance of David P. Rowland (president), Thomas J. Wieckowski, PhD (first vice president), and Stephanie L. Walsh (archivist) of the Old York Road Historical Society, as well as the earlier assistance of other society members, including Mary Washington and her late husband, Jack Washington. I'm also immensely grateful to the Cheltenham Township Historical Commission for its help over the years.

I welcomed the brainstorming and researching about the cemetery established in Guineatown (and the disposition of the 75 mostly African American remains buried there in the Glenside–Edge Hill area of Cheltenham Township) with local historians, researchers, and community leaders; they included Dr. Wieckowski; David Harrower; and Betty Smith; as well as Terry Buckalew, noted for his outstanding research and documentation concerning the Bethel Burying Ground Project in Philadelphia that's associated with the historic Mother Bethel African Methodist Episcopal (AME) Church led by the pastor and a noted denomination historian, the Reverend Mark Kelly Tyler, PhD.

Earlier explorations for my books about Camp William Penn, where the largest amount of federal black soldiers trained for the Civil War in Cheltenham Township, helped me with researching Montier-Bustill-Bowser family members who were associated with the facility. The prior assistance of researchers and others preserving the legacy of Camp William Penn included the late Perry Triplett; Joyce Werkman; James Paradis, PhD; Robert D. Hicks, PhD; and Edward G. McLaughlin of the Citizens for the Restoration of Historic La Mott (CROHL), as well as members of the 3rd Regiment Infantry United States Colored Troops (USCT) re-enactors led by such officers as Joseph Becton and the late Joseph E. Lee. The researcher-scholars James Elton Johnson, PhD, and William Chambrés were invaluable for their expertise concerning Camp William Penn.

Vestry member and Historical Committee co-chair Ginny McCracken of the Trinity Church Oxford, in Philadelphia, was tremendously helpful with archival and historical research concerning the Penrose, Morrey, and Montier families.

Meanwhile, Timothy H. Horning, public services archivist for the University Archives at the University of Pennsylvania, was exceptionally helpful; Ray Smith, weekly archives volunteer for the Springfield Township Historical Society, provided detailed information regarding local historical property owners and much more. Superb graphic assistance was provided by Stacey Swigart, director of the Atwater Kent Collection, Drexel University, in association with the Lenfest Center for Cultural Partnerships. I'm also deeply appreciative of Lynn Clouser Waddell, director of the Drexel Founding Collection (of art) at Drexel University.

Integral to the book's completion was the very fine assistance of the dedicated staff members at the Historical Society of Pennsylvania, the Historical Society of Montgomery County, as well as the Philadelphia City Archives, Department of Records; the Schomburg Center for Research in Black Culture; Thomas Jefferson Foundation, Inc.'s Slavery at Monticello initiative; and the Princeton & Slavery Project sponsored by Princeton University.

And I am enormously obliged for the graphics help of The University of Vermont's Barbara Wells, managing creative director, in the Division of Strategic Communication, Sonja Lunde, director, and Isabella Anastasio of the Fleming Museum of Art and Kristen J. Nyitray, director, Special Collections & University Archives, Stony Brook University. Exceptionally helpful were Thea Richard, senior manager, federal and international partnerships, America250, and Matthew Hindra, cofounder of USA Warrior Stories, Inc.

My sincerest appreciation is extended to the Philadelphia Museum of Art and to everyone there for providing generous support, including Kathleen

A. Foster, PhD, The Robert L. McNeil Jr. senior curator of American Art and director of the Center for American Art; Lucia Olubunmi R. Momoh, Constance E. Clayton Curatorial Fellow; as well as Jason Wierzbicki, conservation photographer, Division of Conservation; and Jonathan Hoppe, digital asset librarian, Library and Archives.

My deepest gratitude goes to Janice Sykes-Ross, executive director of the Paul Robeson House & Museum (West Philadelphia Cultural Alliance), for her visionary leadership and providing a wealth of information and expertise.

I commend the committed staffs led by Terry Snyder, PhD, visiting associate professor and chief administrator of the Haverford College Libraries including Sarah Horowitz, curator of Rare Books and Manuscripts and head of Quaker and Special Collections, Lutnick Library, and Daniel DiPrinzio, chief communications officer, Arcadia University, for their immense contributions. The archival and library staff at Arcadia were especially beneficial.

I thank the Emmy-winning Karen Smyles, producer of the documentary *The Montiers: An American Story*, PBS, WHYY-TV, along with the Montier homestead's former owner Helene Huffer, current residents Jerome McGoey and Susan Kawakawa, and J. Scott Laughlin, agent, Berkshire Hathaway HomeServices, Fox & Roach Realtors. I give thanks also to Catharine Boland Erkkila, PhD, managing editor, Society of Architectural Historians, Archipedia and Buildings of America, and nephew Kristopher Scott, for outstanding photographic images, as well as my son, Donald Scott, Jr., for his overall assistance and support. Indeed, the unwavering encouragement and multi-faceted help of my beloved wife, Willetta ("Billie") West-Scott, are immeasurably appreciated.

Offering her invaluable research and superb insight was the Morrey–Bustill–Montier–Miller family historian Joyce Mosley, an author (*Gram's Gift*) and distinguished member of the National Society of the Daughters of the American Revolution (DAR), etc., who is also devoted to the Paul Robeson House & Museum in a wide range of historical and administrative activities.

I would like to express my deepest gratitude to the late William Pickens III; his beloved wife, Audrey Patricia Pickens; and their children, Pamela Alison Pickens, the late William Pickens IV, and John Montier Pickens, for sharing personal recollections and resources, as well as for carrying the family legacy through their magnanimous spirits. I am indebted to their generous support and inspiration; without it, I would never have been able to complete the writing of this book.

About the Author

Don "Ogbewii" Scott Sr., a graduate of the Columbia University Graduate School of Journalism and the historically black college, Cheyney University of Pennsylvania, has written books and contributed to others via such publishers as Oxford University Press, Houghton Mifflin, Schiffer Publishing, The History Press, Arcadia Publishing and the Smithsonian Institution's affiliate, The Senator John Heinz History Center in Pittsburgh.

His history articles have appeared in *Medium.com*, Montgomery Newspapers' Digital First Media & MediaNews Group, *The Philadelphia Inquirer*, *The Philadelphia Bulletin*, *The Philadelphia Tribune*, *The Miami Courier*, *The Miami News*, *Fort Lauderdale News & Sun Sentinel*, *Delaware County Daily Times*, Chester County's *Daily Local News*, *America's Civil War*, *The Quarterly Journal of Military History* (MHQ), *American Visions*, *Ancestors* (the magazine of the National Archives of England), *Wharton* magazine, *The Pennsylvania Gazette*, *Black Enterprise*, and *Everton's Family History Network*, as well as a range of websites, including *Afrigeneas.com*, which published the first national story about the Montier family, written by Scott in 2004.

Scott has contributed stories to three acclaimed book projects, including the *African American National Biography*, edited by Henry Louis Gates Jr. and Evelyn Higginbotham of Harvard University and Oxford University Press; *The Jim Crow Encyclopedia: Milestones in African American History*, a Houghton-Mifflin publication; and *The Civil War in Pennsylvania: The African American Experience*, edited by Samuel Black, director of the Museum of African American History at The Senator John Heinz History Center.

As a journalist and author, Scott has also covered topics ranging from his South Carolina and Georgia Gullah-Geechee ancestors and corporate media mergers to Civil War history focusing on antislavery abolitionist journalists and black soldiers in the conflict that he's examined in two books, including about Camp William Penn, the first and largest federal institution to train Northern-based black soldiers during the Civil War. Scott's 384-page book, *Camp William Penn: 1863–1865*, was updated as an ebook by Schiffer Publishing in 2021.

His televised, radio, and in-person presentations were hosted by The Molefi Kete Asante Institute, Independence Mall National Historic Site, the National Archives regional center in Philadelphia, the United States Department of Labor, United States National Energy Laboratory, Temple University, Dickinson College, the main branch of the Philadelphia Free Library, the Library Company of Philadelphia in conjunction with the Historical Society of Pennsylvania, the Union League of Philadelphia with the Abraham Lincoln Foundation, African Methodist Episcopal Church–First District Plaza, the Community College of Philadelphia (CCP-TV), WHYY-PBS, WURD (black-owned radio station), PCN-TV, and The National Civil War Museum. Several presentations were cosponsored by the Pennsylvania Humanities Council and Pennsylvania Historical and Museum Commission.

Scott has also been a history lecturer in Pennsylvania's Commonwealth Speakers' Program and researcher for the Pennsylvania Humanities Council. The retired assistant professor of English at the Community College of Philadelphia has taught at Temple University, Peirce College, and Cheyney University, his undergraduate alma mater and the first institution of higher learning for African Americans originally known as the Institute for Colored Youth, founded 1837 in Philadelphia. Scott resides just northwest of Philadelphia in the historic community of Cheltenham Township, where Cremona Morrey Fry and her descendant Montiers planted their illustrious roots.

Morrey-Bustill-Robeson-Montier Family Tree (condensed)

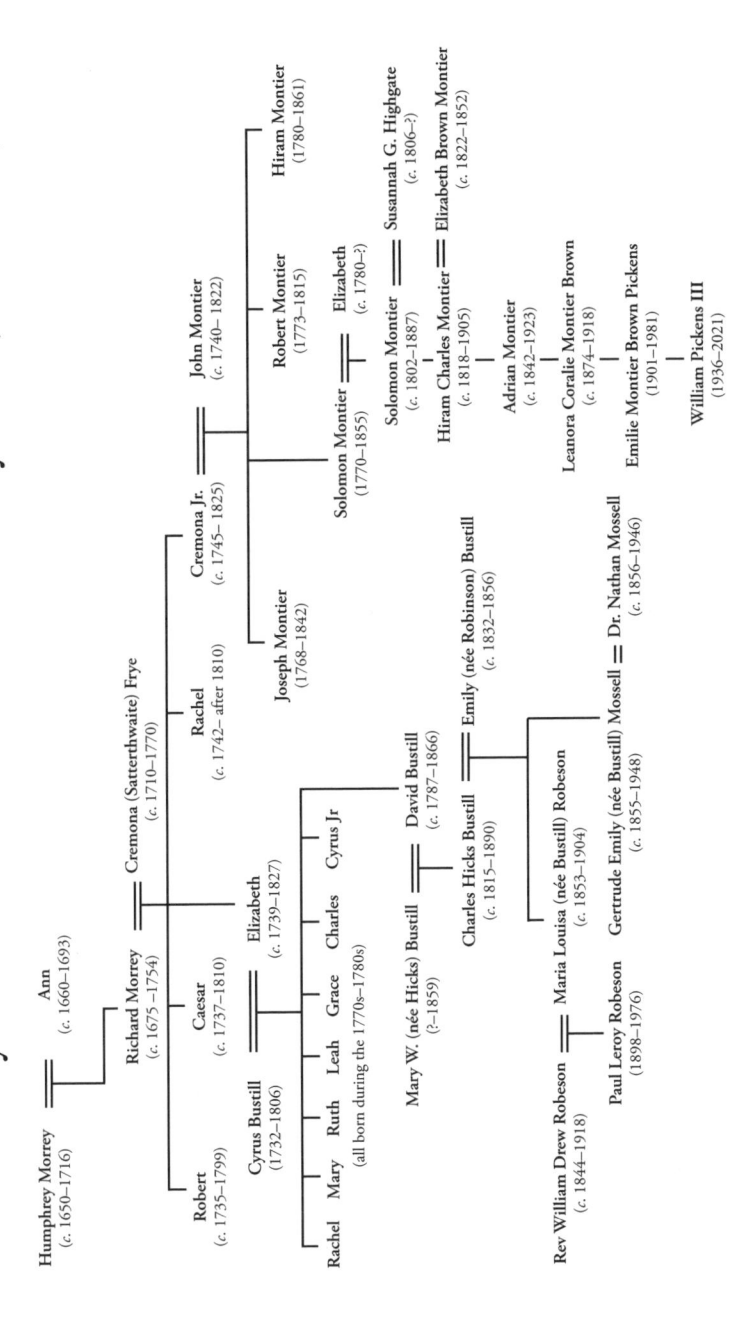

Humphrey Morrey (c. 1650–1716) = Ann (c. 1660–1693)

├── Richard Morrey (c. 1675–1754) = Cremona (Satterthwaite) Frye (c. 1710–1770)
│   ├── Caesar (c. 1737–1810) = Elizabeth (c. 1739–1827)
│   │   ├── Robert (c. 1735–1799)
│   │   └── Cyrus Bustill (1732–1806)
│   │   └── Rachel, Mary, Ruth, Leah, Grace, Charles, Cyrus Jr (all born during the 1770s–1780s)
│   │   └── David Bustill (c. 1787–1866) = Mary W. (née Hicks) Bustill (?–1859)
│   │   └── Charles Hicks Bustill (1815–1890) = Emily (née Robinson) Bustill (c. 1832–1856)
│   │   ├── Maria Louisa (née Bustill) Robeson (c. 1853–1904) = Rev William Drew Robeson (c. 1844–1918)
│   │   │   └── Paul Leroy Robeson (1898–1976)
│   │   └── Gertrude Emily (née Bustill) Mossell (c. 1855–1948) = Dr. Nathan Mossell (c. 1856–1946)
│   └── Rachel (c. 1742–after 1810)
│
└── John Montier (c. 1740–1822)
    ├── Cremona Jr. (c. 1745–1825)
    │   └── Joseph Montier (1768–1842)
    ├── Robert Montier (1773–1815) = Elizabeth (c. 1780–?)
    │   └── Solomon Montier (1770–1855)
    │   ├── Solomon Montier (c. 1802–1887) = Susannah G. Highgate (c. 1806–?)
    │   └── Hiram Charles Montier (1818–1905) = Elizabeth Brown Montier (1822–1852)
    │   └── Adrian Montier (c. 1842–1923)
    │   └── Leanora Coralie Montier Brown (1874–1918)
    │   └── Emilie Montier Brown Pickens (1901–1981)
    │   └── William Pickens III (1936–2021)
    └── Hiram Montier (1780–1861)

Preface

Circa 1746, Cremona "Mooney" (Satterthwaite) Morrey Fry likely strode proudly about her 198 acres of land[1] in what is today Cheltenham Township around eight miles northwest of Philadelphia—akin to one of England's earthy "country market towns." Indeed, just a couple of years earlier, in 1744, a British visitor noted that Philadelphia's environs were quite rudimentary but predicted terrific advances: "I could not apprehend this city to be so very elegant or pretty as it is commonly represented. In its present situation it is much like one of our country market towns in England," he said, before further commenting: "I believe that in a few years hence it will be a great and flourishing place, and the chief city in North America."[2] Indeed, as Philadelphia morphed into the "Athens of Mankind,"[3] "Mooney" must have felt an unparalleled sense of relief and accomplishment as an African-descended and liberated woman of color.

Her new homestead probably encompassed green pastures, fertile farmland, bountiful woodland, and wandering streams branching from the brisk-moving Tacony—or Tookany—Creek, derived from the native Lenape people's name "Tawacawonick"[4] or "tèkëne," meaning "forest" or "wilderness."[5] According to my 2009 The History Press book (*American Chronicles* imprint), *Remembering Cheltenham Township*, "Home to the Lenape [or 'original people' of the Native American 'Delaware' tribe] for thousands of years was the land that would be called Cheltenham."[6] In fact, one of the earliest acquisitions of land by Pennsylvania's Quaker founder, William Penn, in that area from the Lenape was consummated on July 14, 1683, when "purchase was made of [chiefs] Neneshickan, Malebore, Neshanocke, and Oscreneon for the lands lying between the Schuylkill and Pennepack streams, and extending as far northwest of Conshohocken, but now better known as Edge Hill."[7] The Edge Hill area, early on, became renowned for "the most considerable elevation" and "fertile loam," as a place "where limestone abounds, among the best in the county."[8] The sweeping panorama was "described by some [very early European] explorers as having soaring flocks of birds so thick that they'd blot out the sun and schools of fish so plentiful that quiet waters seemed to be boiling as they swam by. The earth was worshipped and honored."[9]

Late 17th-century Quaker homesteads, more than a few utilizing slave labor, would one day give way to 19th-century "Philadelphians" seeking to find "splendid locations for dwellings on the hill sides where exquisite views of fine scenery [were] spread before their porches and windows in summer and winter in the varied beauty of the seasons."[10] One of the so-called city folk among the growing interracial working classes was "sugar baron" William Welsh Harrison, whose Horace Trumbauer-designed mansion (patterned after England's Alnwick Castle) rose in the late 19th century in the vicinity of Cremona's homestead on what today is Arcadia University's campus.[11] A bit further east on nearby Cheltenham estates were Jay Cooke, the financier of Union forces during the Civil War,[12] as well as Edward M. Davis, a prolific land investor affiliated with the Union League of Philadelphia, and his dynamic mother-in-law, the Quaker antislavery abolitionist and women's rights advocate Lucretia Mott.[13] She personally denounced the persecution of indigenous Americans to Cooke and his visiting friend, President Ulysses S. Grant, at Cooke's mansion.[14]

Mott's early-Victorian home in Cheltenham, called Roadside, stood adjacent to Camp William Penn, where the largest number of African American federal soldiers trained for the Civil War from 1863 to 1865.[15] A recruiter and 1863 speaker at Camp Penn was the preeminent black leader of the period, Frederick Douglass; also associated with the historic facility were the Underground Railroad icons William Still and Harriet Tubman.[16] Tubman would one day marry a veteran soldier, Nelson Davis, from the 8th United States Colored Infantry, one of 11 regiments consisting of almost eleven thousand warriors who trained at the facility[17]—including some of Cremona's descendants.[18]

Indeed, Cremona's descendant Cyrus Bustill Miller Jr.[19] joined the 24th United States Colored Troops (USCT) on March 23, 1865,[20] where he very likely heard Harriet Tubman address the regiment there on April 6—about a week before Lincoln's April 15 assassination—concerning her "thrilling" escapades. A local *Christian Recorder* reporter wrote: "It was the first time we had the pleasure of hearing her. She seems to be very well known to the community at large, as the great Underground Rail Road [sic] woman, and has done a good part to many of her fellow creatures, in that direction." The journalist further noted: "During her lecture, which she gave in her own language, she elicited considerable applause from the soldiers of the 24th regiment U.S.C.T., now at the camp. She gave a thrilling account of her trials in the South, during the past three years, among the contrabands and colored soldiers, and how she had administered to thousands of them, and cared for their numerous necessities."[21]

It's even quite possible too that a "runaway" enslaved black man from a North Carolina plantation who would one day graduate from Pennsylvania's historically black Lincoln University with a theology degree—William Drew Robeson (1844–1918)—joined the 45th USCT of Camp William Penn in 1864.[22] William was destined to marry another descendant of Cremona, Maria Louisa Bustill (1853–1904). The couple would give birth to the iconic African American leader, Paul Robeson (1898–1976).[23]

Some of Cremona's 19th-century descendants are on record for helping such self-liberating African Americans by way of the Underground Railroad. The Morrey–Bustill–Montier family historian and author Joyce Mosley writes that her ancestor, Cyrus Bustill Miller, was an antislavery activist and Underground Railroad operative. Furthermore, "Elizabeth Bustill Miller and her husband, Jacob C. White, Sr., were also leaders in the black community," she writes, with White owning such properties in the Philadelphia area as "Lebanon Cemetery—where people of color were buried with dignity." Mosley says that such abolitionists and local leaders of the Underground Railroad, including some of her other ancestors, met at cemetery offices with the likes of William Still, reputed to be the "father of the Underground Railroad," according to *The New York Times*. Still, Mosley said, kept detailed notes hidden at Lebanon about the escapes of African Americans; these became the basis of a landmark book, *The Underground Railroad*. The remains at Lebanon, a stop on the Underground Railroad, were reportedly relocated to the historic African American cemetery, Eden, in Collingdale, Pennsylvania, Mosley wrote, just outside of Philadelphia, after Lebanon closed in 1903.[24]

The 13-acre Camp William Penn also attracted noted freedom fighters like artist-activist David Bustill Bowser, yet another descendant, who designed and made the camp's regimental flags and whose grandfather, Cyrus Bustill, had baked bread for George Washington's Continental Army[25] and was reportedly duly recognized for his service, including quite possibly a silver dollar given to him by Washington, according to a few sources.[26] Elements of Washington's army, on its way to Valley Forge in December 1777 during the Revolutionary War, fought in the battle of Edge Hill near the developing black community, Guineatown, on or near Cremona's earlier sprawling property; the combat took place in the vicinity of her historic land, where more than a few progeny and other African Americans lived and were put to rest in an associated graveyard,[27] variously known as the "Cemetery for Colored Folks"[28] or the Montieth Cemetery, among other monikers.

In an extraordinary act three decades earlier, such lush land was bestowed to Cremona, an African-descended woman of color, in 1746[29] by her acknowledged Caucasian marital partner, the English-cultured "Gent" Richard Morrey,[30] one of the wealthiest and most powerful men in the Philadelphia area that would become the birthplace of American democracy in 1776. And that is despite the incredible and exceptionally complicated dynamics that she certainly had to navigate as the reputed common-law[31] wife and former slave to Richard and his father, Humphrey Morrey, the first mayor of Philadelphia, appointed by a provincial council in 1691 at the behest of the commonwealth's Quaker founder, William Penn.[32]

According to an array of sources, Cremona and Richard produced at least four or five mixed-race or "mulatto" children[33] during a period when such miscegenation was quite risky legally and even conceivably a threat to their physical well-being.[34] Yet the bodacious union persevered for at least a decade,[35] probably in part protected by Richard's shrewdness,[36] affluence, and influence, as one of the most unique and enigmatic interracial alliances in United States history.

Notably, however, as a woman of African descent, "Mooney" or Cremona's very survival, as well as the couple's conjugal relationship and their children's subsistence certainly depended on what had to be her remarkable intelligence, insight, and some say tantalizing beauty.[37] Indeed, early on, the mixed-race children of such interracial relationships, even in the so-called liberal confines of the Quaker stronghold of Philadelphia, could be forced into various degrees of apprenticeships or even enslavement, as well as brutal punishment.[38]

As Cremona (Satterthwaite) Morrey Fry surveyed her expansive property that day in 1746, despite the challenging days that were surely to come, she nevertheless had reason to envision great hope beyond the horizon—with extraordinary vision and valor.

Introduction

The absorbing interracial relationship involving Richard Morrey (1675–1754), the British-born Caucasian son of Philadelphia's first mayor, the wealthy Quaker Humphrey Morrey (circa 1640–1715), essentially begins with Richard likely igniting a historic union with a woman who had been enslaved by the Morrey family, Cremona (circa 1710–1770), sometimes described as "Negro Mooney." She had been initially kept in bondage, probably primarily in what is today Cheltenham Township, in southeastern Pennsylvania's Montgomery County.

However, although many legal documents such as wills refer to Cremona as "Negro," other circumstantial sources indicate that she was mostly, if not entirely, of Native American ancestry—specifically Lenape, the indigenous people who had inhabited southeastern Pennsylvania for thousands of years. Despite the preponderance of evidence indicating Cremona was a black woman, it's even possible that she was of African, European and Lenape descent.

Nevertheless, Richard and Cremona, by way of their extraordinary interracial relationship, had up to five mixed-race children from approximately 1736 to 1746 who usually took on the Morrey surname or a variation, such as "Murray," like their mother, Cremona.

Indeed, as a young woman, Cremona, born before or about 1710, may have carried the surname or maiden name Satterthwaite, with some sources indicating that was her given or first name. Interestingly, the name Satterthwaite has been historically linked to Native American and/or European families with some involved in the enslavement of Africans.

While various sources indicate that Cremona's parents were Native American, others declare they were enslaved Africans who were abducted from Africa, otherwise referred to as "Guinea" by Europeans, particularly the central West African coast. And although most accounts insist that either Humphrey or Richard Morrey liberated the enslaved Cremona and her children, there is some evidence indicating that Cremona was the impetus for their emancipation.

One of Richard and Cremona's children, also named Cremona, would marry John Montier, an African-descended man likely of Caribbean heritage, and the couple would build a residence at the dawn of the American Revolution that still stands today on the 300 block of Limekiln Pike in Cheltenham Township's Glenside neighborhood, also referred to as Edge Hill.

Although Richard Morrey was married and had children with his British-descended wife, Ann, whose maiden name was likely Turner, Richard had at least another relationship and remarried in 1746 when or about the time his marital bond with Cremona appeared to have fractured; but still, in one of the most unfathomable—and some say honorable acts in American history—Richard then passed to Cremona almost two hundred acres near where Arcadia University of Glenside is situated today, perhaps an indication of his deep affection for her. Others believe that Cremona likely negotiated and craftily navigated the contours of their relationship and the generous terms of the couple's separation, despite—as a woman of color—probably being exploited as an enslaved worker and then employee of Richard Morrey.

Meanwhile, extended family included the Burlington, New Jersey, native Cyrus Bustill, who married Richard and Cremona's daughter, Elizabeth Morrey. Formerly enslaved by a white attorney, Samuel Bustill Jr., who consummated a relationship with Cyrus's enslaved mother, Parthenia (depending on the source), Cyrus—also said to be of Native American ancestry—became a black activist, educator, and entrepreneur. There was also David Bustill Bowser, an antislavery activist during the 19th century and Civil War, who created the colors or flags for the 11 African American regiments at Camp William Penn in Cheltenham, where various distinguished family members trained.

In fact, the interracial relationship between Richard and Cremona Morrey gave birth to or was otherwise tied to generations of the most esteemed African Americans, some also reportedly with Native American ancestry. Direct and indirect descendants include the Bustills, Mossells, Millers, Pickenses, Browns, and Robesons. On that note, one of the more recent members included the great Paul Robeson, a renowned African American scholar, lawyer, diplomat, athlete, singer, and actor, born in Princeton, New Jersey, in 1898, who transitioned to the ancestors in Philadelphia in 1976 during the nation's bicentennial. The story also involves modern descendants, including the Pickenses of New York, whose ancestor William Pickens Sr. cofounded the National Association for the Advancement of Colored People and served as its first field secretary along with being an associate of the eminent black scholar and visionary activist W. E. B. Du Bois.

One celebrated extended family member, the Philadelphia physician Dr. Nathan Francis Mossell, who founded the pioneering Frederick Douglass Hospital for blacks in the city, married the Morrey–Bustill descendant Gertrude Bustill, a renowned journalist. Dr. Mossell was also the first African American graduate of the University of Pennsylvania's School of Medicine. His niece, Sadie Tanner Alexander, became the first black woman to graduate from Penn's law school and the first national president of the historic black sorority, Delta Sigma Theta. Her father, Aaron A. Mossell, was the first black to graduate from Penn's school of law. Further, the African Methodist Episcopal Church bishop, Benjamin Tucker Tanner, was Alexander's maternal grandfather whose son was the famous black painter Henry O. Tanner. Sadie's husband, Raymond Pace Alexander, was the first African American graduate of Penn's Wharton School of Business.

The late William Pickens III, a corporate executive and founder of the New York City-based Paul Robeson Foundation, was instrumental in researching his Morrey–Robeson–Pickens–Brown–Montier family relationships with the encouraging help of his late wife, Patricia, and adult children, Pamela Allison Pickens, the late William Pickens IV, and John Montier Pickens. Book author Joyce Mosley has served as the family historian, carrying on the tradition of their pioneering genealogist ancestor Anna Bustill Smith (1862–1945), who wrote accounts of the family history in the *Journal of Negro History*, founded and edited by the "father of African American history," Carter G. Woodson.

Pickens III said his mother, Emilie Brown Pickens, ignited his passion for family history when she told him stories as a tot sitting on her lap, a tradition that she continued with Pickens's own children. The family's history has also been importantly documented by way of the celebrated portraits of Hiram and Elizabeth Montier, painted about 1841 by artist Franklin R. Street. Found under the bed of an aging family member, Joseph Montier, the images now hang at the Philadelphia Museum of Art as very rare portraits of such affluent 19th-century African Americans.

Remarkably, near or on part of Cremona Morrey's land, a small black town known as Guineatown developed with an associated cemetery ultimately containing the remains of about 75 people, likely including early family members such as Cremona Sr. and her namesake daughter, the younger Cremona. The disposition of those remains has been controversial because they have not been found following a supposed 1963 road-widening project on Limekiln Pike (in the Glenside section of Cheltenham Township within the community of Edge Hill), a sad legacy of what's happened nationally to African American cemeteries being trivialized and much worse.

Although no one absolutely knows the depth of their union and exactly why the remarkable common-law marital relationship between Cremona and Richard Morrey ended after a decade—considering whether Cremona felt coerced or not and how the couple negotiated the terms of that relationship—it led to an African American dynasty that still thrives today.

Don "Ogbewii" Scott Sr.

CHAPTER I

The Early Life of Cremona Morrey

Navigating Momentous "Landmines"

So, who was Cremona [Satterthwaite] Morrey Fry ancestrally, ethnically, culturally, and otherwise? Was Cremona's parentage solely African, as some reports seem to indicate? Or was she partially European and/or Native American based on assertions of her father, and possibly mother, being "Indian"? Is it true, as various sources propose, that Cremona's parents hailed from the Delaware or Lenape tribe, documented as being the primary people occupying land in the Philadelphia area, or "Delaware Valley," well before the arrival of European settlers and the enslaved Africans?[1] Were her parents a mixture of African, European, and Native American heritages?

Leaving aside whether Cremona was attractive or beautiful as a "Negro" woman with primarily African features or mixed with European and/or Native American characteristics, the reality is that physical attractiveness of enslaved women often meant unrelenting sexual exploitation, regardless of the marital status of male slaveholders.[2] In other words, if a black woman—doubly jeopardized during such racist and sexist periods for being female and a person of color—was endowed with so-called physical beauty, it could be viewed as a curse by family members and even the woman herself. Although countless black women with strong and beautiful African features certainly suffered from such sexual predation, mixed-race women were sometimes preferred by white enslavers.[3] President Thomas Jefferson very likely comingling with his wife Martha Wayles Jefferson's teenaged half-sister, the biracial and fair-skinned Sally Hemings, is a prime example of such a relationship, resulting in at least several biracial children, documented as "extremely likely" by various researchers following DNA evaluations.[4]

"For the world and time in which she lived, the African American Hemings had attributes associated with white standards of beauty," writes Annette Gordon-Reed in her Pulitzer Prize-winning book, *The Hemingses of Monticello:*

Multiracial mulatto women lived throughout the Western Hemisphere, where slavery was prevalent, including in Barbados, where Cremona's parents may have been enslaved after being abducted from Africa. Some sources indicate that Cremona was part African and Native American. (Wikimedia Commons)

An American Family. With Sally Hemings and her half-sister Martha, Thomas Jefferson's wife, described as being fair-skinned with long, straightish hair well below their shoulders, it's quite possible "that Sally Hemings was a light-skinned, very obviously black woman—someone whose racial makeup could be immediately discerned upon looking at her—a 'bright mulatto.'"[5] Perhaps, Cremona, or "Mooney," as she was colloquially nicknamed or known as, possessed such physical characteristics, especially considering accounts that her veins pulsed with the blood of Africans, the indigenous people of Pennsylvania, and possibly Europeans.

Nonetheless, despite sketches and 19th-century paintings depicting Cremona Morrey's Montier descendants, including Hiram Montier,[6] as light-complexioned or "mulatto," there's a distinct possibility that Cremona was more bronze, browner, or darker-toned, similar to some of her contemporary and descendant family members, especially if her parents were abducted directly from Africa, as contingent evidence seems to indicate.[7]

Realizing that Cremona's relationship with Richard Morrey and her origins are provocatively enigmatic, some of the inferred research indicates that "Cremona, or 'Mooney,' was born in 1710 to parents who had been kidnapped in Guinea and sold into slavery," writes Gwendolyn DuBois Shaw, a distinguished scholar, author, and art historian.[8]

Perhaps, further knowledge about Cremona's ancestry and identity can be ascertained via her name, according to the researcher-scholar Reginald H. Pitts:

> The name "Cremona" is an odd name, even to present-day ears. However, the name falls into the tradition of naming slaves after Greek and Roman historical figures, or after characters in classical literature. The travesty did not start with the American colonies, as the ancient Romans themselves renamed their slaves after the deities of the conquered peoples. So, this tradition, faithfully followed by the patrician slaveholder of the colonies—who would have

had, as part of his education, a thorough grounding in the classics—resulted in slaves bearing names like Caesar, Pompey, Dianna, Cato, Venus, Psyche or Scipio (after Scipio Africanus, the Roman general who led the first armies to Carthage in North Africa), or after other worthies such as literary giants Horace, Virgil, Ovid, or Terence.[9]

Cremona's bloodline was very likely African because she is clearly identified as "Negro" in official documents and even a newspaper advertisement of the day, keeping in mind that there have been other assertions that her parents were African; however, Cremona's name may have been provided by someone deeply respectful of or involved in European traditions and cultures. An example is that the name "Cremona" has roots to Italy and the town of Cremona, in northern Italy, dating back to its founding in 218 BC by Roman military forces.[10] The name could have also been provided based on, or in memory of, the War of Spanish Succession, when at the start of the 18th century the French army general, François de Neufville, the 2nd Duke of Villeroy, made Cremona his headquarters[11] before being seized at the residence of the world's preeminent violin craftsman—Antonio Stradivari.[12] Thus, it's quite possible that the provider of Cremona's name certainly was familiar with European news and history, and therefore could have been partial to or primarily of European descent or heritage.

Cremona's possible maiden name of Satterthwaite may also provide some evidence concerning her potential European heritage, keeping in mind that the surname has been associated with an ancient English family, among the earliest in Europe involved in the international slave trade[13] and within Europe itself. And there are stories, some with elements that seem to be quite a stretch, indicating that Cremona's background was European and Native American. "Accounts described Richard Morrey, the original owner of the land (and of some of the first settlers), as a general officer in either the British or Revolutionary army who owned over a thousand acres in four Montgomery County townships."[14] According to the source, Morrey supposedly married and had children "with a comely Indian maid." There's also the anecdote of Cremona being the daughter of a "John Murray" whose wife was "the daughter of a chief of the Delaware (or Lenape), bearing the name of 'Satterthwait,'"[15] possibly making Cremona's racial makeup partially European and Native American.

However, more than likely, Cremona Morrey must have lived a challenging life filled with potential life-altering "landmines" as a primarily black woman. That's even if she had been initially working for the Morreys as an enslaved house servant in what is presumed to be comfortable accommodations compared to field workers or farm hands.[16]

Modern artistic impression of Cremona Morrey, born circa 1710. (Geni.com/MyHeritage.com)

To understand the conditions under which Cremona may have lived, it's worthwhile to note the experiences of two other black women: Betty and Dinah. Also enslaved in the Pennsylvania homes of wealthy Quakers—Betty working for Israel Pemberton Sr. and Dinah for Provincial Councilor William Logan—these women likely lived and worked under similar conditions as Cremona during the early 1700s. They certainly endured hardships but lived in better conditions than their agrarian-working counterparts, according to the writer-scholar Jean R. Soderlund:

> Both of the slave women ... Betty and Dinah, worked for families of rich

Pennsylvania's founder, William Penn, signed treaties with the Lenni Lenape natives soon after his arrival during the early 1680s. (Library of Congress)

Philadelphia Quaker merchants, and therefore their lives were substantially different from the situation of sisters living in the plantation areas to the south, or even of black women working in rural Pennsylvania. In the West Indies, South Carolina, and the Chesapeake, the larger majority of black women worked from sunup to sundown in fields growing sugar, rice, tobacco, and grain.[17]

According to Soderlund, black enslaved women such as Cremona, Dinah, and Betty would have "cooked, cleaned, washed and ironed laundry, kept fires, gardened, looked after children, and served as maids. Some also sewed and made cloth." Soderlund further cites the example of a "14-year-old girl," perhaps paralleling Cremona's likely early childhood enslavement, who "knew housewifery, knitting, sewing, and could read."[18]

Because of their close proximity to the "owners" and their wives—who too often reacted jealously and sometimes violently against such black women pursued by their proprietor husbands for sexual gratification—such enslaved women were stuck in perilous circumstances, as noted in the autobiographical narrative of Harriet Jacobs (circa 1813–1897), enslaved by the Norcom family. "Her time with the Norcoms is a large part of her autobiography—especially the sexual harassment she received from Dr. Norcom, the evil 'Dr. Flint' in her narrative," whose wife retaliated against Jacobs with torturous mental and physical abuse. Noted as one of the most important such compositions authored by an enslaved woman, "Jacob's narrative is very frank about Norcom's frequent sexual advances and threats, and makes explicit the particular hazards slave women faced, which are often only alluded to in men's slave narratives."[19]

In fact, perhaps there is nothing more emblematic to this story than the unpredictable circumstances that impacted the life of Cremona (Satterthwaite) Morrey Fry, as well as her contemporaries, and ancestors as primarily people of color deleteriously impacted by the near annihilation of native cultures and the perpetuation

Harriet Jacobs (1813–1897) wrote an 1861 autobiography detailing the sexual, physical, and mental abuse black women endured while enslaved. (Wikimedia Commons)

of slavery's horrors from rape to brutal mutilations and even murder. Cremona's parents reportedly being "kidnapped" in 1710 from "Guinea" certainly impacted her life's paths commencing in the Motherland, perhaps in the northern West African coastal country that is today the Republic of Guinea. Or "Guinea" may have referred generally to the continent or west coast of Africa.[20] Descendants of Richard and Cremona Sr.—including their great granddaughter and noted teacher Maria Louisa Bustill as well as Maria's famous son, the great black activist, intellect, and entertainer Paul Robeson—were descended from the Bantu people of Africa, according to Martin Bauml Duberman, the award-winning biographer of Robeson whose father, William Drew Robeson, was an escaped slave, Union soldier, and preacher.[21] Originally known as Alkebulan by some native Africans,[22] the African continent was exploited by way of the intercontinental forced enslavement of Africans from the early 15th into the 19th century.[23]

Soderlund confirms that black women were in the Philadelphia area even before the arrival of such Quakers as William Penn and Humphrey Morrey, who likely "owned" Cremona before his heir, son Richard Morrey, Cremona's future partner. "Slavery had existed on the Delaware, and African women had lived in the region since before William Penn came in 1682," Soderlund writes.[24]

Indeed, "Africans had been in the Delaware Valley before the arrival of William Penn," mindful of when "the Swedes had African slaves in their settlements along the Delaware River as early as 1639. When Penn arrived a quarter-century later, he and many of his fellow 'Purchasers' brought slaves, or arranged to have them brought into the colony."[25] In fact, "records from the Dutch colony of New Amsterdam show that in 1639, a convict was sentenced to serve among the blacks at the South (Delaware) River," an indication of African-descended people in the area at that time. "This is the first documentation of slavery in the area that would become Pennsylvania."[26]

To get a better understanding about who Cremona Morrey was as a person, it's imperative to briefly examine some of the historical and social dynamics of the period that often revolved around slavery before delving deeper into such issues in upcoming pages of this book. For example, a notable slaveholder was Humphrey Morrey's friend William Frampton of New York City, where Morrey likely had property after first settling in Oyster Bay, New York. Frampton was later "one of the 'First Purchasers' of Cheltenham Township, who received a letter from a sea captain concerning the delivery of slaves," scholar-researcher Pitts notes, quoting the sea captain: "'Sir, I desire you to take into your Custody ye six negroes wch Wm Haig has given you a bill of sale'" by way "'of my Employers Mr Charles Jones Junr & Company [to] dispose of and sell them to the best advantage.'"[27] In fact, "Humphrey Morrey (also referred to as Merry) was another significant First Purchaser" in Cheltenham, located about a dozen miles northwest of central Philadelphia. Other Cheltenham "First Purchasers" also owned slaves, such as Tobias Leech, who cofounded and named Cheltenham with Richard Wall after their native town, England's Cheltenham in Gloucestershire, during the late 1600s. Leech "sailed up the Delaware in 1682 on the ship, *Bristol Factor*," that "accompanied the ship 'Welcome,' which carried William Penn," Pennsylvania's founder, according to the Cheltenham Township website.[28]

The noted historian Gary B. Nash writes "that in December 1684, just three years after the coming of the Quaker founders of the colony, a shipload of 150 African slaves arrived in Philadelphia." Nash continues: "Transported by a Bristol mercantile firm, the slaves were eagerly purchased by Quaker settlers who were engaged in the difficult work of clearing trees and brush and erecting crude houses in the budding provincial capital." That initial slave-transporting ship has been identified as the *Isabella*, according to a range of sources.[29]

The Quaker Richard Wall built his home soon after arriving during the early 1680s in what would become Cheltenham Township. Some of the earliest Quaker meetings in the region were held there before moving on to the nearby Abington Meeting. (Kristopher Scott)

Nash further notes: "So great was the demand for the slaves, according to one prominent settler, that most of the specie brought to Philadelphia by incoming settlers was exhausted in purchasing the Africans." He then provides estimates concerning the total number of enslaved Africans in Philadelphia during the late 1600s and early 1700s. "Thus, at a time when the population of Philadelphia was probably about 2,000, some 150 slaves became incorporated into the town's social structure." These enslaved Africans could have included Cremona Morrey's parents, who may have been initially held in bondage at the Philadelphia estate(s) of the Morreys or at their sprawling "country" residence in Cheltenham. "Although little evidence is available to indicate the extent of slave importation in the next few decades [following 1705], a survey of inventories of estates from 1682 to 1705 reveals that about one in fifteen Philadelphia families owned slaves in that period."[30]

And although the number of slaves in Philadelphia or the "Delaware Valley" fluctuated over the ensuing years depending on duty or taxation prices and other variables, according to historian Nash, the "beginning of the Seven Years' War in 1756 [when Cremona would have been about 46 years old if born in 1710] marked the onset of a decade in which slavery and slave trading reached their height in colonial Philadelphia."[31] Some estimates indicate then that up to one in four Philadelphia merchants owned slaves. "The tax assessors' lists also reveal that slaves composed more than three-quarters of the unfree labor in the city in 1767 and that slaveholders outnumbered servant holders more than two to one," Nash says. "The five-year period between 1755 and 1760, when almost no indentured servants entered the colony and most of those already there completed their terms of servitude, serves to explain this emphasis on black labor," Nash continues. "For at least a brief period in the early 1760s slaves may have represented as much as 85 to 90 percent of the city's bound laborers."[32]

Additionally, Nash writes that "after visiting the city in 1750, Peter Kalm, the Swedish botanist, noted that in earlier decades slaves had been bought 'by almost everyone who could afford it, the Quakers alone being an exception,'" at least initially. "Kalm added that, more recently, Quakers had overcome their scruples 'and now ... have as many Negroes as other people.'"[33] Further, about "1243 slaves entered the Delaware River in the seven-year period 1759–65," writes Darold D. Wax. "Nearly half of these arrived in 1762, the summit of the Pennsylvania slave trade. Fully three quarters of the slave influx was made up of blacks acquired in Africa and brought directly to the Philadelphia area." Yet, Wax notes that before "the late 1750s slaves entering Pennsylvania came via the West Indies and South Carolina. They were shipped north on consignment or carried on locally-owned vessels that brought sugar and other island produce home for sale."[34]

Perhaps Cremona's parents, after being abducted from Africa, could have been transported to Philadelphia after first landing at South Carolina's Gadsden's Wharf in the Charleston harbor, where a huge majority of African slaves were "processed," earlier spending time in the Caribbean, very often in Barbados.[35] "Robert Venable, an African-American native of Philadelphia born in 1736, is on record as saying that he never saw any slaves 'arrive direct from Africa, but enough came round by Barbadoes [*sic*] ... saw them sold at the [London] Coffee House.'"[36]

It's also possible that Richard Morrey directly, or indirectly via "brokers," purchased a significant number of human beings at the London Coffee House or by way of other venues, including from "private owners." Morrey's estate was reportedly gargantuan:

> On a plantation of almost eight hundred acres, there were probably a large number of "Negros" belonging to Richard Morrey. It is not likely that he purchased them fresh off the boat from Africa, as has been surmised. There was not much call for slaves who would not understand even the simplest command in English, or were not used to Western ways.[37]

Slave auctions were held at London Coffee House, which served as an eatery, lodge, and meeting place at Front and High Streets in central Philadelphia near the State House that would become Independence Hall. (Wikimedia Commons)

The Caribbean islands were designated as locations to "break" or acclimate native Africans to slavery. Therefore, slavery in the West Indies and Barbados was reportedly mindbogglingly barbaric. A 1791 lithographic print titled "Barbarities in the West Indies" suggests sadistic punishments including starvation, deadly whippings that literally stripped flesh from bones, and tossing enslaved Africans into the vats of boiling sugarcane used to make rum.[38] "The planters ... were provided with many new ways to keep their slaves in line," according to Maalik Stansbury's 2016 article, "Barbados Slave Codes." "They had the right and the authority to chastise, whip, brand, lacerate, cripple, set them on fire, or murder them with no negative consequences" because "during this time the English common Law, which included the right to a jury and judge was not offered to the Africans."[39] Although there's no clear evidence that Cremona Morrey had been enslaved in Barbados, if her parents had been, then how might their experiences or trauma have impacted them or their daughter in what has been termed as "Post-Traumatic Slave Syndrome" consisting of slavery's pain and anguish transmitted to successive descendant generations?[40]

Such brutality and its impact were certainly considerations of English-born Benjamin Lay (1682–1759), a contemporary of Cremona and Richard Morrey, who protested slavery by interrupting the Friends meetings, destroying goods made with slave labor, and even temporarily kidnapping the children of

Benjamin Lay was a Quaker who, during the early 18th century, demonstrated against slavery throughout the Philadelphia area. He lived in a cave in the Cheltenham and Abington areas. (Library of Congress)

Cheltenham-area Quakers, likely including some meeting at Richard Wall's house (above), supported what became known as the first official protest against slavery in America that was organized 1688 in nearby Germantown. (Kristopher Scott)

slaveholders. Described as a hunchbacked dwarf, Lay was one of the earliest Quakers to oppose slavery in America, among a few others:

> The Society of Friends had been ambivalent toward slavery, with some advocating and supporting it, and others—a decided minority—opposing it on grounds that true Christians would not own slaves, and those who did should immediately free them. By 1745, the situation had reversed itself, thanks in part to the famous antislavery petition of Francis Daniel Pastorius and the Mennonites of Germantown [this 1688 event is described by some sources as being the first "official" protest against slavery in America], which had been rejected out of hand, but led directly to other Quaker antislavery writers and agitators such as George Keith, Ralph Sandiford, and William Southeby, all of whom were met with the daunting response from their fellow Friends—"It is neither just nor convenient to set them at liberty."[41]

Lay was widely recognized for witnessing and writing about the horrors of that institution in Barbados after sailing there with his wife, Sarah, and opening a small store or waterfront retail establishment during the early 1700s before ultimately relocating to Philadelphia. In fact, "during an 18-month sojourn as a shopkeeper in Barbados, he saw an enslaved man kill himself rather than submit to yet another whipping; that and myriad other barbarities in that British colony both traumatized him and drove his passion for antislavery," wrote historian and author Marcus Rediker in his September 2017 *Smithsonian* magazine article, "The 'Quaker Comet' Was the Greatest Abolitionist You've Never Heard Of."[42]

In his 1737 antislavery book published by Benjamin Franklin, Lay noted the horrors that the starving enslaved Africans "thick as Bees" endured and too often succumbed to, including brutal fighting for rotting food sometimes distributed by his wife, Sarah: "She was a tender-hearted Woman, and, as I said, would be very often giving them something or other; stinking Biscuits which sometimes we had in abundance, bitten by the Cockroaches; or rotten Cheese, stinking Meat, decayed Fish which we had plenty of in that hot Country," Lay wrote.[43] "Yet the poor Creatures would come running, and tearing, and rending one another, to get a part in the scramble of that which I am sure some Dogs would not touch, much less eat of … and so ravenous were they, that I never saw a parcel of Hounds more eager about a dead Carcase [*sic*], than they always were."[44] But Lay himself admits to becoming uncontrollably angry when some of the starving enslaved Africans resorted to stealing from his establishment. "Sometimes I could catch them, and then I would give them Stripes [traditionally administered with a leather whip] …, but I have been sorry for it many times, and it does grieve me to this day, considering the extream [*sic*] Cruelty and Misery they always live under."[45]

Beginning in the early to mid-1400s Africans were enslaved in Europe and then throughout much of Western Hemisphere, including the Caribbean, South America, and North America.[46] And that's despite many slaveholders being Quakers who eventually were among the first Europeans to oppose slavery in what would become the United States of America.[47]

Actually, there is some documentation that Cremona and also some of her descendants may have been practicing Quakers[48] like Pennsylvania's founder, William Penn (who was also an early Pennsylvania slaveholder), and many of his associates, including some of Cremona's Morrey enslavers. Quakers, so called "because they trembled before God,"[49] followed the teachings of Leicestershire, England-native George Fox (1624–1691), who in 1652 founded the Religious Society of Friends. The itinerant preacher "exhorted seekers to heed the voice of Christ within, to be honest in business, compassionate to the needy, and to share in the free ministry of the true church."[50]

The beliefs of Fox and his rapidly growing following ignited their often-brutal persecution by opposing religious and political traditionalists; one of the most prominent Fox supporters was William Penn, granted land (that became Pennsylvania) in America by King George because Penn's father, Admiral William Penn (1621–1670), had served the Crown. The elder Penn had, for one thing, acquired Jamaica,[51] one of many Caribbean islands where many thousands of Africans would be enslaved. Strikingly, Penn established Pennsylvania as a haven for those seeking the very freedom that would be initially granted to the indigenous Lenape, a subgroup of the so-called Delawares.[52] Later, however, they were essentially robbed of their land and pushed to western hinterlands, even sometimes placed in bondage, by the European settlers[53] as the so-called settlers increasingly enslaved Africans.[54]

After learning about fellow Quaker William Penn's experimental colony, Pennsylvania, that purportedly offered freedom and equality for all, Lay with his wife, after a brief residence back in England, relocated to Philadelphia only to learn that slavery was hypocritically alive and well. They witnessed slave auctions and family separations, and Native Americans were being increasingly castigated. "Benjamin and Sarah looked forward to joining William Penn's 'Holy Experiment,'" Rediker writes. "Like the many thousands of others who had sailed to 'this good land,' as he called Pennsylvania, they anticipated a future of 'great Liberty.'" Rediker further notes: "Philadelphia was North America's largest city, and it included the world's second-largest Quaker community." It would also feature the greatest concentration of free blacks in the country.[55]

However, after living "in England, where the sights of slavery were few, Lay was angered when he arrived in Philadelphia"[56] and likely witnessed those slave auctions being held at and in the vicinity of London Coffee House, established in 1754 near Front and Market Streets.[57] It was a very well-known enterprise area frequented and inhabited by the likes of the Morreys; President George Washington; and the famous American scholar, statesman, politician, and scientist Benjamin Franklin—all slaveholders. During America's Constitutional Convention, Washington recalled in his diary that on Tuesday, June 12, 1787, he "Dined and drank Tea at Mr. [Robert] Morris's," and then "went afterwards to a concert at the City Tavern."[58] This was just one of many times that he and other prominent convention attendees patronized the establishment near Second and Walnut Streets, erected in 1773 only a few blocks from London Coffee House.[59]

Franklin visited Lay's abode[60] in a cave where he lived after moving from a locale that had been closer to the city; he relocated several miles northwest of central Philadelphia near York Road and Green Lane in "Branchtown."[61] That would have been about four miles southeast from Humphrey and Richard Morrey's country estate in Cheltenham where Cremona and other people of African descent were or had been enslaved. There are other indications that later Benjamin Franklin and other top officials visited Lay in a similar or second

The Revolutionary War's battle of Edge Hill was fought on or adjacent to land where the African American community of Guineatown once stood. (Library of Congress)

cave dwelling to which he probably moved during the 1730s in what is today Abington Township. The second cave was previously thought to be located near the Abington Friends Meetinghouse that Lay sometimes attended or "along [what is today] Chelten Hills Drive" in Cheltenham, although local historians now believe Lay's cave was located somewhere between Manor College and the Alverthorpe estate in nearby Jenkintown.[62] Lay and his wife are buried in a graveyard adjacent to the Abington meetinghouse and the associated Abington Friends School near a state historical marker and tombstone inscribed with "BENJAMIN LAY—1682–1759, SARAH LAY—1677–1735 (EXACT LOCATION OF GRAVE UNKNOWN)." [63]

Indeed, there's also a possibility that Cremona's parents, if the presumption concerning their African or Guinean origins is correct, came directly from the west coast of Africa to the Philadelphia port where they would have been disembarked, cleaned, and auctioned at or in front of London Coffee House or a similar nearby facility where the so-called colonial elite, probably including Humphrey and his son Richard Morrey, would congregate, drink spirited beverages, and even vote.[64] Various accounts indicate that people living in or visiting what was then central Philadelphia could smell—well before a vessel was actually sighted or reached the Philadelphia dock—the stench of human waste that enslaved Africans lay in while chained in the bowels of ships cruising across the Atlantic for up to two or three months and then sailing up the Delaware River. "Witnesses in near proximity reportedly said they could catch a whiff of the distinctive stench that every well-traveled mariner in that ... age knew: the reek of closely-packed bodies, human misery, captivity and death."[65]

As an early African-descended inhabitant of the Philadelphia area, did Cremona Morrey while maturing into a young woman witness the arrival of such vessels during the early 1700s or monitor the slave auctions at or near London Coffee House? Was she, in fact, a victim of those human sales on the proverbial "auction block"? Could she read and keep up with the advertisements in Benjamin Franklin's *Pennsylvania Gazette* newspaper that published runaway slave ads, helping to enrich Franklin as he played an integral role in supporting the institution of slavery—despite ultimately opposing slavery in writing, but keeping blacks in bondage throughout his life?[66] If so, what impact did such experiences and slavery-related ads have on Cremona's psyche and those of other African Americans of the period?

An advertisement from July 12, 1738, when Cremona would have been about age 28 if her estimated birth year of 1710 is correct, clearly indicates that the slave trade in Philadelphia certainly existed: "RUM, SUGAR, and

MELLASSES [*sic*], with some likely Men and Women NEGRO-SLAVES, that have had the Small-Pox, To be Sold by Charles Read, in Philadelphia."[67]

And regarding the escape of an African-descended slave closer to Cremona's Cheltenham home in nearby Whitemarsh, Franklin published in the same July 12, 1738, edition: "RUN away this Morning from *Edward Farmer* of Whitemarsh, a stout lusty Mollatto [*sic*], known in Philadelphia by the Name of Mollatto Jemm alias *James Earl*, has a Scar on his Temple, a wide Mouth and thick Lips, speaks good English." Apparently Farmer was determined to provide details that could lead to Earl's capture: "He was Cloathed when he went away, with a new Duroy Jacket of a dirty colour, lined with a dark blue-grey clour's Shalloon, trim'd with dark collour'd Mohair and Buttons, a fine Shirt, a new fine Hat, a Silk Hankerchief, a speckled Pair of Trowsers, worsted Stockings, and new Shoes and Buckles in them."[68]

The ad, ending with the full name of "Edward Farmer" (1672–1745), a slave owner who would also serve as a scout and interpreter dealing with local Native Americans such as the Lenape, also concludes by offering a monetary reward: "Whoever takes up and secures the said Mollatto [*sic*], or brings him home to his Master, or puts him in the Workhouse of Philadelphia, shall have Five Pounds Reward, paid by—EDWARD FARMER."[69]

It's more than probable that Farmer knew of the Morreys and perhaps had dealt with them, as well as Samuel Morris (1708–1770), who had served as Philadelphia's sheriff and owned the adjacent Hope Lodge estate in Whitemarsh, part of which was acquired from Farmer's sprawling land holdings. Morris, in the following March 5, 1751, *Pennsylvania Gazette* advertisement, seemed quite anxious to rent central Philadelphia real estate and sell three African-descended human beings: "To be lett, by SAMUEL MORRIS, in Second-street, A Commodious Tan-yard, on a navigable part of the Dock, containing 26 vatts, besides 3 large lime-pits, &c. all under cover, with a loft that will contain 2 or 3 hundred cords of bark." Morris advertised that he had "also 3 Negroe men to dispose of, well acquainted with the tanning business; and one of them excellent currier. And a quantity of good upper, foal [*sic*], bridle and harness leather, by small or large parcels."[70]

Likely of particular interest to Cremona would have been a *Gazette* advertisement of June 29, 1738, concerning an interracial runaway, probably of African descent, mirroring her possible mixed-race ethnicities: "RUN away on the 20th Inst., from Joseph James of Cohansey, a Servant Man named Lazarus Kenny, is a swarthy Fellow, his Father being a Molatto [*sic*] and his Mother a white Woman." The advertisement continued:

> He is pretty tall and well set, his Hair cut off: Had on a Felt Hat, grey Kersey Coat and Vest, old Leather Breeches, an old homespun Shirt, yarn Stockings, round toe'd Shoes and brass Buckles. He took a large white Stallion that trots altogether, with an old black Saddle and good Snaffel Bridle. Whoever secures the said Servant and Horse so that they are had again, shall have *Forty Shillings* Reward and reasonable Charges, paid by—*Joseph James*.[71]

There were more than a few enslaved Africans on properties within several miles of where Cremona Morrey had been initially held in bondage, according to Theodore W. Bean's 1884 *History of Montgomery County, Pennsylvania*, based on "a variety of advertisements once circulated in this county," including the tragic sale of a one-year-old infant boy:

> Richard Bevan gives notice, in the *Pennsylvania Gazette* of July 24, 1751, that he has for sale, "near the Gulf Mill, a likely negro man about thirty years of age, fit for town or country business. Also a negro girl about fifteen years of age." John Jones, of the "Manor of Moreland, near the Crooked Billet," announces in the same paper of October 12, 1752, that he has for sale "a likely negro woman, about twenty-nine years of age, had the small-pox, and understands country business well. Also a negro child, a boy, one year old."[72]

Cremona would have also been particularly impacted, if she could read or somehow was apprised of such transactions and advertisements concerning the enslavement of black females since she was an African-descended young woman, including another June 29, 1738, *Pennsylvania Gazette* ad: "To be SOLD by the said Thomas Howard, a couple of likely Negro Girls, one Bermudas [*sic*] Born, the other Antigua, they can do any kind of Household Work, and are fit for Town or Country."[73]

In fact, as previously noted, black women such as Cremona Morrey were among the earliest Africans to arrive in the Philadelphia area, including, the parents of "Alice," one of the most colorful and long-lived people in local and American history. "Her parents, from Barbados, arrived here in 1684 on the Isabella, the first slave ship to reach Philadelphia," writes researcher-scholar Constance Garcia-Barrio. "Colonial women of color shaped history and paved the way for others." Indeed, at "age 5, Alice began serving drinks and oysters in a tavern and lighting pipes for its patrons, according to Susan Klepp, a retired Temple University history professor. Legend has it that when Alice lit a pipe for William Penn (1644–1718), he tipped her one pence, about 75 cents [in] today's money."[74]

Notably, "Alice, known variously as Black Alice and Alice of Dunk's Ferry," was quite a remarkable person, according the website of The Library Company of Philadelphia, founded by Benjamin Franklin in 1731 "as a subscription library supported by its shareholders," primarily affluent white male colonists. She "was a native of Philadelphia and a slave, born to parents who had come from Barbados. She is said to have been 116 at the time of her death in 1802," mathematically making her birth year about 1686, just several years after William Penn arrived in 1682. "In extreme old age Alice," a lifetime member of Christ Church, "received many visitors who enjoyed hearing stories about early Philadelphia and its famous first settlers, including William Penn and Thomas Logan."[75]

In his 2001 book, *African Americans in Pennsylvania: Above Ground and Underground*, the preeminent black Pennsylvania historian Charles Blockson described Alice as "an amazing African American" who "vividly recalled the original wooden structure" of Christ Church whose members also included such colonial powerhouses as Benjamin Franklin and Dr. Benjamin Rush, the foremost physician of the burgeoning colony. "The ceiling of it could be touched with her lifted hands. The bell, to call the people to worship, was hung in the crotch of a nearby tree. At the age of 10, Alice's slave owner then moved her to Dunk's Ferry, 17 miles up the Delaware River in Bucks County. She later collected tolls at Dunk's Ferry Bridge."[76]

Incredibly, Alice was "remembered riding on horseback, galloping to Christ Church at the age of 95," Blockson noted. "She vividly remembered William Penn, and survived George Washington, the first President of the United States," passing away in Bristol of Bucks County, Pennsylvania, on earth for well past a century.[77]

It's quite likely that Thomas Forten (1740–1773),[78] father of the wealthy free-black sailmaker James Forten (1766–1842),[79] monitored such advertisements and witnessed slave-ship arrivals in Philadelphia during the mid-1700s. As the grandson of an enslaved African who more than likely sailed up the Delaware River in bondage during the 1680s and somehow later obtained emancipation or self-liberated himself,[80] Thomas was probably born free and would have been also a contemporary of Cremona and Richard Morrey. Thomas's freeborn son, James Forten, would eventually fight in the Revolutionary War and help to start in Philadelphia what may have been the first major civil rights organization in America, the Free African Society, after becoming quite wealthy by acquiring a sail-making enterprise from Robert Bridges, a white man likely with abolitionist leanings. That organization gave birth to two pioneering black religious institutions anchored by the Mother Bethel African Methodist Episcopal Church founded by Richard Allen and the African Episcopal Church of St. Thomas, established by Absalom Jones, both highly respected social activists, preachers, and theologians who had been slaves.[81]

In fact, descendants of Cremona and Richard Morrey would become prominent members of both denominations that were at the forefront of the antislavery and Underground Railroad movements, including their great grandson, Hiram Charles Montier Jr. (1818–1905), as reported in *The Philadelphia Times* (September 5, 1882 edition): "The meeting of colored Independent Republicans, called by Robert Purves [sic], William Still and forty-eight other prominent colored men, which was held at Liberty Hall on Lombard street, below Eighth, last night, was attended by one of the best-dressed and most intelligent-appearing audiences of colored men ever assembled in this city," the newspaper reported. "Conspicuous among those who lent their names to the movement as vice presidents and occupied seats upon the platform were: Robert [Purvis], F. P. Main, E. E. Birchett, Robert Williams … and Hiram Montier." The unidentified writer noted that attempts to disrupt the meeting were fervent and somewhat effective: "They did not succeed in silencing the Independent speakers, but they did create a great noise and confusion when the meeting was about half over, and for a time it looked like breaking up in a row. About a dozen policemen from the Nineteenth district station house were present on duty, and while they made a pretence [sic] of remonstrating with the roughs they appeared to be more in sympathy with the rowdies than to make any determined effort to preserve order."[82]

However, curiously, an 1820 United States Federal Census report indicates that a "Hiram Mauntier," possibly Hiram Jr.'s father, Hiram Montier (1780–1861), who was the son of Cremona Jr. and John Montier, had two male youngsters identified as "Slaves" within a household of 10 people living in his Cheltenham home on the northwest outskirts of Philadelphia.[83] That's keeping in mind that some early blacks acquired others in bondage with the distinct intention to liberate them. There's also a possibility that the two youngsters were classified as slaves because of colonial-era laws requiring interracial children in Pennsylvania into forced labor or servitude until they became young adults. Considering the antislavery abolitionist and pro-civil rights activities of Richard and Cremona Morrey's descendants, including the Bustills, Douglasses, Millers, and Robesons, the two "Slaves" may have been relatives or somehow associated with the Montier family who were acquired so they could be emancipated, perhaps via the Underground Railroad. Or they could have been leased out to Elizabeth and Hiram Montier by a nearby slaveholder until their freedom could be purchased but actually living as free blacks or mulattos within the couple's household.[84] "Masters routinely hired out their slaves, which further added to the labor system's flexibility and the regional impact of slavery," notes James Gigantino in *The Encyclopedia of Greater Philadelphia*. "The hiring-out system allowed slaves to move throughout the region on long and short term contracts to various masters."[85]

About the time that Hiram's grandmother Cremona Morrey was purportedly born in 1710, "slaves constituted almost twenty percent of Philadelphia's population," according to Gigantino, who further notes that "the number of slaves increased until just before the American Revolution, reaching 1,375 in 1770 or just over eight percent of the total population."[86]

In fact, just two decades later, George Washington, as the first president of the United States, would bring nine enslaved Africans to Philadelphia, where he served his initial term in the Executive House (1790 to 1797), leased from the financier of the Revolutionary War—and future United States treasurer—Robert Morris, a slaveholder who also reportedly co-owned a shipping and trading company, Willing, Morris & Co., that bought, transported, and sold slaves. "Washington's presidential household included nine enslaved Africans from Mount Vernon," his plantation in Virginia, according to historian Edward Lawler Jr. Those enslaved Africans included Hercules, his chef reputed to have been trained in France, as well as Washington's wife Martha's "body servant," Oney Judge. Both of these enslaved blacks ultimately successfully escaped bondage, almost certainly with the help of antislavery activists in Philadelphia's large free-black population.[87]

Although Oney Judge decided to flee the Washingtons' bondage, other black women remained enslaved or as free persons for their prior "masters" after their apparent abolition or liberation, quite notably Cremona Morrey. Still, there's at least one noted case of a black woman not choosing liberation, according to Soderlund: "Sometime before 1750, and perhaps as early as 1720, Rachel Pemberton, the wife of long-term assemblyman and Quaker leader Israel Pemberton Sr., offered freedom to her slave Betty," Soderlund writes. "The black woman refused the offer, preferring to remain with the family."[88]

However, that was the exception for such women, though some obviously remained in the white host family's household for economic and familial reasons. "Later in the century, in the spring of 1776, another wealthy Quaker couple, Provincial Councilor William Logan and his wife, Hannah, discussed freedom with their slave Dinah. In this case, however, the black woman broached the subject," Soderlund notes. "The Logans had already freed her daughter Bess, but they seem to have been saddened by Dinah's request [to be liberated] because she had been in Hannah's family since she was a child and they considered her a part of the family."[89]

Such circumstances help to illuminate the conditions in which Cremona [Satterthwaite] Morrey Fry may have lived and the dynamics that she considered as an enslaved African, then liberated employee of Richard Morrey who reportedly bought her own freedom presumably from Richard for £20 by or before 1746.[90] Some sources indicate or imply that Richard liberated her without money changing hands, perhaps before or during their romantic union.[91] Her considerations had to be based on the nature of that relationship and how it was initiated and persisted for almost a decade from about 1736 to 1746. Was it truly an egalitarian relationship with Cremona feeling no pressure to become what was essentially Richard Morrey's common-law wife? Is it at all possible for someone in Cremona's circumstances not to feel even one iota of coercion—especially considering that women and African Americans were virtually powerless legally and otherwise during Philadelphia's colonial period? It's likely that she did feel some level of coercive pressure. The question is, to what degree?

Considering such circumstances and her "Negro" and/or mixed ethnicity, Cremona Morrey must have been a woman of extraordinary courage and intellectual prowess. And despite her mate Richard Morrey's prominence, which probably shielded her from the prejudicial wrath of colonial society, his gender and skin color placed him at the apex of that society while Cremona—a woman of color—was at the bottom. Whether her heritage was primarily African or

This deed, found at Haverford College, details Richard Morrey's leasing almost two hundred acres for 500 years to Cremona, with various stipulations. (Quaker & Special Collections, Haverford College)

included a notable amount of Native American ancestry, Cremona had to be constantly cognizant of and concerned about such dynamics, including the potentially devastating consequences of her relationship with Richard rupturing from internal and external pressures that were likely quite formidable.

Exploring Cremona's Possible Links to the Lenape, Satterthwaites

Various genealogical and historical sources indicate that part of Cremona's parentage or ancestry included Native Americans of the Delaware or Lenape tribe, perhaps one or more of those predecessors intermarrying or intermixing with the European Satterthwaite family with deep Quaker roots in England.[92] Indeed, although there's growing evidence that indigenous Americans were enslaved and exported to distant colonies in greater numbers than previously realized, "Native Americans were occasionally among the enslaved [in America] until at least the middle of the eighteenth century," according to researcher-writer James Gigantino, "but most enslaved people were Africans or African descendants."[93]

Still, there were instances of Native Americans and African Americans intermixing and having children who were held in bondage, not far from where Cremona Morrey was probably initially enslaved in Cheltenham. In the July 24, 1751, issue of Benjamin Franklin's *Pennsylvania Gazette*, a prominent colonist and Pennsylvania Supreme Court justice paid for an advertisement seeking an absconded mixed-race "slave," according to Theodore W. Bean's 1884 *History of Montgomery County*: "Dr. Thomas Graeme states that 'a mulatto slave, named Will, about twenty-nine years of age, being of a Negro father and an Indian mother,' ran away from his plantation in Horsham township. 'Whoever secures him in any goal shall have five pounds reward and reasonable charges paid.'"[94]

Graeme, as well as his superior, Sir William Keith, appointed governor of Pennsylvania, held multiple slaves in bondage, as did the cofounder of Cheltenham, Tobias Leech—including enslaved Africans assigned only single names such as Ben, Cuffy, Betty, Cate, Cuggs, Busso[95]—whom Cremona Morrey may have known since Leech lived on an estate near the Morreys' residence where she was enslaved and then employed. The trio of slaveholders also probably dealt with or interacted with local Native Americans, in particular the nearby Lenape (whom the English called the "Delaware"), inhabiting the land for thousands of years, before the arrival of the European colonists: "They were a nomadic people belonging to the Algonquian language family."[96]

Important tribes within this language group also included the Ojibwa, Blackfoot, and Shawnee. The Lenape were divided into three bands of sub-tribes: the Minsi (or Munsee, "People of the Stone Country") inhabited the northern part of Pennsylvania, the Unami ("People Who Live Down-River") inhabited the central region of Pennsylvania, and the Unalachtigo ("People Who Live by the Ocean") inhabited the southern area of Pennsylvania. The Lenape who inhabited the land that became Philadelphia spoke the Unami dialect.[97]

As "Penn's colony" began to take off during the early 17th century, it appears that many servants in Pennsylvania were indentured and from a variety of ethnicities, including white, black, and Native American, despite the growing number of enslaved Africans. Initial regulations imposed on such servants appeared to be somewhat equitable or less stringent than in other comparable colonies:[98]

> In Penn's colony, all servants had to be registered with full names, wages, and pay clearly documented. There was a strict requirement that no servant could be kept past the time of indenture. They were to be "kindly treated" and provided with the "customary outfit" at the time they were freed. Those servants included Native Americans and blacks as well as indentured whites.[99]

It's likely that the three indentured groups found time to intermix and even intermarry as they sometimes lived and worked in close quarters, again conjuring up the likelihood—especially considering European Satterthwaites living in the vicinity, most practicing Quakers in what is today nearby Abington Township—of Cremona (Satterthwaite) Morrey Fry's mixed race. In fact, it appears that Native Americans, at first, were given extra consideration, perhaps as the original custodians of the land: "In addition, Indians were provided with legal channels to redress grievances. Any person who 'injured' an Indian would be punished, and any planter who was injured by one should 'not be his own judge upon the Indian.' Conflicts between the two parties were to be settled by a committee of six white men and six Indians."[100]

Tragically, though, the pretense of "Brotherly Love" would not persist, as briefly discussed earlier. "Peaceful relations between the European settlers and the Lenape would disintegrate, however, not long after Penn's death in 1718," according to Licht et al.[101] "The Lenape famously lost all claims to the terrain they had inhabited for centuries in the fraudulent 'Walking Purchase' deed of 1737. After purchase agreements with William Penn, the Lenape moved outward, but soon these lands would be claimed by growing numbers of European settlers in the countryside around Penn's Philadelphia," Licht et al. further note. Soon after, "Penn's sons reinterpreted an accord that Penn had reached with the Lenape in 1686, insisting that the Penn family claim extended a full day-and-a-half's walking distance. Sending out so-called 'walkers' to determine the extent of their asserted domain, the Penn family seized ownership of lands sixty-five miles to the north and west of the earlier purchase agreements, effectively adding 750,000 acres to the family estate."[102]

Yet, clearly, the enslavement of African-descended people, including those mixed with Native American heritage, would expand: "The enslavement of Africans was tolerated under the auspices of educating and religiously training them," Jack Schick notes.[103]

Indeed, was it possible for Cremona's heritage to be at least partially Native American?

One unsubstantiated online Ancestry.com entry identifies "Cremona SATTERTHWAITE" as being born on October 27, 1710 in Catawba County, North Carolina, ultimately passing away 1770 in Pennsylvania's Montgomery County. Her father is identified as "Delaware Indian Fivekiller," born 1674 in Cherokee, Alabama and dying in 1741. Her mother, in that entry, is unidentified. Cremona's "Spouse," however, is listed as Richard Morrey, living from 1675 to 1754. "Cremona SATTERTHWAITE married Richard MORREY and had 2 children," the entry says,[104] obviously not the four to five children numbered in other sources. Furthermore, there appears to be uncertainty concerning whether her supposed father was ethnically "Cherokee" or "Delaware."

Although most genealogy sources do not identify Cremona's possible Native American mother, a "Private User" via genealogy website Geni.com (among a couple of other online sources), in May 2022 identified her maternal parent as "Tame Doe," presumably of the Lenape tribe. According to the Geni.com source, Cremona is also listed as the "Wife of Richard Morrey" and "Mother of Rachel Morrey; Elizabeth Bustill; Cremona Montier; Caesar Morrey[105] and Robert [Lewis] Morrey." Her "Occupation" is described as "negro servant," despite both parents seemingly identified as Native American.[106] Still, is there a possibility that either or both potential Lenape parents were of African and Native American ancestry?

Some modern descendants have identified or implied Cremona as having Native American ancestry, although one prominent family member, the late William Pickens III, previously said that he believed she did not. According to Daniel DiPrinzio, descendants participated in a spring 2022 program at Arcadia University, including Joyce Mosley, a descendant of the Morreys, Bustills, Millers, and Montiers. "Born Cremona Satterthwaite in 1710, Cremona Morrey was an 18th-century Lenape/black woman who was formerly enslaved on the Cheltenham estate of Philadelphia's first major, Humphrey Morrey (appointed in 1691 by William Penn)," DiPrinzio writes. Richard then "entered into a relationship with Cremona, who took his last name. While the nature of their relationship is not fully clear, the couple had five interracial children during the 1730s and 1740s, and she was willed the land by Richard Morrey."[107]

There's also the possibility that the enslavers of Cremona's parents were British Satterthwaites, or associated with one of their slave-dealing enterprises. Indeed, some of the European Satterthwaites were likely involved very early in the transatlantic slave trade, according to various sources. Benjamin Satterthwaite of England, who was deeply involved in the Caribbean slave trade, made the following observations in a letter written to his stepfather during the summer of 1740, just a few decades after Cremona was born: He wrote that a primary competitor, "Morecroft [or Moorecroft] has so many Guineamen [slavers] to load that he's engaged several plantations for the crops of sugar this year, which is expected to break very high. The Liverpool and Bristol men I believe will make a fleet and go without convoy." Benjamin

Arcadia University's 2018 to 2022 panel discussions focused on Morrey, Montier, and Bustill African American families, highlighting the interracial relationship between Cremona and Richard Morrey. William Pickens, III speaks (sitting in the center) as WHYY-PBS television's producer Karen Smyles moderates from the podium. (Arcadia University)

The Grey Towers administrative building is located at Arcadia University in the vicinity of land that was owned by Cremona Morrey. (Wikimedia Commons)

Satterthwaite was "born in Leeds the son of a Quaker, Thomas Satterthwaite and his second wife Mary," according to "The Letter Book Of Benjamin Satterthwaite Of Lancaster, 1737–1744," read by M. M. Schofield to The Historic Society of Lancashire & Cheshire in 1960.[108] "In the 1740s Benjamin was in Barbados, not only participating in the slave trade, but also acting as an agent for Gillows of Lancaster (a local furniture makers [*sic*]) in the West Indies," according to Art UK's caption of an oil-painting portrait of Benjamin Satterthwaite (1718–1792) sporting a serious, ruddy face; a slender nose; silver hair with arching brown eyebrows; and a white ruffled shirt, ivory vest, and high-collar dark blue or black jacket.[109]

Further, according to Schofield, Henry Laurens, a Charleston, South Carolina, slave trader who followed John Hancock as the president of the Second Continental Congress, noted that "slaves" were "sold there [South Carolina] from the Gambia, owned by 'Satterthwaite and Inman.'" Schofield added, "Some of the slaves had been sent from Barbados by the firm of 'Law, Satterthwaite and Jones,'" another indication of the Satterthwaites' involvement in the slave trade.[110]

Interestingly, however, the first Satterthwaites to arrive in America "came from England in the colonial days, and located in the exact spot where the city of Philadelphia now stands," says the introduction of the 1887 book of remembrances compiled by F. S. Stickney, *Fenner Bryan Satterthwaite, Together With The Obituary Proceedings Of The Washington Bar, Etc.* "Joseph was the first to turn his course southward. He came to North Carolina, and settled in that section of Beaufort county called Pungo, then known by its Indian name, Machipungo, before the Revolution. From him was descended in the third generation Fenner Bryan Satterthwaite, who was born on the 6th of March, 1813." The Satterthwaites came from "people who had fled from persecution," presumably because they were Quakers, "to the wild retreat in the woods of Carolina, then an unnamed province." Stickney described the Satterthwaites as "a liberty loving people … grown up in her [North Carolina's] borders."[111]

However, that adoration for liberty apparently did not extend to the enslaved Africans that Fenner Satterthwaite (1813–1875) owned, despite his supposedly amiable attitude during interactions with them, family, and friends: "He was a genial host, a thoughtful parent, a kind master," Stickney wrote. "His slaves, his family, and his friends were devoted to him."[112]

Stickney ended his introductory passage with a story about Satterthwaite that reflects a disturbing paternalistic attitude regarding slavery and assumes that the enslaved were innately happy with their circumstances of serving slaveholders:

Only a few weeks before, he had attended in the cemetery the burial of one of his faithful slaves—Carey. Many white persons were present, and when the last spade-full of earth had been thrown on his grave, he raised himself up from his revery [*sic*] and addressed those who had come to honor the funeral of this poor negro. He first spoke of his faithfulness and noble example; then of the precarious tenure we have on life, ending with the query—*who should be next?* He wept, and all wept; it was a solemn day. He was next. If we end well is not the race successful?[113]

Fenner Bryan Satterthwaite died in 1875, a decade after the United States Civil War that essentially ended slavery, at least on paper, following his marriage to Annie E. Laughinghouse and having almost a dozen children.[114] He also served in the House of Representatives from Beaufort County and had been an attorney, studying law under John S. Hawks before being admitted to the North Carolina Bar in 1843, according to the Fenner Bryan Satterthwaite Papers, 1857–1913, held at the North Carolina Digital Collections.[115]

Meanwhile, despite a branch of the Satterthwaites settling in North Carolina, it's clear that some remained in the Philadelphia area according to *The Pennsylvania Gazette*, the newspaper published by Benjamin Franklin who significantly profited from runaway-slave advertisements placed in the paper.[116] In fact, as mentioned earlier, Franklin enslaved several blacks throughout his lifetime, perhaps some that Cremona Morrey may have known or heard about, keeping in mind that Franklin also sporadically supported antislavery abolitionist causes.[117]

Estate affairs of the late William Satterthwaite were described in Franklin's Philadelphia-based newspaper on Thursday, June 7, 1753: "By virtue of a writ to me directed, will be exposed to sale by way of publick vendue, at the house of Joseph Inslee, in Newtown, on the 14th day of June next, a messuage and plantation, situate in Soleberry township, Bucks county, containing one hundred acres … lately the property of William Satterthwaite, deceased, now in the hands and custody of William Biles, administrator to the estate of said Satterthwaite," the advertisement says.[118]

According to the "Satterthwaite family papers" held at the Haverford College Quaker & Special Collections repository, William Satterthwaite was born about 1709, approximately the time of Cremona's birth, to Esther and Michael Satterthwaite. William apparently traveled from England and settled in Pennsylvania, marrying Pleasant Mead in 1736.[119]

However, a conflicting account of William's marriage and life appeared in the article "A tale of fractured love on Lumberville's Coppernose Hill," published on April 18, 2016, in the *Bucks County Courier Times* by columnist Carl LaVO: "Bill was an idealistic young schoolteacher and poet in England in the 1700s.

Then love walked in. In the midst of a wild storm, he offered overnight shelter to a female student," LaVO wrote. "The torch was lit. 'The imprudence of their step dawning upon them next day, they set sail for Philadelphia,' according to a letter about the couple written by Samuel Preston in 1826."[120]

Subsequently, the couple settled in Solebury, in "the picturesque village of Lumberville on the Delaware River. They built a home at the foot of a red sandstone hill overlooking the river. There they settled and had a baby. That's when things began to fall apart," according to LaVO, as Satterthwaite's wife became crankier and quite an "extravagant" spender, nearly ruining her husband financially, before attempting to poison him. Even his attempt to be consoled by a powerful slaveholding Quaker friend, Jeremiah Langhorne, did not help circumstances.[121]

After Satterthwaite was reportedly bitten by a rattlesnake and became deathly ill, his wife took the opportunity to elope with another man. It is then, according to LaVO, that "two villagers" actually "sent for Nutimus, the great Lenape Indian chief and medicine doctor [associated with the Delaware tribe]," who ultimately healed Satterthwaite.[122]

Although the blood of Cremona (Satterthwaite) Morrey Fry, a "Negro" daughter of the Motherland, might have been amalgamated with the Satterthwaites of Europe and others, she would survive the throes of human bondage in America, and ascend to become one of the very few black landowners with such expansive property in North America, despite the marital and other challenges that she would endure. Her perseverance and survival carved trailblazing pathways for her illustrious descendants. Along the way, Cremona (Satterthwaite) Morrey Fry's African and supposed indigenous-American bloodlines would merge with that of the so-called white aristocracy, in a place where the very concept of America was developed with significant governmental structural roots to the Native Americans' Iroquois Confederacy. The Natives' contributions are explored by Cynthia and Susan Feathers in "Franklin and the Iroquois Foundations of the Constitution":

> In 1744, envoys from Maryland, Pennsylvania, and Virginia met in Lancaster, Pennsylvania, with delegates, or *sachems*, of the Six Nations of the Iroquois Indians. During the discussion, the Iroquois leader Canassatego advocated the federal union of the American colonies, exhorting the colonists: "Our wise forefathers established a union and amity between the [original] Five Nations. This has made us formidable. This has given us great weight and authority with our neighboring Nations. We are a powerful Confederacy and by your observing the same methods our wise forefathers have taken you will acquire much strength and power; therefore, whatever befalls you, do not fall out with one another."

The Featherses further note: "When an Indian interpreter and old friend of Benjamin Franklin's brought him the official transcript of the proceedings, Franklin immediately published the account."[123]

Meanwhile, just a mile or two from where the African American identity was seeded and nurtured and later blossomed at Congo Square, then on the outskirts of central Philadelphia, African slaves were also inspected like common cattle before being sold on auction blocks at and near London Coffee House not far from the Philadelphia wharf, during the early 1700s. "Slaves were brought to [Washington] square," which became known as Congo Square, "once a month before they were sold to buyers in Pennsylvania and elsewhere," noted the late author-historian Charles Blockson, regaled as one of the nation's foremost collectors of African American memorabilia and rare books that are housed at Temple University's Charles L. Blockson Afro-American Collection. "At 'Congo Square,' slaves and freed African Americans could be seen [weekly on Sundays according to various other sources] praying, dancing, cooking traditional African foods, and conversing in various languages."[124] This was a scene that Cremona Morrey may have witnessed or even joined in early Philadelphia as those Africans buried their deceased via African rites. Along the way, those Africans began to develop unique African-English dialects to communicate and even rhythmically danced together to echoing drumbeats worshipping their ancient deities and bygone ancestors despite the often-deleterious challenges.[125]

Soon their simmering multicultural stew of Africanisms and the dynamism of leaders in the growing black community would ignite some of the first African American civil rights and religious institutions in America, all vital for establishing the African American identity. Richard S. Newman, in his book *Freedom's Prophet: Bishop Richard Allen, the AME Church, and the Black Founding Fathers*, focuses on the formation of the African American identity and the pioneering civil rights group the Free African Society, founded by Philadelphian theologians Richard Allen and Absalom Jones in 1787:

> One of the most important social characteristics of African society, communalism served as the foundation for free black culture in early national America. Connections between past and present, between African heritage and American realities, remained omnipresent to black founders like Allen. Nearly every major free black institution created in the urban North following the American Revolution had the word "African" affixed to it, from Masonic lodges to educational groups to benevolent societies.

These included the church that Allen founded, the Mother Bethel African Methodist Episcopal, and the African Episcopal Church of St. Thomas, which

Jones organized.[126] Indeed, Cremona's likely deep awareness—despite her comparative fortunes regarding land ownership—of the perils and diabolical injustices of slavery pertaining to the transatlantic slave trade and her parents' apparent abductions from Africa bring to mind a young and pioneering African American poet who was also kidnapped and enslaved before being emancipated, Phillis Wheatley (c. 1753–1784) of Boston:

> Should you, my lord, while you peruse my song,
> Wonder from whence my love of Freedom sprung,
> Whence flow these wishes for the common good,
> By feeling hearts alone best understood,
> I, young in life, by seeming cruel fate
> Was snatch'd from Afric's Fancy'd happy seat:
> What pangs excruciating must molest,
> What sorrows labour in my parent's breast?
> Steel'd was that soul and by no misery mov'd
> That from a father seiz'd his babe belov'd:
> Such, such my case. And can I then but pray
> Others may never feel tyrannic sway?[127]

Cremona's courageous survival and her progeny's ultimate thriving meant that they, as some of the first African Americans, would also give birth to a pioneering African American town—Cheltenham's Guineatown—that would be the genesis of the most esteemed blacks in the region, the United States, if not the world. A nearby sacred burial ground, the Montieth Graveyard—sometimes referred to as the Edge Hill Cemetery or Montier Cemetery—would also be established with up to 75 graves, where local historians believe Cremona and many of her brethren would be put to rest there in the rich, fertile soil that they had nourished with their lifeblood as enslaved and eventually liberated people in a distant land, the American republic for which they were so very much the essence and backbone.

CHAPTER 2

The Privileged English, New York, and Philadelphia Quakers

Humphrey and Richard Morrey

When Humphrey Morrey, the future first mayor of Philadelphia, was born about 1640 or 1650 (sources vary), in or near Cheshire, England, the country's political, religious, and social circumstances were in upheaval. There were immense "stresses and fractures" concerning "the collapse of the government of Charles I, the disintegration of the Church of England, and the accompanying panic that swept through much of the country on the eve of the English civil war."[1]

Approximately two hundred thousand lives were lost during that debacle and subsequent conflicts through 1651 between supporters of the monarchy and those opposing it, "directly or indirectly ... making it arguably the bloodiest conflict in the history of the British Isles."[2] Such conditions led to and may have even inspired the creation of the Quaker religion that Humphrey would adopt shortly before or after migrating to America. "Quakerism started in England in the second half of the 17th century, during the aftermath of the English Civil War; a time when many people were interested in radically reshaping religion, politics and society."[3] Spurred by the leadership of their founder, George Fox,

George Fox, the founder of Quakerism in England, attracted such followers as William Penn and Richard Morrey, as well as Richard's father, Humphrey Morrey, the first mayor of Philadelphia (circa 1691). The Quakers migrated from England to Philadelphia to escape persecution and pursue religious independence. (Wikimedia Commons)

"early Quakers started preaching around the North of England, and then further afield around Britain, gathering followers who were convinced by their radical ideas."[4]

Although various sources provide conflicting birth dates and at least one indicates that "no records have been found of Humphrey's birth,"[5] Ancestry.com's "Cheshire, England, Parish Registers, 1538–1909," records a "Humphray Morrey" being baptized on December 6, 1648, in Audlem, Cheshire, England; his father is identified as William Morrey, but his mother is not listed.[6]

Assuming Humphrey's father was born during the first or second decade of the 17th century, there are at least several William Morreys listed in Cheshire and other English baptism records who might be prime candidates for being Humphrey's father. One was baptized in 1614 at "All Saints, Newcastle-Upon-Tyne, Northumberland," England, with a father—who would have been Humphrey's grandfather—identified as Thomas Morrey, but no mother listed.[7] Yet, another William Morrey with an unidentified mother was baptized on November 21, 1619, at "Malpas, Cheshire, England"; his father is identified as Hugh Morrey.[8] And then there was William Morrey, baptized January 6, 1612, at "Wybunbury, Cheshire, England," again, with no mother listed.[9]

Meanwhile, the Morrey or Murray surname has an exceptionally deep history in the United Kingdom. "The surname Morrey was first found in Moray, where the Clan founder, Freskin [likely of Flemish ancestry], received a grant of the lands of Strathbrock in 1100 AD," in what today is Scotland, according to HouseofNames.com. "The ancient Pictish-Scottish family that first used the name Morrey lived in the county of Moray in the northeast of Scotland, but some historians describe the Clan's forebears as originally Flemish, some as Lowland Scots," the site says. "More enlightened research places them as [descendants] of MacAngus de Moravia, who was descended from King Duncan of Scotland and who was the first Earl of Murray."[10]

However, Humphrey Morrey's ancestry may have been partially or largely French, as some family-history sources suggest about the Morreys' or Morrays' deep ancestry. "Presumably of French Huguenot ancestry, he may have more recently come from 'Brereton, in the County of Chester, in Olde England,' where a number of his relatives lived."[11] In fact, according to the preeminent black history scholar Carter G. Woodson, the pro-black scholar and educator Anthony Benezet was one of the most prominent people of Huguenot ancestry settling in the Philadelphia area during the 17th and 18th centuries. Benezet was "born in St. Quentin in Picardy in France in 1713," just a few years after Cremona's presumed birth in 1710. "He was a descendant of a family of Huguenots who ... saw themselves denounced and persecuted as heretics and finally driven from the country by the edict of Nantes."[12] Though Benezet, reputed to be an unparalleled teacher, scholar, and intellect, did not initially advocate for the immediate liberation of enslaved Africans, he would become increasingly active in the antislavery movement;[13] Benezet would also allow African Americans to attend his school, including Richard Allen (1760–1831), the founder of the African Methodist Episcopal Church denomination in Philadelphia who had been enslaved with his family by Pennsylvania's chief supreme court justice, Benjamin Chew.[14]

Considering that Humphrey's "first known child" was "baptized in 1661 in London," likely after he "married a woman named Ann," his plausible age then mathematically was about 20 or 21 years old if born in 1640 (although some sources indicate he was born in 1650). In fact, "his brother Leonard lived in Buerton, Cheshire, and it is probable that Humphrey was born there." Humphrey and his wife Ann had several children. "He named his sons Humphrey, John, Leonard and Richard,"[15] the same "Richard" who would one day inherit a large portion of his father Humphrey's estates in America, along the way developing a relationship with the "Negro" family servant, Cremona Sr. "Richard Morrey was baptized in February 1675, in London, the son of Humphrey and Ann Morrey," presumably traveling with his parents to America by ship within seven to eight years before or by 1683. "He was baptized at the church of St. Bartholomew the Great in Smithfield" and "was the youngest of their known children and only one of two to survive to adulthood. He first came to New York as a child with his parents before 1683, then moved to Philadelphia with them."[16]

In fact, Sue Long, who says she is a modern Morrey descendant, has conducted much research that correlates with other historical accounts concerning Humphrey Morrey and his son, Richard. Long, who said that she is descended from Matilda, the daughter of Richard Morrey and his first wife, Ann (with the possible surname or maiden name of Turner), provided this author with family history data in an email dated June 11, 2013, focusing initially on Richard's father Humphrey and his first wife, also named Ann. "They had several children, including Richard, baptized at St. Bartholomew the Great in London around 1660 to 1665. An interesting time to be having children in London, what with the plague and the great fire." Long continued: "Humphrey bought land in Cheltenham, at the north end of the township, and the land in Philadelphia that made him wealthy, because of the ground rents." Meanwhile, their "son John married Sarah Budd and died fairly young."[17]

Most historical sources indicate that, upon arriving via ship in America about 1683, perhaps at the New York or New Amsterdam harbor, Humphrey Morrey and his family, along with friend William Frampton, initially resided in Oyster Bay, New York, and/or Manhattan, likely as farmers or yeomen. Later they probably became merchants. Humphrey was born "in England about 1650" and identified as "a Quaker" who "probably settled first in New York, removing to Philadelphia before 1685."[18] However, "before he came to Philadelphia … there are indications that he was a native of Rhode Island. He was a merchant in New York in 1684, and the following year he came to Philadelphia and continued in business as a merchant, or shopkeeper."[19]

Still, "at some point Humphrey and Ann left London and moved to New York, presumably taking their two surviving children with them [John and Richard]," probably after gravitating to the growing anti-establishment Quaker movement, perhaps suffering increasing persecution for being labeled heretics by traditionalists aligned with the Church of England and monarchy: "It is not known when they became Quakers and little is known of their life in New York. Some have speculated that they lived in Oyster Bay, Long Island, where there was a small Quaker community."[20]

Interestingly, however, more than a decade before Humphrey Morrey and his family may have lived in Oyster Bay, the founder of Quakerism, George Fox, actually visited Quaker congregants there in 1672 when Fox performed a miracle of sorts, according to the book, *History of Long Island from its Discovery and Settlement to Present Time*: "The celebrated George Fox, a man equally distinguished for his moral character, intelligence, and courage, visited America in 1672, and, as has been above remarked, paid a visit to this town [Oyster Bay]." The book says that "this extraordinary individual" had just spent "a few days in the city of Philadelphia, and [was] passing from thence through the province of New Jersey." According to Fox's own words in his "private journal":[21]

> At length we came to Middletown, an English plantation in East Jersey, where there were some Friends; but we could not stay to have a meeting, being earnestly possessed in our spirits to get to the half yearly meeting of Friends at Oyster Bay in Long Island, which was near at hand. We got to Gravesend, where we tarried all night. Next day got to Flushing. The day following we reached Oyster Bay. Several from Flushing and Gravesend accompanied us. Thence to Shelter Island and Fisher's Island; but could not stay, for the mosquitoes, which abound there, and are very troublesome. We returned to Oyster Bay, where we had a very large meeting.[22]

Soon, Fox would describe a miraculous event that Morrey and his friend William Frampton must have heard about and greatly admired if they were indeed residents of Oyster Bay and members of the local meetinghouse. (Although Humphrey Morrey's local membership has not been documented by this author, Ancestry.com records indicate that Frampton attended the "Half Year's Meeting at Oyster Bay, Long Island."[23])

> From Oyster Bay we went about thirty miles, to Flushing, where we had a meeting of *many hundred people*. Friends went to a town in Long Island, called Jamaica, and had a meeting there. We passed from Flushing to Gravesend, about twenty miles, and had three precious meetings there. While we were at Shrewsbury, John Jay,[24] a Friend of Barbadoes [sic], who came with us from Rhode Island, fell from his horse and *broke his neck*, as people said. Those near him took him up for dead, carried him a good way, and laid him on a tree. I got to him as soon as I could, and concluded he was dead.[25]

It's then that Fox took matters into his own "hands," performing a remarkable deed with "good faith":

> Whereupon I took his head in both my hands, and setting my knees against the tree, raised his head two or three times with all my might, and *brought it in*. He soon began to rattle in his throat, and quickly after, to breathe. The people were amazed, but I told them to be of good faith, and carry him into the house. He began to speak, but not know where he had been. The next day we passed away, and he with us, about sixteen miles, to a meeting at Middletown, through woods and bogs, and over a river, where we swam our horses. Many hundred miles did he travel with us after this.[26]

Meanwhile, further exploring Humphrey Morrey's marital status, it's worth clarifying that "John Budd," identified as "Sheriff of Philadelphia County, 1706–7," had a "sister Sarah [Budd] Morrey," who is acknowledged in the online 1913 book concerning the Kyn family of "New Sweden [Philadelphia]," as the "wife of Humphrey Morrey, from New York, sometime Member of the Provincial Council of Pennsylvania and first

George Fox traveled widely as a Quaker evangelist, including to Barbados, where slavery was prevalent. Quakers were among the first Europeans to oppose slavery, despite William Penn and other early Quakers enslaving Africans. (Wikimedia Commons)

known Mayor of Philadelphia."[27] On that note, there's evidence that "Anne Morrey, Humphrey's wife, died in 1693, leaving him with two sons [John and Richard], both grown men, or nearly so." So, Humphrey may have remarried another or different "Sarah" following the death of "Anne" or "Ann." However, "John Morrey, who seems to have been the eldest son, married Sarah Budd in Philadelphia on May 29, 1689. Three of their four children failed to survive childhood, and John himself, probably in his early thirties, died on September 10, 1698"[28] in Philadelphia.[29] John had apparently not only followed his dad Humphrey into the brewery business, but also named his son Humphrey Morrey[30] in honor of his father, Philadelphia's first mayor.

Deplorable environmental, health, and other conditions were likely contributing causes of the earlier Morrey children's very short lifespans, tragically not uncommon in England at the time. Another source confirms that during the "1660s Humphrey and Ann were living in London, where several of their children were baptized at St. Bartholomew the Great, in Smithfield," founded in 1123 as a monastery chancel.[31] "If this was their home parish, they were living north of the City in a suburb." London, then surrounded by a wall going back to the AD 43 days of Roman occupation and jammed with hordes of people, was without an effective sewer system. Life there and in the surrounding areas, such as Smithfield, would have been quite challenging environmentally with animal and human waste along walkways and alleys, as well as rampant vermin and insects. Indeed, "in 1665 London was struck by the bubonic plague, in its last major eruption in England," causing more than one hundred thousand deaths.[32]

Still, Humphrey Morrey and his wife Ann's family persisted, despite the often horrific circumstances:

> The baptisms of Humphrey's children extended from 1661 to 1675, suggesting that he spent much of his young adult life there [in the London vicinity]. It is possible that Humphrey and his brother Leonard were in business together in London. A Leonard Morrey, probably Humphrey's brother, had a son Richard baptized at St. Martin in the Fields in December 1674, just two months before Humphrey's son Richard's baptism. In all Humphrey and Ann had five children baptized at the church of St. Bartholomew the Great, plus another son, John, who was apparently not baptized there.[33]

However, life still was not easy by any stretch of the imagination, even if the family tried to temporarily escape their miserable circumstances. They could have departed the London area "for the countryside," perhaps traveling further to Buerton, which would have been "a week's travel by horses; it was 170 miles north of London."[34] Indeed, conditions in the London area must have been quite horrible for the family to decide to travel the rugged highways that often meandered through dense forests inhabited by lawless thugs and highwaymen, as described in a particularly savage account in a 1674 pamphlet, "Bloody News from Yorkshire," that details the robbery and murder of traveling merchants:

> According to him [the unidentified writer] on 21 January fifteen butchers "rid out of the City of York" on their way to Northallerton fair. They "took with them very considerable sums of money, each man according to his ability and occasions." About sixteen miles from York an "ambuscado was laid" when the fifteen overtook a gentleman and rode with him for a while. Then in "a place where the way was very narrow" the gentleman started to sing; the fifteen butchers joined in and that was the signal for nineteen other highwaymen to appear with their swords drawn. "Dam ye ye Dogs deliver was the first word of command," but the butchers, "a sort of rugged people not to be huff'd out of their Money with big words" refused. A battle ensued in which the highwaymen shot and killed seven of the butchers, tied up the rest and robbed them of £936.[35]

Meanwhile, the "death rate from the plague peaked that summer [in 1665] and many people returned in the spring of 1666" when "Humphrey and Ann" with their children "were living in London" again, likely based on "when another child" that year "was baptized at St Bartholomew." Ironically, however, they arrived during "the year of the Great Fire, the second calamity to strike the city in two years. Much of the center city burned, but the suburban slums did not."[36] The destruction was apocalyptic: "'Oh the miserable and calamitous spectacle!' wrote John Evelyn in 1666, 'mine eyes ... now saw above 10,000 houses all in one flame.' The conflagration he witnessed 2–5 September destroyed much of the medieval metropolis, swallowing 400 streets, 13,200 houses, 87 churches, and 44 livery halls."[37]

Such conditions, on top of the political and religious persecution of members of the Quaker religion that the family may have joined by then with thousands of other oppressed English, likely spurred the Morreys to leave England for the so-called New World, enticed by offers of religious freedom, land or property ownership, and economic prosperity in such colonies as New York and especially William Penn's Pennsylvania or "Penn's woodlands." Yet, choosing to leave England and traveling across the mighty Atlantic in relatively fragile and extraordinarily unsanitary ships were not for the faint of heart during the 17th and 18th centuries, as described by the indentured servant Gottlieb Mittelberger in 1754:

> When the ships have for the last time weighted their anchors near the city of Kaupp [Cowes] in Old England, the real misery begins with the long voyage. For from there the ships, unless they have good wind, must often sail 8, 9, 10 to 12 weeks before they reach Philadelphia. But even with the best wind the voyage lasts 7 weeks.

> But during the voyage there is on board these ships terrible misery, stench, fumes, horror, vomiting, many kinds of sea-sickness, fever, dysentery, headache, heat, constipation, boils, scurvy, cancer, mouth-rot, and the like, all of which come from old and sharply salted food and meat, also from very bad and foul water, so that many die miserably.[38]

And although the Morreys likely brought some of their own provisions onboard the unidentified vessel that they voyaged on to reach America about the year 1683, they certainly were not immune from the brunt of suffering:

> Add to this ... hunger, thirst, frost, heat, dampness, anxiety, want, afflictions and lamentations, together with other trouble, ... [and] the lice abound so frightfully, especially on sick people, that they can be scraped off the body. The misery reaches the climax when a gale rages for 2 or 3 nights and days, so that everyone believes that the ship will go to the bottom with all human beings on board. In such a visitation the people cry and pray most piteously.[39]

After their arrival in the colonies, perhaps via the New York harbor, probably sometime during 1683, "Morrey, along with his counterparts [and] William Frampton," who may have by then been living in "New York City, and Edward Shippen, Sr., of Boston, bought property in the colony of 'Penn's Woods.'" They likely targeted Pennsylvania because it was an early haven for Quakers, "with Morrey and Frampton becoming among the first two 'Proprietors' of Cheltenham Township." It wasn't long before "Humphrey Morrey purchased his initial 250-acre grant on May 23, 1683," probably not long after settling in the commonwealth. "Morrey moved his family to Pennsylvania from his home at Oyster Bay, Long Island. He brought his wife Anne, their two sons, and all of their possessions down to their Philadelphia home, 'a large Timber House, with Brick Chimnies [sic].'"[40]

Humphrey's move to Philadelphia was likely also due to the fact that the city "afforded a better field for mercantile pursuits than New York," suggests Josiah Granville Leach's 1894 article "Colonial Mayors of Philadelphia: Humphrey Morrey, First Mayor, 1691–1692." "That he brought with him a considerable estate and that happy accompaniment, a good reputation, and that he was forthwith assigned rank among the prominent men of the city, are indicated in events succeeding his arrival."[41]

Within a few months, according to Leach, "Morrey was appointed a justice of the peace, by virtue of which commission he became also one of the judges of the County Courts. This appointment is noted on the records of the Provincial Council, under date November 6, 1685." It appears that Morrey's rise within governmental ranks was meteoric, because he "was elected to the Assembly" in 1687 and again in 1690. The next year, in 1691, he was chosen to be Philadelphia's first mayor by the council with Proprietor William Penn's approval.[42]

Humphrey Morrey's likely "account book," acquired in 2020 by the Manuscript Division of the Library of Congress, provides exquisite details about Morrey's activities and life in Philadelphia. Enveloped in "a leather cover folded like a wallet, which closes with a brass clasp," the book can be found in a special collection at the Library of Congress. "Its 63 pages contain a merchant's business transactions from 1684 to 1699. While the owner of this volume failed to record his name on it, the transactions point to Quaker merchant Humphrey Morrey, a New Yorker who was attracted to William Penn's Quaker experiment and resettled in Philadelphia." During "the mid-1680s" Morrey "was living between Chestnut and Walnut streets on the Delaware River, where he owned a large house, a warehouse, and a wharf." Remarkably, although "Philadelphia was growing into a busy trading port, one could still keep a flock of sheep there, as Morrey did."[43]

In fact, "under date Sixth month 16, 1690 ... 'the Petition of Humphrey Morrey and James Fox for themselves and in behalf of others concerned in a flock of sheep in Philadelphia was read, Requesting a Convenient piece of land somewhere about the town for keeping them.'" Responsible authorities very generously, according to the quoted petition, "Ordered that about Sixty acres be laid out in Squares between the Broad Street and so far towards Delaware as conveniently may be, so that it be near Dock Street and Walnut Street."[44]

Morrey apparently was also gifted at penmanship, as well as diversified in business, even trading with Native Americans, and quite interested in their

This leather carrier was owned by Humphrey Morrey, holding very important financial, retail, and real-estate documents. In addition to being a retailer of various goods that included liquor or "spirits," Humphrey invested in real estate throughout the region via acquisitions from William Penn. (Library of Congress)

language for trading or business-enterprise purposes: "The first pages of this book, written in a hand that would have been familiar to William Shakespeare, date from a time when William Penn was still in Pennsylvania, just two years after founding the colony. Most pages document the buying and selling of goods, including imported wine and local 'Indian corn from the mill.'"[45] Yet Morrey was also involved in philanthropy, surely an indication of his growing wealth and affluence. "Contributions toward the construction of two Quaker meeting houses are recorded. So are expenses associated with the repair of the Chestnut Street wharf, which Morrey owned, the building of a counting house and other buildings, and the construction of a ship," which prompts questions about whether the ship and Morrey were involved in the transatlantic slave trade. "There is also a recipe for a cordial, probably a byproduct of Morrey's wine importing business."[46]

Intriguingly, several "pages are devoted to a vocabulary of the language of the local Lenape Indians. The Lenape were among the people who lived in the area claimed by William Penn for at least ten thousand years before he arrived in 1682," generally accommodating and accepting the European settlers but as highlighted earlier, ultimately suffering a range of abuses inflicted by the newcomers. "As a trader, Morrey engaged with nearby Indian tribes. In 1697 he was one of a group of Philadelphia merchants who wrote Penn about a plan to organize a settlement on the Susquehanna River in order to benefit from the fur trade carried on by the Lenape Indians there," quite aware that it was necessary to learn Native American words to communicate and conduct business. "This vocabulary focuses on trade, including translations into English of numbers one through ten, and phrases, including: 'what hast got' and 'I will give so much.'"[47]

Such interactions, in fact, conjure up questions about whether Cremona Morrey, the future common-law spouse of Humphrey's son Richard, may have been part of a transaction between the Lenape or a third party resulting in her early enslavement by the Morreys. Researcher-writer Reginald H. Pitts, quoting, Clinton A. Weslager, the esteemed "historian of the Delawares," which included the Lenape tribe, noted: "Many of the old village sites … had been abandoned as the white settlements expanded, and in some areas it was not healthy for an Indian to make an appearance after dark for fear a slave trader might seize him and sell him into slavery as he would an itinerant Negro." He continued: "Some Negro slaves had escaped their masters and found refuge in Indian villages, and there had been black intermarriage with Indian women. The children of such marriages were always in danger of being sold into slavery, and that created new fears of mixing in white society."[48]

Although some sources indicate that there is no absolute proof that Humphrey Morrey had slaves based on them not being listed or identified in his will and other official documents, given the amount of property and arable land that he owned, it's practically beyond doubt that he was directly or indirectly involved in the "peculiar institution" of slavery, as well as younger family members. For example, Humphrey's namesake grandson clearly ordered inventory produced via slave labor, including "Rum from Barbadoes" as a major Philadelphia distiller in 1726, according to the "Distilling Accounts [of] Humphrey Murrey & Edward Shippen," among many of such original records in the Special Collections Department at Haverford College. In addition to paying "William Allen in part for his own molasses," the account also lists "Muscovado sugar," a slightly refined or unrefined brownish sugar used to make dark rum.[49] Plus, more than a few powerful individuals with government positions or influence were able to shield their tax liabilities, including slaves, as well as take advantage of "hiring" or "leasing" enslaved labor from others without recording the specifics. Yet, there is at least one instance of the elder Humphrey Morrey going on record about his misgivings concerning slavery. In or about the year 1698, Humphrey "signed a letter from Philadelphia Monthly Meeting to Friends in Barbados to dissuade Quakers there from exporting Negroes to Pennsylvania."[50] It's quite noteworthy that Humphrey Morrey did, in fact, go on record opposing the importation of enslaved Africans relatively early, perhaps influenced by such pioneering Quaker antislavery abolitionists as John Woolman and Benjamin Lay. However, it's also important to note that although such early Quakers as William Penn expressed doubts about the morality of slaveholding, they held African-descended people in bondage; in fact, despite the likes of the so-called Founding Fathers Benjamin Franklin, Thomas Jefferson, and even George Washington writing about their supposed dislike of slavery, they were notable slaveholders during their lifetimes.

Like many early Americans, Humphrey Morrey probably viewed taxes as antithetical to what was believed to be the "great American experiment" and felt disdain for tyrannical control via governmental taxation and other perceived interferences concerning politics and religion, especially considering that Quakers in England had been brutally beaten, tortured, and imprisoned as heretics while also suffering tremendous financial losses.[51]

> Reflecting the values of the day, a prominent nineteenth-century historian, Richard T. Ely, wrote that "one of the things against which our forefathers in England and in the American colonies contended was not against oppressive taxation, *but against the payment of any taxes at all*" [emphasis added]. Those who braved the hardship of travel across the Atlantic and who tamed a wilderness on their own did not relish paying taxes to any government.[52]

Given Morrey's wealth, power, and prestige, did he simply not record his possible enslaved "property" to avoid taxation—if in fact during that early colonial period he was required or mandated to pay such taxes on the enslaved at all? It's clear that Pennsylvania's proprietor, William Penn (also an enslaver), catered to such wealthy colonists to help ensure the colony's growth via land purchases or speculation and the development of enterprises that would attract even more immigrants. There were also incentives to attract lower-income colonists who often did not report taxable "property" because related laws or regulations were not stringently enforced, as earlier discussed.[53]

> At the close of the seventeenth century, residents of Pennsylvania with real estate and personal assets worth less than £30 were exempt [from paying taxes]. Adult males worth less than £72 paid a reduced poll tax of 6 shillings. Even these low rates were vigorously resisted as farmers consistently undervalued their property and overvalued their produce, the means of payment. The colonial governor of New York warned the English Crown in 1688 that attempts to strengthen tax enforcement or impose new taxes would result in the departure of his subjects to other colonies.[54]

So, despite indications that the two were already increasingly prosperous in New York before departing for Philadelphia, it's quite plausible that one of Humphrey Morrey and William Frampton's reasons for leaving New York was "high taxes for frontier defense. When paired with low wages, many New Yorkers found themselves short on cash and fled New York for a more favorable economy and better working conditions in Pennsylvania."[55] More than likely, the pair's prosperity was in large part due to holding African-descended people in bondage, thus limiting long-term labor costs. "Although no direct evidence exists to show that Humphrey Morrey ever held slaves, tradition insists that they worked his land in Cheltenham, possibly making the first attempts at herding sheep and mining for iron ore."[56]

Virtually without doubt, Humphrey Morrey's son, Richard, as well as other heirs and descendants, certainly did use such slave labor, as we'll explore soon.[57]

Unequivocally, "Humphrey Morrey was extremely well off for his time," and considered to be part of the so-called colonial elite. "The 1693 Philadelphia County Tax Lists assess his estate at 634 pounds, the seventh highest assessment …. He possessed a virtual barony in Cheltenham, possibly using slaves to work the land."[58] Furthermore, according to *The Pennsylvania Magazine of History and Biography*, one of Morrey's closest associates, William Frampton, absolutely owned and traded in slaves:

> In "Quaker Merchants and the Slave Trade in Colonial Pennsylvania," … the activity of William Frampton in this area is described: "Friend William Frampton, a merchant and operator of a 'Brew house and Bake house' in Philadelphia, was involved in the Negro trade

as early as 1686. In that year, he received instructions from the Bristol firm of Charles Jones, Jr. and Company to sell six Negroes brought from the coast of Africa on the ship Isabella."[59]

As a matter of fact, Frampton's involvement in slavery on many levels has been noted in a range of sources.[60]

Again, these important questions arise: Given Humphrey Morrey's close relationship with Frampton in England, New York, and, finally, Philadelphia, as well as Morrey's reported shipbuilding endeavor, how deeply was Morrey directly or indirectly involved in slavery and its wide-ranging enterprises? Could Cremona's parents have been among the six enslaved Africans referenced in the preceding passages, perhaps even possibly sold or lent by Frampton to his buddy Humphrey Morrey? Considering that Cremona's estimated birth date was 1710, is it possible that almost 25 years earlier her parents might have arrived in 1684 on the slave-ship *Isabella* at the Philadelphia port as two of the reported 150 Africans—to become among the young city's first enslaved Africans?[61]

Meanwhile, during his early business activities, Humphrey Morrey or "Murray" apparently lived in the same central Philadelphia vicinity (where an estimated 25 percent of shopkeepers utilized enslaved Africans) as his New York compatriot William Frampton, who again is confirmed by yet another source to have had "a house, brew-house, and bake-house, of brick, on Front, east side below Walnut." Other neighbors included: "John Wheeler, from New England, on Front, west side below Walnut, by the Blue Anchor," as well as "Samuel Carpenter, Front, west side above Walnut; John Test, north-east corner of Third and Chestnut; Nathaniel Allen, Front, west side above Chestnut, next to Thomas Wynne's; John Day, a good house after the London fashion, of brick, with large front shop-windows, Front, west side between Arch and Race; Humphrey Murray, from New York, a large timber-house, with brick chimneys."[62]

Morrey and Frampton, as relative latecomers to that early Philadelphia business district, were not at first assigned the very best waterfront properties by William Penn, but that would very soon change:

> Two prominent New York Quaker merchants, William Frampton and Humphrey Morrey, were also assigned lots as purchasers. They had been doing business in the Delaware for some years and now looked to establish a base of operation in the rising Quaker community. At the time of their applications all the choice front lots were assigned, so they agreed to take lots elsewhere, hoping that later, if the progress of the place warranted the expense, they might be able to buy front lots from original purchasers. To accommodate the brew and bake house Frampton intended to build, Penn assigned him lot 10 on Delaware Second Street. Its location, immediately south of Pool Street next to the stream flowing into the northern corner of the Swamp, provided him with access to the river. For Humphrey Morrey, Penn

assigned lot 119 on the north side of Holme between Fourth and Fifth Streets, close to the waters of the Coaquannock. Each assignment was predicated on the eventual purchase of country land.[63]

Morrey must have been a sharp and very observant land speculator or investor, because "of the nine lots surveyed during February, only three were on Delaware side. One of these was a second lot for Humphrey Morrey, who was still a resident of New York when, in early January, he arranged to buy the Front lot assigned to the widow Mercy Jefferson, with the 'house thereon erected.'" In fact, the "improved lot, at the southwest corner of Wynne, was surveyed for Morrey in the middle of February, five days after Penn granted him a warrant which added twelve feet to the lot's breath; the excess presumably was the result of a miscalculation by the surveyors when the street was first laid out."[64] As the years passed, Morrey's land speculation activities showed no signs of slowing down: "Within two years, by August 1685, he had acquired several additional town lots .... In 1688, Morrey purchased 350 acres of rural land, [and] a bank lot opposite his Chestnut Street residence and, on December 15, 1689/90, a city lot ...."[65] Humphrey Morrey eventually acquired land throughout Philadelphia, including about seven hundred acres in the Cheltenham area. "Humphrey Morrey had 739 acres in this end of Cheltenham" when "he died in 1715, leaving his lands to his son Richard and his grandson, Humphrey Morrey, Jr. ... Richard Morrey regained the owner[ship] of this portion of his father's estate. In 1734 he was credited with 250 acres," certainly still a decent chunk of land. "He lived till long after, dying between 1755 and 1757. At the latter date Leonard Morrey and Stephen Williams, both his heirs, were the owners of 175 acres, but in 1760 Williams, as the owner of the whole plantation, sold to Robert Greenaway."[66]

After being appointed mayor by the provincial council in 1691 via William Penn, Morrey appears to have been relatively active but to have exercised limited power, according to several historical observers. However, a year later in 1692, "Mayor Morrey bore a conspicuous part in that historical [free speech and freedom of press] controversy respecting George Keith, Thomas Budd, [the pioneering and noted printer] William Bradford [1663–1752], and others, which shook the very foundations of the social, political, and religious world hereabout, and attracted attention throughout the American colonies and abroad," according to writer-historian Josiah Granville Leach, with significant free-press and religious-liberty implications. "He was one of the judges who (on August 24, 1692) caused the arrest of William Bradford, printer, and John MacComb, tavern-keeper, for 'publishing, uttering and spreading a malicious and seditious paper,' and who, on the following day, at a 'private session' of the court, framed the famous proclamation against [a popular Quaker preacher] 'George Keith, and his printed address,' and caused it to be read by the common crier in the market-place."[67] Keith and Bradford, who helped to establish the first paper mill in America with David Rittenhouse in Philadelphia's Germantown,[68] eventually won the case, "arguing for press freedom, and prevailed in the trial when the jury could not agree on a verdict."[69] It's interesting to note, too, that an apprentice of Bradford was John Peter Zenger (1697–1746), "whose famous acquittal in a libel suit (1735) established the first important victory for freedom of the press in the English colonies of North America."[70] Bradford "began a new position as the royal printer" in New York "in 1693," later "printing the colony's first issue of paper currency in 1709 and starting New York's first newspaper, the New-York Gazette in 1725."[71]

Meanwhile, the death of Humphrey Morrey's son John Morrey in 1698[72] left him with one remaining son, Richard Morrey, destined to become heir to much of his expansive properties and wealth. Some historical records indicate that Humphrey also had a daughter named Matilda Morrey (Flannigan). However, those sources might be mistaking Humphrey for his son Richard, who too is reported to have had a daughter, Matilda, eventually marrying and settling in Bucks County, as we'll soon further examine.[73]

> Born about 1675, [Richard] may have been educated in England; he is described in the public records of the day as "Merchant," and later "Gent. Of Cheltenham;" his father had been content to be described merely as "Yeoman." It would appear that father and son did not see eye to eye on many matters. There is evidence that Richard Morrey, like his brother John and many other second-generation Philadelphians of Quaker stock, turned away from the faith of the fathers to the more ritualistic services of the Anglican and Presbyterian churches. This fact would have certainly bothered their father.[74]

Did the slaveholding Richard and some of his peers in fact move away from Quakerism because by then the Friends had increasingly criticized holding slaves, influenced by the activism of such early antislavery abolitionists as Benjamin Lay, John Woolman, and Anthony Benezet? Increasingly, Quakers began to preach against slavery and even punished or sanctioned those among them who persisted in the practice as the 17th century drew to a close. However, despite the absence of documentation that Humphrey Morrey held African-descended people in bondage or used slave labor, "his son and grandsons did," as well as the nephew named for him, "the younger" Humphrey Morrey:

> In his will, Humphrey Morrey the younger [son of Richard's brother John] mentions three slaves. He commanded his executors to see that two slaves, "Cipio" (Scipio) and Moll, receive

50 • THE MONTIERS

their freedom, along with "forty acres off the south end of my plantation in Edgehill now in their possession" that they would live on for the rest of their lives. Morrey further stated that if the two did not like their home, [associates Edward] Shippen and Allen were to find forty acres for them no more than eleven miles from Philadelphia and "build them a little log house" where they could spend the rest of their lives.[75]

Yet, "Humphrey Morrey the younger," kept multiple generations of that family in bondage:

Humphrey also had [yet] another slave named Scipio, who evidently was the young son of Scipio and Moll. In his will, he gives the younger Scipio to his "cousin" John Crapp. In a codicil, Morrey noted that John Crapp had died, so Scipio was to serve Crapp's parents until their death; after that, Scipio was to serve another "cousin," William Paschall for the rest of his (Scipio's) life. These slaves seem to have come to Humphrey from his mother's estate.[76]

Richard Morrey's son Thomas Morrey also verified his father's enslavement of African-descended people, including Cremona:

Thomas Morrey remembered "my father Richard Morrey's servants the Negros" in his will, giving them twenty shillings apiece. It is not known how much was spent in fulfilling his request. Jane Lawrence ("Lorrance"), described as a "spenster of Philadelphia," but who was employed by Richard Morrey, also died about the same time as Thomas. In her will, she mentions a number of legatees, including a bequest of forty shillings to "Richard Morri's [sic] Negro Mooney."[77]

Remarkably, it's likely that the "younger" Humphrey Morrey had "cousins" who were associated with one of the most well-known merchant firms in the Philadelphia area, Allen & Turner, which vigorously participated in the slave trade. "It is probable that [the older] Richard Morrey dealt with his nephew's cousins in trying to find workers and house servants,"[78] possibly preferring to network amongst relatives and close friends. "When Allen & Turner announced they had shipped from 'St. Christopher's Island' [St. Kitt's] in the Caribbean 'a parcel of Fine Negroe Boys and Girls' in August 1732 [when Cremona would have been about age 22 if born in 1710], did Richard Morrey bestir himself and ride the eleven or twelve miles into the city to look for a personal maid for his wife [Ann]? And, amidst that 'parcel' did his eye light upon a young girl whom he decided would fit the bill?"[79] Such questions are difficult to answer. "At this late date, there is no way that we can know when the young girl Mooney first met the [then] nearly sixty-year old landowner Richard Morrey. However, the preceding would seem to be as about as logical a sequence as any other."[80]

After being born and/or "baptized in February 1675, in London," according to Takingthelongerview.org, "at the church of St. Bartholomew the Great in

Smithfield," Richard "was the youngest of their [Humphrey and Ann Morrey's] known [several] children and only one of two to survive to adulthood." Although Richard in about 1683 "came to New York as a child," perhaps about age eight if born in 1675, "with his parents," he "may have gone back to England to be educated," similar to other young males hailing from well-off English families in America. By or around "1695 he married a woman named Ann" when Richard would have been about age 20, assuming again that he was born in 1675; despite some indications that their marriage likely became strained due to Ann's eventual illness and/or Richard's possible extramarital indulgences, the couple would prove to be quite financially savvy. "There are no records of Richard Morrey in Pennsylvania until 1702, when he witnessed a deed of sale by his father Humphrey of a Philadelphia lot. Was he acting as the English agent for his father's trading business until then? The family owned a house in Tower Hill, London, where Richard and Ann could have lived," in an up-and-coming area of newly built homes and businesses owned by the wealthy and affluent, including prosperous shopkeepers.[81] Further, again, did his father Humphrey Morrey's "trading business" consist of doing business in the transatlantic slave trade considering that he was involved with building a ship?

Tragically and as noted earlier, Humphrey's older son, John Morrey, "died [on] September 10, 1698, having married Sarah, daughter of John and Rebecca Baynton Budd, and granddaughter of Thomas Budd, the Free Christian Quaker." In fact, John "was father of ['the younger'] Humphrey, the grandson named in the will of Mayor Morrey."[82]

So, about the time that Richard's father, Humphrey Morrey, died in "171[5] Richard [at around age 40] and [his first wife] Ann were living in Cheltenham, when Richard inherited considerable land from his father Humphrey, sharing some of it with his cousin, the younger Humphrey," one of a number of intra-family transactions that would be executed over many years. "They shared the Cheltenham estate of at least 450 acres and another 400 acres in Gloucester County, West Jersey. Richard got a Philadelphia lot, probably the one on Mulberry Street, while Humphrey received the 'water lot', probably the Chestnut Street property."[83] The duo, Richard and his younger relative, Humphrey (who also reportedly inherited substantial land via the will of Humphrey Sr.), launched a real-estate transacting blitz (with the assistance of Richard's wife, Ann) after they, Richard and Humphrey, "probated the will of the elder Humphrey in May 1716, and the next month" commenced to "sell his land." They also purchased a massive amount of other properties that would soon overextend Richard, almost leading to his financial demise:

> In June 1716 they confirmed a deed of a lot on Mulberry Street sold by the elder Humphrey but never conveyed; they confirmed the sale to Richard Hill, a Philadelphia merchant. In October 1716, Richard sold part of his city lot to Sven Warner, Cordwainer of Philadelphia, conveying the rest to Richard's son Thomas. In 1717 Richard and his cousin Humphrey made a large land purchase of their own, buying rights to 2,000 acres to be laid out from the three daughters of Nathaniel Bromley, a First Purchaser of land from Penn. Two years later, in 1719, Richard, his wife Ann, and cousin Humphrey sold a lot in the city to Joseph Taylor, a Philadelphia brewer. It was the city lot that went along with the Bromley purchase. The next year the Morreys sold another lot from the Bromley purchase to William Branson, joyner, and in 1721 they sold yet another part of the lot to Hugh Cordry, pulley maker. In 1722 Richard and Humphrey partitioned the 2000 acres of the Bromley land, laid out in Wrightstown, Bucks County.[84]

As the major heir to his father's wealth and property, Richard Morrey became quite dynamic as an investor in civic activities in Philadelphia and Cheltenham. He "evidently shuttled back and forth between Philadelphia and his Cheltenham home," likely constructed in the vicinity of the William Harmer[85] estate near what would become Limekiln Pike. "He was an extremely wealthy man. He collected rents on twelve properties in Philadelphia; he bought land of his own, expanding his holdings," obviously operating with superior financial finesse. Meanwhile, Richard's son "Thomas grew to manhood and was sent to England to be educated," while his father became "active in matters affecting the Cheltenham community; his signature appears on a number of documents including a request to open a road from 'Thomas Fitzwater's Limekilns' out to 'Abington Meeting House.'"[86]

Richard's daughter "Matilda and her husband [Anthony Kimble] were married about 1710." Although her "grandfather Humphrey Morrey had been a Quaker," it seems that "his children fell away from the Society and became Anglicans." Matilda may not have been Quaker, as her "marriage does not appear in any Quaker meeting records." Likely due to the inheritances from her parents, grandfather, and brother Thomas, "Matilda and her family lived in Bucks County" where she had "inherited" a substantial amount of property in excess of two hundred acres of land. Much of the acreage was later "passed to her children William, Anthony, Rose, Ann and Mary, along with additional land from Matilda's father Richard and cousin Humphrey." Matilda apparently outlived her husband Anthony, marrying "a man named Carty, and later married again, to a man named Flannagan. She died in 1749 or 1750," without a will, requiring "her heirs" to petition "Orphan's Court to divide the land." The land was subsequently divided among "five claimants," including what appear to be at least a few of Matilda's children.[87] Some of Matilda's descendants apparently still survive today.[88]

Meanwhile, the younger Humphrey, as well as Richard and his wife Ann made a range of other real estate deals, including one during "May of 1720" when "Richard and Ann Morrey made an unusual transaction that reveals something about their marriage and possibly Ann's birth. Thomas Turner of London had conveyed a credit from the stock of the East India company,"[89] a significant international trader of enslaved Africans and spices, "to Richard Morrey, supposedly in a will written on May 11, 1711" amounting to "one-third of a credit" totaling 325 pounds, "a handsome bequest," that both raised an intriguing question and furnished a possible answer:[90]

> What was Morrey's relation to Turner? Given the terms of the 1720 conveyance, it is possible that Turner was Ann Morrey's father. The money was clearly intended for Ann's use. Richard and Ann conveyed one-third part to Job Goodson and John Warder of Philadelphia, who were to invest the money for the use of Ann Morrey. Her husband was not to meddle with it, and it would be excluded from his estate. Ann was to dispose of the profits "at her own will and pleasure." This unusual provision suggested that the profits were to be Ann's because they came from her father.[91]

Furthermore, it's well worth noting that Ann's father had distinct ties to an international slave-trading firm, the East India Company, as revealed in the preceding text.

Indeed, was Ann's potential father, Thomas Turner, somehow related to Joseph Turner, co-owner (with Pennsylvania Chief Justice William Allen) and among the principal operators of the slave-trading and merchant firm Allen & Turner of Philadelphia? Joseph Turner was a member of "Benjamin Franklin's Junto [an influential working-class group of white males dedicated to improving life and city operations],"[92] and Allen was a close confidant and friend of Franklin.[93] The three men cofounded a school, the Academy and Charitable School of Philadelphia, that later became the University of Pennsylvania, for which the trio served as trustees.[94]

Six years following the "1720 conveyance" to Richard's wife Ann by her possible father, Thomas Turner, in "1726 Richard bought 1,000 acres from Nathaniel Roberts of Kent County, England, for £30," possibly straining Richard's finances and causing him serious "financial trouble" in late 1729. In a complex personal-financial rescue plan he and several associates "set up a trust to cover his debts" that involved conveying "his house and 250 acres in Cheltenham, his land in Gloucester County, a house and lot on Front Street in the city, and several lots on Chestnut Street" to those financial rescuers; the arrangement also required Richard to transfer "to the trustees 984 acres laid out for him on Manahatawny Creek in Philadelphia County with the intention that they should sell it," perhaps if necessary. "From the income of the properties, the trustees were to pay Morrey's debts, make a payment to Ann for her maintenance and that of their son Thomas, and pay a smaller amount to Richard for his 'pocket expenses,'" surely quite a humbling experience for the so-called Philadelphia "gent."[95]

Meanwhile, making matters even worse, Richard would endure the deaths of at least three very close family or household members in 1735,[96] about a decade after purchasing those one thousand acres from England's Nathaniel Roberts in 1726 that may have ignited his financial woes:

> The first to die was his nephew Humphrey, who made his will on 6 August and died about a week later. He left large sums of money to his cousins on the Budd side (his mother was Sarah Budd), and left his uncle Richard and cousin Thomas each £20 per year. The second loss was that of Jane Laurence, who probably died in late September. Jane wrote a will remembering Richard and Ann, their son Thomas, their daughter Matilda Kimble and three of her children, as well as Richard's "Negro woman Mooney." The inclusion of Mooney, also known as Cremona, strongly suggests that Jane was a member of Richard's household.[97]

The "inclusion" also "suggests" that by then Richard was in very close proximity to Cremona or "Mooney," as well as Jane, with Cremona likely serving him as an enslaved servant or already liberated employee and Jane as a "lady" supervisor[98] of sorts, within his Philadelphia and/or Cheltenham households by 1735; that would have been approximately a decade before Richard's wife Ann would expire[99] in or around 1746. Hence, it's quite possible that an extramarital relationship between Cremona and Richard may have begun to blossom well before Ann's demise.

It is difficult to pinpoint exactly when Ann perished, and when Richard began his relationship with Cremona because of the paucity of related historical records. "Ann Morrey died some time [*sic*] between 1735 and 1746. Administration on her estate was granted to her husband Richard,"[100] perhaps an indication that when Ann passed away, her relationship with Richard was not acrimonious, even conceivably harmonious; that's keeping in mind that Richard, as a white male with far more power and influence based on chauvinism and contemporaneous laws that then disempowered or ignored women, would have benefitted ultimately from Orphan's Court or other determinators' rulings dominated by and for white men. "For some reason there is no record of the administration in Philadelphia, but it was noted in England, probably because the family still held property in London."[101]

Richard and Ann's son Thomas perished in 1735. "He made his will in September and died in late October. The fact that Jane and Thomas died so soon after Humphrey the younger suggests that they were victims of an infectious disease," perhaps "malaria, smallpox, measles, pneumonia" or one of the other diseases that "could sweep through a community, especially in the summer months."[102] Cremona's survival of such health threats is surely indicative of her being physically healthy, and family folklore and oral history asserts that she was likely quite vibrant at about age 25 in 1735.

By most estimates, within a year, before or by 1736, perhaps in part due to Richard seeking solace because of his tremendous family losses, a relationship ensued between Richard and Cremona that would reverberate throughout the Cheltenham community, where a likely more modest home rested on the sprawling Morrey estate, and probably to some extent to the halls of power in Philadelphia. That relationship would impact the course of the city's colonial history and give birth to one of the country's first African American family dynasties and the illustrious generations that followed.

Richard Morrey: A Flamboyant "Gent. of Cheltenham"?

It's not hard to visualize Richard Morrey cruising around Philadelphia in an elegant carriage driven by a black or white servant, drawn by one or two purebred steeds during the early to mid-1700s, perhaps headed to dine at the London Coffee House near one of his central Philadelphia abodes. Or perhaps Richard traversed the rugged country roads near his Cheltenham estate as one of the "pink-coated gentlemen" who "traditionally hunted the fox, over hill and dale, on the back of a horse," as the preeminent University of Pennsylvania scholar Digby Baltzell, once described the lifestyles of such colonial Philadelphia "gentlemen." "Riding to the hounds [had] been the Philadelphia gentleman's favorite pastime ever since the eighteenth century," Baltzell further noted.[103] Although it's not likely that Richard's Quaker father, Humphrey Morrey, reputed to be a conservative dresser who avoided the ostentatious as a practicing Friend or Quaker, would have ventured on foxhunts, Richard might have enjoyed such activities as he probably became increasingly drawn to the more liberal Anglican and/or Episcopal churches.[104] Or, perhaps, his lifestyle was a blend of conservative and "bourgeoisie" pursuits.

As Richard's father, Humphrey Morrey, lived his final years that culminated on February 13, 1715 or 1716 at about 76, he may have been a bit worried or disappointed in his son Richard, possibly after earlier sending him to England to be educated. Richard likely moved away from Quakerism upon his return to America, as did more than a few of the children of immigrants who settled in Pennsylvania and other American locales.[105] And that's despite evidence

56 • THE MONTIERS

Philadelphians, possibly including Richard Morrey, often hunted foxes in the Cheltenham vicinity, including in the nearby Philadelphia countryside that became known as Fox Chase. (Wikimedia Commons)

that Humphrey Morrey at times may not have been a fervent participant in Quaker meeting affairs in his twilight years. In fact, "Morrey was not particularly active in Quaker endeavors; after 1698 he does not appear to have attended monthly meetings either in Philadelphia or in Cheltenham."[106] Another reason for the later generation's drift away from Quakerism may have been the early antislavery protests and/or writings of a few Friends; that apparently included Richard's father Humphrey who reportedly liberated enslaved blacks (depending on the source), a movement in its infancy that perhaps initially made the likes of son Richard Morrey quite nervous about losing African Americans' free labor and the consequences of this loss for generational wealth. However, it's possible that Richard may have emancipated the enslaved. Nevertheless, the differences in values between father and son seemed quite real because in "public records" Richard is more often described as a "Merchant," and "later 'Gent. of Cheltenham'"; that's while "his father had been content to be described merely as 'Yeoman,'"[107] even shortly before he expired at the Morreys' Cheltenham estate or home that may have been similar in construction to his Philadelphia abode, likely built during the mid to late 1680s and described in multiple documents as "a large Timber House, with Brick Chimnies [sic]."[108] However, the Cheltenham home was likely noticeably smaller or more compact, perhaps resembling a moderate-sized to spacious farmhouse.

In the Philadelphia and Cheltenham areas there were apparently a range of wood types used for such construction in 1681: "There is variety of Trees in the Country, and many of them, as Oak, Cedar, Chestnut, Wallnut [*sic*], Mulberry, etc. and several sorts that are not in England." Further, according to the 1912 book *Original Narratives of Early American History*: "Their houses are some Built of Brick, some of Timber, [and] Plaister'd ... as in England: So that they have Materials within the Country, to set Themselves at work, and to make all manner of Conveniency for Humane Life: And what they do not Spend, or have to Spare, they sell to their Neigbours [*sic*], and Transport the Rest to the other American-Plantations."[109]

By the 1680s, Humphrey Morrey and other first-generation immigrants did have access to skilled laborers, including "Coopers, Smiths, Carpenters, Bricklayers, Wheel-Wrights, Plow-Wrights, and Mill-Wrights, Ship-Carpenters, and other Trades, which work upon what the Country produces for Manufactures."[110]

During the same late-17th-century period in nearby New Jersey, a variety of goods were manufactured and available, likewise in Philadelphia: "The Country also produces Flax and Hemp, which they already Spin and Manufacture into Linnen: They make several Stuffs and Cloath [*sic*] of Wool for Apparrel [*sic*]: They Tan Leather, Make Shooes [*sic*] and Hats."[111]

An examination of Humphrey Morrey's will that included many of his simple personal items speaks volumes about how he perceived himself and perhaps wanted others to remember him, despite the fact that he "lived in comfort in Cheltenham" with the total value of his non-real estate assets estimated to be about £376:[112]

> As befits a good Quaker gentleman, he did not have an extensive wardrobe: two coats with plate buttons, a riding coat, a vest, an old hat, three shirts, stockings and shoes. He owned 14 coverlets and blankets, piles of sheets, table cloths and napkins. His furniture included beds, chests of drawers, tables, stools, and cane chairs. His kitchen was stocked with pans, tongs, kettles, pots, and a frypan. He ate off of pewter dishes and drank from a silver tankard, and drank his cocoa in cups trimmed with silver. His livestock included three horses, twelve cattle, 29 sheep and lambs. He still kept his house in the city, but with only one room of furniture: a bedstead and table, a case of drawers, a few dishes and some candlesticks.[113]

Considering his exceptional wealth and likely pulling away from Quakerism and associated lifestyles, what details can we ascertain regarding son Richard's values, as well as his relationship with Cremona Morrey, his black "common-law wife"? To reach meaningful hypotheses concerning these questions, we'll examine the wealth, household dynamics, and lifestyle of Richard, and soon we'll also focus on and compare circumstances of other white men who had relationships with enslaved black women.

Without doubt, as a primary heir to his late father Humphrey's substantial estate(s), Richard was exceptionally wealthy with notable business ties throughout the region and stretching across the sea to England where he and his wife, Ann, still had several investments and properties during the early and mid-18th century. Although records are scarce regarding his residence in Cheltenham, it's worth repeating that it was likely "a simple home" and "sparsely furnished,"[114] situated near the residential property of William Harmer. Following his father Humphrey's death in 1715, "Richard and his nephew Humphrey split most of the Cheltenham property, Richard receiving 'half of the land joining to William Harmer.'"[115] In addition to the original 250 acres that had been "laid out" for Humphrey Morrey by William Penn in Cheltenham, Humphrey "added to his Cheltenham land by buying 100 acres from Thomas Fairman" in 1684. And again, after purchasing more land from Fairman in 1686, Humphrey "in 1692 completed his Cheltenham tract with another 109 acres from John and Susanna Colley."[116] Remarkably, "he eventually acquired over 700 acres stretching from the present Cheltenham-Springfield Township border east toward the present Washington Lane, as well as city lots in Philadelphia bordered by Front and Second Streets and Chestnut and Walnut Streets, where he constructed rental property."[117]

The September–October 1735 will of house manager "Jane Larrance [sic],"[118] residing with the couple in either their likely sizeable Philadelphia or smaller Cheltenham abode, identifies more than a dozen people in the household, including "Negro: Mooney," also known as Cremona, Richard's so-called "mistress." Jane is recognized as a "Spinster" within the "County of Philadelphia,"[119] which then included Cheltenham and other modern suburban areas. Prominent in the will is Richard Morrey, identified as "Executor," as well as an apparent co-executor, Job Goodson.[120] Others identified in the household include Thoms [sic] Barlow, Job Goodson, Richard Gullom, Mary Hicks, Tho. James, Ros Kemble, Ann Kemble, Richard Matildo, Richard Murrey [sic], Thomas Murrey [sic], Ann Nash, Hester Spencer, and Francis Woodkins.[121] Ann Morrey's name is conspicuously missing from the will, perhaps because of a life-threatening illness, or due to familial and or personality conflicts.

As a member of Philadelphia's so-called colonial elite, the almost exclusive province of white men (the exception being a few Caucasian widows and wealthy single heiresses), Richard Morrey would have been in the thick of such society. That's especially considering that his father, Humphrey Morrey, had been the first mayor of Philadelphia with business and platonic ties to the founder of the city and the Commonwealth of Pennsylvania, William Penn. That circle would have included other powerbrokers who were often slaveholders—as were some of the Morreys and William Penn. At his Pennsbury estate in Bucks County, not far from Morrey's properties in Cheltenham, Penn enjoyed landscaped gardens and a spacious mansion and "owned black slaves" who "played a significant role in Pennsbury's creation and maintenance." Those enslaved workers included "at least eight slaves," including "laborers with [structural] building" skills. "'Peter' was trained as a gardener," however, and most of the enslaved "seem to have been mainly agricultural workers and household servants, including Parthenia who did the laundry."[122] The personnel dynamics at Pennsbury were probably quite similar to those in Richard Morrey's household, where the intimate relationship with Cremona, likely commenced. In fact, "Pennsbury's 'garrets' [or attics] in 1701," almost a decade before Cremona's estimated birth in 1710, "held multiple beds and accouterments for sleeping, though Mrs. Penn's sidesaddle also resided there when not in use, perhaps because it was too valuable to be kept in a barn."[123]

Similarly, Samuel Morris's nearby Whitemarsh estate, the Georgian-style Hope Lodge, likely also had enslaved workers living in close quarters to him, according to sources. "At Hope Lodge, a farmhouse as much as or more than a bourgeois country seat, one large room served as storage, and a smaller space with a fireplace served as quarters for a Negro house slave, James Nettle."[124] Perhaps Cremona initially lived in similar accommodations within Richard Morrey's home. The close proximity of the enslaved workers or indentured servants to the white proprietor and his family led to more intimate communication and relationships, for better or worse. For instance, "Stenton's three finished garret [attic] rooms, two of which had fireplaces, accommodated the eight to ten servants employed by James Logan. Servants also slept in one of the smaller rooms on the second floor."[125]

Richard Morrey and his wife Ann, who would have lived within their abode conceivably quite close to Cremona and other servants and enslaved Africans, were likely noteworthy players in the city's "hereditary upper class, based on business wealth and power," further remarked Baltzell in his classic 1958 book, *Philadelphia Gentlemen: The Making of a National Upper Class*.[126] "Philadelphia was ruled by a small Quaker oligarchy during the late seventeenth and early eighteenth centuries," Baltzell asserted. "A small group of men," including Richard Morrey's father Humphrey, "held most of the important positions, were [often] related by marriage ... and made their fortunes over the seas, as daring merchants and traders [including in the transatlantic slave trade],

60 • THE MONTIERS

or inland with the Indians, whom they treated well from the very start."[127] As examined earlier and as time passed the indigenous people were treated horribly, swindled out of their land as well as too often enslaved, brutalized, or outright murdered, if they had not perished due to then novel European diseases.

As mentioned earlier, but examined in more detail here, the Morrey family was "also well-connected with marriages [to] prominent members of the 'Philadelphia elite' such as the Budd family,"[128] notably Humphrey and Ann Morrey's son—Richard's older brother John—marrying Sarah Budd.[129] Destined to also become a slaveholder, "the younger Humphrey Morrey [son of John and Sarah] became a merchant and a distiller in Philadelphia. Through his mother, Sarah Budd Morrey, who lived until 1720, he was related to Edward Shippen III, like him the grandson of a well-off Quaker merchant and wealthy in his own right, and William Allen, a rising young lawyer and merchant." Similar to the elder Humphrey Morrey, "Shippen and Allen would become mayors of Philadelphia," with Shippen rising to "become Pennsylvania's Royal Governor and Allen its Chief Justice."[130]

Sarah's father was the British-born William Budd, who settled about 1678 in Burlington, New Jersey, described as "a large locator of lands," presumably a land speculator or investor. Sarah's brother, Thomas, "held many important trusts in the Province. When the first form of government was established by the Proprietors, he was selected, with others, to assist the Governor to establish a code of laws suitable to the maintenance of order," later moving "to Philadelphia" where he "continued his business as a merchant till his death, in 1697."[131]

Like Richard Morrey, Israel Pemberton, the enslaver of "Betty" who had turned down his offer for emancipation early in the 18th century likely due to concerns about how to subsist,[132] and other second-generation colonists whose fathers had migrated to America about the time that Penn arrived in 1682 became quite wealthy via inheritances and/or by way of their own volitions. Pemberton, "whose father had migrated from Lancashire, England, in 1682, was born in the county of Bucks, just north of Philadelphia," Baltzell chronicled. "As a young man he came down to Philadelphia and became one of the city's wealthiest merchants. Israel Pemberton, his brother-in-law, James Logan, and Isaac Norris were the leading members of the Quaker oligarchy during the second quarter of the eighteenth century"[133] when Cremona Morrey would have matured into an apparently alluring young woman, perhaps with mulatto features accentuated likely by unmistakable "Negro" characteristics visually.

Most of such white colonists migrated into Pennsylvania and Philadelphia from places near and far due to a range of reasons related to topography, economics, religious and political freedom, as well as other factors. "Furthermore, Pennsylvania, because of its middle position" geographically on the Eastern Seaboard, "its religious toleration, and its almost immediate economic success, attracted settlers not only from all parts of Great Britain but from earlier colonies as well," a prime example being Richard Morrey's father, Humphrey, becoming an almost instant financial success before quickly ascending to become Philadelphia's first mayor in 1691. Some, such as Humphrey who had been a successful merchant in New York after emigrating from England, arrived in Philadelphia with a sizeable amount of capital that often was acquired via slave economies and the transatlantic slave trade. "Gentry-class settlers of early Pennsylvania can be identified as coming from both Jerseys, Maryland, New York, Virginia, Connecticut, Massachusetts, Rhode Island, Antigua, Barbados, Bermuda, and Jamaica,"[134] where interracial relationships involving white men and enslaved black women, although often outwardly or publicly criticized, were prevalent because of the burgeoning numbers of "mulattos" or mixed-race African Americans and other factors, as previously discussed.

An examination of a few of those relationships and comparing them to what we know about the union between Richard and Cremona should be quite telling.

CHAPTER 3

A Forbidden Relationship Develops during Racially Explosive Times

Perhaps Richard Morrey's eyes began to drift toward and then fixate on his young "Negro" servant, Cremona or "Mooney," as she blossomed into womanhood during the mid to late 1720s or early 1730s in the relatively close quarters of the Morrey residence on the sprawling Cheltenham estate stretching across emerald grounds and meadowlands inundated with livestock and caretaker domestics, both indentured and enslaved. Maybe the embers of passion began to ignite as Mooney cooked and served him during mealtime, or while she performed other chores around the household. Richard may have even watched her from afar walking towards a well to retrieve water or executing other physical duties, increasingly enraptured by her curvaceousness, by her alluring or intellectually witty personality.

Cremona was essentially legally powerless in America as a young black woman living in two circumstances during certain phases of her life: in bondage or as a liberated employee[1] who either bought her own freedom or was voluntarily emancipated, perhaps by Richard.[2] As she matured, perhaps "Mooney" began to realize that, with her growing physical and cerebral maturation, she indeed did wield a substantial amount of power and influence over Richard if judiciously exercised, as well as depending on his temperament. Perhaps Cremona began to realize that she possessed something that most men, including Richard, utterly desired. "The historiography of slavery has long since moved beyond the notion that slave owners were deity-like in their omnipotence and that slaves really were actual chattel, like pieces of furniture lacking conscience and will," writes Annette Gordon-Reed in her National Book Award-winning *The Hemingses of Monticello: An American Family*,[3] which largely focuses on the reported interracial romance between one of America's most revered Founding Fathers, Thomas Jefferson, and his maturing African-descended servant, Sally Hemings, half-sister to Jefferson's wife, Martha Wayles Skelton Jefferson. "It is now well recognized that within their admittedly limited sphere, enslaved people helped shape the contours of the master-slave relationship, both as actors and as reactors."[4]

Still, despite such acknowledgments, forced relationships and sexual coercions were well documented during slavery, with some scholars questioning whether there could ever be an unconditional love between a so-called slave and her master. In fact, such relationships could be morbidly perverse and lurid based on the ugliest of racist and sexist stereotypes: "Throughout the period of slavery in America, white society believed black women to be innately lustful beings," a belief system that still exists today in Western spheres. "Because the ideal white woman was pure and, in the nineteenth century, modest to the degree of prudishness, the perception of the African woman as hyper-sexual made her both the object of white man's abhorrence and his fantasy. Within the bonds of slavery, masters often felt it their right to engage in sexual activity with black women." Tragically, some black women, often to survive and possibly obtain freedom, relented to such advances. "Sometimes, female slaves acquiesced to advances hoping that such relationships would increase the chances that they or their children would be liberated by the master. Most of the time, however, slave owners took slaves by force."[5]

Mixed-race mulatto women, even in Brazil (where about 40 to 50 percent of all abducted Africans were enslaved in the Americas), were often pursued by elder European colonists or enslavers. Richard Morrey was about thirty years older than Cremona when his relationship with her commenced in about 1736. (Wikimedia Commons)

Did the 1735 deaths of Jane—a platonic and managerial centerpiece of Ann and Richard Morrey's household—and Thomas—their son, whom both parents presumably deeply loved—help lead to the disintegration of the marital relationship between the couple while prompting Richard's apparently open and novel romance with Cremona? After all, such unexpected deaths of offspring placed enormous emotional pressure often saturated with guilt on the surviving parents—despite Thomas likely being a young unmarried adult in 1735[6]—and that burden must have been compounded by the loss of their household supervisor, Jane. In addition there are indications that Ann's father, likely Thomas Turner of England, may have been quite guarded and cautious or concerned about Richard for one reason or the other because he clearly wanted a major part of his financial legacy to be directly distributed to his daughter, Ann, although she was married to Richard.[7] Did such concerns place even more strain on Ann and Richard's potentially fragile marriage?

Assuming Richard Morrey's wife Ann died in 1736, or perhaps 1735, it's quite possible that he was distraught, depending on the nature of his relationship with her—especially about the time she passed away. However, if Richard had been for some time grooming Cremona for romantic companionship or if he commenced that relationship before Ann's death, then his feelings for Ann might have been neutralized when she died considering that he had found solace, as well as possible sexual gratification, or amorous relations with "the young slave girl,"[8] Cremona. Yet, just like in the case of Sally Hemings, it's quite possible that Cremona possessed a substantial amount of realized power as a woman aware of men's needs and desires, especially considering that she and her children would obtain liberty and the remarkable amount of land that Richard passed on to her.

Another possible pressure on Ann and Richard's relationship could have been religious differences. In fact, Ann, likely a practicing Quaker (despite Richard probably moving away from the Friends based on Quaker records during that period scarcely bearing his name, perhaps an indication that he at least tolerated or even early on supported the institution of slavery), "made a will and left a legacy to Abington Monthly Meeting."[9] Relatedly, "minutes of the meeting noted the legacy," with Ann declaring, "'I give and bequeath unto Abington Monthly Meeting the sum of 5 pounds, the Which legacy this mtg is given to understand is in the hands of Henery [sic] Vanaken of Phila, wherefore James Paul our Treasurer is appointed to receive the said legacy of the said Friend and place it to the common stock of this mtg and to give a receipt in the name and behalf of this mtg for the same.'"[10] So it's important to underline that Cremona, Ann's assumed marital or romantic competition, may have been a practicing Quaker; yet records regarding Cremona's participation or attendance as an enslaved African-descended person or free black woman might have been quite minimal or nonexistent since many early Quakers also maintained racist views, possibly rendering Cremona invisible or even actively disdained because of her intimate relationship with Richard. It is however virtually beyond doubt that Cheltenham's Quaker-dominated community in which Cremona and Richard lived on the Morrey "country estate" was quite aware, but comparatively more tolerant, of the eyebrow-raising interracial relationship. "Richard Morrey's liaison with his servant probably scandalized his neighbors, most of whom were small farmers, with many of them being members of Abington Monthly Meeting."[11]

Based on the terms of young Thomas's will—which seemed to vastly favor his mother financially, compared to his father Richard—was Thomas already aware of a possible relationship between the servant Cremona and his father—especially considering that Cremona's first child was born in 1736, likely fathered by Richard?

> Thomas' will revealed some of his life and that of his family. He left his father Richard any books he wanted. He left his mother Ann the rents of a house at Tower Hill, London, to be given after the death of his parents to cousins in Cheshire. He left 200 acres on Neshaminy Creek in Bucks County to his sister Matilda Kimbal [sic] and an adjoining 200 acres to her children.[12]

This information is corroborated in Josiah Granville Leach's 1894 article "Colonial Mayors of Philadelphia," in *The Pennsylvania Magazine of History and Biography*.[13]

Interestingly, Thomas must have felt affection for some of his parents' black servants too, perhaps including Cremona, as well as had a clear interest in groundbreaking scientific endeavors based on his gift to a renowned figure in United States science history:

> He left his microscopes to Christopher Witt, and money to his father's servants and Negroes. He left £2 to the minister of St. Thomas Church at Whitemarsh to preach the funeral sermon. The picture is of an unmarried Anglican gentleman living a comfortable life with his books and scientific devices, fond of his family and generous to his servants. Christopher Witt was an especially interesting acquaintance for Thomas. He worked as a physician, cast horoscopes, and was a friend of the botanist John Bartram. His library in Germantown was filled with books on philosophy, "natural magic," and divining. Perhaps he used Thomas' microscopes to study the plants of Bartram's garden.[14]

Given the circumstances, the presence of the young and reportedly vibrant Cremona within the household was likely quite irresistible to the aging and possibly despondent Richard. Despite it being impossible to determine exactly how the relationship developed, given Richard's advanced age of about 60 in 1735 and authority over the much younger Cremona as her employer or "master," it's likely that he was initially the aggressor—especially given the racial and gender dynamics of the period. As a black woman, Cremona would have been particularly vulnerable so not likely to initially risk zealously pursuing a relationship with Richard. It's estimated that Richard's wife Ann Morrey "died some time [sic] between 1735 and 1746," when the liaison between Richard and Cremona probably developed, and one hypothesis is that Cremona may have still been a teenager due to some uncertainty about her birthdate:[15]

> Although it is not known when she [Cremona] was born [despite some estimates of 1710], it can be guessed that by 1735 she was young, possibly not yet out of her teens, and attractive, maybe already the mother of a child. Richard Morrey may always have been aware of the maid's evident charms; perhaps, one day, he turned around and took a long look at her. He then may have found that the solicitous servant was young and nubile, and that his blood could run as hot as it had in his younger days. Somehow, in some manner, the master and the servant started an affair that would last for nearly ten years and result in either four or five children.[16]

Still, given the above scenario, the question is, to what degree did Cremona feel coerced, especially considering that Richard was or had been her enslaver and then employer, as well as ultimately Cremona's historically unique and ultra-generous benefactor? How and why did Cremona succumb to or accept the likely advances of the much older Richard, even when he was quite possibly still married to Ann? What sort of pressures might Cremona have felt or received from Richard's wife Ann, especially if "mistress" Cremona and wife Ann were living in the same household? Again, there are more than a few documented cases of such black women enduring and sometimes succumbing to horrific hostility and violence by jealous white wives who often controlled nearly every domestic aspect of such households.[17] Of course white women during that period had limited rights compared to their husbands,[18] despite having virtually absolute power over black domestic workers, especially if they were enslaved.[19]

Remember there have been questions about Richard Morrey's faithfulness and marital relationships based on his reported marriages to two other women, including his first wife Ann (Turner) whom he married "about 1695," who probably passed away before or about 1746.[20] Likely after Ann's passing, Richard also had a matrimonial relationship with Sarah Allen Beasley, a marriage that began in 1746,[21] about the time Richard provided Cremona with the 198 acres of land and probably separated from Cremona and the couple's children, at least very likely on a full-time familial basis. Indeed, had

Richard's romantic or intimate relationship with Sarah commenced before he and Cremona broke up?

Meanwhile, there are some examples of wealthy white men having affectionate, visible, and sustaining marriages or relationships with black women while supporting the couples' children, including William Purvis (1757–1826), the father of the noted Philadelphia antislavery abolitionist, entrepreneur and investor Robert Purvis (1810–1898). As the middle child of three sons born in Charleston, South Carolina, to the free black woman Harriet Judah (1785–1869) and father William, a British-born cotton dealer, Robert said his dad implanted in him a deep disdain for slavery. In addition to being sent to Philadelphia at about age nine or 10 and enrolled in the Pennsylvania Abolition Society's Clarkson School, the light-complexioned Robert was later educated at the Amherst Academy in Massachusetts. Robert would return to Philadelphia, blessed with a hefty inheritance from his deceased father, to become extraordinarily active in helping runaway slaves escape via the Underground Railroad. Robert also associated with other leading freedom fighters, including William Still, Lucretia Mott,[22] and, quite remarkably, Hiram Charles Montier (1818–1905),[23] a great-grandson of Cremona [Satterthwaite] Morrey Fry and Richard Morrey.

Other such interracial relationships involving enslaved or formerly enslaved women, more than likely coerced by varying degrees, are well known in American history—from Founding Father Thomas Jefferson having a child-producing relationship with his late wife's half-sister, Sally Hemings, to Aaron Burr's "secret wife," Mary Emmons—all among liaisons that we'll explore. Indeed, a modern descendant of the Morreys, Montiers, and Bustills, Joyce Mosley,[24] says she also descends from the Burr–Emmons union.

Again, such relationships were not without risks, ranging from adverse publicity and political exploitation to various punishments, depending on the socioeconomic statuses of those involved. Both Cremona and Richard lived during a period when their relationship put them in immense jeopardy—at least on paper: "In 1726, in order to control the relatively large local slave population and to discourage owners from freeing their slaves, the Assembly passed a black code that required £30 surety bond for manumission, forbade intermarriage between whites and blacks, and restricted the freedom of both slaves and free blacks to travel, drink liquor, and carry on trade," circumstances that the couple probably monitored, despite Richard's stature perhaps shielding them somewhat from such penalties.[25] In fact, Pennsylvania had passed a strict miscegenation law outlawing interracial marriages in 1725, when Cremona would have been about age 15 if born in 1710.[26]

Moreover, penalties for interracial relationships were recorded and sanctioned well before 1725. Daniel Rolph's 2011 article "Black History Month: Inter-Racial Marriages and Relationships in Colonial Pennsylvania" notes:

> Even though the above Richard Morrey would live as husband and wife with a slave woman, the Pennsylvania colony and surrounding area, were by no means, "bastions of benevolence" when it came to the inter-racial relationships of its citizens. As early as 1677 a white servant was indicted, for being *"contrary to the Lawes of the Government and Contrary to his Masters Consent hath ... got with child a certaine molato wooman Called Swart anna,"* while in 1698 the Chester County, Pennsylvania Court forbade the "mingling of the races." Plus, the "Minutes of the Abington Monthly Meeting," for 1693, records the course of action taken against a "Negro Man ... And a white woman for having a Baster Childe ... *she being examined, Confest the same: ... the Court ordered that she shall Received Twenty one laishes on her beare Backe ... and the Court ordered the negroe never more to meddle with any white woman more uppon paine of his life."*[27]

The risks for participating in such liaisons in William Penn's land of so-called equality could be quite costly; although Richard Morrey's powerful standing in the community likely afforded him and Cremona substantial immunity from such punishments, other less affluent folks deemed guilty of such liaisons could and did face perilous statutory consequences.

The Statutes at Large of Pennsylvania, Section VIII, for 1725–1726, emphatically declared:

> Be it further enacted ... That *if any white man or woman shall cohabit or dwell with any negro under pretense of being married, such white man or woman* shall forfeit and pay the sum of thirty pounds or be sold for a servant ... and *the child or children* of such white man or woman *shall be put out to service as above directed until they come to the age of thirty-one years ... and if any free negro man or woman shall intermarry with a white woman or man, such negro shall become a slave during life ... and if any free negro man or woman shall commit fornication or adultery with any white man or woman, such negro or negroes shall be sold servant for seven years ... and the white man or woman shall be punished as the law directs in cases of adultery or fornication.*[28]

Further, if a "Magistrate" or religious authority such as a preacher dare officiate the marriage of such interracial couples, the fine would be an astounding "one hundred pounds!"

Restrictions placed between the two races were not simply confined to the subject of marriage or cohabitation within the "City of Brotherly Love." The "Middletown Meeting" records for Bucks County, Pennsylvania, on the "6th of the Third Month, 1703," also stated how "Friends are not satisfied with having negroes buried in Friends' burying-ground," and again in 1738 the same meeting declared that "deceased Negroes [are] forbidden to be buried within the grounds of the graveyard belonging to this Meeting."[29]

It's likely, however, that such relationships were more prevalent than traditional historical resources might suggest, according to the noted African American jurist A. Leon Higginbotham Jr. in his classic book, *In The Matter of Color: Race & The American Legal Process: The Colonial Period*.[30] "While there is much speculation as to the extent of interracial sexual activities occurring in Pennsylvania," the renowned scholar Edward Raymond Turner notes in his 1910 doctoral thesis for Johns Hopkins University that "there had doubtless been some [interracial] intercourse from the first.' One tract of land [in the region] ... was known as 'Mulatto Hall.' Despite the prohibitions of the 1725–1726 statute it 'did not succeed in checking cohabitation, though of marriages of slaves with white people there is almost no record," Higginbotham points out, quoting Turner.[31]

Meanwhile, Higginbotham notes, "advertisements for runaway slaves indicated that there were 'very many' mulattoes."[32] Benjamin Franklin's *Pennsylvania Gazette* had no shortage of such ads focusing on mixed-race or mulatto blacks, some literate and refined according to European standards, perhaps like Cremona Morrey culturally and socially.

On July 21, 1748, the *Gazette* ran an advertisement seeking the return or apprehension of "a Negro man" and "Mulattoe wench" who had escaped, likely together, from a Bucks County slaveholder. "RUN away, on Sunday Night last, from David Lindsay, of Northampton, Bucks county, A Negro man, named Dove, about 30-years of age, of middle stature, pretty much pitted with the Small-pox, and talks pretty good English: Had on a whitish coloured kersey jacket, buckskin breeches, grey stockings, without the feet, old shoes, and steel buckles in them," Lindsay's advertisement said. "Also run away at the same time, from said Lindsay, a Mulattoe wench, named Kate, about 16 years of age, of low stature, and can talk very good English: Had on, a linsey gown, and linsey petticoat. Whoever takes up and secures said Negro and wench, so as they may be had again, shall have Twenty-shillings reward for each, and reasonable charges, paid by DAVID LINDSAY."[33]

A November 16, 1752, advertisement focused on selling "a Strong able Negroe wench, and her son, a fine boy, about 7 months old, the wench is about 26 years old, has had the small pox, and is an excellent cook, a good washer, and very fit for either town or country business," conceivably a description that may have characterized Cremona in earlier years if she had already given birth to Robert Lewis, her reported first child, via another suitor before her relationship with Richard. The 1752 ad continued offering for sale "a Molattoe girl, about 16 years of age, has had the small-pox and measles, cooks and washes well, and very fit for any gentleman service," seemingly with sexual connotations, "that may have occasion for such a girl." Interestingly, the ad ends with a note, presumably from Benjamin Franklin: "Enquire at the New-Printing Office."[34]

The phrasing and sexual connotations in the advertisement directly above provoke uncomfortable but necessary questions about the intimate disposition of Cremona's relationship with Richard Morrey. Did Richard consider her to be "very fit for any gentleman service," including sexual exploitation? Did the relationship develop into a more common-law marital bond after the much older Richard coerced Cremona, during or after her enslavement, leading to her first pregnancy? How much were such interracial relationships secretly or publicly accepted in Northern settings and even among white spouses of such so-called gentlemen maintaining relationships with black women? How visible was the relationship between Richard and Cremona? The evidence seems to dictate that Richard's relationship with Cremona was certainly more noticeable and obvious to local observers in Cheltenham and quite possibly his first wife, Ann, but shielded to a large degree from his affluent comrades in Philadelphia, due to Cheltenham's relative remoteness from the power center of the city.

In fact, as quiet as such affairs were kept, while being accepted with the proverbial "wink of the eye," perhaps that most well-known Philadelphian from the colonial period through to today, Benjamin Franklin, may have maintained sexual relationships with black women, according to Higginbotham:

> Throughout the colonial literature there is a continuous debate as to whether interracial sexual relations occurred primarily between blacks and "servants, outcasts, and the lowlier class of whites" or whether it included the master class as well. Turner believes that the stigma of such illicit intercourse in Pennsylvania would "not generally seem to rest upon the masters." But it is perhaps not without significance that one of Pennsylvania's leading statesmen, Benjamin Franklin, "was openly accused of keeping negro paramours."[35]

And Benjamin Franklin was not the only so-called Founding Father reputed to have had sexual relations with black women. There was also Thomas Jefferson, the third president of the United States and primary author of the Declaration of Independence, who reportedly wrote much of the historic document in 1776 proclaiming "that all men are created equal" on the second floor of a central-Philadelphia brick home (owned by Jacob and Maria Graff) where he held an enslaved African American likely on the third level or in the attic, 14-year-old Robert Hemings,[36] a brother of the black mistress with whom Jefferson had several mixed-race children, according to a range of scholarly sources.

Thomas Jefferson appears to have been much more clandestine regarding his relationship with Sally Hemings compared to Richard Morrey's more visible

72 • THE MONTIERS

and acknowledged union with Cremona. Still, Jefferson's intimate proclivities can provide some important comparative insights into the dynamic ties between Cremona and Richard Morrey, despite Jefferson's involvement with Hemings occurring several decades after Cremona and Richard's union. Nonetheless, there are striking similarities. Like Richard Morrey, Thomas Jefferson was much older than Sally, and Sally, like Cremona, by many accounts, was a mixed-race "Mulatto," with Sally "described by one slave as 'mighty near white,' 'very handsome,' with 'long straight hair down her back.'"[37]

> When Jefferson went to France in 1785 he took only his eldest daughter Martha. When the youngest, Lucy, died in Virginia, Jefferson requested that his second daughter, Mary (Polly), be sent to Paris with a middle-aged slave woman who had had smallpox. Instead she was accompanied by [the teen-aged] Sally Hemings. She was given a modest salary and apparently tutored in French along with her brother James, Jefferson's valet.[38]

Notably, despite Jefferson's doubts about African Americans' intellectual capacities and his belief that they were physically as well as mentally inferior to whites, he probably initiated a relationship with his black, teenaged servant:

> There is subtle evidence in Jefferson's journals, letters, and account books to indicate that in 1788 the forty-five-year-old widower, lonely after the return to London of his intimate artist friend Maria Cosway, fell in love with the blooming young quadroon, half-sister to his dead wife. Madison Hemings, Sally's third son, in an important but long-neglected memoir, reported that his mother became Jefferson's "concubine" in Paris, and that when he was called home, Sally was "*enceinte* [or pregnant] by him." Since by French law she was free, Sally refused to return until Jefferson promised that he would free all her children at twenty-one. A son was born shortly after her return to Monticello in December 1789.[39]

It is also worth considering the interracial liaison between Aaron Burr Jr., a Revolutionary War veteran officer and the former United States vice president who killed fellow Founding Father Alexander Hamilton in an 1804 pistol duel, and Mary Emmons, a native of India. "In 1787 or before, Colonel Burr," although by then married to Theodosia Prevost, who had inherited slaves from her late husband James Marcus Prevost, "commenced a relationship with Mary Eugénie Beauharnais Emmons," a woman of color and enslaved servant in his household, wrote an African American descendant of that relationship, the noted scholar and author Sherri Burr, Esq., in the 2020 article "Aaron Burr J. and John Pierre Burr: A Founding Father and his Abolitionist Son."[40] Author and family historian Joyce Mosley, in addition to descending from the Bustills, Morreys, Montiers, and Millers, also marvels about her ties to the Emmons and Burr families. Emmons was born in Calcutta, India, "around 1760," about a decade before Cremona Sr.'s estimated 1770 death. She "first migrated to Haiti, where her original Indian name was abandoned to become Eugénie

Beauharnais, and then to the United States, where that name was changed to Mary Emmons." It's likely that Emmons had been enslaved in Haiti by Theodosia's former husband, James Prevost, who died in 1781 of yellow fever in Jamaica. Theodosia's probable inheritance of Emmons essentially made her the enslaved property of Burr, Theodosia's husband. Although "Mary Emmons became part of their household," it's likely that "Theodosia was ... already afflicted with cancer and her health steadily declined until her death in 1794."[41]

Meanwhile, "Burr Jr.'s children with Mary Emmons, Louisa Charlotte born in 1788 and John Pierre born in 1792, survived to adulthood and had produced children and grandchildren who were living when Burr Jr. died at

Duelist and former United States vice president Aaron Burr Jr. and his wife, Theodosia Bartow, were married when he began a relationship with Mary Emmons, an enslaved woman native to India. Two mixed-race children were born of that relationship. (Wikimedia Commons)

the age of 80 in 1836," descendant Sherri Burr noted. In fact, "it is true that Burr Jr. impregnated Mary Emmons twice while he was married to Theodosia Prevost. That both his wife and servant gave birth during the same year (1788) indicates Burr Jr. was having intimate relations with both women around the same time."[42]

Burr Jr.'s political career soared. "When Burr Jr. and Thomas Jefferson received Electoral College votes in the 1796 presidential election, Louisa Charlotte and John Pierre were born," Sherri Burr notes. However, "Burr Jr. kept his family of color secret throughout the entirety of his political life,"[43] similar to what his fellow politician Jefferson unsuccessfully tried to do regarding his child-producing relationship with the mixed-race African American Sally Hemings:

> In the election of 1800, when his children of color were about twelve and eight, Burr Jr. tied with Jefferson in the Electoral College. At the time, electors did not vote separately for president and vice president; rather, the person with the highest votes won the presidency and the second-highest won the vice-presidency. Because Jefferson and Burr Jr. both won 73 electoral votes (the incumbent John Adams won only 65 votes), the election was decided by the House of Representatives. After 36 ballots and the intervention of Alexander Hamilton, who

threw his support behind Jefferson, the primary author of the Declaration of Independence became the nation's third president and Burr was elected its third vice president. Both men sworn into the nation's two highest offices were fathers to children of color.[44]

Yet, a persistent rivalry between Alexander Hamilton and Aaron Burr would culminate on July 11, 1804, when the two "met on the dueling grounds at Weehawken, New Jersey, to fight the final skirmish of a long-lived political and personal battle. When the duel was over, Hamilton would be mortally wounded, and Burr would be wanted for murder,"[45] charges that did not result in prison, despite Jefferson's attempts to get Burr convicted for treason. When Burr Jr. migrated to Europe for four years near the end of the first decade in 1800s, his children "John Pierre was 18 and his sister Louisa Charlotte was 22." John would become a barber and was exceptionally active in the antislavery movement while helping African Americans via the Underground Railroad; his sister Louisa also became active in the black community, and she served as a housekeeper. "Unlike three of Thomas Jefferson's children of color who married into white society, Louisa Charlotte and John Pierre both married free blacks in Pennsylvania."[46]

Both siblings became exceptionally active progressives, despite significant challenges and dealing with family tragedies. "Louisa Charlotte married Frances Webb, a founding member of the Pennsylvania Augustine Education Society," likely associating with extended family members of the Montiers and Bustills. And remarkably, "the Webbs also became active participants in the Haytian Emigration Society to encourage Free blacks to migrate to Haiti (then Hayti)." Tragically, "Louisa Charlotte and her husband were returning from the island in November 7, 1826 when their daughter Mary Webb died at the age of two." However, "their youngest son Frank J. Webb became an adult," writing "'The Garies and Their Friends,' the second published novel by an African American author, in 1857. The novel included a preface signed by Harriet Beecher Stowe, the author of *Uncle Tom's Cabin*."[47]

John Pierre Burr, the biracial son of Aaron Burr Jr., was an antislavery abolitionist and helped enslaved blacks via the Underground Railroad. (Wikimedia Commons)

Meanwhile, Louisa Charlotte's brother, John Pierre, "married Hester (Hetty) Elizabeth Emery" at the historic African Episcopal Church of St. Thomas in Philadelphia in 1817. In fact, "Hetty was the daughter of John Emery, who had served as a private in Pennsylvania's Fifth Regiment during the Revolutionary War," including at Valley Forge with George Washington's Continental Army. His "barbershop became a station on the Underground Railroad" while he and Hetty also helped to hide "self-liberating slaves in their Philadelphia home at Fifth and Locust (then Prune) streets in the attic, a cave in the cellar, and a deep hole in the backyard at night."[48] John Pierre additionally interacted and organized with prominent members of the Pennsylvania Antislavery Society, including the indomitable Lucretia Mott, whose Roadside estate in Cheltenham was just a couple of miles from Guineatown, the black community that sprouted on and near Cremona Morrey's 198 acres. "A literate man, John Pierre served as an agent for William Lloyd Garrison's abolitionist newspaper, *The Liberator*, and he published the Journal of the American Reform Society." Resolutely, before his death, John Pierre signed "a petition, along with famous abolitionist Frederick Douglass, to encourage free black men to join the U.S. Colored Troops to fight in the Civil War," with his son John Emery Burr joining the 41st U.S. Colored Troops of Camp William Penn, the first and largest Northern-based federal facility to train African American soldiers during the war.[49] After their deaths, Louisa Charlotte and John Pierre were buried at the historic African American cemetery in Delaware County, Pennsylvania, called Eden; Matilda Burr married into the Bustill family, according to Mosley.[50]

As the years and then decades passed, the family expanded to include such notable African Americans as Sherri Burr and Joyce Mosley, exposing and documenting the interracial legacies of their family lines: "On September 29, 2018, the Aaron Burr Association voted unanimously to formally acknowledge that Aaron Burr Jr. had fathered two children by Mary Emmons and that all their descendants are legitimate members of the Burr family," Sherri Burr notes. "This vote was memorialized in the headstone affixed to John Pierre's gravesite and consecrated on August 24, 2019, in the presence of the Sons of the American Revolution Color Guard at Eden Cemetery outside of Philadelphia"[51] where several of the Montier and Morrey family members also rest.

It's striking that Aaron Burr and Thomas Jefferson both tried to shield their relationships with women of color, even as these relationships led to the births of multiple biracial children. Burr was initially more successful with the cover-up while Jefferson was exposed early on by a crusading—some say "muckraking"—journalist, James Thomson Callender, who had worked for Philadelphia publications. Although Richard Morrey's relationship with

Cremona occurred decades earlier, his union with her appeared to be more aboveboard, with Cremona and some of her children even taking on a variation of Morrey's surname. Perhaps most telling is Richard's bequeathment to Cremona of the almost two hundred acres that were obviously meant to sustain her and the children, despite his soon marrying another woman. There is little to no evidence that Jefferson or Burr left such legacies for their "women of color" and children. Yet, before drawing conclusions, let's focus on yet another interracial relationship that produced biracial children.

Just after the mid-18th century, likely during Cremona's lifetime, Dido Badaracka, the grandmother of one of Philadelphia's greatest antislavery abolitionists, Robert Purvis, was born in Africa, possibly between 1754 and 1766, then soon abducted and taken to America as a teenaged slave. Badaracka's grandson, the mixed-race Purvis, came to the world "on August 4, 1810," in Charleston, South Carolina's "The Neck" neighborhood, characterized by some as "a place of lawlessness" that "was home to many free blacks, and the black mistresses of white slave owners," according to Margaret Hope Bacon's 2007 book *But ONE Race: The Life of Robert Purvis*. Robert Purvis's father, "William Purvis, a white cotton merchant, and his mixed-race wife, Harriet Judah, lived" in the area "on Elizabeth Street from time to time. The couple had three children; Robert was the second."[52]

According to Purvis, his mother Harriet "was the daughter of" Badaracka, "'a full-blooded Moor.' Purvis described her as a woman of 'magnificent features and great beauty. She had crisp hair and a stately manner.'"[53]

Around "the age of twelve, she [Badaracka] was captured [possibly about 1776] by a slave trader, along with an Arab girl," as the story goes. "Both girls had been lured to go a mile or two out of the city where they lived to see a deer that had been caught. They were seized, bound, placed on the backs of camels, and carried to a slave market on the coast. Here they

The dynamic Philadelphia antislavery abolitionist and wealthy entrepreneur Robert Purvis was the son of a white cotton broker and mulatto mother. The couple reportedly had a lifelong committed relationship. (Wikimedia Commons)

were loaded onto a slave ship and transported to Charleston, South Carolina in 1766," just a few years before Cremona Morrey would die about 1770 after remarrying an African American and former slave, John Fry. Although the "Arab girl" was set free—"to keep peace with the Barbary pirates" since "in none of the British colonies were Arabs or Moors enslaved"—Purvis's grandmother "Dido was sold to a white woman, a Miss Harriet Deas, who educated her." Purvis's grandmother Dido Badaracka was "treated" more or less "as a companion," with Deas declaring "that Dido was to be freed and given an annuity of $60 when Miss Deas died" about "nine years later."[54] In fact, after her emancipation "when she was nineteen, Dido married a German, Baron Judah,"[55] probably of Jewish ancestry, an indication that two generations of interracial marriages preceded Robert Purvis's birth:

> When Dido was still a young woman, Purvis said, she had attracted the attention of Baron Judah, a member of a prominent Jewish family. There was such a person living in Charleston at the time, who may have been Purvis's grandfather. Baron or Baruch or Barry Judah (1763–1830) was the third of ten children of Hillel Judah, a German Jew, and his wife Abigail Seixas Judah, a Sephardic Jew, originally from Spain or Portugal. This family moved to Charleston sometime between 1766 and 1783, becoming part of a tiny Jewish community.[56]

It's probable that about 1783, when Sephardic Jews had already moved to Charleston making it the "second largest population" of them in America outside of New York, the couple, Dido and Baron, met. "Purvis stated that they were married in a Methodist church, but this would have been unlikely. Many white men had black mistresses, but interracial marriage was extremely rare and frowned upon," Bacon wrote. "The Judahs were a prominent and proud Jewish family and owned slaves at the time. It is probable that Dido was either a slave in this family, or an indentured servant," servitude circumstances that seemed somewhat parallel to Richard and Cremona's initial relationship. "Whatever their relationship, Baron and Dido had two children, Harriet and a son who was possibly named Daniel. Harriet, born in 1785, became Robert Purvis's mother. A third child of Harriet's, Mary, had a different father."[57]

Just as Richard and Cremona's relationship ultimately ended, so too did Baron and Dido's romance conclude. Baron moved on to yet another union that produced children with an unidentified woman. "The relationship between Baron and Dido ended in 1790, when Baron moved with the rest of his family to Savannah, Georgia, and then on to Richmond, Virginia in 1791," Bacon noted. "In Richmond, Baron Judah became a prominent merchant and citizen, a devoted husband and father of at least four children. According to 1820 records, he kept one slave, Mary. He may have owned others but such records were destroyed in the Richmond fire during the Civil War."[58]

Early on, Robert Purvis said that his British-born father, William, implanted in him a deep disdain for slavery—despite his father and mother Harriet's involvement in the abhorrent institution. "Although Robert Purvis probably never knew this, his mother, Harriet Judah, was a slaveholder," Bacon noted. "In February and March 1812, when Robert was a baby, she sold a black girl named Betty, aged ten, and bought an African girl named Bella and a black girl named Jenny. Though some free blacks bought relatives as slaves in order to save them from white owners, this was not the case with these two girls," Bacon wrote. "It is possible that she dealt in slaves as a way of helping her lover William Purvis."[59] Furthermore, "in 1819, William purchased a family of slaves from a South Carolinian slaveholder," one of several transactions that documented his ownership of slaves, despite Robert later indicating that his father did not. "It may be that Robert never knew of these transactions," Bacon theorized. "It may also be that William acquired slaves reluctantly and divested himself of them quickly."[60]

According to Bacon, there is considerable confusion about whether Robert Purvis's mother Harriet was in fact born a slave based on the likelihood that her mother, Dido, probably was not officially liberated. The children of enslaved women were considered to be slaves too. "It may be that William never legally freed her, since the laws for manumission were becoming increasingly rigorous," Bacon wrote. "It was impossible, for instance, after 1810 to free a slave unless one could demonstrate his/her ability to be self-supporting. This eliminated the possibility of freeing one's children."[61]

Nonetheless, it appears that Harriet's relationship with William was deep and authentic, harmony that Robert Purvis would have likely observed and relished. Despite his continuing involvement in slavery, Robert's father, William, began to plan for his interracial family's escape from Charleston's intense slave society in which his sons could have been victimized in a myriad of ways, including lifetime enslavement. Following the death of his brother, Burridge Purvis, who was also William's business partner, William prepared to take action. William's "growing uneasiness about dealing in slaves, plus the growing harshness of the slave owners, caused William Purvis to decide to leave ... and move to England or Scotland, where he felt his three sons could be properly educated," Bacon wrote. "In 1817, he sold his business. In 1819, he took his little family to Philadelphia, intending it to be a temporary stop while he settled his complicated financial affairs. He planned to buy a home for them in Scotland or northern England."[62]

By "1826, his [Robert's] father died, leaving him $120,000,"[63] an astonishing amount for the period, especially for a biracial African American. Robert Purvis returned to Philadelphia, blessed with a hefty inheritance from his deceased father, to become a deft real-estate investor. He was also extraordinarily active in helping runaway slaves escape via the Underground Railroad and associated with other leading freedom fighters, including William Still, Lucretia Mott,[64] and, quite remarkably, Hiram Charles Montier, the great grandson of Cremona [Satterthwaite] Morrey Fry.[65]

Along the way, Robert became "acquainted with his counterparts in the black elite who were to play a role in his later life," leading to his later marriage to Harriet Forten, the daughter of one of Philadelphia's wealthiest and most important black rights activists, James Forten, who had fought in the Revolutionary War and cofounded the Free African Society (FAS). In fact, in 1792 he likely met some of James Forten and his wife Harriet's children at the historic and pioneering African Episcopal Church of St. Thomas,[66] one of the first black churches in America founded by the African American preacher and bishop (and cofounder of FAS), Absalom Jones.

And as fate would have it, Robert Purvis would also associate with descendants of Cremona Morrey, the Bustill family,[67] from which the magnanimous Paul Robeson would rise. "Another family whom the Purvis boys came to know was that of Robert and Grace Douglass," Bacon wrote. Indeed, Grace "had been brought up as a Quaker by her father, Cyrus Bustill,"[68] who was the baker credited with assisting George Washington's Revolutionary War army and likely lived in Cheltenham's Guineatown, the historic black neighborhood that would develop on or near 198 acres that Richard Morrey bequeathed to his black partner, Cremona or "Negro Mooney." "Along with her children, she [Grace] attended Quaker meetings regularly, though she was never invited to join."[69] Robert Douglass, however, was an elder of the First African Presbyterian Church,"[70] founded by the former slave, the Reverend John Gloucester, who associated with the formerly enslaved Pastor Jones and the dynamic black preacher, Richard Allen. In fact, Allen was another cofounder of FAS and the Mother Bethel African Methodist Episcopal Church that is today a worldwide denomination. Both Jones and Allen would become founding bishops in their respective historic churches.[71]

Without doubt, Robert Purvis's father, William, displayed a unique and enduring love for his wife, Harriet, a former slave, despite both being complicit in the horrific institution of slavery.

Yet, Robert Purvis's previously enslaved maternal grandmother, Dido Badaracka, seems to not have received the same consideration from her partner, Baron Judah. Ultimately, not only did Baron leave Dido with children that included Robert Purvis's mother Harriet, but he also moved to another city and started a new family. It's not clear if he left Dido with any type of substantial financial or real estate legacy—and if he did, it was not likely comparable to the two hundred acres that Richard Morrey bequeathed to Cremona.

As noted, Aaron Burr and Thomas Jefferson both hid and did not acknowledge their relationships with Mary Emmons and Sarah "Sally" Hemings, respectively, and their resulting biracial children. And there's certainly minimal evidence that either woman received a substantial financial legacy, although some sources purport that Jefferson made provisions for Hemings and her children to eventually be emancipated. Sally Hemings, according to most sources, was never officially emancipated; although her surviving children were liberated when they reached age 21.

Despite some descendants and other observers believing that Richard and Cremona's relationship was "transactional" and even exploited it's worth repeating that Cremona and at least a few of her children took on a variation of Richard Morrey's surname,[72] perhaps an indication that Richard tentatively or even substantially accepted his somewhat limited public relationship with her and their biracial children. Courageously, perhaps, and virtually unprecedentedly, it's worth repeating Richard ultimately left Cremona almost two hundred acres clearly meant to provide a means of sustenance for her and the children—despite likely suddenly leaving Cremona and their kids to marry another woman in 1746. Richard's departure from Cremona is still controversial among some of his descendants and modern historical analysts.[73] Meanwhile, however, there is little to no evidence that Jefferson or Burr left such legacies for their "women of color" and children.

Comparatively speaking, Richard Morrey seemed to display parts of the characteristics that have been attributed to all the above-described Caucasian men in their interracial relationships with women of color, including those enslaved of African descent. However, particularly noteworthy is Richard essentially passing to Cremona two hundred acres of land with conditions that have been interpreted by some as an indicator of his once deep love and respect for Cremona. He materially supported his former "common-law wife," Cremona, and their children, to a degree like Robert Purvis's father, William Purvis, as well as remained with her and their progeny for at least a decade. It seems that Richard also agreed to or made arrangements for Cremona and ultimately her children's liberations, despite the likelihood that Cremona herself negotiated the emancipations, as well as acquiring the almost two hundred acres. Indeed, some descendants and historical observers believe that there were likely strong elements of Richard coercing Cremona given his power over her as an elder white man who initially held her in bondage, then later became her employer.[74] And that's despite the possibility that Richard may have been already involved romantically by the mid-1740s with Sarah Beasley, the woman he married in 1746, presumably shortly after abruptly leaving Cremona.

Richard's relationship with Sarah seemed to be largely based on conducting business such as the selling of much property in the Philadelphia region, including in Cheltenham, at least until his death in 1754. Indeed, was Sarah and Richard's union primarily a relationship of "convenience"? Some observers believe so. Did Richard, for one reason or the other, feel compelled to leave Cremona and marry Sarah, despite still having deep feelings for Cremona? Regardless, Richard's departure is somewhat reminiscent of Baron Judah leaving Robert Purvis's grandmother, Dido Badaracka, with children, including Purvis's mother Harriet. Conversely, Robert Purvis's father, William Purvis, seemed to display and provide an unconditional love for Harriet, Purvis's mother, and sons, including for Robert, by relocating the entire family to Philadelphia with plans to then move everyone to England where his sons would be educated; it seems that William Purvis unconditionally loved and accepted his biracial family. Richard and Cremona's relationship, however, certainly seemed to be conditional and transactional by the time it ended in 1746.

Indeed, Cremona and Richard Morrey appear to have ultimately navigated exceptionally complicated matters of interracial romantic relationships, gender, and class interwoven within the atrocious institution of forced enslavement and eventual liberation. It seems that Richard's "love" or infatuation for Cremona and the children fizzled and became increasingly negotiable, perhaps by Richard and Cremona as demonstrated via their likely Hemings/Jefferson-style "treaty." Circumstances seem to indicate that Cremona and Richard had developed a relatively unique, but conditional relationship, conjuring up a very important question: Can there be true love with conditions? "As we travel the path of life towards this true love, we will experience lesser forms of love in its many guises," asserts writer Jeff Thibodeau, despite others declaring that all "love" and life itself are conditional. "These guises are all forms of conditional love, and because of the limits created by conditions, they fall somewhere short of the infinite depth of true love."[75] Yet, even with such conditions and the need for a couple to go separate ways, can the sacrifice of the relationship itself be a deep expression of true love?

The relationship between Richard and Cremona was not without risks or challenges—especially for Cremona, an African-descended woman—despite the likelihood that Richard's affluence and wealth as a white man minimized their criminal exposure. Higginbotham illustrates that black men maintaining romantic relationships with white women were almost always guaranteed extraordinarily harsh punishment compared to white men having such relations with black women[76] that too often involved rape, a practice that was one of the most traumatic and dastardly during the slavery era and beyond:

> In a 1702 case, for example, a Bucks County court found a Negro slave called Hugo and a white woman named Sarah Cooper guilty of committing fornication. Sarah had had a bastard child, evidently from this union. The court ordered that Hugo be "whipped with twenty one lashes upon his bare back well laid on" and that Sarah receive the same punishment. However, had Sarah been able to "pay a fine as the law in this case directs," the court noted, she could have escaped the corporal punishment. Thus, in this case the court gave the white defendant the option to pay a fine and avoid the corporal punishment that was mandatory for the black.[77]

Higginbotham elucidates further that "the court imposed some punishment on both Hugo and Sarah," but in another situation and ruling involving a white man and black woman, the outcome was markedly different, noting that "the court in the Duckett and Anna case imposed no penalty on either defendant for committing (interracial) fornication." Higginbotham concludes: "This decision not to pardon the defendants [Hugo and Sarah] may have been attributable to a growing hostility toward interracial premarital sex and to the fact that Hugo was a black male and Sarah a white female, while Duckett was a white male and Anna a black female."[78]

In fact, the penalty of death was not out of the question for black men having amorous relationships with white women, according to Higginbotham, as evidenced by a case about a dozen years before Cremona Morrey's presumed 1710 birth:

> In 1698 a Chester court took an even harsher view toward the "commingling" of the races. A black man and white woman were charged with having a bastard child. Both parties testified that the white woman had "intised" the black and promised to marry him. While the court held that the white woman should receive "twenty one lashes on her beare Backe" it also "ordered the negro never more to meddle with any white women *upon pane of his life.*" Thus, a second conviction of the black for having premarital sex with any white female could have led to his execution, even if both parties had acted voluntarily.[79]

If accused or convicted of attempting rape or murder, or committing such actions, the penalties for a supposed African-descended perpetrator were nothing less than barbaric, including castration or executions:

All blacks—both "free" and enslaved—found guilty of attempts to rape a white woman or maid were to be castrated. Those convicted of "robbing, stealing or fraudulent taking or carrying away any goods, living or dead"; or carrying "any guns, swords, pistols, fowling pieces or other arms or other weapons whatsoever, without his master's special license"; or meeting in groups over four were all to be publicly whipped.

For crimes such as raping a white woman or maid, committing murder, buggery, or burglary, all blacks could be executed. Here, the legislature obviously deemed the state's interest in "controlling" blacks of paramount importance. With the exception of murder, these crimes were not capital for whites until 1718.[80]

Higginbotham, while further noting the disparity in punishments for relationships between white women and black men versus white men and black women, certainly illuminates such circumstances between the likes of Richard, a Caucasian man, and Cremona, an African-descended woman:

> The [above Chester court] decree illustrates the fact that interracial premarital [and presumably mixed-race marital] sex was cause for brutal punishments, and that those punishments were imposed only on the black male violators; the court certainly did not threaten the white woman with loss of *her* life for future sexual violations. The ruling also suggests that interracial sex between black males and white females was the object of harsher punishments than interracial sex involving white males and black females, for it is unlikely that these punishments would have been imposed in the latter type of relationship. It is inconceivable, moreover, that a court would ever have executed or threatened to execute a white man for engaging in sex with a black woman.[81]

Considering Richard's immense affluence and wealth that were certainly tied to his late father, Humphrey Morrey, being the first mayor of Philadelphia with close business ties to Philadelphia's so-called colonial elite, as well as Richard's advanced age compared to Cremona being so young and perhaps most importantly considering her black ethnicity, chances of him being criminally or otherwise punished were practically none. Yet, Cremona, despite her protective perch as the paramour or common-law wife of Richard who was not likely to face charges, must have both realized that she was essentially at the complete mercy of Richard and likely endured a degree of consternation from some of her white neighbors. Higginbotham notes that black women were essentially considered to be at the bottom of the social and political hierarchy. A case in Chester County, Pennsylvania, particularly demonstrates the mortal punitive dangers that a black woman such as Cremona Morrey could face at the behest of a white landlord or landowner:

> Our review of the seven Chester County cases indicates that the commissioners' major priority was protecting the interest of the property class. The most harsh penalty was imposed on slave Phobe, apparently a woman who was charged with "burglariously entering house of

Thomas Barnard and stealing divers goods." She was sentenced to be hung, and apparently was, in fact, hung. She was valued at fifty-five pounds and per a court order her owner, Joseph Richardson, received that amount from the provincial treasurer.[82]

Even the slight possibility of facing deleterious consequences if Richard became bitterly estranged from her, or somehow fell in disfavor among the politically powerful, would have been ominous for Cremona and her children. She more than likely knew that "free blacks convicted of marrying whites were sold into slavery, and their children into servitude until the age of thirty-one," according to Higginbotham.[83]

Given the prospective draconian penalties for Cremona, it appears that she—and her children—shouldered much of the potential risk for her relationship with Richard, especially if at any point their relationship turned bitterly sour and Richard decided to remove his likely protective shield from around Cremona and their children. Cremona had to definitely consider whether she believed the so-called union with Richard was largely built on lust reflecting the perception of many white males that black women were hyper-sexual "jezebels" who were ripe for the proverbial harvest whenever they pleased—or was "Richard Morrey, Gent.," truly in love with Cremona and a dedicated father to their children?

During her early years, it's possible that Cremona Jr. was not literate considering that her mother, the elder Cremona, signed the 1772 deed settling the intra-family property dispute with an "X" and thus may not have been able to teach her daughter how to read or write. Indeed, it appears that Richard Morrey's possible failure to help Cremona become literate likely provides perspective regarding how he felt about her as a woman and perhaps as an intellectually equivalent human being—that might reveal negative racial and/or gender biases that were quite prevalent during that era. In fact, in the mid to late 18th century, much more emphasis would have been placed on teaching male family members such skills, including free-black males, often the biracial offspring of such interracial relationships. As noted, a few of such Murray males were able to sign their names on the 1772 deed, perhaps thanks to literacy skills they developed while serving as apprentices. It's also notable that no records or accounts have been found indicating that Richard Morrey provided for or invested in educating his biracial children. Nonetheless, "a substantial number of freed men and women resided in the town [Philadelphia] nearby. Some owned property and were married in the Anglican and Lutheran churches, and many had learned to read and write."[84] Although a noticeable number of free blacks were then literate in the Philadelphia area, Cremona Jr. and her sisters, like most African American women, would have been primarily relegated to learning domestic skills such as cooking, washing, sewing, and a variety of other menial tasks.

The elder Cremona undoubtedly walked an incredible tightrope of survival with exquisite intelligence and perhaps uncanny shrewdness that led to her acquiring substantial property from Richard, despite what amounted to substantial conditions or developments causing her to lose much land over the years. In fact, to reiterate, Richard, after his "finances were apparently mended" by 1745,[85] essentially bestowed to Cremona almost two hundred acres of land in 1746,[86] as well as Cremona along the way purchasing her freedom presumably from him for £20, an arrangement that likely led to the liberation of their children some time before 1746.[87] The critical question is considering Richard's assumed love for Cremona, why would she be required to purchase her own freedom (even at such a nominal cost) and not simply be liberated by Richard, as some sources indicate? And why did Richard ultimately leave Cremona, and presumably their children, to marry another woman in 1746, the very same year that he bequeathed her two hundred acres of land?

Meanwhile, throughout the years spanning from the arrival of Africans in Philadelphia as early as the dawn of the 18th century through 1746, the year Richard deeded to Cremona 198 acres and then quickly married Sarah Beasley, and the decades following, racial and living conditions in Philadelphia were abhorrent for African-descended people. One bill that was introduced, but failed to pass in 1700, "the Trial of Negroes," included "a harsh measure providing death, castration and whipping for punishments, and forbidding the meeting together of more than four Negroes. ... In 1706 another act for the trial of Negroes was passed and allowed," wrote W. E. B. Du Bois in his landmark book *The Philadelphia Negro: A Social Study*. The "act" mandated "that Negroes should be tried for crimes by two justices of the peace and a jury of six freeholders; robbery and rape were punished by branding and exportation, homicide by death, and stealing by whipping; the meeting of Negroes without permission was prohibited." The "Act of 1726," when Cremona would have been just age 16 if born in 1710, established "for the Better Regulation of Negroes in this Province," directly addressed such interracial relationships as the one that Richard and Cremona would develop before or by the end of the next decade. "This act was especially for the punishment of crime, the suppression of pauperism, the prevention of intermarriage, and the like—that is, for regulating the social and economic status of Negroes, free and enslaved."[88]

Furthermore, "the Act of 1726 declared the hiring of their time by Negro slaves to be illegal, and sought to restrict emancipation on the ground that 'free negroes are an idle and slothful people,' and easily become public burdens."[89] Specifically, Du Bois noted:

> The Act further provided penalties for the harboring of Negroes by each other; for trading or dealing with each other without license—all on pain of being sold into slavery if unable to pay fine; also provided penalty of £100 for anybody who should marry a Negro and white person; £30 for Negro caught living in marriage relation with white person, in such cases Negro to be sold into slavery for life.[90]

And Cremona was likely quite aware of her vulnerabilities and other regulations that forbade the free gathering, described as "tumults," of African Americans, probably to curtail spirited outdoor funeral rituals or other occasions with sacred or celebratory African chanting, singing, drum-playing, and dancing. Du Bois observed the growing consternation of Philadelphia's powerful whites concerning such activities: "1738, July 3. Slave tumults. Draft of Ordinance to suppress tumults of slaves considered in Philadelphia City Council …. 1741, August 17. Tumults of Negroes. Order made by Philadelphia City Councils to suppress disorders of Negroes and others on court house square [that ironically became the nation's Independence Hall] at night."[91]

Flagellation was one of many forms of cruel and dehumanizing punishment used to subjugate the enslaved by their masters. (Wikimedia Commons)

In fact, there are indications that African-descended people persistently gathered for camaraderie, entertainment, and solidarity in the face of unrelenting racism and brutality, making white observers and politicians even more nervous, leading to increasingly stricter laws: "Especially in Philadelphia did the Negroes continue to give general trouble, not so much by serious crime as by disorder," wrote Du Bois. "In 1732, under Mayor Hasel, the City Council 'taking under Consideration the frequent and tumultuous meetings of the Negro Slaves, especially on Sunday, Gaming, Cursing, Swearing, and committing many other Disorders, to the great Terror and Disquiet of the Inhabitants of this city,' ordered an ordinance to be drawn up against such disturbances."[92]

Such gatherings sometimes included Native Americans and mixed-race African Americans, Du Bois continued, arguably the former and latter possibly being Cremona's combined ethnicities: "Again, six years later, we hear of the draft of another city ordinance for 'the Effectual suppressing Tumultuous meetings and other disorderly doings of the Negroes, Mulattos and Indian servts. and slaves.'" Gatherings after dark seemed to be especially feared as indicated "in 1741, August 17, 'frequent complaints having been made to the Board that many disorderly persons meet every ev'g about the Court house of this city,'" noted Du Bois, perhaps acts of defiance aimed at the seat of authority. There were "'great numbers of Negroes and others'" that "'sit there with milk pails and other things late at night,'" apparently pounding African or indigenous-American beats or rhythms. Du Bois further noted that once the era's white elite concluded that "'many disorders are there committed against the peace and good government of this city,' Council ordered the place to be cleared 'in half an hour after sunset.'"[93]

Punishment for even the smallest infractions could be quite severe. Virtually any Caucasian "person whatsoever," had the "power to take up Negroes, male or female, whom they should find gadding abroad on the said first days of the weeke, without a ticket from their Mr. or Mrs., or not in their Compa [company], or to carry them to gaole [jail], there to remain that night, … without meat or drink, and to Cause them to be publickly whipt next morning with 39 Lashes, well Laid on, on their bare backs, for which their sd. Mr. or Mris. Should pay 15d. to the whipper."[94]

Yet, contrary to traditional historical documents and books, instead of completely succumbing to such harsh laws, African-descended people in the Philadelphia area consistently resisted and even violently protested the abhorrent conditions. "In 1706 a slave is arrested for setting fire to a dwelling; in 1738 three Negroes are hanged in neighboring parts of New Jersey for poisoning people, while at Rocky Hill a slave is burned alive for killing a child and burning a barn. Whipping of Negroes at the public whipping post was frequent, and so severe was the punishment that in 1743 a slave brought up to be whipped committed suicide."[95] Taking one's own life was an act of defiance that allowed such African descendants a final measure of controlling their destiny with the belief that death would allow them to return to the Motherland and the ancestors.

An enslaved person's suicide was even documented in Cheltenham several years after Cremona Morrey's death, circa 1770. The March 17, 1775, edition of *The Virginia Gazette* noted that a "Negro man" resorted to hanging himself while trying to deal with the pressures of enslavement.[96]

88 • THE MONTIERS

This sheet music illustration by artist Ephraim W. Bouve portrays the preeminent African American anti-slavery abolitionist Frederick Douglass escaping from enslavement in 1838, along the way stopping in Philadelphia before moving on to Massachusetts. (Library of Congress)

Such acts of defiance happened well beyond Cheltenham and the Philadelphia region, occurrences that most European colonists were quite cognizant of and greatly feared—even in the Philadelphia area. Benjamin Franklin's *Pennsylvania Gazette* and other early-American newspapers often carried the sobering news of black revolts. "The beginning of chattel slavery in North America birthed something else: Rebellion," writes Erin Blakemore. "Enslaved people didn't just engage in passive resistance against slaveholders—they planned and participated in armed revolts. Between the 17th and 19th centuries, enslaved Africans and African Americans in British North America and the United States staged hundreds of revolts."[97]

Just two years after Cremona's estimated 1710 birth, a 1712 rebellion of enslaved Africans "in New York City killed at least nine white slave holders, while in 1739, up to 100 black people in colonial South Carolina participated in the Stono Rebellion, the largest slave uprising in British North America," Blakemore notes. "The revolt resulted in some laws intended to discourage uprisings and rein in brutal slaveholders, but fomented fear of black rebellion. The colonies already had strict slave codes designed to govern the behavior of enslaved people. In response to the Stono Rebellion, laws became increasingly draconian."[98]

It's under such incredibly challenging conditions that a black woman and white man joined hands, despite their obvious ethnic, class, and age differences, to essentially live together as husband and wife—countering the racist conventions of the day. And despite the immense pressures that Cremona must have felt, perhaps wondering if she had simply accepted Richard's frivolous passions and lust or true and unconditional love, they would conceive up to five biracial babies together, according to most sources, likely to the consternation of most, and at the very least, the indifference of others. Very few whites during that period would have been able to stomach such an unusual and unlawful union. One day, despite the industrious mixed-race children that Cremona bore, the reality of their cruel world would likely come roaring back.

CHAPTER 4

Richard and Cremona's Visible, Child-Producing Union

Although we will likely never know the exact nature or depth of Cremona's relationship with Richard, there's some evidence that Richard authentically loved Cremona as she bore their multiple children for about a decade, according to a key descendant and other historical observers. Indeed, despite enduring questions about the exceptionally complicated dynamics of Cremona and Richard's bond that may have been arguably or partially predicated on a slave–master and/or employee–employer relationship, the late Dr. William Pickens III postulated that Richard's passing to her of about two hundred acres of land and other considerations are clear indications that they likely had a deeply loving and reciprocal relationship.[1] Or, was Richard much more mercenary, motivated primarily by satisfying his sexual proclivities and need for female companionship but feeling morally obligated to provide support for Cremona and their children after his departure?

The relationship between Thomas Jefferson and Sally Hemings, his teenaged quadroon "slave," was publicly ridiculed in a press caricature attributed to James Akin. (Alamy)

There is some circumstantial evidence that possibly indicates Cremona was deeply impacted emotionally by Richard's departure from their common-law relationship (and the children), depending on when she became involved in a subsequent matrimonial relationship since sources provide conflicting timelines, some indicating that Cremona married a previously enslaved African

American, John Fry or Frye, within one to two years of Richard's departure; other sources say it was several years or almost a decade. "She did not marry for eight years, until after Richard's death, suggesting that she had an emotional bond to him." Nonetheless, there is no clear evidence, however, that Cremona was in love with Richard or heartbroken for multiple years after he remarried. "Unfortunately, we have nothing in Cremona's words to tell us how she felt."[2]

Regardless, Richard's first and second wives, Ann (Turner)[3] and Sarah Beasley, respectively, were likely quite aware of the relationship that Richard had with Cremona, according to some historical observers. The Morrey–Bustill–Montier family historian and author Joyce Mosley believes Richard Morrey's first wife, Ann, was likely still living in the couple's residence when the relationship between Richard and Cremona started, perhaps shortly before 1736 when Cremona probably began giving birth. The relationship, even after Ann's death, was probably tolerated in the Cheltenham area because it was heavily populated by antislavery Quakers, Mosley postulates. "I mean she could walk around the community and get the protection of having the last name [Morrey or Murray]. She was accepted." In fact, according to the online source Takingthelongerview.org, "it is hard to believe that his [Richard's] wives, Ann and later Sarah, would not have known about it …. This liaison, between an older man and his dependent slave, is unsavory."[4]

Cremona, too, must have been strongly drawn to Richard, say some observers, insisting that the relationship was reciprocally loving by pointing to the number of children she bore with Richard, as well as her likely being quite impressed by his prodigious material support and presumed protection from deleterious racist antagonists. And as examined briefly earlier, others believe that there could never be a loving reciprocal relationship between a slaveholder and the enslaved, even if that servant became eventually liberated and worked as a paid employee; the worker could still be subject to exploitation or coercion, they argue. What would have been Cremona's fate[5] had she rebuffed Richard's advances, assuming that he was the one who initiated the relationship? Indeed, at the heart of the supposed romantic relationship between Richard and Cremona is an inescapable question: Was the relationship consensual? "It is not clear whether it was consensual on her [Cremona's] part or whether [Richard's first wife Ann] condoned the relationship."[6]

Still, another intriguing dynamic to consider is whether there were co-existing but clearly contradictory elements regarding the relationship between Cremona and Richard, despite the couple procreating:

> The relationship between slaves and their masters could, at one and the same time, be governed by exploitation and affiliation, submission under the master's authority and intimacy. It was

characterized by what may be called a mutual dependency: the master was dependent on the slave's loyalty and the slave dependent on the master's maintenance and humane treatment of him [or her]. While slaves had to bow to their master's wishes under the constant threat of punishment, they could also become indispensable to them, function as their confidants, and be party to their secrets.[7]

Cremona and Richard's children, as well as descendants, weren't and are not alone considering such dynamics that impact the majority of most modern African Americans whose ancestors were enslaved and too often victimized. Such issues are often discussed by descendants of historic interracial relationships, including whether there could have ever been a true, unconditional love between an enslaved or formerly enslaved person and the so-called master during such anti-black and proslavery eras. Julius "Calvin" Jefferson, an African American descendant of Jefferson and Hemings, told *The New York Times* in 2018, "Being a slave owner, no matter how you cut it, that's a crime against humanity," adding that Jefferson "justified it in his mind. Slavery was legal, and he believed in the rule of law. Sometimes, at the Monticello reunions, we get into arguments about it. Some people believe slavery is slavery, and no matter what you say, Thomas Jefferson owned slaves. They are not going to look at the personal relationships between Thomas Jefferson and his slaves."[8]

However, Julius Jefferson further opined, "I really believe that Thomas Jefferson believed that all men were created equal,"[9] a phrase he wrote in the Declaration of Independence of 1776 in Philadelphia where the father of Richard Morrey—Humphrey Morrey—served as the first mayor of the infant metropolis 75 years earlier, beginning in 1691. In fact, as Jefferson wrote those immortal words on the second floor of what was then a farmhouse that still stands in Philadelphia's historic district, remember he held in bondage on the third floor an ancestor of Julius, Robert Hemings who was the brother of his very young mistress, Sally.[10]

Brenda Yurkoski, another black descendant of Jefferson and Hemings, told the *Times* that she really ponders about the relationship between the American statesman and Hemings: "If I could ask Thomas Jefferson anything, I'd ask, 'Did you have feelings for Sally?' Because he left nothing behind. This man wrote everything down. Everything. He knew that people would be looking back at him …. As descendants, and because of his character, we want to believe that it wasn't just a slave-master rape situation. I don't know why we want to believe that. But we do. We just do."[11]

The late William Pickens III, a prominent descendant of Cremona and Richard Morrey, although acknowledging that Cremona was originally enslaved by the Morrey family, often reemphasized that their relationship was primarily loving and deep. However, Pickens's son, John Montier Pickens—who was named after the likely Caribbean-born John Montier, the husband of Cremona Sr.'s daughter (also named Cremona)—believes that the relationship between Richard and the elder Cremona was certainly conditional and that the potentially coercive slave-master power that he probably held over her must be acknowledged. Co-descendant Joyce Mosley[12] agrees that such relationships were certainly conditional and quite possibly predatory,[13] perspectives shared by some modern descendants of Thomas Jefferson and Sally Hemings.

"One of my dad's sisters did not want to talk about the Jefferson thing at all," Yurkoski told the *Times* in 2018. "Aunt Alice was a proud Black woman and she felt, 'Why would I want to embrace that legacy? He owned her.' She couldn't get past that. But I look at it as, 'Sally Hemings accomplished something amazing for her children, which was freedom.'"[14]

At the heart of such matters, considering the possible dynamics ranging from true or conditional love to devious victimizations, there's no doubt that such black women as Sally Hemings and her much earlier predecessor, Cremona [Satterthwaite] Morrey Fry, knew, despite the often-overwhelming challenges and such infernal racism, their survival would and must preserve future generations.

Destined to document her horrific sexual abuse and hardships as an enslaved black woman, Harriet Jacobs (1813–1897), described as "a light mulatto," probably like Cremona, in a runaway slave advertisement, was born in Edenton, North Carolina. She eventually escaped the sexual torment of her so-called master, Dr. James Norcom, in June of 1835 after hiding in a small crawlspace for seven years at her nearby free grandmother's residence, later illuminating her initial escape to Philadelphia, abuse, and life in the 1862 autobiography *Incidents in the Life of a Slave Girl*:[15] "For my master, whose restless, craving, vicious nature roved about day and night, seeking whom to devour, had just left me with stinging, scorching words; words that scathed ear and brain like fire," she wrote. "O, how I despised him! I thought how glad I should be if some day when he walked the earth, it would open and swallow him up," Jacobs continued. "He tried his utmost to corrupt the pure principles my grandmother had instilled. He peopled my young mind with unclean images, such as only a vile monster could think of .... But he was my master. I was compelled to live under the same roof with him .... He told me I was his property; that I must be subject to his will in all things."[16]

The horrifically abused and enslaved "Patsey" in the autobiography of Solomon Northup, *Twelve Years a Slave*, was described as "the offspring of a

'Guinea nigger.'"[17] Northup was essentially kidnapped as a Northern free black man living in Washington County, New York, with his family and tricked into slavery in 1841 after being lured by two white men, then held and brutally beaten in a Washington, DC, slave pen before being shipped to the Deep South to Avoyelles, Louisiana. On the plantation of his so-called master, Edwin Epps, Northup monitored Epps's repeated and vicious sexual exploitation of Patsey, who was often also brutally beaten by Epps with a flesh-stripping whip and assaulted with life-threatening violence by Epps's jealous wife:[18]

> She [Patsey] had a genial and pleasant temper, and was faithful and obedient. Naturally, she was a joyous creature, a laughing, light-hearted girl, rejoicing in the mere sense of existence. Yet Patsey wept oftener, and suffered more, than any of her companions. She had been literally excoriated. Her back bore the scars of a thousand stripes; not because she was backward in her work, nor because she was of an unmindful and rebellious spirit, but because it had fallen to her lot to be the slave of a licentious master and a jealous mistress. She shrank before the lustful eye of the one, and was in danger even of her life at the hands of the other, and between the two, she was indeed accursed.[19]

After his miraculous 1853 rescue Northup further wrote in his memoir that was made into an Academy Award-winning 2013 "Best Picture" film for which Lupita Nyong'o (with Kenyan roots) won Best Supporting Actress for her role as Patsey and Chiwetel Ejiofor (of Nigerian ancestry) won Best Supporting Actor for playing the title role as Northup: "The enslaved victim of lust and hate, Patsey had no comfort of her life."[20]

Briefly re-examining the Gordon-Reed analysis more deeply, Sally Hemings (similar to Cremona Morrey) could have begun to recognize her growing empowerment interpersonally and socially as a beautiful young woman when enslaved at the Jefferson Monticello estate in Virginia; soon "Dashing Sally," as described quite visibly in media reports, was required to serve Jefferson in France during a five-year period in 1787. However, that's when, according to French law, she could have legally and successfully declared her freedom, but instead likely negotiated terms of her enslavement, and possibly for her future children, should she return to America with Jefferson. Instead of being "cowed" by Jefferson's affluence and power that was greatly diminished in France, Sally's "treaty" with her so-called master "sounds much more like the handiwork of a smart, if overconfident, attractive teenage girl who understood very well how men saw her and was greatly impressed with her newly discovered power to move an infatuated middle-aged man."[21]

Such "treaty" circumstances could have applied to Cremona's earlier relationship with Richard Morrey. Yet, there were certainly monumental caveats, including reports that Jefferson had impregnated Sally Hemings while in France when she was still a teen and considered by him to be his enslaved servant, certainly harkening of coercion at the very least, or statutory rape, at least by today's standards. Furthermore, Sally's "mother was not there to tell her that such spells rarely last forever," Gordon-Reed concluded, also hypothesizing that it's not likely that Jefferson had raped or forced himself upon her in France, or she would not have returned to America nor maintained a long-term relationship with him that resulted in the birth of up to five or six children.[22]

The 1804 Akin political rendition of Hemings is reported to be the only known original of her image. (Wikimedia Commons)

The dynamics between Richard Morrey and Cremona, or "Mooney," were likely quite similar in certain ways, despite notable differences; both Morrey and Jefferson would remain partners with their respective black "paramours" for multiple years, and Jefferson was documented as being very despondent after his wife Martha passed away in 1782 at just age 37 as a relatively young woman, as did Richard's wife, Ann, expiring at a comparative early age almost a half-century earlier possibly leaving Richard in a state of mourning, at least to some degree.

Richard Morrey's much earlier relationship with Cremona certainly did not receive the media notoriety or visibility that the Jefferson–Hemings union generated, partially based on a vengeful "muckraking" journalist, James Thomson Callender, writing a "series of newspaper articles alleging that Thomas Jefferson had children with Sally Hemings." Intriguingly, despite substantial criticism that Callender had "an axe to grind," he initially "established himself as a journalist in Philadelphia" for the *Philadelphia Gazette*, criticizing "elements of the U.S. Constitution that he believed were undemocratic, such as the election of the president through the Electoral College." Callender also insisted "that the Senate was flagrantly unrepresentative because it was not directly elected by the people, and blasted George Washington, who had 'debauched' and 'deceived' the nation by promoting himself as a popular idol." Still, during "Callender's career his writings were rabidly partisan."[23]

As Jefferson's neighbors and Monticello workers noticed the remarkable resemblance between him and Sally Heming's biracial children, the same probably also happened when Cremona bore Richard Morrey's children during the decade stretching from about 1735 to 1745.[24]

Yet, in both cases, there arose questions regarding paternity. For one reason or the other, Cremona and Richard's supposed son, Robert, took on the surname of Lewis, perhaps because he did not have fond feelings for his purported father, Richard, or possibly because he, Robert, may not have been fathered by Richard after all. Meanwhile, as mentioned earlier, "Lewis's brother Caesar and sisters Elizabeth, Rachael," as well as the younger Cremona, "took the surname of Murray, similar to their father Richard's last name, Morrey."[25] Did the spelling variation in the names signify that there was some sort of animosity or strained relationship between father Richard and his biracial offspring, perhaps having to do with how they felt about their father's remarriage? Could Richard and Cremona's reputed eldest child, Robert Lewis, have taken on his surname because he harbored similar feelings? There is yet another possibility: "Robert Lewis, born sometime between 1733 and 1735, may have taken his last name from one of the many neighboring Welsh farmers in the area [whom Robert may have worked for in some capacity]. ... Robert seems to have worked on farms in the area of Guineatown for a number of years."[26]

Robert's brother Caesar may have been required to work as an apprentice or as an enslaved worker until age 31,[27] according to regulations or laws that targeted interracial offspring. After being sent to work in New Jersey, there's a possibility that Caesar "was sold or employed by the Penroses and assigned that surname," likely before establishing his own shoemaking and shoe repair enterprise. "The Penrose family was active at the center city Episcopal Parish, Christ Church,"[28] where such so-called colonial elite as Dr. Benjamin Rush and the quintessential Philadelphian, Benjamin Franklin, were parishioners. Sometime during or after working for the Penroses, "Caesar would have come to Trinity [Church, Oxford],"[29] which was established and still is located in what is today Philadelphia just east of Cheltenham and where the likes of the township's cofounder, Tobias Leech, attended services. Today Leech is buried in the adjoining burial ground that also contains blacks formerly enslaved by Leech. Caesar, who is also buried in the cemetery, was apparently quite active in the church, serving as sexton for more than a half-century. "If correct, Caesar lived a long life, more than half of it at Trinity, seeing us through the American Revolution."[30]

Founded in 1696, Trinity Church Oxford had roots in the Church of England. Many Cheltenham-area settlers attended by way of a thoroughfare—now known as Church Road—that dissects the township. (Wikimedia Commons)

According to the New Jersey Historical Commission, a Caesar Murray certainly had been enslaved in Burlington, New Jersey, then rose to be quite prosperous as he purchased the freedom of very close family members: "Caesar Murray of Burlington County served twenty-five years as a slave before he was given his freedom. A shoemaker by trade, he opened a business in this field and employed from three to five apprentices and several artisans in his shop," including other African Americans.[31] "His skill and diligence earned him not only a leading position in the business community in Burlington but attracted many customers from the surrounding country and Philadelphia."[32] Caesar "used the profits to buy the freedom of his wife and children, to build them 'a genteel commodious home' and to educate his children. One of his sons, Robert Murray, became a shoemaker on his own."[33]

Although such work arrangements or indentures were sometimes voluntary for whites, Caesar or Robert or any of their siblings, as free black or interracial youngsters, could have been forced into such circumstances, according to Pennsylvania law. The "indenturing of free black children assured whites that the new 'freedoms' of free blacks were not equivalent to the inherent liberties assured all whites." And relatedly, "all children of a free black could be sold into servitude until their twenty-first (for females) or twenty-fourth (for males) birthdays, thereby potentially removing every free black child from his family during his childhood."[34] Although it's debatable whether Robert Lewis was forced into some type of forced indenture, that may have very well depended on his relationship with Richard, especially considering whether Richard Morrey was his blood-father or not, or the possibility that they were estranged.

As a reminder and to add some perspective about such conditions in the Philadelphia area for African Americans during the decade stretching from 1735 to 1745, when Richard and Cremona's children were born, construction of the "Pennsylvania State House—later known as Independence Hall" was completed and the "first Assembly meeting [was held] there in 1735."[35] It was not uncommon for blacks and others to be held or punished by public whippings, and sometimes executed, at the state house site or at the jail on High Street (later named Market Street). The notorious Walnut Street Jail at the rear of the state house complex was built by 1790 to alleviate crowded conditions at the High Street Jail (constructed circa 1718 when Cremona Morrey was about eight years old).

Although the African-descended Caesar (Morrey) Penrose served as sexton of Trinity Church Oxford for about half a century, church member and cofounder of Cheltenham Township Tobias Leech kept in bondage the likes of Ben, Cuffy, Betty, Cate, Cuggs, and Busso. A ceremony in 2007 was dedicated to honoring such enslaved persons, some buried in the church's graveyard. (Donald Scott Sr.)

Furthermore, during the 1730s, "most of the blacks in Pennsylvania had been recently imported. Few white Americans, in Pennsylvania or elsewhere, thought that slavery was wrong." In fact, just three enslaved Africans were freed or manumitted by Philadelphians during the 1730s, according to Quaker records. "Perhaps others were released during their masters' lifetimes,"[36] similar to Cremona and her children, "but relatively few blacks were freed before 1740." Yet, there's clear evidence that the Quakers began moving slowly away from practicing slavery. "Although most Quaker merchants withdrew from the trade in the 1730s after a period of controversy within the Society of Friends regarding the morality of importing and trading slaves, merchants of other religious persuasions gladly accommodated the growing demand."[37]

Despite the very difficult challenges that the biracial children of Cremona and Richard likely faced, their presumed reputations as the couple's offspring with Cremona ultimately becoming a comparatively well-off African American woman with substantial land, probably provided them with a bit of social or even legal protection and limited opportunities.

Specifically, at relatively young ages, Robert Lewis with his brother Caesar may have been "apprenticed to a shoemaker, possibly neighbor Reynier Tyson."[38] If so, Robert may have been a free black or liberated before or by 1745, when Tyson apparently died.[39] Born in 1659 in Kaldenkirchen, Herzogtum, Rhineland, Germany,[40] Tyson "was of the Society of Friends, but was for a short time associated with the Mennonites," according to the publication "Colonial Families of the United States." The source also notes that he: "Sailed from Crefeld, Germany, on the 'Concord,' arriving at Philadelphia, 6th Oct. 1683, with his brother, Derrick Tyson," as well as with an extraordinarily notable soon-to-be antislavery abolitionist and founder of Germantown, "[Francis] Daniel PASTORIUS."[41] Other sources, however, indicate that Pastorius sailed on the ship *America*, arriving in 1683. Meanwhile, Tyson "is named in Penn's Patent of 12th Aug. 1689 as one of the original incorporators of Germantown," where Pastorius, as well as a group of Quakers and Mennonites, participated in the first official protest of 1688 against slavery in America.[42] In Abington, Tyson apparently acquired or "bought 250 acres of land," along the way marrying "Margaret KUNDERS of Germantown,"[43] today an exceptionally historic section of Philadelphia. "From 1683 to 1707 were erected the stone houses of Thones Kunder, Jacob Telner, Isaac Dilbeck, Francis Daniel Pastorius, Jan Doeden, Jacob Schumaker, and other[s] like, but doubtless the most pretentious house of the early settlement, was that of Hans Milan, built in 1690, and later incorporated in 'Wyck.'"[44] Is it possible that Tyson maintained antislavery sentiments based on his association with the Quakers and possible links to Pastorius? Would such social circumstances make him more amenable to accepting a black apprentice considering the general racist conventions of the period?

Reynier Tyson, after purchasing the 250 acres in Abington, stayed there "the remainder of his life," eventually "serving as an elder of Abington Monthly Meeting from 1725 until his death, on September 27, 1745 and its representative in the Quarterly Meeting for many years. He and his wife Mary had nine children,"[45] but were apparently still able to accommodate Robert

Lewis's possible apprenticeship, despite some historical documents indicating that Tyson was a "yeoman."

Yet again, Robert Lewis may have also been employed or apprenticed to the breadwinner of a white family, presumably when he was quite young, perhaps to a farmer and merchant, Robert Lewis, for whom Cremona's son Robert may have adopted or received his name. "As previously mentioned, his last name may have come from any of the neighboring Welsh farmers, or specifically from Robert Lewis, a Philadelphia merchant," Pitts hypothesizes. "Lewis, a Quaker, owned property in Pennsylvania and New Jersey near Burlington, and had three sons; Nathaniel, Robert Jr., and William." Indeed, the family was quite colorful in more ways than one. "Robert Lewis Jr. 'of Byberry' joined Abington Meeting in 1773 and was thrown out two years later 'for participating in war-like activities.'" In the intervening time, "William Lewis followed in his father's footsteps, becoming a wealthy merchant. He was also a Justice of the Peace for the City and County of Philadelphia, and was acting in that capacity when the deed of trust turning over Cremona's land to the trusteeship of Isaac Knight Jr. in 1772 was recorded," conjuring up intriguing questions: "Could our Robert Lewis have been sent to live with the Lewis family, changing his last name in the process? Could he have been a half-brother of William Lewis, or rather, a playmate and friend with whom he spent his childhood?"[46]

Robert Lewis would go on to play a leading role in his own extended family, but he also became an exemplar of the community, bolstered by his elder status, no doubt, as indicated by his name's appearance on the "deed of trust":[47]

> At any rate, the deed of trust marks the first appearance of Robert Lewis of Guineatown in public records. He reappears with surprising regularity for the next twenty-seven years. As the eldest, he seems to have taken the dominant role in all family matters, and it was probably through his efforts that the deed was drafted and signed. His wife was an African American known only as Jane, and between them they had four sons and seven daughters.[48]

Cremona and Richard's other children also led intriguing but challenging lives as biracial African Americans while the institution of slavery persisted in Pennsylvania, despite the commonwealth's early movement towards gradual emancipation.

Caesar, born about 1737, was probably also "apprenticed to a shoemaker,"[49] perhaps involuntarily if still enslaved or forced due to his interracial status as mandated by laws impacting free and enslaved African Americans; if emancipated, he could have been voluntarily indentured. "Once completing his indentures, twenty-five year old Caesar Murray left for Burlington, New

Jersey, where he set up shop as a shoemaker and cordwainer (bootmaker)," certainly quite challenging for an African American then due to a range of racist conventions or beliefs. "While there he fell in love with a slave woman named Elizabeth, whom he married," determined to purchase her freedom. "He worked years to save up enough (120 pounds) to free her and their three children, Rachel, Joseph, and Robert …. He owned a house on Pearl Street in the city of Burlington, and had three to five apprentices in his shop at various times," which must have been quite satisfying given that years earlier he had been in their proverbial "same shoes." Apparently, among the apprentices "was his son Robert Murray; another was his nephew Solomon Montier." When Caesar died at the dawn of the 19th century in 1799, he "had 'acquired a considerable reputation for his care, dexterity and industry, as well as considerable property.'"[50]

Elizabeth, born about 1739, became "a maid for Nicholas and Sarah Waln; they wrote a letter of testimony for her in [the] 4th month [of] 1773. Elizabeth later married Cyrus Bustill, a prosperous black business man [sic] and founder of a school for black children" who also taught at the institution. "It is said that Cyrus," a baker, "donated bread for Washington and his troops,[51] and that [the northeast Philadelphia neighborhood of] Bustleton is named for him."[52] Interestingly, "Elizabeth and Cyrus lived as Quakers but were unable to join as members because of their race." Yet, such discrimination would not stop them or future generations from ascending to great heights in such a debilitating and racist society. As will be discussed in greater details later, "One of the descendants of Cyrus and Elizabeth was Paul Robeson," the great scholar, diplomat, activist, "actor and singer."[53]

Rachel, born about 1742, would later marry Andrew Hickey.[54] They "were married in Philadelphia at Gloria Dei (Old Swedes') Church in Southwark on June 21, 1771," eventually changing "their surname to 'Hick,' and later 'Hicks.'" Along the way they settled in "Swedesboro, New Jersey with a family of seven or more—Josiah and Isaiah (twins), William Stratton, and Charles, the sons; Elizabeth (or Eliza), Mary W., and Rachel, the daughters—at the time they sold their Guineatown property." By "1796, the family moved to a farm in Deerfield Township in Cumberland County, New Jersey, near the village of Gouldtown," an African American community like Guineatown that had origins in an interracial relationship involving Elizabeth Adams, "granddaughter of John Fenwick, the founder of Salem, New Jersey," and a "Quaker gentleman" with platonic ties to William Penn. Elizabeth reportedly gave birth to "a son as the result of an affair with an African whose name may have been Anthony Gould, or 'Gool.'"[55] In fact, a "branch" of the Bustill

Pickens III and his wife, Patricia, witnessed the prepping of the portraits of Hiram and Elizabeth Montier at the Philadelphia Museum of Art, found under the bed of one of Pickens's elder relatives. (William Pickens III Archives)

family, described as "descendants of the Leni [sic] Lenape Indians," settled in South Jersey. "There they developed rich farm land and one of the youths selected as his wife the daughter of the first governor of New Jersey, Governor Fenwick, who gave to this daughter a tract of land known as Gouldtown," notes a biography of the eminent African American physician Dr. Nathan Francis Mossell[56] of Philadelphia, who married Gertrude Bustill, a descendant of Cremona and Richard Morrey.

Cremona Jr.—Richard and Cremona Sr.'s youngest daughter, who was named after her mother—was born in 1745. She was destined to marry, "some time prior to 1772, more probably about 1765,"[57] John Montier, believed to be formerly enslaved on one of the French-speaking Caribbean islands such as Haiti, perhaps brought to America not long before the Revolutionary War era approached. They would have four sons, including "Joseph (1768–1842), Solomon (1770–ca 1855), Robert (ca 1773–ca 1815) and Hiram (1780–1861)."[58]

One thing appears to be certain, despite questions about the degree to which Richard was in love with or dedicated to Cremona and their children: the couple gave birth to an exceptionally important African American family legacy that would expand exponentially.

CHAPTER 5

Richard Passes to Cremona Nearly Two Hundred Acres before His Death

As Cremona may have realized that Richard Morrey's amorous pursuits were getting quite serious, she perhaps weighed the pros and cons of being in a relationship with someone not only several decades her senior but who wielded great "authority" over her, regardless of whether she was enslaved or a self-liberated employee. It's especially noteworthy that Richard, born about 1675, would have been about age 60 if the relationship with Cremona commenced in 1736; Cremona, if born about 1710, would have been about age 26.[1] How exactly did she negotiate the early then later terms of the relationship that apparently led to her acquiring almost 200 acres?

As examined briefly earlier, conceivably the relationship between Richard Morrey and Cremona (Satterthwaite) Morrey Fry began as an emotional and physical attraction or attachment, at least the latter probably from the much older Richard Morrey's perspective. Feasibly, it commenced as Cremona performed the services of a chambermaid, like what Sally Hemings endured a generation later as such a servant for the American statesman and politician Thomas Jefferson. "Hemings was Jefferson's concubine, a woman who bore him six children, of whom four survived. Hemings' role was to attend to Jefferson's clothing and his chamber, which probably brought her into the main house often—and in very close proximity to Jefferson and his bed."[2]

Several decades before the Hemings–Jefferson relationship, as Richard Morrey likely pursued Cremona, it's possible that she began to negotiate small favors that eventually led to conditions for self-liberation, to become "a free woman, having 'for twenty-pounds' bought her freedom."[3] Twenty pounds was comparatively quite a nominal emancipation fee for that period, perhaps an indication of Richard's goodwill. The "Bargain & Sale for 500 years, Richard Morrey to His Negro Woman Cremona Morrey," found at the Philadelphia City Archives, stipulates: "Richard Morrey of Cheltenham Township in the

This "Emancipation and Freedom Monument" of a liberated black woman holding her baby was designed by Thomas Jay Warren. It stands on Brown's Island, Richmond, Va., and is mindful of Virginia's Sally Hemings and Cheltenham's Cremona Morrey reaching valiantly for precious freedom. (Wikimedia Commons)

County of Philad.—Gentleman Sendeth Greetings—Know ye that the said Richard Morrey as well as for and in Consideration of the good & faithful Service unto him done and performed by his now freed Negro Woman Mooney—otherwise Cremona Morrey's—as of the Sum of twenty Pounds unto him will & Truly paid by the said Cremona at & before the Sealing & Delivery hereof."[4] Such a so-called transaction would have been still repulsive in its acknowledgment that a price could be assessed for a human being, as earlier addressed. That Cremona might be required to pay any price for her own freedom speaks volumes about Richard's attitude concerning the legitimacy of the institution of slavery and the relationship that they may have maintained with each other. Nonetheless, although there aren't indications that Cremona was brutalized by Richard, when "navigating lives of privation and brutality, enslaved people haggled, often daily, for liberties small and large, from rare personal time to less harsh treatment for themselves or family members, even to being set free."[5]

Furthermore, perhaps as the relationship became more serious, transitioning from Cremona being Richard's possible "concubine" and then the couple having children together—essentially living as husband and wife—Cremona's bargaining power almost certainly increased exponentially. It's quite possible that Cremona began to negotiate the liberation of their offspring too, perhaps along the way realizing first his immense attachment to her and the children and later that Richard was straying from the relationship. Bluntly, Cremona could have negotiated those notable transactions—including a "treaty" as described in Hemings's case.

In addition to negotiating the purchase of her own freedom and her children's, Cremona may have indirectly or directly suggested the 1746 deal with Richard that provided her with almost two hundred acres of land, an unprecedented development in the annals of American history. "Cremona, basking in her new status as a free black woman—which may have also freed her children—and the mistress of almost two hundred acres of ground was placed in [a] unique, not unpleasant, situation."[6] Yet, it's important to reiterate that some sources indicate that Richard actually liberated Cremona.[7]

Nevertheless, the wording of the transaction(s) seems to suggest that Cremona's liberation and the resulting transference of land to her were cleverly pre-arranged business agreements. The very deed of January 6, 1746, transferring for "one peppercorn" the nearly two hundred acres of land to Cremona, in part, reads: "Know ye, that the said Richard Morrey, as well for and in consideration of the good faithful service unto him done and performed by his now freed Negro Woman Mooney otherwise known as Cremona Morrey … do bargain and sell for consideration of one peppercorn" for the acreage, noting that the operative words are "his now freed Negro Woman Mooney."[8] Pitts maintains: "For the lack of a certificate of manumission—a document expressly stating that the bearer was a free man or woman—the deed itself would suffice."[9] Still, arguably, that transaction and wording also strongly imply that despite their prior relationship and shared children, Cremona negotiated much of the agreement knowing that by 1746 Richard was about to break off the relationship—or had already done so.

Archival evidence seems to support that the lease transaction was being considered as early as "January 1745," according to a Haverford College Quaker Special Collections document with telling details: "Lease from Richard Morrey to Negro Mooney alias Cremona for 198 Acres of Land ... for the Term of Five Hundred years—under a peppercorn Rent."[10]

However, the document also stipulated: "Two thirds of this Land descending after the Death of Richard Morrey to the Heirs or Devises of Humphrey Morrey, the same way divided of in the Partition, and about one third of the 198 Acres was left in the possession of the Negro Mooney, which she still holds."[11] Below the handwritten text, "proved and recorded in the Recorders Office at Philad.,"[12] is a diagram consisting of essentially two interconnecting box-like figures, one representing the 68 acres "now possessed by Mooney" and the remaining larger portion of about 130 acres.[13] In short, does the wording seem to suggest that Richard Morrey's heirs were empowered to take control of two-thirds of the 198 acres that had been leased to Cremona following Richard's death in 1754?[14]

Although Cremona was initially permitted to lease 198 acres at a nominal cost "for 500 years," conditions or subsequent transactions appear to have reduced the amount of property and length of possession time provided by "Richard Murrey to his Negro woman Cremona (or Mooney)" to 200 years and "about 1/3" or "68 acres which included their House & Improvements."[15]

A July 23, 1767, sheriff-sale advertisement in Benjamin Franklin's *Pennsylvania Gazette* noted that Cremona and her second husband, John Fry or Frye, were trying to retain or hold on to 45 acres of land within a much larger parcel that had been put up for sale, "situate in the township of Cheltenham, in the county of Philadelphia, containing 243 acres and 89 perches; bounded by lands of Evan Thomas, Issac Tyson, and land of Richard and Humphrey Morrey, and others." The property apparently was the "late part of the estate of Robert Greenway, deceased, seized and taken in execution by WILLIAM PARK, Sheriff."[16]

A notation following the advertisement further noted: "N.B. Certain two Negroes, viz. Money [sic] and Fry, claim 45 acres of the premises above mentioned, which they hold on lease for 200 years, great part of which term is yet unexpired."[17]

Two decades earlier, someone and/or something had certainly convinced or forced Richard to make extraordinary decisions. "At any rate, due either to external pressure from his neighbors, or from internal doubts as to the course his life was taking, in 1745 Richard Morrey decided to change his way of life," apparently, about then, terminating his common-law marital relationship with

> BY virtue of a writ of levari facias, to me directed, will be sold, by publick vendue, at the London Coffee-house, on Thursday, the 23d day of July instant, at 6 o'clock in the evening, a certain messuage, plantation and tract of land, situate in the township of Cheltenham, in the county of Philadelphia, containing 243 acres and 89 perches; bounded by lands of Evan Thomas, Isaac Tyson, and land of Richard and Humphrey Morrey, and others; late part of the estate of Robert Greenway deceased, seized and taken in execution by
>
> WILLIAM PARR, Sheriff.
>
> N. B. Certain two Negroes, viz. Money and Fry, claim 45 acres of the premises above mentioned, which they hold on lease for 200 years, great part of which term is yet unexpired.

In 1767, not long before her death in about 1770, the elder Cremona and her second husband, John Fry, were trying to hold on to their land, according to this announcement in *The Pennsylvania Gazette*. (William Pickens III Archives)

Cremona. "He made plans to leave Edgehill and move to Philadelphia. In a 'clearing-the-decks' gesture, he disposed of some of his Edge Hill property."[18] Morrey made several significant transactions that included major swaths of land that today include portions of Philadelphia's northeast and northwest sectors, as well as the adjoining southeast Montgomery County where Cheltenham Township is now situated:

> On September 28, 1745, "the said Richard Morrey for and in consideration of the meer good will and affection that he hath for his kinsman" Leonard Morrey,[19] grandson and namesake of old Humphrey Morrey's brother, deeded over a tract of land totaling 326 acres, 143 perches, and situated along the "south side of a road laid out between the churches of Oxford [Trinity Church Oxford at the corner of Oxford Avenue and Disston Street in the Mayfair section of Northeast Philadelphia] and Whitemarsh [St. Thomas] [dividing Richard Morrey's land from his other land]" and bordered by the holdings of Job Howell, William Nice, Joshua Harmer, Evan Thomas, and Henry Slingow.[20]

Essentially, "Richard and Ann sold 700 acres in Cheltenham to Leonard [Morrey][21] for 5 shillings, a nominal sum to make it a legal contract," quite probably. "The land adjoined Richard's other Cheltenham land."[22]

About 90 days later, "on January 22, 1746," the apparently determined "Morrey went before Charles Brockden, the Philadelphia County recorder of deeds," and the historic words for the deed required to transfer the 198 acres to "his now freed Negro Woman Mooney otherwise Cremona Morrey" were recorded by Paul Isaac Voto, Brockden's "deputy"; Cremona received "a conveyance subject to ground rent," that included the sprawling property "'with all and singular the buildings, improvements, ways, woods, waters, watercourses, rights, liberties, privileges, or hereditaments and appurtenances whatsoever thereunto belonging.'" Essentially, the arrangement made "Cremona the effective owner, though the land remained Morrey's. The deed may have been so structured to avoid restrictions on ownership of property by blacks."[23] Although the imperfect arrangement certainly had its weaknesses, it was exceptionally significant, certainly indicating that Richard had considerably more than casual feelings for Cremona even as their romantic or marital relationship obviously fell apart. "It was then known that a lease had been made by Richard Murrey to his Negro Woman Cremona (or Mooney) for 500 years of 198 acres."[24]

Cremona's land likely included portions "of old Humphrey Morrey's original 250-acre grant of 1683," granted by Pennsylvania's founder, William Penn, spanning "from the present Cheltenham-Springfield township border east to what is now Waverly Road and south to what is" today "Cheltenham Avenue." Specifically, her domain "was located roughly at what is now the corner of Willow Grove Avenue (then 'Mermaid Road' or 'the great road leading from Abington to Church Road') and Limekiln Pike (then 'Limekiln Road') and then proceeding east on Limekiln Pike to about the present intersection of Limekiln Pike and Waverly Road; from that intersection south on Waverly to Church Road, and then Church Road west to the intersection with Willow Grove Avenue."[25]

Cremona's acquisition of the land with the supposed terms that she and her descendants had initial rights to it for 500 years, had to be quite gratifying—albeit with conditions. The property could also provide the livelihoods and capital that the young African American family initially led by a single mother needed to sustain itself; Cremona likely at first relied on her offspring or hired help to assist with the chores, but by 1754 she would reenter a marital relationship with a formerly enslaved African American, John Fry or Frye.[26]

After the death of Richard's wife Ann Morrey, probably before 1746, in June of that year, "Richard married Sarah [née Beasley] Allen, a widow, at Trinity Church in Oxford,"[27] today in the lower northeast sector of Philadelphia. "Richard had been raised as a Quaker, but at some point he had fallen away. He does not appear in the records of Abington Meeting or Philadelphia Meeting .... When she married Richard, she was the widow of an Allen."[28] It wasn't long, however, before the couple dealt with pressing business concerns:

> In 1752 Richard and Sarah went to court to solve a problem. His father Humphrey had left Richard the Philadelphia lots with their valuable yearly quitrents, but they were entailed in the male line. That is, Richard owned them but could not sell them; they could only be passed down to his male heirs. That must have seemed feasible in 1716 when Humphrey

died, but after 1735, when both Thomas and his cousin Humphrey died, there were no male heirs in the Morrey line. Richard and Sarah went to the Court of Common Pleas for a common recovery, an elaborate legal fiction which circumvented the terms of the bequest.[29]

The implication is that Richard and Sarah were quite savvy businesswise. So, was their relationship predicated more on business endeavors, rather than romance, especially considering that Richard was advancing in age and Sarah was an aging widow? The following seems to support their likely sophisticated financial acumen and influence within the political structure. The arrangement "involved a token sale of the property, a 'straw man' who appeared in court briefly then disappeared, and a judgement from the court that the actual owner should recover the land in fee simple, with the right to sell, instead of fee tail. Now Richard and Sarah were free to sell the rents," including "to Israel Pemberton" for a hefty 550 pounds. "On August 1753, Richard and Sarah sold a lot 'on the Northern Bounds of the said city' to William Chancellor for £500, as well as a property in Cheltenham."[30]

Remarkably, the couple appeared in front of an exceedingly well-known historical figure in the process of conducting business—none other than the Founding Father, scholar, and quintessential entrepreneur, Benjamin Franklin:

> The twenty ninth day of January in the year one thousand seven hundred and fifty three Before me Benjamin Franklin Esq One of the Justices Came the within named Richard Morrey and Sarah his Wife and Acknowledged the within written Indenture to be their Deed and desired Same may be Recorded ... this Deed the said Sarah thereunto Voluntarily Consenting she being of full Age Secretly and apart examined and the Constraints thereof first made known unto her Witness my Hand and Seal the Day & Year above said.—B. Franklin [followed by a circular hand-drawn seal] Recorded the 29th day of March 1753.[31]

Richard, with the assistance of his wife Sarah, continued to sell property in 1753 throughout the region, including in Philadelphia's central business district as "the only Surviving Son of the Said Humphrey [Morrey] of which Lot he the Said Richard having lately conveyed one hundred and twenty one foot messuages" in the vicinity of "Second Street unto John Mifflin, Thomas Rubut [and Israel Pemberton]." The value of the transactions amounted to "the Sum of five hundred and fifty Pounds lawful Money of Pennsylvania unto them [Richard and Sarah Morrey] well and truly paid by the said Israel Pemberton at & before the sealing and Delivery hereof."[32]

Perhaps beginning to feel quite "under the weather," "in August 1753, Richard Morrey made his will, after a long and eventful life." At 78, a relatively old age for that early American period, Richard had "outlived his first wife and his only son." And perhaps with Cremona as a diminishing memory and Richard being quite satisfied with the substantial land (with notable conditions) that he had in essence bequeathed to her, Richard "left all his property to his wife Sarah, and made her and her brother John Beasley the executors" of his estate, "with William Chancellor and Jenkin Jones as overseers."

Richard Morrey passed away "not long after,"[33] probably "between August 30, 1753, and January 3, 1754."[34] For his funeral, "Joshua Harmer, a Quaker neighbor" in Cheltenham whose land was adjacent to Cremona's, "was asked to be a bearer at the funeral." However, Harmer "refused, saying that there were younger men more fit for the purpose," perhaps a rejection due to his allegiance with his neighbor Cremona and the possibility that he did not appreciate Richard's abrupt departure and remarriage? Or, was Harmer concerned about Quaker sanctions for participating in Anglican burial rites? Nevertheless, "the sexton gave him a pair of gloves anyway, as was the custom for bearers at an Anglican funeral. Joshua was reported to Abington Monthly Meeting for taking the gloves against the rules of the Society of Friends, and he had to make acknowledgement of the fault."[35]

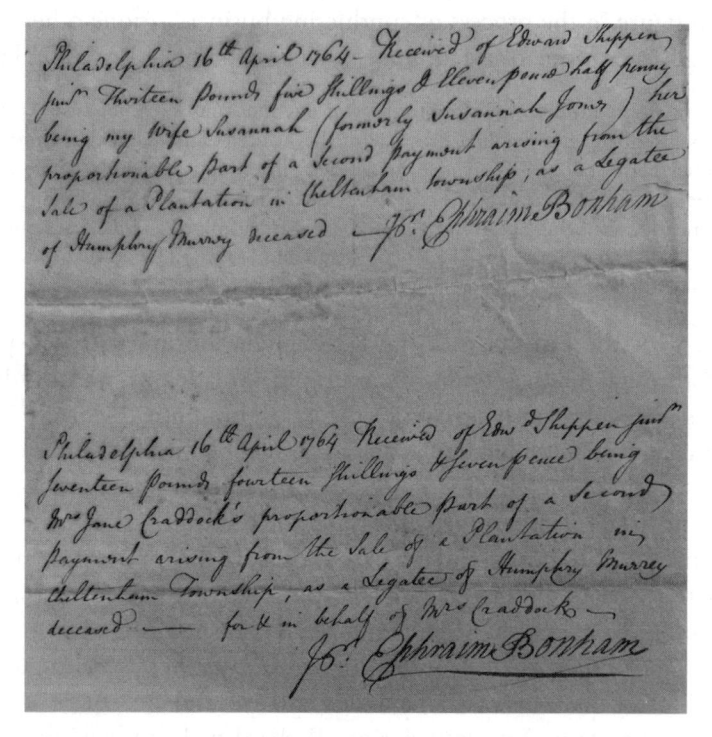

After Richard Morrey's death in 1754, a Cheltenham "plantation" that had been bequeathed to him was apparently put up for sale. (Quaker & Special Collections, Haverford College)

By the time "inventory of Richard's estate was taken on February 11, 1754," his wife "Sarah Morrey was also dead" with "her brother John Beasley" acting "as the surviving executor." Cremona, by then, would have been about age 44, if born in 1710. And based on the inventory of Richard and Sarah's household belongings, they were likely living in grander accommodations compared to Richard's years with Cremona in the smaller residence on their farm estate in Cheltenham, assuming that Richard and Cremona lived under the same roof for a period of years. "In [Richard and Sarah's] main house, in northern Philadelphia, they had walnut leather chairs, prints on the walls, a clock and looking glass, a Delft punchbowl, a mahogany oval table, spice box, and ample linens," among other items. Further, "they still had a simple home in Cheltenham, sparsely furnished," perhaps the very place where Richard had lived with Cremona and presumably their children. The Philadelphia residence "was offered for sale in an ad [of May 2, 1754] in the Pennsylvania Gazette: 'House where Richard Murray, dec'd, formerly dwelt, near the northern bound of Phila., bounded on W. by ground of George Royal and on E by land of Jonathan Zane, for sale; apply to William Chancellor in Market St."[36]

In the end, "Richard Morrey appears not to have been buried within the confines of a graveyard, but on a small plot of ground situated on what is now Willow Grove Avenue, one mile south of Edge Hill" in Cheltenham just a stone's throw or two from where his relationship with "his now freed Negro Woman Mooney" had been consummated.

CHAPTER 6

Brave New Horizons

Challenges as a Land-Owning Black Woman Moving Forward

Cremona and Richard Morrey's home may have resembled the house of Tobias Leech, a cofounder of what became known as Cheltenham Township. Hailing from Gloucestershire, England's town of Cheltenham (that's recognized and celebrated today as the "twin" of Pennsylvania's Cheltenham), Leech also "owned" enslaved blacks who worked at his homestead and large mill which was likely powered by the nearby Tacony Creek. (Cheltenham Historical Photograph Collection)

When Richard Morrey died about 1754, there were very few liberated black Northern women who were able to gaze proudly across their own land. And there were virtually none, outside of Cremona Morrey, with acres that happened to be located in Cheltenham, founded and named by English settlers after their hometown in Gloucestershire, England, where "a church is known to have existed ... as early as 1603."[1] Through or near Cremona's substantial property flowed a number of swift-running creeks—the Neshaminy, Tacony and Pennypack—that derived their names from the languages of the land's original inhabitants. Cheltenham had been "the hunting ground of the

Lenni Lenape Indians, whose headquarters were on a bluff, overlooking the Neshaminy [creek], near Newtown, Pennsylvania."[2]

The powerful water currents propelled the vertical wheels of gristmills, some established a half-century earlier in Cheltenham by the likes of the town's cofounder and Cheltenham native Tobias Leech, "an English country gentleman," near the dawn of the 18th century. One of Cremona Morrey's grandsons, Solomon S. Montier, would marry Susanna G. Highgate, the daughter of one of the earliest black millers in the region, if not the country, Moses Highgate. Leech, initially a Quaker slaveholder who would leave the Friends or Quaker religion like Richard Morrey and ultimately join the nearby Trinity Church Oxford in Philadelphia with roots to the Church of England, "bought 604 acres in Cheltenham Township adjacent to Richard Wall on August 9, 1706,"[3] not far from Cremona's eventual estate where she "settled"[4] with her biracial children. Cremona was likely still emotionally impacted by Richard's departure, as well as his marriage to Sarah (Beasley) Allen[5] (at Trinity Church Oxford[6]) and his ultimate death.

With no definitive indications about whether Richard and Cremona's breakup was acrimonious or not, it's difficult to determine her exact state of mind. Nor is it clear exactly when she would develop a relationship with a nearby African American man, John Fry, and be blessed again with the miracle

The Richard Wall House was an early core of Quaker activities, including religious meetings, not long after those English settlers arrived from Cheltenham, Gloucestershire, England during the early 1680s. (Kristopher Scott)

of childbirth. "After Richard Morrey left Edgehill for a new home and a new wife, Cremona and her children settled down on her land,"[7] with some of the children likely old enough to help with the many required chores.

At some point "after—the date is unknown—she married a former slave named John Fry ... or Frey." Possibly, "his name may signify that he was once owned or employed by John Fry, a prosperous farmer of Abington Township," noting that "the black John Fry's appearances in the early township tax lists find him entered as 'Old Free Negro,' 'Old Fry Negro' and 'Old Negroe Fry,' leading one to consider that he could have originally been called 'Free John' or 'John Free' which was changed to 'Frey' and then 'Fry.'"[8] Considering that Takingthelongerview.org indicates that Cremona married Fry (sometimes spelled Frye) about 1754, eight years after[9] the circa 1746 breakup with Richard, if she and John Fry had more children Cremona would have been age 44 at the time of Richard's 1754 death or the approximate year that she may have remarried. Nonetheless, "Cremona and John Fry would have at least one surviving child, a son named Joseph; there may have been more that failed to survive to maturity."[10] Indeed, is it possible that Cremona began having children with Fry even before Richard's departure—or shortly after Richard began to court or married Sarah (Beasley) Allen?

Although "next to nothing is known about John Fry, or Frey," one of his descendants may have been the African American Albert Fry, born about 1845 in Philadelphia and who died on November 15, 1887. Albert, who could have been more recently descended from the abovementioned son of John Fry named Joseph, was then buried five days later on November 20, 1887, in "Edge Hill";[11] he was interred likely in the segregated family cemetery in Guineatown variously identified as Edge Hill Cemetery, Montieth Cemetery (sometimes spelled Monteith), and even "the Colored Cemetery in Glenside" or "Cemetery for Colored Folks," that was officially established via a "1798 indenture."[12] Albert had been living as a "Single" man in "Ward 23," then encompassing Philadelphia's "Somerton" area, according to FamilySearch.org.[13]

Although a "John Fry" is listed in the 1790 census as a Montgomery County resident, it's possible that the reference is to the European American individual who may have been the employer or so-called master of the African-descended John Fry or Frye whom Cremona Sr. would marry after Richard Morrey's death. Nonetheless, a John Fry would serve in the renowned Pennsylvania Rifle Regiment during the Revolutionary War, commanded by Colonel Samuel Miles (1740–1805). Miles became a Philadelphia mayor and purchased more than 160 acres in Cheltenham, "where he died at the age of 67 on December 29, 1805."[14]

Probably before or by the mid-1750s, Cremona Morrey Fry's daughter, "the younger Cremona," was "being courted by John Montier" when "the small group of African Americans living on the grant from Richard Morrey numbered about twenty" in what would become the historic community of Guineatown. It wasn't long before "John and the younger Cremona married and soon had two sons, Joseph, born about 1768, and Solomon, born in 1770."[15] Solomon Montier would become the forefather of Dr. William Pickens Sr., the first field secretary of the NAACP and an extended relative of the great African American activist, entertainer, and scholar Paul Robeson.

The end of a momentous era would come when "tragedy struck" and "Cremona Fry, probably not yet sixty, died about 1770."[16] Indeed, "Cremona entered and became possessed of the said Messuage & Tract of Land and died leaving the said John Fry her husband in possession thereof," notes the original "Indenture" at the Philadelphia City Archives.[17] "And Whereas it was intended by the said Richard Murrey that the said Lands should go among his said Children but by the Second Marriage of the said Cremona that intention was in some measure defeated and some Difference has arisen."[18]

Cremona's widower, John Fry, would soon marry "Margaret Reiter (Riter, Righter)," who "was a daughter (probably the eldest) of George Reiter (1729–1794) of 'Chresheim, Germantown Township,'" and "owned land adjacent to Cremona's grant."[19] If Margaret was of European ancestry, as circumstances seem to indicate, then the African American John Fry's union with her would have also represented a rare interracial marital relationship.

John Fry's new marriage to Margaret would open a Pandora's box of sorts leading to quite a "family crisis":

> Cremona's children became concerned regarding the fate of their mother's property. Under the prevailing legal theory of the period, when John Fry married Cremona, he also gained the same interest in any property that she held, making them co-owners (tenancy by the entirety). The survivor would become the full owner of the property. Had Cremona left a will stating her intentions as to the final disposition of the property, there might not have been a quarrel. However, Cremona died intestate, and under the law, John Fry, as her husband, was the owner of the land. After his death, if he had not sold property before then and died intestate, title would go to Joseph Fry, his eldest son, and any other children John Fry would have with his new wife. Cremona's children by Richard Morrey would be completely cut off. They decided to challenge their stepfather's right to the property.[20]

To resolve the outstanding issues, Cremona's children took an approach recommended much earlier and consulted respected Quaker neighbors affiliated with the Abington Friends Meeting House. With roots in the Gloucester Monthly Meeting in England, Abington Friends first met at the Cheltenham residence of Richard Wall,[21] reputed in 1979 when it "was placed on the National Register of Historic Places" to be "the oldest house in Pennsylvania which had continuous family residence to that date."[22] Meanwhile, "in his will, old Humphrey Morrey had requested his son [Richard Morrey] and grandson [the younger Humphrey Morrey and offspring of Richard's brother John] to resolve their differences not 'by going to law but [by] apply[ing] themselves to the Monthly Meeting at Philadelphia' who would appoint two members to end 'such Differences as may arrive between them,'" an indication of how Quakerism still influenced the younger generation, at least to some degree. "Fifty-five years later, his grandchildren followed this advice, and approached local Quaker landowners to help them resolve this problem," including Isaac Knight Jr.,[23] whose "father had inherited" 250 acres in what is today nearby Abington Township. "Knight's father had inherited this property and about 1725," following the examples of Cheltenham cofounders Richard Wall and Tobias Leech, "constructed a mill at the present corner of Rice's Mill Road and Glenside Avenue, which under various owners, stayed in business well into the Twentieth Century."[24]

A resolution, essentially allowing proceeds and land to be split between the intra-family adversaries, was described "in [the] deed, dated January 23,

The New Cheltenham Mill was one of many powered by the nearby Tacony Creek. (Wikimedia Commons)

1772," just a few years before America's 1776 Declaration of Independence from Britain that would result in the Edge Hill area being swept up into the final phases of the Revolutionary War:

> Now for a putting an End to all disputes, and for the sake of Equity, this Indenture Witnesseth that the said John Fry, Robert Lewis, Caesar Murray, Elizabeth Murray, Andrew Hickey and Rachel, his wife, John Mounteer [Montier] and Cremona his wife and Joseph Fry for and in Consideration of Thirty Shillings unto the John Fry, Robert Lewis, Ceasar Murrey, Elizabeth Murrey, Andrew Hickey and Rachel his Wife John Monteer and Cremona his Wife and Joseph Fry by the said Isaac Knight at and before the Sealing and Delivery hereof well and truly paid the Receipt whereof is hereby acknowledged, have and each of them hath granted bargained Sold released & confirmed.[25]

Interestingly, the above agreement represents "the first known appearance of John Montier's name in public records."[26] As briefly discussed earlier, "[t]he deed was signed by all parties—Elizabeth Murray, Rachel Murray Hickey and Cremona Murray Montier signed with an 'X,' as did their stepfather, John Fry,'" likely an indication that Cremona Sr.'s daughters couldn't write and more than likely weren't literate, perhaps suggesting that Cremona Sr. herself was not literate either, having failed to pass literacy skills on to her female children. However, "the rest of the men carefully signed their names." Indications are that Caesar and Robert did become literate.[27]

Meanwhile, the resolution required that the contested "property" be "sold to Isaac Knight who would allow John Fry to live there for the rest of his life, and then divide the property among Cremona's children, including Joseph Fry," the son he had with the elder Cremona. In fact, "John Fry's other children would not be slighted; in an unrecorded deed dated December 19, 1771, George and Elizabeth Reiter sold four acres 'along the Road from Chestnut Hill to Susquehanna' [Mermaid Road, now Willow Grove Avenue] to Margaret Fry, John's second wife, thereby providing for her two sons, Abraham and Solomon Fry."[28]

Yet, Cremona, despite the monumental challenges of navigating as a black woman in early America's proslavery and racist society, made remarkable strides that provided the foundation for forthcoming dynamic African American generations. Cremona's descendants became some of the most industrious and prosperous African Americans in Cheltenham's Guineatown, as well as the region and what would become the United States.

John Fry's life would come to an end in 1788,[29] around 18 years after Cremona died. Soon after John's death, Isaac Knight "sold off about 122 acres of the original grant," raising about $1,200 in capital. "The remaining 76 acres were held for the use of Cremona's children," with the acquired funds and land "apportioned into fourteen acre plots" that were handed "over to the children" on July 23, 1789.[30] In fact, "Rachel Murray Hickey and her husband Andrew received a plot located next to Margaret Fry's four acres on Willow Grove Avenue opposite what is now Glasgow Quarry." Meanwhile, land "belonging to Elizabeth Murray Bustill and her husband Cyrus came next, stretching to the intersection with Limekiln [Pike]."[31] Right next to the Bustills' property was "that of Cremona and John Montier"; and just across the street "were the twenty-eight acres belonging to Robert Lewis" and Guineatown's "burying ground,"[32] bordering Limekiln Pike, with "Cremona's offspring" receiving "each" approximately "two hundred dollars,"[33] valued at about $7,000 today, depending on inflation rates.[34]

Despite the racist hardships that people of color undoubtedly faced, some members of the Montier family began to branch out to other areas in the region; the Montiers, Bustills, and others associated with the historic Guineatown continued to survive, and often thrive, in the very Edge Hill community where General George Washington and his Continental troops would fight British forces for their own independence that ironically and hypocritically helped to preserve the institution of enslaving Cremona Morrey's African-descended brethren. "Even so, the founders were deeply conflicted over slavery," writes Nikole Hannah-Jones in her Pulitzer Prize-winning essay "DEMOCRACY" and groundbreaking book *The 1619 Project*. "So when it came time to draft the Constitution, the framers carefully constructed a document that preserved and protected slavery without ever using the word," she points out. "In the key texts for framing our republic, the founders did not want to explicitly acknowledge their hypocrisy. They sought instead to shroud it."[35] Despite the tremendous odds, the Montier family would miraculously persevere and build on the foundation that Cremona Sr. built with unparalleled craftiness, ingenuity, and apparent love of self and family. And that was as the Americans would retreat to nearby Whitemarsh and then Valley Forge where they, including a notable contingent of African Americans, would barely survive a horrendously brutal winter.

CHAPTER 7

Cremona Jr., Her Marriage to John Montier, and the Genesis of the Bustills

Cremona Jr. and her husband, John Montier, of Afro-Caribbean ancestry, began building this handsome home along Limekiln Pike about the time of the American Revolution. (J. Scott Laughlin, BHHS, Fox & Roach Realtors)

During the two decades following Cremona Morrey (or Murray) Montier Jr.'s 1745 birth[1] as the youngest daughter of Richard and Cremona Morrey, there was a "rapid growth of slavery" in the Philly area. The climax would have been about the time of the elder Cremona's 1770 death that "occurred at precisely the time the pre-Revolutionary abolitionist movement, centered in Philadelphia and led by John Woolman and Anthony Benezet, was reaching its climax."[2] Born 1720 in New Jersey's Burlington County, Woolman was a prominent anti-slavery Quaker and preacher who traveled extensively throughout the mid-Atlantic orating and writing about the evils of slavery.[3] Benezet, of French Huguenot ancestry, also vehemently opposed slavery and educated many African Americans in schools that he established, leaving "the bulk of his estate to the 'Free School for the Black People of Philadelphia'" when he died in 1784.[4]

In fact, during that consequential mid-18th century, Cremona and her siblings almost certainly performed various farm chores on their mother Cremona Sr.'s homestead, but at a certain point "Robert and Caesar were apprenticed as shoemakers, possibly to neighbor Reynier Tyson." Adventurously, "Caesar Murray later relocated to Burlington, New Jersey, working as a shoemaker and cordwainer. Robert likely worked on farms in the Guineatown area [in Cheltenham] for more than a few years,"[5] as well as probably continued helping on his mother's property with sisters Elizabeth, Rachael, and Cremona Jr.

Yet, somehow, the younger Cremona met and developed a relationship with the African-descended John Montier, who was probably initially enslaved in the Caribbean, circumstantially from a French-speaking island, such as Martinique or Haiti. In fact, "his descendants thought that he was originally from the island of Hispaniola (Haiti), and that the name was originally pronounced 'Mon-tee-ay' rather than 'Mounteer.'" Nevertheless, "there were Montiers—who may have been Scottish rather than French, living in Lancaster County, Pennsylvania, who moved to Westmoreland County and served in the militia during the American Revolution. John may have been a part of that family."[6] Primarily, however, John Montier's "descendants maintain that he was originally from Haiti, and spoke French more readily than English."[7]

The Montier surname appears to have roots in the French surname Dumontier, "from du Montier" or "'Le Montier,' apparently from the name of several places in the north of France."[8] Among other Du Montiers or Dumontiers, a "Denis Bernard Du Montier" was apparently born in 1636 in Beauvais, Oise, Picardie, France, according to Geni.com.[9] A variation of the Montier spelling—"Mounteer"—indicates that it is a "topographic name from Middle English" or "monter," referring to "'dweller on the mount or hill.'" That's comparable to "Mount (of French Huguenot origin): altered form of French Montier.'"[10] Although a variation of Montier was locally referred to as "Moneith," that spelling is "Scottish" and a "habitational name from the earldom and province of Menteith in Perthshire named in Gaelic as 'hill (above) the Teith'" or a "river name of obscure origin."[11]

Remarkably, there are also historical assertions that a John Montier living in Cheltenham was tied to a Montour family with mixed Native American ancestry in Pennsylvania and elsewhere. According to numerous sources, a John Montour was the son of Andrew Montour, of European and indigenous-American heritage, who served as an interpreter and negotiator and fought in several early American conflicts. "Captain Andrew Montour was thrice married, first to a grand-daughter of Chief Allumappees, hereditary sachem of the Delawares," according to Charles Augustus Hanna's 1911 book *The Wilderness Trail: The Debatable Land*.[12] Andrew's second marriage was "to an Indian woman whose English name was Sarah. At one place in the Pennsylvania records, his wife's name (in 1768) is given as Catherine." Nevertheless, "John Montour, the oldest son of Andrew, was born about 1744," likely to Andrew and his first wife. "He was educated by Provost Smith at the Philadelphia Academy," a forerunner of the University of Pennsylvania, "and seems to have lived with his father at Fort Pitt at the time of the latter's death." John would distinguish himself in the military, taking part in the Dunmore War of 1774; "in 1775, as Captain John Montour, [he] asked compensation for the lands of his father,"[13] Andrew, who received correspondence from an up-and-coming commander of "Virginia Forces," George Washington, dated September 19, 1755. In the letter, Washington requests to meet with Andrew, instructing him to "bring some Indians along" and adding: "If you think it proper … bring Mrs. Montour along with you." Andrew's son, John, eventually "served in the Revolutionary Army, in the West, and commanded a company of Delaware warriors in 1782, under Colonel Brodhead, being distinguished for his valor and friendship to the American cause." And John reportedly received a substantial amount of acreage in Ohio, likely as "compensation" for his father's land, but eventually settled in "Cheltenham Township, Montgomery County, PA, on the outskirts of Philadelphia. Although he lived there more than thirty years, he kept his Ohio lands."[14] Sources are contradictory and not explicit, however, concerning the possibility of John being married to Cremona Jr. or anyone else during his supposed time in Cheltenham.

Nonetheless, a "John Montier arrived in Cheltenham Township in the late 1760s and married Cremona Murray," likely quite a notable event for Guineatown's inhabitants, and began having children—Joseph, Solomon, Robert and Hiram—starting in 1768 through 1780. The couple built a historic home in what is today the 300 block of Limekiln Pike in Glenside's Edge Hill neighborhood in Cheltenham "on the old Montier grant; tradition insists that their [original] section was built about 1771."[15]

As *Philadelphia Magazine* reported in 2019 when the Georgian-style colonial home, expanded over the years, was put up for sale, "Cremona and her husband John Montier, a free African American, built a two-story barn and a house sometime after 1772," when America's Revolutionary War conflict with the British began to boil. "Their son Hiram would expand the house over the years as he prospered as a bootmaker in Philadelphia."[16] The "two-story

Rooms with fireplaces, such as this one in the Montier house, were the center of family activities that included cooking, eating, and, of course, keeping warm. (J. Scott Laughlin, BHHS, Fox & Roach Realtors)

More formal interactions were likely held in such living spaces, including receiving guests. (J. Scott Laughlin, BHHS, Fox & Roach Realtors)

structure built in the late 1700s" is today "part of the current home, which was expanded in the 19th century. The barn was eventually expanded into a private residence."[17] In fact, the "original portion of the house" now serves as a den, while an 18th-century springhouse on the property has been used for gardening. The four-bedroom home, today totaling 3,647 square feet, has five working fireplaces—at least a couple probably dating to the Revolutionary War era—and also features wood floors, exposed beams, and crown molding, according to online real estate descriptions.[18] An owner of the residence had been documenting the house's history in order to pursue historical site designation(s) via the Pennsylvania State Historic Preservation Office.[19]

In fact, not long after John and Cremona likely began to complete the initial phases of building their home, American colonists' struggle to break away from England reached a fever pitch. "There's little doubt that the" growing number of Guineatown's African American "inhabitants ... and other Cheltenham citizens heard the gunshots of British and American forces as they clashed over the Edge Hill highlands in the vicinity of the Montier home ... on December 7, 1777."[20] And although there's no indication found so far that blacks in the community officially assisted American or British forces in combat, perhaps due to the pacifist Quaker influence in the area, that possibility cannot be ruled out, especially considering questions about whether the above-mentioned American warrior John Montour and John Montier were the same individual, despite notable doubts.

In the Guineatown area, "both armies reportedly drank from a spring at the intersection of what is today Church Road and Washington Lane during the combat."[21] Tragically, while "British forces moved toward Philadelphia and positioned themselves to overtake Washington's forces, Hessian soldiers fighting with the English king's forces 'committed great outrages on the inhabitants, particularly at John Shoemaker's ... a well-to-do farmer and miller, whose home and grist mill was beside the York Road.'"[22]

Apparently, the "British were outraged as Howe's troops frustratingly looked for an opening in the American lines, soon lighting torches and burning local residences, clearly riling residents in Philadelphia's Germantown and even in the Cheltenham vicinity."[23] A top priority for both battling armies was to take the high ground, meaning that the heights of Guineatown and Edge Hill were prime targets. "The American and British forces fought and maneuvered to take the highlands of the Edge Hill area with both sides suffering about forty casualties,"[24] surely an indication of intense fighting. "Two American commanders, General John Cadwalader and Colonel Joseph Reed, were rescued by a squadron of American troops led by Captain Allen McLane, when they were pinned down in a wooded area and about to be captured or killed."[25] And although "the Continental army's Morgan's Rangers, known as very adept sharpshooters, conducted guerilla-type maneuvers, the British were able to hold their own before both sides withdrew."[26]

Washington's Continental Army forces retreated to nearby Whitemarsh "where the British were planning to attack." Depending on the source, the "Hope Lodge" estate of Samuel Morris, reputed by various sources to be a slaveholder (while others contend he likely was not), served as a temporary hospital for Washington's beleaguered troops.[27] As the story goes, "a local Quaker woman, Lydia Darragh, reportedly heard the plans for the attack and walked over snow-covered roads and gave her information to Lieutenant Colonel Craig and General Elias Boudinot at [the] Rising Sun Inn. Washington was warned by soldiers who likely traveled up York Road and then west on Church Road in order to reach Washington's Whitemarsh headquarters quickly."[28]

Consequently, "American forces by December 19, were forced to leave and camp in Valley Forge for a brutal winter without sufficient rations, which would lead to virtual starvation and the brink of defeat. Yet the mighty efforts of citizens like the black baker Cyrus Bustill,"[29] noted to be at one time a Guineatown resident who married Cremona and Richard's daughter Elizabeth Morrey, ironically, would help to save the Americans who manifested the institution of slavery while seeking freedom for themselves. "During the American Revolution, Bustill risked his life to take bread to George Washington's starving troops at Valley Forge," notes the acclaimed African American historian Charles Blockson, whose work focused on Pennsylvania's blacks. "It's said that Bustill," recognized as a "Black Founding Father" who helped to start the pioneering civil rights group the Free African Society (FAS) during the late 18th century in Philadelphia, "received a silver piece from Washington."[30] Bustill assisted Washington's primary baker at Valley Forge, Christopher Ludwick (1720–1801), within "a second company of bakers" in February 1778 with the approval of Congress.[31]

Although born in 1732 outside of the immediate Philadelphia area,[32] Cyrus Bustill, a practicing Quaker and former slave who purchased his own freedom, would become a central figure for many of Guineatown's inhabitants and others—blacks and whites—far beyond the community's boundaries. That's because he was destined to become a community leader, entrepreneur, Revolutionary War patriot, educator, and black activist. After marrying Elizabeth Morrey, the daughter of Cremona Sr. and Richard Morrey, they then reportedly purchased property in Guineatown.[33] The couple's residence and land was "adjacent" to the properties of Elizabeth's siblings, including Cremona Jr. and her husband John Montier, plus brothers Caesar Murray and Robert Lewis and their families.[34]

Elizabeth and Cyrus continued to raise children there, despite marrying as comparatively older adults for that time period, because Cyrus did not want his offspring to be born as slaves; if he had earlier married an enslaved woman and remained one himself, their children, according to the law, would have been considered slaves. "He 'would not perpetuate a race of slaves'; so he did not marry early in life."[35] In fact, when Cyrus was reported to have owned property in Guineatown[36] several years following the Revolutionary War, his leadership and influence within African American communities in the Delaware Valley were likely well recognized and appreciated as local Quakers increasingly opposed slavery.

Although some sources indicate that Cyrus was born to an unidentified "slave woman" and "Samuel Bustill, Jr."[37] of Burlington, New Jersey, on February 6, 1732, Cyrus Bustill came into the world enslaved "in the family of [the] colonial official" Samuel Bustill Sr.[38] Various other sources however indicate that son Samuel Jr. likely fathered Cyrus via a relationship with one of the estate's enslaved women by the name of Parthenia.[39] "Samuel Bustill Sr. died in 1742; in order to pay his debts, provide a dowry for his granddaughter, and an income for his spinster daughter, his will called for the dissolution of his estate by selling off most of his holdings, including five 'negroes—Dina, Parthenia, Hester, Cyrus and Cato.'"[40]

Young Cyrus endured some of the poignant travails of slavery, but somehow persevered and eventually thrived:

> Ten years old Cyrus was sold to John Allen, Sr. of Trenton, who promised the boy that he would be freed upon Allen's death. When Allen died in 1753, his widow promised to free Cyrus after *her* death, if he would stay on. Cyrus consented, but after Mrs. Allen's death in 1758, her son John Allen Jr. callously informed Cyrus that the young black was still a slave and would remain so. To Cyrus's rescue came one Thomas Pryor, Jr. of Philadelphia, a Quaker by faith and a baker by vocation, who first offered to hire Cyrus, paying Allen for the use of the slave's services. Allen refused, so Pryor after putting up part of his money along with Cyrus' life savings, bought Cyrus from Allen.[41]

Either as part of the so-called transaction or due to Cyrus's supposed further obligation to Pryor, Cyrus was additionally held "as a slave for a period of seven years" when "Pryor used the time to teach Cyrus the mysteries of the craft of baking" that essentially served as "an apprenticeship."[42] It's during that time that "Cyrus met Elizabeth Murray, who was working as a domestic in the home of Quaker merchant Nicholas Waln. Cyrus and Elizabeth were married at Christ Church in Philadelphia on April 20, 1773," although other sources indicate they were married at a location in Cheltenham's Guineatown as we'll explore soon. The couple "reared a family of eight children, Rachel, Mary, Ruth, Leah, Grace, Charles, Cyrus and David."[43]

Notably, "Cyrus Bustill, as the records will show, conducted his bread, cake, and biscuit business many years with credit and profit," according to an account that appeared in Carter G. Woodson's *Journal of Negro History*, written by one of Cyrus's descendants, his great-granddaughter Anna Bustill Smith (1862–1945), renowned as a trailblazing African American genealogist who documented[44] her family's highly esteemed history.[45] She further noted in the journal—founded by Woodson, who became renowned as the "Father of African American history"—that "Cyrus moved to Philadelphia, and still conducted his baking business" in the first block of "Arch Street," near the city's Delaware River waterfront.[46]

Smith provides a statement in the article from Thomas Falconer, "contractor for supplying troops at the above mentioned port" in Burlington, New Jersey, dated May 1, 1782, indicating "that Cyrus Bustill has been employed in the baking of all the flour used at the port of Burlington and that he has behaved himself as a faithful, honest man and has given satisfaction such as should recommend him to every good inhabitant." She concluded: "This was a patriotic contribution to the struggle of the Continental forces," reiterating that Bustill "received a silver piece as a souvenir, from General George Washington. A member of the family," whom Smith did not identify, "still preserves it."[47]

At Valley Forge, "700 to 720 Patriots of African descent," primarily from "Rhode Island, Connecticut, and Massachusetts units" were among Washington's troops who endured the brutal winter and other horrendous conditions that undoubtedly included racism. "Each unit commander determined whether he would accept black enlistments. Even with these restrictions, Black people continued to fill both military and civilian support roles. Many fought in integrated units, which would not occur again until the Korean War, about 170 years later."[48] Notably, "Black people joined the fight against the British, even before the official formation of the Continental Army." Among these was Crispus Attucks of Boston, who, according to historian George Washington Williams, "'was the first to open the hostilities between Great Britain and the colonies—the first to pour out his blood as a precious libation on the altar of a people's rights'"[49] when he was killed while confronting British forces at the Boston waterfront. "Yet, Congress did not authorize their [African Americans'] recruitment until January 1776," leading to an estimated "five-to-eight thousand" African Americans participating in the war.[50]

Although there were other blacks with Pennsylvania roots at Valley Forge, Stacey Williams (c. 1742–September 21, 1820) was "the only known Black veteran who joined a Pennsylvania Continental unit and left behind a pension narrative," according to the Valley Forge National Historical Park.[51] "Williams enlisted on April 29, 1777 in Newtown, Pennsylvania. He served in the 6th Pennsylvania Regiment 'commanded by [Lieutenant Colonel Henry] Bicker and afterwards by [Lieutenant Colonel Josiah] Harmar [of the] Pennsylvania Line and in the company commanded by Captain [Jacob] Humphries," notes the National Park Service. "Williams encamped at Valley Forge and fought in the Battle of Monmouth Courthouse and in South Carolina with the Southern Campaign. After the war, he settled in Middletown Township in Bucks County, Pennsylvania."[52]

Moreover, "in Philadelphia the British had a 'Company of Black Pioneers,' consisting of some seventy-two 'privates,' fifteen women and eight children," many of them likely accepting the British offer of African Americans joining their forces in exchange for liberation from slavery. "Under the command of Captain Allen Stewart this contingent was clothed by the army, each man receiving in September 1778 a great coat, hat, sailor jacket, white shirt and winter trousers."[53]

Yet, there were other Pennsylvania blacks who served, including a native of Conshohocken in Montgomery County where Cheltenham was also founded. "Edward Hector, of the Third Pennsylvania Artillery, took part in the Battle of Brandywine in September 1777," according to historian Benjamin Quarles. "When the American army was pulled back, Hector disobeyed the order to abandon wagons. Making use of arms left on the field by fleeing soldiers, he protected his horses and his ammunition wagon, bringing them safely in," Quarles notes. "Fifty years later the Pennsylvania legislature gave him a $40.00 donation."[54]

Gad Asher, whose grandson, the Reverend Jeremiah Asher, became the pastor of Shiloh Baptist Church in Philadelphia and who would serve during the Civil War as a chaplain for the 6th United States Colored Troops of Camp William Penn, where some of the Morrey–Montier descendants trained for battle at the facility in Cheltenham, replaced his so-called Connecticut master during the Revolutionary War. According to Jeremiah's 1850 memoir, *Incidents in the Life of The Rev. J. Asher*, Gad in about 1735 was "'stolen from the coast of Guinea when four years of age,' and destined for enslavement in colonial Connecticut." Although an agreement was made that Gad would be liberated after fighting in fierce battles that apparently cost Gad his eyesight, the slave owner "reneged" on his promise, forcing Gad to purchase his freedom by working many more years. "Grandfather Gad would pass the burning torch of his Old Testament religious fervor to his grandson, Jeremiah," who ultimately died just after the

Civil War in Wilmington, North Carolina, likely of malaria or typhoid fever with many of his flock of soldiers. A staunch antislavery activist who had employed at his church one of the earliest and most acclaimed black singers, Elizabeth Greenfield (the former slave known as the "Black Swan" and destined to sing for Camp William Penn's African American Civil War regiments and even Queen Victoria in England), left behind a wife and several children, as well as a devastated congregation and activist community.[55]

Perhaps the most well-known African American Revolutionary War hero from Philadelphia was James Forten, whose ancestors would befriend and even marry descendants of the Bustills and Morreys. "Of the Negroes serving on the privateers the best known to history was James Forten who while not yet fifteen enlisted as a powder boy on the *Royal Louis*, commissioned by Pennsylvania in 1781," notes historian Quarles. "On her second cruise the *Royal Louis* was captured by the frigate *Amphyon*, assisted by two other British vessels. Young Forten became a playmate of the son of the *Amphyon*'s commander, but the powder boy resisted efforts to persuade him to renounce his American allegiance,"[56] Quarles continues. "As a consequence he was sent to the floating dungeon, the Jersey, where he spent seven months before being released in the general exchange of prisoners which took place as the war drew to a close." Incredibly, following "the war Forten [became] a sailmaker in Philadelphia,"[57] after being apprenticed by a white sailmaker named Robert Bridges who sold Forten his business. One of Forten's grandsons named for Bridges, Robert Bridges Forten, who was the father of the acclaimed educator and diarist Charlotte Forten Grimke, would also enlist in a Camp William Penn regiment, the 43rd United States Colored Troops, along with several Montiers who joined other affiliated Union forces. Similar to Chaplain Asher, he would die of disease. James Forten ultimately amassed "a fortune of $100,000, a portion of which came from his invention of a device for handling sails."[58] As a dedicated antislavery activist, "Forten spent some of his money in support of reformist movements," including cofounding the Free African Society in Philadelphia, as well as "the William Lloyd Garrison wing of the abolitionist crusaders."[59]

Meanwhile, although Cyrus Bustill "and his family attended the Fourth and Arch [Streets] meeting" of the Quaker Friends, he seems to have gravitated to a pioneering African American church founded by the formerly enslaved Absalom Jones, also a cofounder with Bustill and other influential blacks of the Free African Society on April 12, 1787:

> In the Annals of the first African Church in United States, the Protestant Episcopal Church of St. Thomas, 1862, it is said: "Cyrus Bustill was generally respected for his uprightness, and much relied upon by his brethren for his sound judgement. He was the first to relinquish his

claim in the old Society in behalf of the church. This noble act appears to good advantage in view of his religious sentiments, which accorded with those of the Friends."[60]

As he aged, Cyrus Bustill was still driven by purpose and determined to improve the lives of his African American brethren. "He finally retired from business and built a house on Third and Green Streets, where he opened a school and taught."[61] Just after the dawn of the 19th century, Cyrus Bustill died, but his wife, obviously intelligent and assertive, persevered:

> After Cyrus' death on February 8, 1806, just six days past his seventy-fourth birthday, Elizabeth undertook the operation of the beerhouse, appearing as owner and proprietor in the city directories, and later ran a millinery store on Arch Street with one of her daughters, Grace Bustill Douglass. As old age crept up, Elizabeth lived quietly in the house on North 3rd Street with the family of her youngest son David and his wife Mary W. (Hicks) Bustill, with others of the family close by. Elizabeth Murray Bustill survived all of her family, dying August 10, 1827 in her eighty-fourth year.[62]

Following the Revolutionary War, Cremona and John Montier's relationship seemed to have flourished as they accrued more property, affluence, and likely much respect in the tight-knit Cheltenham community of increasingly antislavery Quakers as the 18th century drew to a close. Neighbor "Isaac Knight, Jr. sold fourteen acres to Cremona Montier,"[63] as noted previously, "and, gave her two hundred dollars, part of her bequest from her parents."[64] However, "the land was in her name, not jointly with her husband." Yet, "John appears in the Cheltenham Township Tax Lists as the owner. The 1791 list shows John 'Mountier' with thirteen acres, his own 'dwelling,' one horse and two cows."[65] John purchased an additional "three acres from his brother-in-law, Caesar Murray," on December 23, 1794. "This land lay adjacent to the Montier land. Therefore, by 1800, John and Cremona Montier owned between them fifteen acres,"[66] enough to sustain themselves and their maturing children, some who likely still lived with them. "On this land, the Montiers farmed their crops, raised their sons, and lived quietly for the almost sixty years of their lives together. Their sons grew up, acquired a smattering of book learning, and, one by one, set off to make their way in the world."[67]

Of Richard and Cremona Morrey's proud descendants, including the offspring of Cremona Jr. and John Montier, some would become integral participants in early 19th-century black liberation movements spearheaded by the likes of Frederick Douglass, William Still, Lucretia Mott, and William Lloyd Garrison with co-descendant family members such as David Bustill Bowser. They'd join forces with other freedom fighters like Robert Purvis. Their courageous work necessarily included educating themselves, their children, and African American brethren, earlier foundational steps that James Forten,

David Bustill Bowser was a popular antislavery activist, artist, and designer of flags for the 11 African American regiments that trained at Cheltenham's Camp William Penn during the Civil War. Other extended family members trained at the historic facility. (Library of Congress)

Maria Louisa Bustill, a descendant of Richard and Cremona Morrey, was the mother of the renowned Paul Robeson, a dynamic scholar, actor, attorney, civil rights activist, and athlete. (Wikimedia Commons)

his progeny, and his close friends, including Cyrus Bustill, would also pursue. "James Forten had probably known [the highly esteemed educator] Grace Bustill Douglass from childhood" because "she was the daughter of Cyrus Bustill,"[68] who had purchased land and property in Guineatown[69] via his marriage to Elizabeth Morrey, a daughter of Cremona and Richard. Cyrus's "wife, Elizabeth Morey, was the daughter of an English aristocrat [Richard] and a Native American woman [Cremona Sr.]," notes historian-scholar Julie Winch,[70] keeping in mind that other sources identify her ethnicity otherwise or are ambiguous. Grace and her husband, Robert Douglass, "a [likely formerly enslaved] prosperous barber from the Caribbean island of St Kitts," whom she married in 1803, were known to have "a high regard for education, and both agonized over their children's schooling."[71] That struggle for education and upward mobility would become the hallmark of many future generations, including for iconic African American activist, scholar, and entertainer Paul Leroy Robeson, born in Princeton, New Jersey, on April 9, 1898,[72] whose schoolteacher mother, Maria Louisa Bustill, was the great-granddaughter of Elizabeth Morrey and Cyrus Bustill.[73]

CHAPTER 8

The Development of Guineatown and Early Flourishing of the Montiers and Other Residents

The Eagle Hotel was likely the hub of activity for Guineatown-area residents, including the Montiers, serving early on for meetings, grabbing meals and spirits, and probably such activities as voting. It also served as a stagecoach stop. (Pennsylvania State Archives)

Cremona and Richard's union in early America—notwithstanding the many intricacies and challenges during a time when such relationships were illegal, socially challenging, and potentially punishable with imprisonment or vigilante deadly "justice"—led to the establishment of one of the earliest African American towns in the United States just northwest of Philadelphia in what is today Cheltenham Township's Glenside community of Edge Hill in Montgomery County, Pennsylvania—a significant portion of which was earlier known as Guineatown.[1]

Future family branches stemming from Guineatown included the NAACP's first field secretary and W. E. B. Du Bois's advisor, Dr. William Pickens Sr., during the early 20th century. And as noted earlier, there was also Anna Bustill Smith (1862–1945), a cousin of the famous black actor, singer, scholar, athlete, and diplomat Paul Robeson (1898–1976); she was an African American descendant of the early Bustills and Morreys who was acclaimed as a pioneering black genealogist focusing on her esteemed family's multiracial lines, writing about the formidable challenges and accomplishments of her family. Remember Smith provided valuable data in the *Journal of Negro History*, founded and edited by Carter G. Woodson. In fact, Smith wrote that she possessed "the Family Record of [her great-grandfather] Cyrus Bustill (still preserved)." Furthermore, Smith said that her documentation included "the birth and marriage notice of Elizabeth Morrey," Cyrus's bride and a daughter of the elder Cremona and Richard Morrey. "My Father's records (still preserved in his own writing) tells of Satterthwait her Mother and of Richard Morrey, an Englishman, her Father," Smith wrote, apparently asserting that Cremona was originally known as "Satterthwait."[2]

Meanwhile, Smith's father, Joseph Casey Bustill (1822–1895), was the son of Mary Hicks and David Bustill,[3] who had been born to Elizabeth Morrey and the formerly enslaved Burlington, New Jersey, native Cyrus Bustill (1732–1806).[4] Cyrus later owned property[5] or real estate interests[6] in Guineatown, considering his wife Elizabeth's upbringing and associations in the area before or even after the couple relocated to Philadelphia following his early 18th-century enslavement in New Jersey. In fact, an article in the January 27, 1900, edition of the *Herald* newspaper, based in Frankford, Pennsylvania, indicates that Cyrus and Elizabeth were actually "married at Edge Hill,"[7] where Cheltenham's Guineatown was located. "Franklin Haynes Jones, an Indian of intelligence, who is well informed, claims that his maternal great-grand-father, Cyrus Bustill, was an early settler"[8] in the Bustleton section of Philadelphia, a community arguably named for Cyrus, where he built one of the original dwellings, at least according to several sources.[9] Although the *Herald* article asserts that Bustleton was named for "one of its inhabitants—a bustling woman, who was an early riser," that woman may well have been Cyrus's daughter, also named Elizabeth, otherwise known as "Bustling Bess" because of her talkative effervescence.[10]

Intriguingly, while the publication says that Cyrus "was a full-blooded Indian, born in that old Indian settlement and council fire, Burlington, N.J.,"[11] most sources indicate that Cyrus was born to an enslaved African woman,[12] Parthenia, and the white "English-born" Burlington attorney,

Samuel Bustill.[13] Some sources, though, indicate that Cyrus's mother was essentially an unknown enslaved black woman. Nevertheless, although a few sources say Elizabeth and Cyrus married at Christ Church in Philadelphia, after purchasing his freedom, the *Herald* notes, "Cyrus Bustill married at Edge Hill, Sattawatwee, sister of Nattawatwee, the popular chief of the Lenni Lenape tribe (original people)."[14] Again, the assumption is that "Sattawatwee" was actually (or became known as) Elizabeth. However, despite the possibility of having indigenous kinship, indications are that Cyrus and his wife Elizabeth were also African-descended and considered themselves to be culturally black based on their various affiliations, including Cyrus helping to establish in Philadelphia the trailblazing civil rights organization the Free African Society and his involvement in pioneering black churches such as the Reverend Absalom Jones's African Episcopal Church of St. Thomas[15] and the Reverend John Gloucester's First African Presbyterian Church.[16]

In fact, Smith confirmed in a related *Journal of Negro History* article that Cyrus "married Elizabeth Morey, daughter of Satterthwait, an Indian maiden of the Delaware tribe, who lived on the banks of the nigh river bearing their name, and with whom William Penn made his famous treaty for 'Penn's Woods.'" Smith added, "She [Elizabeth Morrey] was free as himself, and both were familiar with the manners and customs of the Friends."[17]

The community that would become Guineatown and their home base seems to have had roots dating back to the start of the 18th century.[18] "Guineatown centered at the junction of Limekiln Pike and Willow Grove Avenue, and at this time probably consisted of little more than farms, a small house or two, and the Eagle Hotel, built about 1711 and described as a 'great popular house with farmers.'"[19] In fact, "as the eminent local historian Horace Mather Lippincott[20] described it, the Eagle and its counterparts were 'the first common center .... Men frequented the taverns to meet their neighbors and discuss the news and business of the day ....'"[21] This was similar to the Founding Fathers and other upper-echelon counterparts fraternizing in central Philadelphia at the City Tavern or London Coffee House, where early colonists also voted and held slave auctions.[22] Although evidence has not been uncovered indicating that such slave sales were held at the Eagle Hotel, the establishment "not only provided lodging, ... but served as a substitute for our present clubs and business exchanges."[23] One eyewitness observer, while strolling along Limekiln Pike in 1917, recalled Guineatown's interracial quaintness, including an African American church. "The old part of the village is on the pike and includes the Eagle Hotel, several stores, a fire house, with a large steel ring for an alarm, a blacksmith shop and several very ancient homes," the observant pedestrian noted. "There are two churches in the village, a negro Baptist and the Edge Hill Presbyterian."[24]

Conceivably, some of Guineatown's residents of color frequented the Eagle Hotel's tavern, quite possibly including an early African American miller and farmer residing in the area, Moses Highgate, whose daughter would marry into the Morrey-Montier family.[25]

With the name "Guineatown" probably derived from the word "Guinea," which was often used when referring to the African continent or natives of that land, other nearby communities where African-descended people lived bore similar or identical names. "The term was probably a derogatory one, but was not unique in referring to an area where African Americans" resided. "For example, Witherspoon Street in the borough of Princeton, New Jersey, where blacks lived from Revolutionary times was first called 'African Lane.'" Furthermore, "plots of land in Radnor Township in Delaware County, owned by James Miller and Caesar Waters," identified as "two blacks, were also called 'Guineatown.'"[26] The "Hamlet of New Cassel" that is today "in the heart of Long Island's Nassau County, about 20 miles from Manhattan," is among the island's oldest African American villages .... Over the years, the area had many names, including Guinea Town, after the Guinea Coast of Africa, the ancestral home of some of the early settlers."[27] Closer to home, "people formerly enslaved by the Hugg family" in the Camden County, New Jersey, vicinity "founded the community of Guinea Town in the area that later became Bellmawr in the late eighteenth century, and others founded settlements of Davistown and Hickstown in Gloucester Township [New Jersey]."[28]

Nonetheless, the community referred to as Guineatown within Edge Hill spanned throughout the western part of what is today's Cheltenham Township's Glenside neighborhood and other nearby areas that included blacks and whites:

> Guineatown was a bustling little village in its heyday, surrounded by the early industries that aided in the growth of Cheltenham Township—the limekilns of the Tysons and the Fitzwaters; the mills on Tookany Creek of the Knights and Paxons; and the farms of the area, owned and operated by the holders of names such as Bradfield, Hallowell, Harmer, Hubbs, Stout, Montier, Lewis and Meredith. In the period after the Civil War, iron foundries and rock quarries were opened, bringing "a measure of prosperity to the Edge Hill region." The village itself, at its time of largest expansion, could claim part of four townships within its borders—Cheltenham, Abington, Springfield and Upper Dublin. Among its residents were a number of African Americans, the number increasing and decreasing according to either the availability of work in the area, or the prevailing racial climate.[29]

In fact, along the banks of Tookany Creek, "there were also several gristmills and a fulling mill in Cheltenham. Other sources indicate that mill communities

THE DEVELOPMENT OF GUINEATOWN • 139

Scenes such as this one were probably characteristic of Guineatown, which was surrounded by farmland often worked by African-descended people. (Wikimedia Commons)

developed in Harmer Hill," that likely included parts of Guineatown, "near the intersection of Church Road and Limekiln Pike, as well as Milltown in what is today Cheltenham Village,"[30] one of the earlier settled communities in what is today in eastern Cheltenham Township. "And there were other milling enterprises, including C. Hammond's Tacony Edge Tool Works, which produced hammers and sledges; Rice's Mill; and … Knight's Mill, also known as Paxsons Mill."[31] Richard Wall, the township's cofounder, also operated a farm among the mills along a tributary of the Tookany. "Joined in marriage to the Shoemaker family, the Wall-Shoemaker clans owned the corn gristmill on the nearby Tacony Creek, while descendants of the Walls occupied the house until 1847, followed by the Boslers. The house [among the oldest in the township and still standing today] was added to and/or redesigned in 1730, 1760 and 1805."[32]

The genesis and legacy of Cheltenham's Guineatown was greatly intertwined with the children of Cremona Sr. and Richard Morrey (and their marital relationships), leading to the growth of associated African American families bearing the names of Fry, Montier, Bustill, Hickey, and Highgate. The mid-18th-century marriage of Elizabeth Morrey, daughter of Richard and Cremona Sr., to Cyrus Bustill was a case in point; and as mentioned earlier, a generation later, Solomon S. Montier marrying the daughter of the black miller and farmer Moses Highgate would prove to be quite consequential.[33]

THE MONTIERS

It's quite possible that residents of Guineatown passed by or even worked at such locales at the Shovel House, a manufacturer of shovels. Nearby, the African American Moses Highgate married into the Montier family and operated a mill, becoming one of the first black people to do so in the state, if not in America. (Old York Road Historical Society)

Apparently, as the years passed immediately following the American Revolution, the number of African Americans in the area dwindled, perhaps due to nearby factories curtailing production of equipment and material for the war. "The 1790 Federal Census finds the number of blacks living in the Guineatown area to be about twenty-two persons." Indeed, additional "African Americans in the Guineatown area were the two sons of Margaret Fry; Cuffee or Cuff Gardner, who headed a household of 'Free people other than Indians' numbering six, and Ralph Smothers, who headed a household of three." In other nearby communities, likely

The Shovel House still stands today in Cheltenham as one of the oldest such structures in the state. (Kristopher Scott)

with African Americans who interacted with Guineatown's black occupants occasionally, were "Thomas Clemens (or Clements), whose family lived in upper Dublin Township in succeeding census enumerations; the family of William and Elizabeth Robinson, who evidently worked for Upper Dublin resident Isaiah Hubbs … and Isaac Palmer, whose family name seems to have survived in both Cheltenham and Abington Townships down to the present day."[34]

African Americans would reside in the Guineatown and Cheltenham areas throughout the 18th and 19th centuries, some immigrating from outside of the Philadelphia region and others native to the area, including Cyrus Bustill, born in Burlington, New Jersey. Although born in 1800 in Maryland, according to the 1850 federal census, Marvina Bower, age 50, identified as "Black" and "African American," appeared to be employed in the household of the Cheltenham-based John Britton, age 30, labeled as "White." John's likely wife was 29-year-old Precilla Britton, born in 1821, also described as "White." The Brittons' children or those living within their household ranged from age one to six, likely keeping their probable black housekeeper Bower and John's wife quite busy. Curiously, living within the household was one-year-old Julia Britton, also identified as "Black" and "African American."[35] The question is, who were Julia's parents? It's not likely that the black worker, Marvina Bower, would have given birth to the one-year-old child at age 49 to 50. Did John Britton have the child with a younger black woman outside of his marriage with "Precilla"? Was the child born to one of his nearby Britton relatives who had a relationship with a black woman, and then John and Precilla decided—or were asked—to adopt Julia for one reason or another? Or, were the Brittons actually light-complexioned African Americans mistakenly labeled "White" by census takers?

Meanwhile, also living in Cheltenham, adjacent to the Brittons and perhaps not far from or within Guineatown, was the African American Hill family. Born 1819 in Pennsylvania, Harper Hill, age 31, was the apparent head of household and married presumably to Frances Hill, age 29, with both identified as "Black" and "African American," according to the 1850 federal census. Living in their home were their implied children John Hill, nine, born in 1841; Rachel Hill, seven, born 1843; Will Hill, four, born in 1846 and Thomas Hill, two, who came into the world in 1848. The presumed father, Harper Hill, worked as a "skin dresser,"[36] more than likely a tanner or currier who prepared animal skins for manufacturing or sale.

Meanwhile, several decades before the 1850 federal census, "Robert Lewis and [his brother-in-law] John and [sister] Cremona Montier stayed in the area, while the others … sold off their property at various times." Local landowners, mostly European Americans, "would profit most" from the departures and resulting property sales. "Isaiah Hubbs, a fifty-two year old merchant farmer and stonemason, was … a member of the Presbyterian Church in Abington, [who] bought ten acres of ground from Caesar Murray on July 12, 1790, and later bought the entire plots of the Bustills and the Hickeys, totaling thirty-four acres." Then there was "Abner Bradfield, a forty-five year old Bucks County Quaker," who "bought thirteen and a half acres in Guineatown from Robert Lewis on January 10, 1793," as the yellow fever epidemic raged in the Philadelphia area, forcing President George Washington to leave his "Executive House" in central Philadelphia with his cabinet and cadre of enslaved African Americans to seek refuge in nearby Germantown. "Eventually Bradfield would own fifty-eight acres in the area, including the plot he bought from Lewis and thirty-three acres purchased from Isaiah Hubbs. This transaction concerned the parcels Hubbs purchased from Caesar Murray, Andrew and Rachel Hickey and Cyrus and Elizabeth Bustill."[37]

Without doubt, Cremona (Murray or Morrey) Jr. and John Montier's children and their various bonds would be crucial to the further development of that pioneering African American community. Most would eventually move beyond the area, but some would ultimately be buried in a family cemetery with up to 75 graves adjacent to or within the Montier homestead that also served as a resting place for other community members. The graveyard, known variously as the Montier, Montieth, or Edge Hill cemetery, etc. was likely segregated and mostly reserved for the African descended, and was co-established in c. 1795–1798 by the oldest sibling of Cremona Jr., Robert Lewis.[38] Lewis's name, in fact, appears first in the 1772 "deed of trust" that settled the property dispute between Cremona Sr.'s children and the subsequent offspring of her widower husband, John Fry, with his new wife, Margaret Reiter. [39]

One of the couple's daughters would marry a son of Cremona Jr. and John Montier. "Joseph Montier, the eldest son, married his first cousin, Mary Lewis and stayed on the farm with his parents."[40] Meanwhile, "Solomon and Robert seem to have ventured to Burlington, New Jersey, where Solomon was probably apprenticed to his uncle, Caesar Murray, to learn the art of shoe and boot making,"[41] a skill that would serve him quite well in future years.

Robert, however, would pursue a more menial line of employment that ironically allowed him to pursue scholarly endeavors with a well-known Quaker family within the Philadelphia upper-class society. "Robert went to work as a servant in the house of Samuel Emlen, a wealthy Quaker merchant.[42] The Emlens were an established and influential Philadelphia family engaged in a variety of businesses," with antislavery abolitionist leanings,[43] providing an opportunity for Robert, obviously assertive and able to navigate within Eurocentric cultural environments. "A Burlington Quaker, William Allinson,[44] one of the executors of Caesar Murray's estate, was also an acquaintance of the Emlens. Robert Montier may have come to Emlen's notice through Allinson."[45]

Robert Montier impressed key members of the Emlen family. "Robert Montier was described by Susannah, Samuel Emlen's wife, herself a descendant of English Quakers,[46] as being 'remarkably intelligent, civil and obliging,'" obviously indicative of his intellectual acumen and sensitivity to various racial dynamics. "He capably performed his household duties …, 'tho' he often exercised my patience by spending much of that time in reading which I thought he ought to have employ'd in rubbing my tables and chairs,'"[47] Susannah Emlen remarked with a tone that might be interpreted by some as a sort of racial matriarchy reminiscent of plantation mistresses. Yet, "the Emlens encouraged his bookishness by giving him the run of their library." Regardless, Robert certainly had the wherewithal to cleverly dish it right back at the likes of Susannah Emlen. When he requested a particular book, likely having to do with the constellations or solar system, Susannah offered Robert "'a pamphlet in which there was an explanation intended for young persons." She described what happened next: "He looked over it and to my question if that would do, answered 'thank ye Ma'am. I am acquainted with all the Phenomena.'"[48]

Apparently, Robert was so assertive that he even proposed a business partnership with an acquaintance, who was also reportedly African American, that Samuel Emlen agreed to finance for "100 Pounds."[49] It appears, however, that Robert's chosen partner was unscrupulous and the "venture proved unsuccessful," propelling the business into bankruptcy.[50] Robert, to his credit, began to pay back Emlen his share of the debt, until it was eliminated.[51] The experience, however, did not seem to deter Robert from seeking financial independence and pursuing entrepreneurship:

> Robert Montier tried his hand at another profession, and was successful. He became a beer bottler—a novel profession for those times. In those days, beer was sold from breweries in barrels, not bottles. Proprietors of taverns and inns, as well as those who did their own brewing and distilling, had to place their brew in easily portable containers. Although there were glass works that made bottles, rare was the business that took orders from brewers or tavernkeepers to place their brew inside the bottles at the glass works.[52]

Robert clearly saw an immense opportunity and capitalized:

> Here is where Robert Montier and his associates came into the picture. Robert and his fellow bottlers took orders from his clients to bottle and cork their brew. Once used, they would be returned to the bottler to be refilled.[53]

Robert's persistence and ingenuity helped him to prosper by running his pioneering firm "in a cellar on North Front Street in Philadelphia" by bottling "beer, ale, and porter."[54] However, at not much more than 40 years old, "Robert Montier died suddenly, probably in the late summer of 1815," leaving "behind his wife, Rachel (Lewis) and ten children, the youngest aged four."[55] And regrettably, although he had operated the enterprise for almost two decades, "he was still renting the bottling cellar at the time of his death," and he "died without a will."[56] Ultimately, although it took two years or more for his cumbersome estate[57] to be valued and settled, "after his creditors had been paid, his heirs received the tidy sum of $1503.79."[58] Robert was likely buried in the Edge Hill "family burial ground,"[59] among his progenitors, which probably included Cremona Morrey and other kinfolk and Guineatown inhabitants.

Robert's siblings, in general, also chose to pursue financial independence via the trades and entrepreneurial ventures. "Hiram Montier, the youngest, about thirty-five and married to Susan (Lewis) together with their five children were living in Edge Hill (at this time still called Guineatown)," became a shoemaker, but also likely farmed. Meanwhile, Robert's mother Cremona Jr. and father John Montier, as well as "brother Joseph and his sister-in-law Mary, along with other relatives, field hands or boarders resided with them in the family home."[60] In fact, Ancestry.com's "1820 United States Federal Census" reveals that a "Hiram Mauntier" resided in his Cheltenham residence among a total of 10 individuals, including two young "Slaves".[61] However, as discussed earlier, there is a distinct possibility that Hiram harbored and eventually purchased the freedom of the two enslaved children because they may have been relatives.[62]

There are certainly indications that Hiram's household struggled during the early years of his marriage as he proverbially "tried to make ends meet." Indeed, "Hiram, although trained as a shoemaker, probably helped out on the family farm and on other farms in the area," despite "his children's names repeatedly" appearing "on the township 'Poor List'—a listing of school-age children whose parents were unable to pay the taxes that financed the township-sponsored grammar school." Consequently, "the education of these children was therefore to be underwritten by the township."[63]

However, a couple of years after the 1820 census, Hiram Montier's fortunes figuratively and literally improved. "On May 7, 1822, he bought a farm from his brothers-in-law, David and Amos Lewis, for $450, assuming the mortgage on it." Situated "across Limekiln Pike from his birthplace," the land that Hiram acquired totaled "seventeen acres," in addition to "the seven acres he had received from his brother Joseph in 1825," giving "him a total of twenty-four acres. After Joseph's death, Hiram" would relocate to nearby "Germantown, where others of his family were living."[64]

In 1850, when Congress passed the notorious Fugitive Slave Act[65] that threatened the liberty of even the free blacks living in Guineatown while inevitably leading to the Civil War's armed conflict, Hiram's industrious daughter, Jane, "purchased a building lot on Centre Street in Germantown; four years later, she sold it to her brother, Charles, after having erected a two-story house on it." The structure, in the 300 block of East Rittenhouse Street, "would be the Montier home for over one hundred years" before it was "demolished in 1960."[66]

As Cremona Jr. and John Montier aged in Guineatown, "Joseph Montier, the eldest son … seems to have handled most of the duties around the farm. He paid the yearly taxes, reporting in sometimes with his father or brother, Hiram," as well as on occasion "with his brother-in-law, David Lewis."[67] And as another indication of the Montier family members' thirst for upward mobility, "on August 5, 1807, Joseph bought a small lot off Limekiln Pike 'near the schoolhouse' from the two sons of the late George Leonhart, Sr."[68] Yet, he wasn't finished with such purchases: On April 1, 1812, the year America waged war again against the British with African Americans serving both sides in hope of achieving freedom and equal rights,[69] Joseph "bought an adjoining parcel from neighboring farmer, Isaac Bradfield," totaling five acres, on which he built a home.[70]

Joseph's brother, Solomon M. Montier, was also quite hardworking but prolifically roamed the region to work and live with his growing family in various locales, unafraid to test the proverbial "new waters." Upon completing his shoemaking apprenticeship in New Jersey, Solomon "returned to Guineatown as a shoemaker and cordwainer, and then married Elizabeth Lewis."[71] The couple had "at least" a half-dozen children, embarking "on an odyssey that lasted about thirty-five years" and took them to various locales within the region.

As early as 1802, Solomon lived on Crown Street, not far from Philadelphia's central district and the Delaware River. However, by 1810, according to the federal census that year, he resided with his family of five in what is today South Philadelphia near "7th and South Streets,"[72] specifically in the historic Moyamensing community. "About five or six years later, Solomon moved his family back to the Guineatown area, and settled with a large group of blacks on the Upper Dublin side of Edge Hill."[73] Those African Americans, increasing from just 28 in 1819 to 58 in 1820, may have been pursuing work "due to the opening of an iron ore mine or the operation of a forge."[74] In fact, as the 19th century progressed, the area "became a center for ore smelting," specifically by the Edge Hill Furnace Company. And apparently it was quite an operation, run by Joseph E. Thropp, "a native of Valley Forge," who subsequently was "urged to run for Congress, but declined" to do so. "Large hot-blast stoves and furnaces were built in 1869, one stack measuring sixteen by sixty-four feet. The annual capacity of this company was 18,000 tons."[75]

Solomon may have found employment at the forge, perhaps while working as a shoemaker or repairer, in addition to returning to farming. "Along with Thomas Clements, whose family were long-time residents of Upper Dublin, Solomon Montier was enumerated with his wife and six children; also his nephew, William Lewis and cousin Peter Knight and Richard Harding."[76]

Interestingly, as an older couple, it's quite possible that Cremona Jr. and her husband, John Montier, may have even resided with their son Solomon, as he practiced his shoe business trade, while the family undoubtedly dealt with issues ranging from social, political, and employment challenges to such seemingly mundane affairs as taxes on the family dog:

> Solomon Montier probably made shoes and boots for the small colony; his parents may have lived with him and his family. In the 1818 Upper Dublin tax list, John Montier appears, paying a "dog tax" on one dog, breed not given. Four years later, in 1822, "Sollom Mounteer paid a tax for one dog, possibly the same one his father had paid for. In 1827 Solomon's name is listed, but a line is drawn through it; possibly, the dog died or ran away."[77]

Sadly, as their land holdings dwindled to about 20 acres due to various property and acreage sales, Cremona Jr. and John Montier would not survive beyond the 1820s, with John succumbing in 1822 and "Cremona on July 31, 1825,[78] at the age of eighty."[79] Apparently, they "both died intestate."[80] Their son Joseph, however, skillfully handled estate matters.[81] "He very adequately dealt with the Montgomery County Orphans Court in Norristown, becoming administrator of his mother's estate, according to courthouse records."[82]

As a coheir of the estate, Joseph's brother Solomon was able to pursue and establish his shoe enterprise after relocating with his family to Philadelphia.[83] Solomon's four sons included Joseph (2nd), Richard, William, and Hiram, all trained to be shoemakers by their father.[84] Hiram, the elder Joseph's nephew who would be depicted in one of the celebrated dual 1841 portraits painted by artist Franklin R. Street, the other painting featuring his new bride, Elizabeth Brown, was the ancestor of the William Pickens Sr. line of the Montiers.[85]

The elder Joseph's death in 1842[86] would come about a year after his nephew, Hiram Montier, and Hiram's new wife, Elizabeth Brown Montier, sat probably at Street's studio for the portraits that were found under the bed of Solomon's son, the younger Joseph, as he grew older in Philadelphia during the mid-1900s.[87] "Joseph [the elder] and Mary Montier continued to live on the family farm in Edge Hill until Joseph's death in late 1842. In his will, written in October 1841, and filed for probate in January of 1843, Joseph made his nephew Solomon S. Montier—his late brother Hiram's eldest son—his residuary legatee, leaving him the family home and farm and most of his money."[88] He also made other notable provisions for his wife Mary and other loved ones, as well as named his nephews as executors:

> I give and bequeath unto my dear wife Mary Montier one bed together with such of my household furniture and kitchen utensils as she may choose to keep for her own use during her widowhood ... [and] the use and occupation of one room on the second floor West corner with the [privilege] thereto and from at all times during her natural life without any hindrance or molestation whatever, and my said wife may have as much fruit growing on my said lot as she may require for her own house use and part of the garden next to the limekiln road for her own use, and I further give and bequeath to my wife the just and full some of thirty dollars to be paid to her annually out of my real estate by my executors hereinafter named.[89]

The will further stipulated that Joseph's "brother Solomon Montier" receive "the sum of Thirty Dollars [or] to his heirs and assigns," as well as other funds and property to be distributed to various kinfolk. "And Lastly I nominate constitute and appoint my two nephews Solomon Montier & Hiram Montier Jr. of Philadelphia to be the executors of this my last will and Testament."[90]

Joseph Montier's nephew, Solomon S. Montier[91] (born in 1802), who was the eldest son of his brother Hiram, would marry "Susanna G. Highgate, daughter of [the pioneering African American] miller Moses Highgate." Solomon, describing "himself variously as a farmer, cook, painter ... and laborer," would live "at the Highgate family homestead for almost twenty years." The family would eventually move to the 500 block of South Sixth Street in nearby Philadelphia where they lived, likely through the Civil War (1861–1865), until "about 1867."[92]

Remarkably, Moses Highgate carved out a very unique niche in the Guineatown vicinity as probably one of few black mill operators in the state and, perhaps in the country, who owned land that he also farmed for a substantial period.[93] It's virtually certain that he was the only such mill operator (or owner) in Cheltenham.[94] Highgate was "a prime example of an African American who became successful with the help of local whites since he apparently bought land and a mill from and with the assistance of neighboring Quakers in 1813."[95]

So, what was the origin of the remarkable Moses Highgate, who obviously was quite a go-getter and trailblazer? "Highgate is first observed 'by name in [the] written record' in the 1798 tax list,'" and may have had "family roots extending to a 'High Gate' plantation in Gloucester County, Virginia ... with several relatives or siblings making their ways northward," among them Moses Highgate. Given the time and the family's possible Virginia origins, it's conceivable that they escaped slavery[96] there, where it was practiced widely by the likes of such Founding Fathers as presidents George Washington and Thomas Jefferson. Perhaps they fled with the assistance of Underground Railroad operators, likely with connections to Philadelphia's comparatively large free African American community and antislavery Quakers, including those living in the Cheltenham–Abington area like Benjamin Lay, a forerunner of such future abolitionist residents as Lucretia Mott and her son-in-law, Edward M. Davis.[97]

It appears, after initially settling in Delaware County's Tinicum Township, Highgate married Mary Dill, who may have been somehow related to an African American head-of-household named Thomas Dill, living in nearby Abington Township, according to the 1810 federal census.[98] The couple may have been the parents of at least a half-dozen children, born between 1785 and 1807. One of those children, Susanna G. Highgate, born 1806, "clearly had connections to Cheltenham's Guineatown because she married Solomon S. Montier, the ancestor of the New York-based William Pickens III, whose grandfather, William Pickens Sr., cofounded in 1909 the NAACP with scholar W. E. B. Du Bois."[99] The couple resided on the Highgate property that was situated along Limekiln Pike to the west, with the estate's "northern boundary" separated from Abington Township "by the present Township Line Road to the north; Jenkintown Road to the west, and Church Road to the south and east." The Highgates' property "was part of the 300 acres that Everard Bolton of Ross, Herefordshire, England received from William Penn on 10 September 1683."[100]

Susanna and her likely siblings appear to have been raised quite well by Moses and his wife Mary, as indicated by their industrious endeavors as free African Americans during a period when most African Americans faced monumental challenges. Their son "Amos Highgate, born in the middle or late 1780s," found work "on farms" throughout the Philadelphia metropolitan area and the surrounding counties. "He married Mary Miller, daughter of James and India Miller of Delaware County's Guineatown, located in Radnor Township."[101] By 1820,[102] "Amos and Mary (Miller) Highgate[103] were living in Willistown Township in northern Chester County" before a decade later moving to Radnor Township.[104] The couple, meanwhile, had generally passed their fervor for industriousness to their children with some becoming property owners themselves:

> Most of the sons stayed in Marple and Newtown townships, working on farms. Two of the older sons, Charles and George W. Highgate, broke that pattern to some extent. Charles, a barber, worked in hotels and other vacation spots in Pennsylvania, New York, and New Jersey, before settling in Syracuse, New York. George worked on farms in Pennsylvania and New York state until he saved enough money to own his own farm near Newtown Square.[105]

Born in 1790 when the first official census of the United States was taken, London Highgate "worked on farms in northern Chester County for about forty years."[106] London and his wife "Catherine (Fuller?)," had "several sons and at least one daughter."[107] London's brother, Thomas D. Highgate, probably "born between 1794 and 1806,"[108] owned and operated a barbershop at "11th and Market streets" in what is today Philadelphia's center-city shopping district. "He was at this location until early 1850"[109] when Congress passed the notorious Fugitive Slave Act.[110]

Meanwhile, "Mary Highgate, born in the early years of the nineteenth century, was married to John Mullen, by whom she had at least three children—Caroline, John R., and 'Mauris' (Morris) V. After living at the mill with Moses Highgate, the Mullens moved to Germantown in Philadelphia County."[111] Susanna's brother, William Highgate, born during the first decade of the 1800s, "opened a grocery [store] on Barley Street (now the 900 block of Waverly Place, between Pine and Spruce streets)." Although William had no children with his wife Mary Hill, he "owned large parcels of real estate in Philadelphia, and his wife was adept in managing them," outliving "him[112] almost forty years."[113] In fact, "the 1880 Federal Census listing for his wife [Mary A. Highgate][114] states that the value of her real estate holdings was thirty-five thousand dollars,"[115] worth more than $1 million today in purchasing power, according to MeasuringWorth.com[116] and other sources.

Meanwhile, until 1860,[117] when the nation began to erupt into the Civil War, Susanna and her husband, Solomon S. Montier, lived on the property that her father, Moses Highgate, had originally bought and operated a mill on for three decades. Moses "seems to have made a comfortable living for himself and his family."[118] However, upon reaching age 70, a remarkable lifespan accomplishment for an African American during the first part of the 19th century, "he appears to have become beset by financial troubles" because on April 13, 1827,[119] he "mortgaged his mill to one David Rorer of Abington. Almost seven years later, Highgate's money problems,"[120] possibly due to Rorer "wanting to call in the mortgage," escalated to the point "that he

[Moses Highgate] was in danger of losing his mill." Still, due to the kindness of a neighbor, Moses had a slight chance of saving his property: "Although a local Quaker widow, Jane Thomson, helped Highgate with finances because she had 'probably known Highgate for most of her life,' that was not enough. 'Moses Highgate lost the mill and the three lots adjacent to it' in 1835 ... but was able to hold on to his house and 'three-quarters of an acre of land, with a horse, a cow, and a dog.'"[121]

Moreover, on January 22, 1835, the "High Sheriff of Montgomery County," John Todd, sold "'a certain grist mill and three tracts of land situate in Cheltenham Township' to Jane Thomson for $2,600,'"[122] essentially because Moses Highgate had defaulted on the property. Consequently, although Highgate had to relinquish the mill and much of the land, "he was able to hold on to the little house he had bought from Dan Hallowell's son, Robert." His "daughter and son-in-law (Mary and John Mullen), their children, and other assorted relatives, friends, hired help, and hangers-on," would also reside with the elder Highgates at various points.[123]

Ultimately, "on October 1, 1837, 'Mrs. Thomson sold the mill to [Jehu Jones Roberts] for $2,600. He worked the mill for about thirty years, eventually selling out to the Roland family,'"[124] despite some of the younger-generation Highgates being able to stay on the property until at least 1860.[125] "Moses Highgate and his family resided in the house near Church Road for a few more years. However, on December 18, 1841, Moses and wife Mary sold the home to their son William for just ten dollars, likely as collateral for a grocery store the son operated and owned." And "less than a year later on July 25, 1842, Moses Highgate died[126] at age seventy-eight from a short but severe illness."[127] He was buried in the Abington Friends Cemetery,[128] an indication that Moses had been following the doctrines of Quakerism, likely sometimes attending the Abington Meeting.

After the property was sold again in 1860, Solomon and Susanna (or Susannah) moved to central Philadelphia in the 500 block of South Sixth Street.[129] Over the years, they "had one son, Sylvester B. Montier, and five daughters."[130] The couple's oldest, Mary Elizabeth, "married New Jersey-born Edward E. Irvin (Erwin), by whom she had a son and two daughters."[131] In fact, born specifically in Edge Hill or Guineatown in 1849 according to her May 3, 1909, death certificate, 60-year-old Mary Elizabeth Irvin was buried in the family and community cemetery along Limekiln Pike a few days later on May 6, 1909. Mary Elizabeth was identified as "Widowed," as well as a "Housekeeper" and "Colored." Her parents were identified as "Solomon Montier" and "Susan Highgate," and her cause of death was listed as "uremia," probably due to kidney disease or failure. During much of her adult years, Irvin had resided in the 100 block of West Duval Street in Philadelphia's historic Germantown community. Funeral services were performed by "Kirk and Nice" company,[132] founded in 1761,[133] likely an indication of Mary Elizabeth Irvin's affluence; the firm, regaled "as the first funeral home in the United States,"[134] in fact was responsible for the burials of more than a few of the Montiers and their descendants at the family graveyard.

Following Mary in age was Anna Matilda, who "married George R. Hilton, by whom she had three children. Both families lived near each other in Germantown."[135] Mary's other siblings, Caroline and Clarissa or Clara, "were dressmakers and seamstresses. Amanda Susanna, although as proficient a seamstress as her sisters, was among one of the first Afro-American schoolteachers in the Philadelphia school system."[136]

Amanda's teaching profession was emblematic of the Montiers, Bustills, and their progeny's insatiable thirst for racial progress and knowledge, but, more importantly, of their commitment to reaching back to uplift their often-castigated African American brethren. As one of their descendants, the great scholar and activist Paul Leroy Robeson, would one day exalt about the goals and dreams of his people: "To be free … to walk the good American earth as equal citizens, to live without fear, to enjoy the fruits of our toil, to give our children every opportunity in life—that dream which we have held so long in our hearts is today the destiny that we hold in our hands."[137]

CHAPTER 9

Hiram and Elizabeth Brown Montier and the Family Dynasties that Followed

Surviving "Through Sunny and Stormy Weather"

The portraits of Hiram and Elizabeth Montier were painted by local artist Franklin R. Street. (William Pickens III Archives)

In 1841, a young married couple sat for their portraits. This might be considered unremarkable; however an African American couple with apparent wealth and affluence engaging the services of a European American artist was certainly an enigma—and exceptional, to say the least—in 1840s Philadelphia. Indeed, "slavery was still partially legal in the state of Pennsylvania"[1] as antislavery abolitionists organized and protested with unparalleled fervor.[2] As Hiram Charles Montier "and his bride, Elizabeth Brown," sat for their portraits, likely in the studio of the English-descended artist Franklin R. Street,[3] racial conditions in the city were in upheaval amid years of brutal riotous attacks on the city's blacks by primarily Irish residents.[4]

"When the Montiers presented themselves to the little-known painter Franklin R. Street to have their portraits made," writes the University of Pennsylvania art professor, curator, and historian Gwendolyn DuBois Shaw, "they were barely of age …: Hiram was twenty-three and Elizabeth was twenty-one. And yet, they both look far more mature and erudite than their youth would imply." The portraits were displayed at the Philadelphia Museum of Art in recent years,[5] via the arrangements of the late descendant William Pickens III[6] before he passed away in 2021.[7] "Each is posed in front of a column, perhaps to suggest strength or stalwartness; a sunrise behind him and a stormy vista behind her may signify the wish for a solid relationship through sunny and stormy weather."[8]

Philadelphia remained a destination for runaway slaves, with escapes often coordinated by the likes of the highly esteemed African American William Still, known as "the Father of the Underground Railroad," and the white Quaker, Lucretia Mott, who would later make her home in Cheltenham, not far from Guineatown. The brief *Philadelphia Ledger* article "A SLAVE SECRETED," appearing in mid-1841 (about the time the Montiers were painted) describes how "a slave was found secreted on board the schooner Marmion as she was leaving New Orleans on the 7th inst. for Philadelphia, and on his person were found pistols, a bowie knife, and $3000 in gold." Obviously this runaway was apprehended before reaching the so-called "Promised Land" of Philadelphia and beyond. "The capturer returned and delivered the slave and money to his master. A Mr. John Lewis has been arrested as the person who secreted him."[9]

In fact, the most well-known and influential antislavery activist of the 19th century, Frederick Douglass, escaped slavery from Maryland's Eastern Shore on September 3, 1838, masquerading as a black sailor or seaman, "traveling north by train and boat—from Baltimore, through Delaware, to Philadelphia."[10] A decade later, in mid-September 1849, the Underground Railroad (UGRR) icon Harriet Tubman also fled the Eastern Shore's slavery via Philadelphia,[11] and like Douglass, conceivably with the direct or indirect help of such UGRR super-operatives as Still and Mott, who relocated from Philadelphia to the Chelten Hills section of Cheltenham in the late 1850s.[12] Douglass would ultimately visit and speak in Chelten Hills during the Civil War to some of America's first black federal soldiers in July 1863 at Camp William Penn, a 13-acre complex (less than three miles from Guineatown) training the largest number of African American troops—about 10,500[13]—including Morrey-Montier descendants. Another of the families' progeny, David Bustill

Patterned after an original photograph, this Camp William Penn recruiting lithograph (poster) was used to recruit African American soldiers throughout the Philadelphia metropolitan area and likely beyond. (Library of Congress)

Bowser, designed and made the regimental flags for most of the 11 regiments originating at the historic facility.[14] Meanwhile, Harriet Tubman would speak at Camp William in April 1865,[15] as well as later marry a soldier from the facility's 8th United States Colored Troops regiment, Nelson Davis, her second husband.[16] Many of the soldiers at Camp William Penn had escaped slavery, some conceivably with the help of Bowser, Tubman, and Still, who operated a store or sutler's post on the grounds of the fort.[17]

As the 1830s commenced, tensions were soon to reach a climax "because of the rise of the national abolition movement, the [financial] Panic of 1837, and the Pennsylvania State Constitution of 1838, which rescinded the free Black vote,"[18] infuriating abolitionists that probably included the Montiers. Meanwhile, racist whites were temporarily satiated concerning the curtailment of African Americans' suffrage or voting because they feared black empowerment and believed the growing numbers of African Americans were taking their jobs, as well as threatening to infringe on nearby white neighborhoods.[19] "Abolitionists within the city, not deterred, constructed a meeting hall known as Pennsylvania Hall on Sixth Street near Franklin Square," that upon completion, "after only four days of operation" was "burned to the ground" by a racist mob "as firemen refused to fight the fire and instead focused on protecting neighboring structures,"[20] events that some of the Montiers may have witnessed or directly heard about from fellow abolitionists.

As African Americans whose ancestors were enslaved, the Montiers likely harbored strong antislavery sentiments, notwithstanding Hiram's father, John Montier, reportedly leaving the island of Saint-Domingue, specifically the northern sector later known as Haiti, before or during the Haitian Revolution (1789–1804) as perhaps a member of the *gens de couleur* or free blacks of mixed African and European ancestry.[21] The *gens de couleur* consisted of some individuals who may have been dedicated to combatting French colonialism and enslavement, while others were clearly part of the slaveholding establishment or supported it to various degrees.[22] The timing of John Montier's supposed departure from what would become the Republic of Haiti during the early 1800s is challenging to confirm since he was said to have married Hiram's mother, Cremona Jr., in America earlier, probably between 1765 and 1772.[23] During or before that approximate 1765–1772 period, John Montier may have departed Saint-Domingue, renamed the indigenous Arawak people's word Hayti (Ay-ti) or "land of mountains"[24] by the victorious revolutionary African-descended ex-slaves determined to get rid of that Eurocentric "Saint-Domingue" label.[25] In fact, it's possible that Montier departed the island for America around 1760, when a Jamaican slave rebellion known as "Tacky's War" occurred, prompting proslavery forces on various Caribbean islands (including Haiti) to establish draconian laws negatively impacting free "people of color" and especially the enslaved black masses.[26]

Nevertheless, Street's striking 1841 images of Hiram Charles Montier and his wife Elizabeth Brown, considering artistic reviews and expert critiques, are rare examples of middle-to-upper-class African Americans being depicted in such elaborate artwork, in this case probably supported by Hiram Montier's shoe- or boot-making enterprise. "While the artist's skills were limited," notes Gwendolyn DuBois Shaw, "particularly when it came to painting the lower halves of his sitters' bodies, he was highly accomplished at rendering their distinct facial features, hair, and skin color; Hiram's aquiline nose contrasting with Elizabeth's more rounded one; her long wavy hair curled into four vines that cascade down her shoulders and his substantial sideburns; her eyes a little darker, his skin slightly lighter."[27] Furthermore, "Street also suggested Hiram's literacy through the inclusion of several books, and Elizabeth's Catholic piety is on view in the form of the golden cross and looped chain at her neck."[28]

Indeed, how did the couple feel about being painted in such privileged environs during a period when many African Americans faced atrocious violence and too often very poor living conditions? And to what degree did their fair-skin color play in relationships with fellow African Americans of darker hues, today, referred to as colorism, as well as with whites such as the artist Franklin Street? Were they consciously or subliminally making dual statements about how such challenging social circumstances could be overcome by allowing a white painter to service them? "Whether it was the artist who suggested that his clients be shown against opulent drapery and classical columns is unknown, but what is readily apparent from the portraits is the couple's satisfaction with being represented as both literate and stylish. The elaborate presentation of Hiram Montier and his bride indicates the commensurate wealth and privilege from which they originated."[29]

Before or by 1850, according to the federal census that year, "the Montiers" were "living near Market Street in what is now called Old City, Philadelphia," slightly north of where most African Americans eked out tough lives during the mid to late 19th century in what is today South Philadelphia encompassing major parts of the 7th Ward where the preeminent black scholar W. E. B. Du Bois researched and wrote his 1899 landmark book *The Philadelphia Negro*.[30] "The whole division into 'poor,' 'comfortable' and 'well-to-do' depends primarily on the standard of living among a people,"[31] Du Bois wrote several decades after Hiram and Elizabeth's family lived in nearby "Old City."

Du Bois further observed: "The very poor," constituting a significant number of blacks, "live in one and two-room tenements, scantily furnished and poorly lighted and heated; they get casual labor, and the women do washing. The children go to school irregularly or loaf on the streets."[32] One underprivileged family, Du Bois noted, resided "in one filthy room, twelve feet by fourteen, scantily furnished and poorly ventilated. The woman works at service and receives about three dollars a week."[33]

In fact, according to Theodore Hershberg in his essay "Free Blacks in Antebellum Philadelphia: A Study of Ex-Slaves, Freeborn, and Socioeconomic Decline," "the antebellum black community was extremely poor,"[34] including about the time that the Montiers' portraits were painted. "The total wealth—that is, the combined value of real and personal property holdings—for three out of every five households in both 1838 and 1847 amounted to $60 or less." Indeed, "there was, in other words, despite a considerable increase in the number of households, both absolute and percentage decrease in the number of real property holders."[35]

Still, according to Du Bois, by the late 1800s, a notable number of African Americans—"47 percent of the population"—hailed from "the great hard-working laboring class" and "live in houses with three to six rooms, nearly always well furnished; they spend considerable for food and dress, and for churches and beneficial societies."[36] However, Hershberg notes: "Between 1838 and 1847 there was a 10 percent decrease in per capita value of personal property, and a slight decrease in per capita total wealth among Philadelphia blacks."[37] Plus, "Blacks were not only denied access to new jobs in the expanding factory [sector], but because of increasing job competition with the Irish they also lost their traditional predominance in many semiskilled and unskilled jobs," Hershberg continues. "The 1847 census identified 5 percent of the black male work force in the relatively well-paying occupations of hod carrier and stevedore."[38]

Meanwhile, an apparently "upper class" black family with "three adults and two children," representing a comparatively small number of African Americans, "keep one servant" and "are the aristocracy of their own people, with all the responsibilities of an aristocracy."[39] However, they were more prone to face isolation from black and white communities, as well as increased economic challenges compared to whites with equivalent or similar incomes.[40] An estimation of Hiram and Elizabeth Brown Montier's class status, when they had their portraits painted in 1841, probably falls within the realm of upper working class, bordering on "upper class." In fact, just "one household in thirteen, or slightly less than 8 percent, among the freeborn owned real property,"[41] as several of the Montier families did during the time. "The poorest half of the freeborn and ex-slave-headed households owned 5 percent and 7 percent respectively of the total wealth; for the wealthiest one-quarter of each group the corresponding figure was 86 and 73 percent; for the wealthiest one-tenth, 76 and 56 percent."[42] That last category likely included some of the Montiers.

Although it's difficult to ascertain exactly how the Montiers and the artist Franklin R. Street became acquainted, a range of online genealogical sources indicate that Street was born in 1816, an exceptionally frigid year in Philadelphia and around the world. Incredibly, that year the global weather was in general exceedingly cold due to a hellacious volcanic eruption on the other side of the world during the prior year. "In April of 1815, the eruption of the volcano Mount Tambora rocked modern-day Indonesia. The blast, nearly one hundred times as large as that of Mount St. Helens in 1980, sent a massive cloud of miniscule particles into the atmosphere ... causing a meteorological phenomenon to which we now refer as the 'year without a summer.'"[43] In the Philadelphia area, where Street came into the world, during "a special meeting of 'The Philadelphia Society for promoting agriculture,' held October (10th mo.) 30th, 1816, it was resolved unanimously, that the Curators ... will procure and give information … which have occurred through the extraordinary season of 1816, and particularly the effects of frost on vegetation.'"[44]

Franklin was born to Thomas Street (1787–1857), who seems to have worked as a bootmaker or repairer[45] and "huckster,"[46] and then a blacksmith, and probable housekeeping mother Deborah Royal (1797–1866), according to FamilySearch.org.[47] In fact, Franklin likely had quite a challenging first year in 1816 during a time when infant mortality was rather concerning, especially through such periods of extreme weather that threatened crops and food security. "In Philadelphia, 'cold and fear' were spoken of as being pervasive by late September [1816]. In most instances people seem to know what they were afraid of: failing crops, animal die-offs or other specific results that could threaten economic well-being,"[48] and even their children's lives. "The child mortality rate in the United States, for children under the age of five, was 462.9 deaths per thousand births in 1800. This means that for every thousand babies born in 1800, over 46 percent did not make it to their fifth birthday."[49] Tragically, in Philadelphia, more than a few child deaths were certainly recorded that frigid year in 1816. William George Klett did not survive for a year after he was born to unidentified parents, succumbing on July 20, 1816 with his age tragically noted as "0"; he was buried in the "Moravian burial ground," likely near Franklin and Vine streets in Philadelphia.[50] A baby who died on February 29, 1816, simply identified as "Bishop," was born in 1815 to James Bishop, acknowledged as the father. The child's mother was not identified. "Bishop" was buried at the "Free Quakers burial ground," near Fifth and Spruce streets in Philadelphia, at the mere age of 1.[51] William Mcmutry, born in 1813 to unknown parents, however, did make it to age 3. He died in November 1816, then was buried at the "Christ Church burial ground," in the 300 block of North Fifth Street in Old City Philadelphia—a cemetery where Benjamin Franklin and other members of Philadelphia's so-called colonial elite were interred.[52]

Although *Jacobsen's Biographical Index of American Artists* does not specifically identify an institution where Franklin Street studied art, it briefly lists his name and birth year of 1816, as well as that he was a "Painter"; further, his hometown of "Phila., PA," as well as the year 1850 and surname or description "Young" also appear following the words "Professional Accomplishments," indicating his residential location, and the 1850 census year he reported working as an artist, probably associated with someone (perhaps a tutor or teacher) bearing the "Young" surname.[53] Meanwhile, *Who Was Who in American Art* describes Street as an "artist" living in Philadelphia, according to the 1850 United States census.[54]

It's possible that Street did receive unofficial training at the Philadelphia Academy of the Fine Arts—or perhaps privately via someone associated with such a recognized art school. There's also a distinct possibility that he was self-taught and/or studied at the academy as an unenrolled student. Essentially founded by the great American artist Charles Willson Peale, "the Academy opened its doors to students [in 1810], offering a fairly typical American art education, largely focusing on charcoal drawings of plaster casts, but by 1812, the board established a Life Academy which introduced human models to the curriculum."[55] One of Franklin Street's contemporaries was the acclaimed portrait artist Thomas Sully (1783–1872), a prominent teacher at the academy,[56] who may have indirectly or directly influenced Street. In fact, about five years before Street was born in 1816, "Sully taught his first painting lessons" locally.[57] Sully was recognized for "painting the crossing of [George] Washington and his troops across the Delaware River (1818), being elected as the [academy's] president" (and reportedly turning down the position), and painting portraits of England's Queen Victoria during the late 1830s,[58] just a few years before Street would finish the Montiers' portraits in 1841. Even if Street had no obvious association with Sully, it is virtually certain that he knew about the famous artist's work and vast reputation.

Franklin Street apparently married Jane Simler, born 1818, also in Philadelphia, on September 25, 1836—just several years before painting the Montiers—at the Old St. George Methodist Episcopal Church.[59] The church has been hailed as "the oldest house of Methodist worship in continuous use in America," its history dating back to 1767, when "Captain Thomas Webb, a veteran of the French and Indian War, organized a Methodist Society in Philadelphia. Two years later, the Society bought St. George's Church," which had been "a Dutch Reformed Church, but was auctioned when the church was unable to borrow enough money to complete the structure."[60] Although St. George did have African American members, two of the most prominent blacks, Absalom Jones and Richard Allen, as well as other African-descended parishioners, departed St. George to start their own congregations, upset with St. George's segregationist policies. Jones and Allen "became the first African Americans granted preaching licenses by the Methodist Episcopal Church" in 1784. "Three years later, protesting racial discrimination, Allen led most of the black members out of St. George's."[61] As revealed earlier, Allen soon founded the Mother Bethel African Methodist Episcopal Church, and Jones started the African Episcopal Church of St. Thomas,[62] denominations that generations of the Montiers or descendants would join. Perhaps Street and the Montiers became acquainted with each other via their associated churches or by way of a referral from one of their fellow parishioners?

Another intriguing question to consider is why Hiram and Elizabeth Montier didn't engage the services of one of the city's African-descended artists, a few of their own relatives among them. One such acclaimed Philadelphia artist was Hiram's cousin, Robert Douglass Jr., the son of Grace Bustill Douglass. Robert "studied portrait painting at the Pennsylvania Academy of Fine Arts with Thomas Sully, the renowned painting artist of the time."[63] And as earlier revealed, Grace's father, the respected black activist and educator Cyrus Bustill, had married Robert's mother, Elizabeth Morrey, who was a daughter of Richard Morrey and the elder Cremona or "Mooney."[64] Grace "was an abolitionist, whose influence was felt in the political and artistic work of her daughter Sarah Mapps Douglas[s]."[65] Robert Douglas[s] Jr's two siblings Sarah Mapps Douglass (older sister), and William Penn Douglas[s] (his younger brother) were artists, and activists who also followed the family antislavery activism tradition."[66] However, it seems that Robert Douglass Jr., as an artist, was particularly qualified and well known, despite dealing with some of Philadelphia's well-documented racism:

> Though his first work was an oil painting of the Pennsylvania State seal, he rose into public prominence with his transparencies of *President George Washington Crossing the Delaware*. This artwork was displayed on Independence Hall to celebrate the centennial of Washington's birth on February 22, 1832. Douglass experienced discrimination at art exhibitions in Philadelphia where racism against African Americans was commonplace and whites considered it normal. For instance, in 1834, Douglass' oil painting *Portrait of a Gentleman* was included in the annual exhibition of the Pennsylvania Academy of the Fine Arts. However, he was prevented from getting into the Academy to view his own work because of his race.[67]

Franklin R. Street died on May 10, 1882, at age 66 and was buried at Odd Fellows Cemetery, once located in what today is North Philadelphia near Twenty-Fifth and Diamond streets, before being reinterred in an unmarked grave on September 5, 1951, at the Lawnview Memorial Park Cemetery in Rockledge, Pennsylvania,[68] just north of Philadelphia. According to his death certificate, Franklin succumbed to "Paralysis," possibly due to a stroke or major cardiovascular event. His occupation was listed as "Painter," and he had been living in the 1400 block of Lingo Street in Philadelphia. The undertaker was identified as Samuel R. Foster of the 1700 block of Federal Street in Philadelphia.[69]

Although Franklin's father, Thomas, died in 1857[70] and was also ultimately buried at Lawnview,[71] Franklin's mother, Deborah (Royal) Street, according to

The painter of the Elizabeth and Hiram Montier portraits, Franklin R. Street, rests with many family members at the Lawnview Cemetery in what is today the Jenkintown–Rockledge area. (Kristopher Scott)

the Philadelphia City Directory of 1861, was listed as Thomas's "widow," then living in the 400 block of North Seventh Street in Philadelphia as the Civil War erupted. Interestingly, listed in a separate entry below her in the directory was "Franklin Street," almost certainly her son.[72] Deborah died on August 13, 1866, and was ultimately also buried at Lawnview Memorial Park. She probably is resting near her husband, who, as of 2023, remained in an unmarked grave, like her painter son, Franklin. Several of Franklin's siblings are also buried at Lawnview, including Maria Deborah Street, William Street, Mary Ann Street, Margaret J. Street, and Jane Francis Toomey.[73] Franklin's mother, Deborah Street, died at age 71 and at the time of her death was affiliated with the Second Baptist Church of Philadelphia.[74] Franklin and Jane Street's son, Francis Street (who was born August 15, 1854, in New York), apparently became an artist or "Painter" like his father Franklin, according to Francis's death certificate, which reveals that he died on February 2, 1912, at age 57 of "endocarditis" complicated by "chronic interstitial nephritis" or essentially kidney disease. Francis's birth in New York suggests that Franklin and Jane's young family lived there for a period after he painted the Montiers' 1841 portraits before relocating back to Philadelphia. When he died at Samaritan Hospital, Francis, as a single white male, had been living in the 1600 block of Ellsworth Street in Philadelphia's Ward 26 before being buried at the Fernwood Cemetery on February 6, 1912.[75]

Francis's mother, Jane (neé Simler) Street, died in 1894 at about age 78, surviving her husband Franklin by more than a decade.[76] The 1886 Philadelphia directory indicates that she was a widow of "Frank [Street]," living in the 1000 block of South Eighteenth Street in the city.[77] After initially being buried at the Odd Fellows Cemetery in Philadelphia, Jane was reinterred like her husband on September 5, 1951, at Lawnview Cemetery in Rockledge, Pennsylvania.[78] Jane had been residing in the 1800 block of Reed Street in what is today South Philadelphia at the time of her passing in 1894.[79]

Jane and Franklin R. Street, despite the major challenges of living in 19th-century America that included the horrific American Civil War (1861–1865), seem to have persevered, as did Franklin's African American portraiture patrons, Elizabeth and Hiram Montier—and so did their other associated family lines,[80] such as the Bustills, Highgates, Robesons, Pickenses, and others. Indeed, some fought in that bloody "War between the States."

Solomon Montier, born between 1842 and 1845 (depending on the source), initially enlisted as a landsman on the USS *Princeton* on November 28, 1863.[81] Solomon, the son of Margaret and William Montier,[82] whose parents were Solomon Montier and Susannah Highgate,[83] served until December 1, 1863, before moving on to the ship *State of Georgia*; he was then "discharged" on September 10, 1864. Solomon again enlisted on the *Princeton* as a landsman on October 27, 1864, however, before joining the crew of the *Sassacus*, staying there until July 31, 1865. He was finally discharged from the *Princeton* on September 27, 1865, several months after the Civil War ended. Illness and, perhaps, racism may have been primary reasons that Solomon served on several vessels, according to his service records. He apparently applied for and fought vigorously for a pension, according to the online "Case Files of Approved Pension Applications of Civil War and Later Navy Veterans, compiled ca. 1861–1910."[84]

As an African American landsman aboard such vessels during the Civil War, including the USS *Princeton*, "a clipper-built ship" constructed in June of 1851 at the Boston Navy Yard,[85] Solomon would have likely been treated as though he were at "the bottom rung of the shipboard ladder,"[86] even below the status of such castigated landsmen who were "adult white-men (over 17)."[87] Considering that a few other Montiers would serve on such ships as landsmen—regardless of skin color—during the war, their "lot ... on board wartime vessels could be ... extremely difficult," and likely exacerbated because of their African-descended and mixed-race roots. "They could usually expect to undertake the most menial of tasks, including things like moving heavy loads, physically maintaining the vessel and cleaning the decks."[88] The brutal truth was that such landsmen crew members—white and black—"were the dogsbodies of Civil War crews. Their lack of experience and maritime knowledge often marked them out for disdain and ridicule from more experienced crewmen."[89] Although there's an indication that he also served on the USS *Juniata*,[90] Solomon Montier likely served his final months on the *Princeton*[91] after it "was taken to Philadelphia where she was stationed as a receiving ship until" October 1866 "and then sold."[92]

At least three other Montier relatives—Robert Lewis Montier Jr., Francis Montier, and Jeremiah Montier—enlisted in the navy for one-year terms during the war as landsmen, according to the "Return of the United States Naval Rendezvous at New York for the week ending, January 2d, 1864."[93] All apparently enlisted on January 2 as native Pennsylvanians; all were described as having black hair and black or brown eyes; their complexions were described as "Mulatto."[94] Each of the trio stood slightly more than 5 feet, with Jeremiah rising the tallest at 5½ feet tall. Francis, then age 21 and whose father was Robert L. Montier, had been working prior to his enlistment as a laborer while his son Robert, 25 years old, was employed as a "Cook." Jeremiah, age 24, worked as a "Farmer." Although Francis was not described as having any "permanent marks or scars," Robert was noted as having scars on his "left cheek, both feet & right shin." Jeremiah had similar markings on his "left knee & left fore arm [sic]."[95]

Shortly after or about March 1864, Jeremiah Montier began serving onboard the USS *Aroostook*,[96] "a 691-ton ... steam gunboat built at Kennebunk, Maine" that "was commissioned in February 1862."[97] Francis also served onboard the ship,[98] likely at the same time as Robert and Jeremiah. In addition to early during the war engaging "Confederate forces on several occasions," by September 1862, "the gunboat served briefly with the Potomac Flotilla before being ordered to the Gulf of Mexico," after Jeremiah had likely joined the crew, to battle "blockade runners." The USS *Aroostook*, "some months after the end of the Civil War ... was decommissioned at Philadelphia, Pennsylvania,"[99] likely about the time that Jeremiah Montier mustered out of the service.

Following their navy enlistments, Robert and Francis enlisted in the United States Cavalry, specifically a regiment within the apparatus of the United States Colored Troops (USCT), the 2nd United States Colored Cavalry. Then 26-year-old Robert Montier, who was recorded as previously serving as a "Seaman," was mustered in on the grounds of Camp William Penn in Chelten Hills on March 9, 1865,[100] near the end of the war and just weeks before Harriet Tubman spoke to the facility's 24th USCT in mid-April; that would have been about the time of President Abraham Lincoln's April 15 assassination. The 24th was the last regiment to depart for battle from Camp William Penn.[101] Described on his muster card dated March 23, 1865, as having black hair and dark eyes and complexion, Robert, born about 1838 or 1839, stood at just "5 ft. 2" inches.[102] Furthermore, instead of joining the 24th USCT or one of the other earlier 10 regiments associated with Camp William Penn,[103] Robert mustered into the 2nd United States Colored Cavalry,[104] likely via a recruiting or "rendezvous" representative of that regiment, perhaps an indication that Robert was familiar with horses.

Similarly, it appears that Robert's younger brother or cousin, Francis Montier, age 21, with similar physical characteristics—although he was, at almost 5 feet 5 inches, a bit taller—also joined the 2nd Cavalry on March 9, 1865, likely at Camp William Penn, as a "Substitute for Wm. A. Lippincott," according to the "Company [L] Descriptive Book." Apparently, Francis, born about 1843 or 1844, had also worked as a seaman as previously noted.[105]

The 2nd Cavalry regiment of the United States Colored Troops division was "organized at Fort Monroe, Va., December 22, 1863," initially serving at "Portsmouth and Williamsburg, Va., till May, 1864,"[106] about a year before Robert and Francis Montier would join the unit. The regiment saw "action near Suffolk," Virginia, on March 10 and was involved in "reconnaissance" patrols in the Blackwater area from April 13 to 15 before joining General Benjamin "Butler's operations on the south side of [the] James River and against Petersburg and Richmond May 4–28."[107] The squadron also helped to capture "Bermuda Hundred and City Point" on May 5 before participating in the "Richmond Campaign June 13–July 31" and "assaults on Petersburg June 16–19." Notably, the unit ultimately served in ferocious battles at Chaffin's Farm and Darby Road through September and October 1864.[108]

The Montiers likely arrived for duty in March or April 1865, starting in the "District of Eastern Virginia at Norfolk, Suffolk, etc." before being "ordered to City Point, Va." They then sailed to "Texas [on] June 10," 1865.[109] Similar to many of the 180 African American regiments, including most of the 11 from Camp William Penn, they served "on the Rio Grande and at various points in Texas till February, 1866,"[110] often engaging Native Americans and lawless ruffians. Despite there being no documentation found thus far indicating that the Montiers joined the fabled Buffalo Soldiers consisting of fierce-fighting African American troops following the Civil War, some of the Camp William Penn soldiers did muster into such units.[111]

And although it appears that Robert was suspected or accused of desertion while stationed at Norfolk, Virginia, on April 11, 1865, he apparently mustered out in good standing with the rest of the regiment in Brazos, Santiago, Texas, on February 12, 1866.[112] Francis also mustered out at this time, having along the way been promoted from private to corporal.[113]

Other extended family members identified as serving in the Civil War included James H. Menoken,[114] likely of the 32nd USCT,[115] although a source indicates that he was affiliated with the 24th USCT[116] that heard an address by Tubman in April 1865.[117] Both the 32nd and 24th were raised at Camp William Penn.[118] The 32nd initially guarded 280 Confederate prisoners on their way to Fort Delaware in Delaware on the steamship *Continental* while sailing "for the seat of war" in South Carolina after departing Camp William Penn on April 23, 1864. The regiment served on several of South Carolina's Sea Islands, including Folly and Morris Islands, the latter locale noted as where the famous black infantry regiment, the 54th Massachusetts, gallantly fought to overtake Fort Wagner on July 18, 1863—a battle immortalized in the 1989 motion picture *Glory* starring Denzel Washington. In addition to participating in fierce fighting during the battle of Honey Hill and other South Carolina conflicts, the 32nd would assist on Hilton Head with helping the first liberated African Americans or Gullah people (retaining many African customs) a few years after the Union's November 7, 1861, invasion of nearby Port Royal Sound. Specifically, they would construct Fort Baird beginning in August 1864 and help to build Fort Howell near the historic black town of Mitchelville, one of the first self-governing African American communities in the United States, which had begun as a refugee camp.[119]

Cyrus Bustill Miller Jr.,[120] another Morrey–Bustill–Montier descendant, joined the 24th USCT of Camp William Penn, on March 23, 1865,[121] about two weeks before Harriet Tubman would address the regiment on April 6, 1865. Enlisting in West Chester, Pennsylvania, and occupationally identified as a "Seaman," similar to his other warrior kinfolk, the Virginia-born Miller was described as a 21-year-old "Mulatto" standing 5 feet 5 inches, with dark eyes and hair.[122]

Meanwhile, one of the Montier relatives who was very closely associated with Camp William Penn and the antislavery movement in the Philadelphia region was David Bustill Bowser (1820–1900). As the painter who designed and made the regimental flags of Camp William Penn's 11 regiments, Bowser "was a very well connected artist who painted images of the abolitionist martyr John Brown and President Abraham Lincoln."[123] He was also the grandson of Cyrus Bustill. "Bowser received an impressive education at a private school led by his cousin, Sarah Mapps Douglass [who became a leader of the prestigious Institute for Colored Youth in Philadelphia],"[124] as well as pursued art with Sarah's brother, Robert Douglass Jr., an associate and likely pupil of the famous artist Thomas Sully at the Pennsylvania Academy of the Fine Arts.[125] Although some scholarly sources indicate that David and Sarah were cousins of the preeminent abolitionist Frederick Douglass, others refute that possibility. Bowser's composition of the regimental flags, likely with the assistance of his seamstress wife, Elizabeth (Lizzie) Harriet Stevens Gray Bowser (1834–1908),[126] even depicting a black soldier killing a white rebel on the flag of the 22nd USCT, was revolutionary and groundbreaking during a period when many Caucasian Southerners wished to see such ebony warriors back in chains and plenty of European-descended Northerners still viewed blacks as inferior and too often inhuman:

> Forty-one years old when the Civil War erupted, Bowser "was an established artist and painter of signs in Philadelphia." Indeed, the "flags were of regimental size and often contained the national arms on the reverse and an allegorical painting depicting various scenes of the black man in uniform." Bowser also designed and made flags for black regiments outside of the Philadelphia area. Further, Bowser "sold albumen photos of both sides of the flags in carte de visite format."[127]

Born to Rachael and Jeremiah Bowser on January 16, 1820, in Philadelphia,[128] Bowser was respected not only for his artistic skills but also black rights activism, working to eradicate segregation with such Philadelphia-based freedom fighters as Robert Purvis, William Still, and Lucretia Mott. One of the Civil War's martyrs, John Brown, a zealous white antislavery abolitionist, actually boarded in Bowser's residence[129] during one of his Philadelphia sojourns before eventually leading the 1859 raid on the federal arsenal in Harpers Ferry, Virginia, that many scholars say sparked the Civil War. Lucretia Mott, at her Roadside home in Cheltenham, just a few miles from Guineatown, harbored John Brown's wife, Mary,[130] and a couple of her children as her husband was being executed on December 2, 1859 for leading that Harpers Ferry assault that included 18 black and white accomplices, several of whom were also hung.[131]

Undoubtedly, one of the African American Civil War soldiers who monitored Brown's execution from afar and other earthshattering news of

The artist David Bustill Bowser designed this flag for the 22nd United States Colored Troops infantry, one of the 11 regiments—consisting of almost 11,000 soldiers—that trained at Camp William Penn in Cheltenham. (Library of Congress)

the day, was William Drew Robeson, whose son—the scholar, actor, singer, orator, and activist Paul Robeson—would become one of the most recognized African Americans in America, if not the world. Born enslaved in 1844,[132] William was "the child of Benjamin and Sabra, on the Robeson plantation in Cross Roads Township, Martin County, North Carolina," but destined to become quite a trailblazer, despite the formidable challenges he overcame. "In 1860, at age fifteen, William Drew had made his escape [with his brother Ezekiel], found his way north over the Maryland border into Pennsylvania, and served as a laborer for the Union Army (making his way back to North Carolina at least twice to see his mother)."[133] A slave schedule associated with the 1860 federal census indicates that a "Slave Owner" named "William Robason," age 29, resided in "Hamilton, Martin, North Carolina,"[134] perhaps an indication that Paul Robeson's father, William Robeson, may have taken on his so-called master's name before escaping.

Online military records indicate that a William Robeson enlisted for a three-year term on August 8, 1864, in the 45th United States Colored Infantry[135] that was one of the aforementioned 11 regiments established for African Americans at Camp William Penn in Cheltenham or Chelten Hills from 1863 to 1865. Although William's age was listed as 20 and "Birth Location" as "Hu[n]-tingdale, Pennsylvania," it's quite possible that he provided that inaccurate geographic information to conceal his status as a self-liberated African American from North Carolina in order to serve with the United States Colored Troops. An entry in the "Regimental Descriptive Book" indicates that Robeson joined Company H, stood 5 feet 5 inches tall with complexion, hair, and eyes described as "Black." His "Occupation" was listed as "Laborer."[136]

Destined to become the father of the great African American Paul Robeson, the Reverend William Drew Robeson was a former slave who likely joined the 45th United States Colored Troops infantry at Camp William Penn. He would graduate from Pennsylvania's Lincoln University before marrying Maria Louisa Bustill, a descendant of Richard and Cremona Morrey. (West Philadelphia Collaborative History, University of Pennsylvania)

Before leaving Camp William Penn to join the climaxing fight to save the Union, perhaps Robeson witnessed three of the facility's regiments—the 127th, part of the 41st, and his 45th—receive regimental flags from artist-activist David Bustill Bowser during ceremonies that featured one of the regimental bands and a range of speakers;[137] a couple of orators hailed from the "'Supervisory Committee'"[138] derived from the Philadelphia Union League that helped to financially establish Camp William Penn. Among the participants and bystanders cheering was likely William Still, "the father of the Underground Railroad," who was a well-known activist and entrepreneur with a dispensary or sutler's post on the facility's grounds.[139] "'At the conclusion, three cheers were given for the Union, for the Supervisory Committee, and the Stars and Stripes,'" according a media report.[140]

William Robeson, likely following his probable service in the 45th USCT, married Richard and Cremona Morrey's great-granddaughter, Maria Louisa Bustill, a marriage that resulted in the birth of the iconic black leader Paul Robeson. William may have well accompanied that distinguished "'first black regiment to march in a presidential inauguration (President Lincoln's [second term])'"[141] on the "'rainy'" day of March 4, 1865, in Washington, DC.[142] "'They were on duty in the city on the occasion of the second inauguration of President Lincoln, the only colored troops in the procession.'"[143] The famous and pioneering black Civil War correspondent for the *Philadelphia Press*, Pittsburgh-native Thomas Morris Chester, noted that the 45th USCT had arrived in Virginia in the Petersburg and City Point areas, according to a September 24, 1864, dispatch: "The 45th U.S.C.T., from Camp Wm. Penn, arrived at City Point yesterday. It looked as if it was made of good material," Chester wrote.[144] In fact, "'on October 13th, the 45th 'participated in the action at Darbytown Road, and on the 27th at Charles City Cross Roads. It was soon afterwards placed in winter-quarters, and until the opening of the spring campaign, was engaged in fatigue and picket duty, in front of Fort Harrison.'"[145]

Remarkably, the 45th USCT would again cross paths with President Lincoln, according to *Bates History of the Pennsylvania Volunteers*: "'Upon the formation of the Twenty-fifth Corps, it was assigned to the Second Brigade, of the Second Division.'"[146] Indeed, "'four companies which had been on duty in the defenses of Washington, were, on the 14th of March, 1865, united with the other companies at the front. On the 26th, the corps was reviewed by President Lincoln and General Grant, and on the following day crossed the James, for active duty with the army of the Potomac.'"[147] The 45th USCT's pace would not slow down. It would fight at Hatcher's Run, then Petersburg by the beginning of April, before penetrating Petersburg with triumphant

Union forces, including other African American regiments, on April 3.[148]

The 45th—likely including Robeson—would "'help ... other African American units to corner Confederate General Lee's forces'" near Appomattox, Virginia, in April 1865, not long before Lincoln's April 15 assassination, the horrific news of which likely devastated Robeson and his brethren.[149] However, just days earlier, "'mighty rewarding had to be the 45th's pursuit of the leader of the Rebel forces, Robert E. Lee, and his compatriots,'" culminating with them witnessing the Confederates' momentous surrender at the Appomattox Court House on April 9, 1865.[150]

Octavius Valentine Catto, a renowned Philadelphia scholar and civil rights activist, was assassinated in 1871 during an uprising of whites as he tried to encourage fellow blacks to vote. (Wikimedia Commons)

Following Lincoln's April 15 assassination, the 45th USCT, like other African American regiments, were sent west, although the 22nd USCT of Camp William Penn was honored first to participate on April 19 in Lincoln's funeral procession—as well as pursuing the president's assassins with other Camp William Penn regiments.[151] In May the 45th moved on to Edinburg, Texas, near the "'Mexican frontier'" before mustering out on November 4. Robeson, probably with the regiment returned to Philadelphia, where they were "'paid and discharged at Camp Cadwalader'" on December 13, as Robeson undoubtedly envisioned future vistas of freedom and opportunity.[152] The road forward would not be easy.

Although it's quite likely that William Robeson received some degree of education while serving in the military, "'at the close of the Civil War, he managed to obtain an elementary-school education and then, earning his fees through farm labor, went on for ministerial studies at the primarily black Lincoln University, near Philadelphia (receiving an A.B. in 1873 and a Bachelor of Sacred Theology degree in 1876).'"[153] While a student at Lincoln, Robeson showed clear signs of fearlessness and that he would not easily acquiesce to so-called white supremacist conventions. "A classmate later described 'the Uncle Tom' tendencies' among many of the students at Lincoln—but singled William Drew out as 'among the notable exceptions.'"[154]

While studying at Lincoln, William Drew met Maria Louisa Bustill, eight years his junior, a teacher at the Robert Vaux School [in Philadelphia]. Her distinguished family traced its roots back to the African Bantu people (as William Drew did his to the Ibo of Nigeria), and in this country its members had intermarried with Delaware Indians and English Quakers. The many prominent descendants included Cyrus Bustill, who in 1787 helped to found the Free African Society, the first black self-help organization in America; Joseph Cassey Bustill, a prominent figure in the Underground Railroad; and Sarah Mapps Douglass, a founding member of the Philadelphia Female Antislavery Society.[155]

Although not likely intimidated by the accomplishments of anyone—black or white—William Drew Robeson was still probably quite impressed with the achievements of his bride's kinfolk:

Louisa Bustill's own sister, Gertrude, wrote for several Philadelphia newspapers (and married Dr. Nathan Francis Mossell,[156] the first black graduate of the University of Pennsylvania School of Medicine (as well as a considerable activist for racial justice) [who cofounded what became known as Mercy Douglass Hospital focusing on treating African Americans in Philadelphia]). When Louisa Bustill married William Drew Robeson in 1878, the impressive legacy of Bustill achievements, past and current, became part of their son Paul's heritage. But it was not the part he emphasized. He always identified more with the humbler lives on his father's side, often alluding affectionately as an adult to his simple, good North Carolina kin—while scarcely ever referring to his Bustill relatives.[157]

After graduating from Lincoln and accepting "the pastorate of the newly formed Church of the Covenant" in Wilkes-Barre, Pennsylvania, in June 1876,[158] William married Maria Louisa Bustill (a direct descendant of Cyrus Bustill and Elizabeth Morrey) in 1878. A year after marrying Maria, William "undertook the pastorate of Witherspoon Street Presbyterian Church" in Princeton, New Jersey, where Jim Crow racism was at its height.[159] "Princeton was a Jim Crow city, and Princeton Presbyterians were no exception. African Americans had long worshipped at Princeton's First Presbyterian Church, in balcony seating,"[160] a segregationist practice of many so-called Christian congregations throughout the United States during that time. "A fire in 1839 destroyed First Princeton's balcony, and the church funded construction of a new church for its African American members, known as the

Pioneering black physician Dr. Nathan Francis Mossell as a young man sits at the far right in this circa 1875 family image, including parents Aaron and Eliza Bowers Mossell (seated in the center) with siblings (from left to right) Mary Louise, Alvaretta, Charles Wesley, Aaron Albert and Nathan Francis. (University Archives, University of Pennsylvania)

Gertrude Elizabeth Harding Mossell sits between her daughters Mazie and Florence. As a distinguished journalist and community leader, Gertrude was married to the trailblazing physician Dr. Nathan Francis Mossell. (University Archives, University of Pennsylvania)

These are esteemed members of the Bustill family, including Charles Hicks Bustill, Gertrude E. H. Bustill (standing), and Maria Louisa Bustill. Gertrude would marry a trailblazing black physician, Nathan Mossell, who founded the Frederick Douglass Hospital, a first for African Americans in the area. Maria, after marrying William Drew Robeson, would give birth to the great Paul Robeson. (University Archives, University of Pennsylvania)

'First Presbyterian Church of Colour of Princeton,' that would report to the General Assembly in 1845 as Witherspoon Street Presbyterian Church."[161] Well acquainted with the degradations of slavery and racial hatred, William Drew Robeson spoke out against such hypocrisy and advocated for the elimination of racist barriers.[162]

When Paul Leroy Robeson was born on April 9, 1898, in Princeton, New Jersey, "his father was fifty-three years old and his mother forty-five. She had already given birth to seven children, five of whom had survived infancy,"[163] probably an above-average survival rate given the challenges of racial discrimination and health disparities between whites and blacks—even in Princeton—near the turn of the 20th century:

> The town of Princeton was a strictly Jim Crow place, with black adults held to menial jobs and black youngsters relegated to the segregated Witherspoon Elementary School (which ran only through the eighth grade; parents who wanted their children to have more education—like the Robesons—had to send them out of town). Emma Epps, a contemporary of Paul's, remembers walking home with a pack of white kids at her heels yelling "Nigger! Nigger! Nigger!" Later in life, Paul scornfully rejected Princeton as "spiritually located in Dixie," and he referred angrily to blacks living there "for all intents and purposes on a Southern plantation. And with no more dignity than that suggests—all the bowing and scraping to the drunken rich, all the vile names, all the Uncle Tomming to earn enough to lead miserable lives."[164]

Just several years after Paul Robeson's 1898 birth, Woodrow Wilson was accused of virulent racism during his United States presidency and before that as president of Princeton University, serving from 1902 to 1910. "On June 26, 2020, the Princeton University Board of Trustees voted to change the names of both the School of Public and International Affairs and Wilson College; the trustees concluded that Woodrow Wilson's racist thinking and policies,"[165] that included discouraging African Americans from enrolling, "make him an inappropriate namesake for a school or college whose scholars, students, and alumni must stand firmly against racism in all its forms."[166]

Yet, Paul also remembered a close-knit African American community with several relatives living close by, including "Huldah Robeson, Nettie Staton, and cousins Carraway and Chance."[167] In fact, "the black community in Princeton was large (15–20 percent of the population) and cohesive, with a sizable contingent from rural North Carolina that continued in its Southern speech and traditions,"[168] that Paul vividly remembered, reflective sometimes in his own bi-linguistic speech patterns that were obvious during future on-stage and film presentations in roles that spanned from requiring so-called standard English to black dialects. "As Paul himself later wrote, blacks 'lived a much more communal life' in Princeton 'than the white people around them,' a communality 'expressed and preserved' in the church,"[169] of which his father was a central figure.

William Drew and Maria Louisa's children over the years included Gertrude (who died in 1880 as an infant) and William Drew Jr., destined to become a physician before passing away early in his career.[170] There were also "John Bunyan Reeve," as well as "Benjamin; Marian; and Paul, the

Paul Robeson House & Museum's executive director, Janice Sykes-Ross, and Joyce Mosley, the noted Morrey–Bustill–Montier family historian, pose amid an exhibition of the great Paul Robeson. Based in the house where Robeson spent his final years with a sister (Marian R. Forsythe), the multimedia exhibits very comprehensively explore Robeson's incredible life and legacy. (Donald Scott Sr.)

youngest child." One of the couple's children "died at birth,"[171] sadly a prelude of devastating times ahead for the couple and their family. As the last born, however, "Paul was the doted-upon favorite, and in later life always spoke of his family with deep affection,"[172] despite rare times when he likely realized and acknowledged some of his kinfolk's faults or imperfections.

In fact, Paul "later credited" his physician brother, William Drew Jr.,[173] "as the most 'brilliant' member of the family and his own 'principal source of learning how to study.'"[174] It seems that Paul Robeson's siblings each had an impact on him, one way or the other:

> Marian, the one girl, became, like her mother, a teacher; Benjamin, like his father, went on to the ministry. The fiery Reeve (called Reed) rejected any traditional path or cautionary attitude; he was the family brawler, the boy who reacted to racial slurs with passionate defiance—and became something of an alter ego to his younger brother, Paul. "His example explains much of my militancy," Paul wrote later in life. He often told me, "Don't ever take it from them, Laddie—always be a man—never bend the knee." As an adult, Paul would look back lovingly on his "restless, rebellious" brother, "scoffing at convention, defiant of the white man's law." But after street fights (Reed carried a bag of small, jagged rocks for protection) and brushes with the police, Reed was packed off to Detroit, became part owner of a hotel, apparently got involved in bootlegging and gambling, and is rumored to have died on Skid Row.[175]

Paul would later profess a deep affection for his mother, Maria Louisa Bustill, born November 8, 1853, in Philadelphia,[176] with ties to the Bustills, Morreys, and Montiers, many of them early black Quakers. In fact, on a few occasions Paul "did … confide to intimates, 'I admired my father, but I loved my mother,'"[177] despite also later admitting a profound love for his father[178]—especially following his mother's tragic premature death. On that note, Paul probably bonded with her up to age six, when she died at just 50 years old in a horrific fiery accident at home. "I cannot say that I remember her, though my memory of other things goes back before her tragic death," Robeson wrote in his autobiography. "I was six years old when she, a near-blind invalid at the time, was fatally burned in a household accident"[179] because an ember or piece of coal from a fire somehow fell on her as she prepared a meal, setting her dress afire.[180] "Fatally burned, she lingered on for several days in great pain," passing away on January 20, 1904, before being buried at the Princeton Cemetery. "Paul … was away at the time of the accident, but his brother Ben was home. Throughout Ben's life, according to his daughter, the mere sight of a flame was enough to upset him."[181]

Perhaps Paul's memories of his mother faded over the years—likely due to the trauma of her death and his young age.[182] Ironically, decades earlier, not long after Maria Louisa's father, Charles Hicks Bustill (1816–1890), married her mother, Emily Robinson, Emily died prematurely, leaving Charles to raise his two infant daughters, Maria Louisa and her sister Gertrude[183] (who was destined to become a teacher and journalist as well as marry the pioneering African American physician, Nathan Mossell).[184] Charles eventually remarried, however, wedding Elizabeth C. Thomas in the Milltown community of Cheltenham near Guineatown in 1873.[185] "Like his father, David," well known as a member of Philadelphia's upper-class African American community, "[Charles] Bustill made his living as a plasterer while also active as a conductor on the Underground Railroad. His home was a frequent stopping place for self-emancipated men and women on their way north."[186] Paul Robeson recalled in his autobiography: "Through the years the Bustills produced many teachers, artists and scholars, and, in the Quaker tradition, took part in running the Underground Railroad by which so many, like my father, escaped from bondage."[187]

And although Robeson did not remember many firsthand details about his mother, Maria Louisa, he learned about her tremendous family history, character, and dedication from "older [Witherspoon Street Presbyterian] church members and other longtime residents" of Princeton.[188] "And they will tell you, too, about my mother, Maria Louisa: how she moved, so strong and tender, in their midst—comforting the sick, mothering the orphaned, collecting food and clothing for the hungry and ragged, opening to many the wonders of book learning," Robeson recalled in his autobiography.[189] "Others have told me of her remarkable intellect, her strength of character and spirit which contributed so much to my father's development and work," he continues. "She was a companion to him in his studies; she helped compose his sermons; she was his right hand in all his community work."[190]

William Pickens III, a prominent descendant who became founder and president of the Paul Robeson Society in New York, recalls that William Drew Robeson while a student at Lincoln University first became familiar with the studious Maria Louisa via the elder Robeson's association with his grandfather, William Pickens Sr., a former slave who had become the NAACP's first field officer and an associate of the great scholar W. E. B. Du Bois, a cofounder of that civil rights organization in 1909. Pickens III also "remembers Paul Robeson ... as a young man singing at family and church events in the New York area."[191]

As a youngster, Paul also recalled his mother's kinfolk gathering for the Bustill Family Association's "annual reunions to which all of the relatives from far and near would come." The gatherings were "held [in 1912] at Maple Grove"[192] in the Philadelphia vicinity. He recalled participating and later reading in a "printed program"[193] various notable family members with clear ties to the Montiers, etc., holding key positions in the association: "My aunt, Gertrude Bustill Mossell,[194] is listed as vice-president of the association," Paul wrote in his autobiography, "and on the program of the day was a reading of the family history by my cousin, Annie Bustill Smith, and speeches by various other members, including an address by 'Mr. Paul Roberson.' (Though this spelling of my name was a printer's error, it is likely that 'Roberson' was the ancestral name of the slaveholding Robersons from whom my father got his name."[195]

And through the years Robeson distinctly remembered his mother's funeral several days after her January 20, 1904, passing.[196] Indeed, "he had a vivid recall of the day of her funeral: 'He remembers his Aunt Gertrude taking him by the hand, and leading him to the modest coffin, in the little parlor" of the residence in the unit block of Green Street "to take one last, but never forgotten look at his beautiful, sweet, generous-hearted Mother.'"[197]

Despite some historical observers noting that Paul Robeson said that he had little to no memory of his mother, Maria Louisa Bustill Robeson, the evidence seems to indicate that he did harbor deep emotional—albeit abstract—memories of her, especially given that he expressed a deep love for his mom.[198] Yet, Paul probably maintained reservations about various members of his maternal family, some described as "bourgeoisie" or "mulatto," hinting of colorism, today defined as "prejudice or discrimination especially within a racial or ethnic group favoring people with lighter skin over those with darker skin."[199] Although debatable, it's worth considering that Paul, at least a couple of his siblings, and Paul's father, William, were darker complexioned and may have experienced unpleasant slights from lighter-toned family members. "The Bustill clan," although certainly not all, "showed disinterest in the 'dark children' Louisa had left behind (she herself had been light-skinned and high-cheekboned, reflecting the mix of African with European and Delaware Indian heritage), which was perhaps another reason Paul identified deeply with his father's uneducated relatives, who treated him with unfailing kindness."[200]

Despite losing his beloved wife, Maria Louisa, in 1904 and his 20-year "Princeton pastorate" at the Witherspoon Street Presbyterian Church a few years earlier in 1901, perhaps due to elements of congregational colorism or bourgeoisie elitism, as well as accusations of financial mismanagement by church members and local Presbytery officials,[201] the now single William maintained a tight bond with his children, including Paul. "At the time of their mother's death in 1904, Ben and Paul were the only children still at home (Marian, next youngest to Paul, was staying with relatives in North

Carolina and studying at the Scotia Seminary for young black women)"[202] as their father struggled to make a living and keep a roof over their heads. "It wasn't until 1907 that Reverend Robeson managed to relocate himself and his two sons to the town of Westfield, but even then economic hardship continued," with father William still persevering amidst so much adversity. "Reverend Robeson worked in a grocery store, slept with Paul and Ben in the attic under the roof of the store, cooked and washed in a lean-to attached to the back of the building."[203]

It was about that time, in 1907, when Paul's father William changed "his denominational affiliation from Presbyterian to African Methodist Episcopal [Zion]," managing "to build a tiny church, the Downer Street St. Luke A.M.E. Zion" sanctuary.[204] Although it was a humble gathering place, Reverend Robeson held "together its flock of rural blacks from the South. They, in turn, helped Reverend Robeson hold together his family. The woman who ran the grocery store downstairs, along with other church sisters and neighbors, brought food from time to time (supplemented by bags of cornmeal, greens, yams, and peanuts sent up by relatives from Robersonville, North Carolina)."[205] Paul once reminisced: "'There must have been moments when I felt the sorrows of a motherless child, but what I most remember from my youngest days was an abiding sense of comfort and security.'"[206] However, it wouldn't be long before Paul's brother, Ben, would leave for college in North Carolina, resulting in the bond between Paul and his father William becoming even stronger, despite a few rough patches along the way:

> In 1910 Reverend Robeson was finally able to re-establish himself in a parish, St. Thomas A.M.E. Zion, in the town of Somerville, New Jersey. By then Ben had gone off to Biddle University (now Johnson C. Smith) in North Carolina, destined from there to enter the seminary and later to become the pastor of Mother A.M.E. Zion Church in Harlem. That left Paul and his father living alone together. Despite a fifty-three-year gap in their ages, the two were mutually devoted, Paul's respect for his father bordering on awe.[207]

In fact, one of the most poignant moments of young Paul's early life was when he disobeyed his father and then tried to escape his dad's appeals by running off:

> I ran away. He ran after me. I darted across the road. He followed, stumbled and fell. I was horrified. I hurried back and helped "Pop" to his feet. He had knocked out one of his most needed teeth. I shall never forget my feeling. It has remained ever present, and I sometimes experience horror, shame, ingratitude, selfishness all over again, for I loved my "Pop" like no one in all the world ... Never in all my life afterwards, and this happened in 1908, when I was ten, did he have to admonish me again.[208]

Paul fondly remembered his father as being rigid and insistent regarding hard work and discipline, but never bitter or inclined to hold a grudge, even when wronged via ignorance, racism, or otherwise.[209] "Paul was expected to play an active role in church life, to shoulder a full share of family chores, to turn in a superlative academic performance—and to work at odd jobs to help pay his school fees."[210] After all, father William maintained a prodigious work ethic and impeccable scruples and refused to forsake his heaven-sent principles, always keeping an open mind for others—including European-descended neighbors. For instance, "Reverend Robeson counted among his friends in Somerville the Woldins, a white family who lived almost directly across West Cliff Street. He and Sam Woldin, who had escaped from czarist persecution of the Jews, would often sit on the porch 'puffing contentedly on pipes or little Recruits or sweet Caporals, sharing tales of their respective flights to freedom.'"[211]

It was probably Paul's observation of his father's open heart for well-meaning blacks and whites alike that led to his own acceptance of diverse races and nationalities as he progressed through school and as an adult, then throughout his unparalleled professional careers. "During his senior year at the Somerville, New Jersey, high school, he achieved the highest score in a statewide scholarship examination to attend Rutgers College (later Rutgers University)," matriculating there in 1915 as the only African American freshman "and only the third" black "to attend the institution."[212] Robeson's immense intelligence and athletic prowess were stratospheric. As "a varsity debater, he won class prizes for oratory all four years, was elected to Phi Beta Kappa as a junior, was one of four seniors chosen for membership in the Cap and Skull honorary society, and was named class valedictorian." And as if that wasn't enough, "the six-foot, three-inch, 215-pound Robeson earned twelve varsity letters in four sports (baseball, basketball, football, and track) and was twice named football All-America (1917 and 1918),"[213] as World War I raged with fellow African Americans serving primarily in menial support roles, but more than a few putting lives on the line at some of the bloodiest battlefronts. That was especially in France for which they received medals for heroism and valor by the French government; many returned to America, however, to face unrelenting racism and even lynchings.[214]

Even as a popular scholar and football player, Robeson experienced a range of "social slights and racial incidents," perhaps an impetus for his "senior thesis" project that "predicted the eventual use of the Fourteenth Amendment to advance civil rights."[215] After all, just a few years following his self-liberated grandfather William Drew Robeson served in the Civil War, the 1868 law "granted citizenship to all persons 'born or naturalized in the

United States,' including formerly enslaved people, and provided all citizens with 'equal protection under the laws.'"[216] In fact, Robeson's "commencement address boldly combined the accommodationist philosophy of BOOKER T. WASHINGTON with the more militant views of W. E. B. DU BOIS,"[217] a radical approach that William Pickens Sr., a Montier descendant, supported as a Du Bois lieutenant[218] who served as the group's first field secretary, remarkably expanding branches from just several to more than 350.[219]

Receiving his bachelor's degree from Rutgers in 1919, Robeson by 1920 enrolled in the Columbia University School of Law. "He helped finance his legal education by playing professional football for three seasons (1920–1922) with the Akron Pros and Milwaukee Badgers." In 1921 he "married Eslanda 'Essie' Cardozo Goode," who hailed from a notable African American family in Washington, DC. She had been working as "a laboratory pathologist at Columbia's medical school; they had one child,"[220] Paul Robeson Jr., born on November 2, 1927.[221] "Recognizing Robeson's lack of enthusiasm for the law and football, his wife urged him to take up acting,"[222] a transition that proved to be quite visionary because, after receiving his law degree, he became "discouraged by discrimination within the firm and the legal profession generally." So, Robeson "quit a few months later, before taking the bar exam, to pursue an acting career."[223]

The decision to change careers would prove to be quite momentous. "Robeson launched his stage career in 1924 in the lead roles in two O'Neill plays, *The Emperor Jones* and *All God's Chillun Got Wings*, the latter a daring drama about interracial marriage," harkening back to the mixed-race heritages of his Morrey-Montier ancestors. Further, Robeson "achieved a spectacular triumph in London in 1930 when he not only became one of the first Black actors to play [Shakespeare's] Othello but also rendered the finest portrayal of the character yet seen,"[224] with an alluring and evocative baritone voice that often had audiences enraptured.

On that note, Robeson became quite acclaimed as a singer who would soon popularize "Negro spirituals"—undoubtedly with his father's down-home church services and North Carolinian enslaved ancestors on his mind—that had been formerly ignored by the wider society and too often among the so-called black elite who were too often ashamed of the music's soul-stirring roots to slavery. "Robeson was also an accomplished singer, and at [wife] Essie's urging he performed at Carnegie Hall in 1925,"[225] as African Americans continued to be lynched and discriminated against throughout much of the country, often protested by William Pickens Sr. "The first soloist to devote an entire concert to Negro spirituals, Robeson both enthralled the sold-out audience

180 • THE MONTIERS

Paul Robeson sings the "Star-Spangled Banner" among workers at the Moore Shipyard in Oakland, California in 1942 during World War II, also telling them: "This is a serious job—winning this war against fascists. We have to be together." (Wikimedia Commons)

and boosted the popularity of the musical genre."[226] Notably, "Robeson steadfastly refused to sing operatic and classical music, preferring to emphasize Negro spirituals and international folk songs,"[227] endearing him to audiences spanning from trade unions in Europe and Russia's working class to African-descended people in America's South and so-called Northern ghettoes, as well as those fighting insidious colonialism in the Motherland, Africa.

Meanwhile, Robeson also made film history, appearing "in eleven motion pictures, including film versions of *The Emperor Jones* (1933) and *Show Boat* (1936) and Hollywood extravaganzas such as *King Solomon's Mines* (1937)."[228] While doing so,

Robeson appeared in the starring role of Broadway's production of Shakespeare's *Othello*, based on a historic interracial relationship, with the actress Uta Hagen as Desdemona. (Library of Congress)

"Robeson chafed at the stereotyping and racial slights suffered by blacks in the movie industry and demanded positive leading roles; he was most proud of his work in *Song of Freedom* (1936) and *The Proud Valley* (1940),"[229] despite some criticism of a few of his film and on-stage portrayals by progressive African Americans such as William Pickens Sr. concerning Robeson's roles in the likes of *Chillun*:

> That indictment was elaborated by William Pickens, field secretary of the NAACP (and dean of Baltimore's Morgan College). Pickens argued that the subliminal theme of *Chillun* was a case *against* racial mixing: in showing how a black boy and white girl first met in a mixed public school and later fell in love, with disastrous consequences, the play pointed a "dangerous" negative moral—"the Ku Klux would pay to have just such a play as this put on." Nor did Pickens spare Robeson. "Some colored people in it? Oh, that's nothing. Colored people are no better than white people. You can hire SOME of them to do anything that the law allows, if you have money enough."[230]

Extraordinarily, however, Pickens's NAACP compatriot, W. E. B. Du Bois, came to Robeson's defense, in effect countering Pickens's remarks. "Other black commentators took issue with this negative judgment—pre-eminently W. E. B. Du Bois, who chided his fellow blacks for being 'tremendously sensitive'—understandably, he acknowledged, since previous portraits of black life had been merely the 'occasion for an ugly picture, a dirty allusion, a nasty comment or a pessimistic forecast.'"[231] However, Du Bois asserted that *Chillun* "was something different and better—human and credible—and [playwright Eugene Gladstone] O'Neill deserved applause for 'bursting through.'"[232]

Meanwhile, Robeson began to evolve politically, largely due to his travels overseas to flee the virulent racism in the United States. "Robeson's political ideas took shape after George Bernard Shaw introduced him to socialism in 1928,"[233] a fateful development that would impact the rest of Robeson's career and life. "To escape American racism, he lived during most of the 1930s in Europe, returning to the United States only for movie and concert appearances." Robeson, in fact, seemed to be intrigued by Russia's brand of socialism. "Impressed by the absence of racial and class discrimination in the Soviet Union during a concert tour in 1934, Robeson subsequently spent extended periods in Moscow, learned Russian, and enrolled his son in Soviet schools."[234] Although he would later be accused of sympathizing with or ignoring the atrocities of fascists, "he became politically active in opposing fascism, imperialism, and racism," even providing "benefit performances in England for refugees from fascist countries."[235] Robeson also "associated with British left-wing political groups, became acquainted with key figures in the West

African Political Union, including Jomo Kenyatta [leader of Kenya's anti-colonial Mau Mau Movement] and Kwame Nkrumah,"[236] another Lincoln University graduate who became the liberator of Ghana from British colonialism, as well as its first president.

As he began to move away from what he believed to be Hollywood's racial stereotypes, "Robeson's political activism" began to draw "criticism but did not" initially "hurt his career, primarily because of the [early] U.S.-Soviet military alliance"[237] that would ultimately deteriorate over the years. "Indeed, he enjoyed his greatest hour as a performer in October 1943 when he became the first black actor to play Othello in the United States," acting in "a then record-setting 296 performances for a Shakespearean drama on Broadway,"[238] before going on a "nationwide tour." Along the way, "Robeson received the Donaldson Award as the best actor of the year." Furthermore, the National Association for the Advancement of Colored People or NAACP "awarded him the prestigious Spingarn Medal" in 1945,[239] perhaps an indication that his relationship with the organization's regaled field marshal and extended family member, William Pickens Sr., had certainly improved.

This iconic image of Paul Robeson was captured by the great film director and photographer Gordon Parks. (Wikimedia Commons)

However, ominous clouds were on the horizon as America's relationship with the Soviet Union began to collapse and Senator Joseph McCarthy's anti-Communist escapades started to dominate Congress and the nation during the 1950s. "The U.S. House of Representatives Committee on Un-American Activities labeled [Robeson] a 'Communist' and a 'Communist sympathizer' and enlisted JACKIE ROBINSON, who in 1947 had integrated organized baseball, to 'give the lie' to Robeson's statement," despite Robinson ultimately articulating their common goals to eradicate racism.[240] Still, Robeson's ensuing castigation and punishment were epic:

> He was hounded by the Federal Bureau of Investigation, and in 1950 the State Department took away his passport, refusing to issue a new one until he signed a non-Communist oath and pledged not to give political speeches abroad. He refused, and his persistent use of the

Fifth Amendment during House and Senate Hearings and the Soviet Union's awarding him the International Stalin Peace Prize in 1952 only exacerbated the public's perception of him as a subversive. Outraged Rutgers alumni demanded that his name be excised from the school's athletic records and that the honorary master of arts degree awarded to him in 1930 be rescinded. He was blacklisted as an entertainer, and his recordings were removed from stores. His income fell from over $100,000 in 1947 to $6,000 in 1952. Unable to travel abroad to earn money, Robeson was forced to sell his estate, The Beeches, in Enfield, Connecticut.[241]

Adding to Robeson's woes were accusations of infidelity, his paramours supposedly including white women cast in his various productions. The rumors caused major issues and separations from his wife, Essie, a noted scholar and author with a doctorate in anthropology, who still "resignedly managed his career in exchange for economic and social status."[242] The death of Robeson's wife in 1965 as the civil rights movement began to swell to a crescendo "ended their long marriage of convenience."[243] Tragically, after years of torment that led to an attempted suicide and dozens of rounds of questionable "electric shock therapy" that "likely caused permanent brain damage," Robeson "moved to Philadelphia, where he lived with a sister. Virtually an invalid and suffering from acute depression, he refused interviews and was seen only by family and close friends."[244]

However, Robeson was not forsaken by legions of his loyal fans and some live-arts dignitaries who realized the incredible sacrifices that he made with the mighty scruples of his beloved father, the formerly enslaved and self-liberated Reverend William Drew Robeson, who remained emblazoned in his memory. "Too ill to attend the '75th Salute to Paul Robeson' staged at Carnegie Hall in April 1973 by leaders in the entertainment and civil rights fields, he sent a recorded message: 'I want you to know that I am still the same Paul, dedicated as ever to the worldwide cause of humanity for freedom, peace and brotherhood.'"[245] Just a few years later, during the nation's bicentennial in 1976, a heaven-sent voice that echoed the sorrows and triumphs of his people through the ages was extinguished[246]—at least as a living and breathing human being—due to complications following a stroke on January 23, an exceedingly frigid day with temperatures plunging in Philadelphia to as low as 6 degrees Fahrenheit. Tragically, despite his soaring accomplishments, Robeson "remains the only two-time All-American not in the College Football Hall of Fame."[247] He is, however, indelibly memorialized in the minds of many as someone willing to make the ultimate sacrifice, despite uncompromising adversity.

Years earlier, not long after earning his degree from the Columbia University Law School in the spring of 1923 and becoming disillusioned with racism in various law practices as a budding attorney,[248] Robeson "continued his football career after graduating" by playing for the professional teams in Akron and Milwaukee; he also "helped coach at Lincoln University with Fritz Pollard, the black All-American halfback from Brown."[249] Although Robeson had not opted to attend his brother Ben and father William's alma mater, Lincoln, as an undergraduate reportedly because he did not want favored treatment,[250] Lincoln University would prove to be central to establishing vital relationships for kinfolk who attended the college in a few of his associated and extended family lines, including the Robesons, Bustills, and Pickenses.

The late William Pickens III, a retired business executive, philanthropist, and fine-arts patron (with his wife Audrey Patricia, née Brannen) who was the proud grandson of William Pickens Sr., the first field secretary of the NAACP, would often reminisce about how his parents, William Pickens Jr., and mother, Emilie Brown,[251] met by way of his dad's illustrious roommate, the soon-to-be famous African American literary giant Langston Hughes.[252] "He was my father's roommate in college," recalled Pickens, founder and the president of the New York City-based Paul Robeson Foundation, during a 2021 MSNBC television interview with journalist Trymaine Lee, noting that Hughes and his mother, then living in the Philadelphia area, had earlier become friends.[253] In fact, Pickens's mother Emilie,[254] a Montier family descendant whose Uncle Joseph Montier had harbored the Montier portraits under his bed for years, became a very early admirer of Hughes's work. "She would cajole him and encourage him," said Pickens during the interview, a conversation in part held in Sag Harbor, Long Island, New York, a historic African American seaside community where the likes of Hughes would read poetry at the Pickenses' vacation home. "And then when he [Hughes] told my father that he had met this attractive woman in Philadelphia, my dad sought her out and finally married her" when "he was still a freshman in law school" in 1930. That was despite his father, William Sr., urging his son to "wait until graduation in 1932."[255]

Nevertheless, the intriguing life of William Sr. became a major impetus and inspiration for William Pickens III, who often marveled about the accomplishments of his beloved grandfather, the son of former slaves. "The proud grandson of essayist [as well as educator and activist] William Pickens Sr., a child of freed slaves who went on to earn Phi Beta Kappa distinction at Yale and be among the first organizers of the National Association for the Advancement of Colored People (NAACP), Pickens [III] had advocacy and activism in his blood."[256]

In his 1911 memoirs, *The Heir of Slaves: An Autobiography*, Pickens Sr. noted: "I was born on the 15th day of January, 1881, according to the recollection of my parents,"[257] previously enslaved Fannie and Jacob Pickens, "a tenant farmer,"[258] in Anderson County, South Carolina. Pickens's "mother worked as a cook and washerwoman."[259] He further noted: "My father in color and hair is African although his features are not prominently African,"[260] Pickens wrote. "My mother's mother, who lived long in our family and 'raised' all of the grandchildren, was a characteristic little African woman, vivacious and longlived, with a small head and keen eyes. She could thread her own needles when she was eighty years of age."[261] Pickens continued: "She lived for forty years with a broken back, the upper part of her body being carried in a horizontal position, at right angles to her lower limbs, so that she must support her steps with a staff if she walked far." Pickens explained: "This was one of the results of slavery. Being a high-tempered house-servant in that system she had been beaten and struck across the back with a stick."[262]

William Pickens Sr. was a pioneering field secretary and cofounder of the NAACP. (Wikimedia Commons)

Yet even such brutality did not dampen the spirit of William Sr.'s grandmother, who was obviously quite beloved by her grandson. "Even in her old age her temper rose quick," and she could be "volatile," but "was a very dear and most helpful grandmother."[263] And according to family tradition, that line of the Pickenses also had Native American blood. "My mother's father, whom I never saw, and who perhaps died a slave, was half Cherokee Indian, his father being a Cherokee. I suppose that his other half was negro, since he was married in slavery to my grandmother."[264]

Meanwhile, William Sr. was in awe of the tremendous work ethic of his mother, Fannie, while noting too that she was also of Native American ancestry. "My mother was an average-sized brown woman, whose features were somewhat modified by her Indian strain and whose hair was black and of a negro-Indian texture,"[265] William Sr. wrote. "She was simply famous for the amount of hard work she could do. As a cook she could get a breakfast in the shortest possible time,"[266] he remembered, and "as a washerwoman she could put out the clothes of a large family by noon. And her work must have been well done, for she could never supply the demand for her services, and she died of overwork at the age of about forty-five," having given birth to 10 children, of which William Sr. "was the sixth."[267]

William Sr. recalled that when he was a child his family, living in Anderson, South Carolina, "was exceedingly poor." The family was often forced to move from the property of one predatory white landowner to the next. "My parents were farmers of the tenant or day-labor class and were ever on the move from cabin to cabin, with the proverbial unacquisitiveness of the 'rolling stone,'"[268] he remembered. "That part of the state was exceedingly poor, with red hills and antiquated agriculture. From such sections of the old South the immigration agent of the West easily induced many negroes to cross the Mississippi into debt-slavery."[269] His parents decided to take the risk, despite the looming harms. "My parents were industrious but improvident, and began early to talk of moving to Arkansas where the soil was fertile and wages high," Pickens continued. "This was possible only by allowing some Western farmer to pay the fares of the family through his agent, and by signing a contract to work on that farmer's land until the debt was paid according to that farmer's reckoning,"[270] which usually meant cheating and grossly overcharging such African Americans to keep them in debt and bound to the land.

Yet, despite the tremendous struggles, even after moving to Arkansas, William Sr.'s outstanding intellect and dedication to schoolwork—when he was able to attend class while often working long hours to help his then widowed father and siblings—were his salvation. While ascending to high school, "I committed my lessons to memory," he wrote. "The lessons in physiology and history I learned verbatim every day, so that I could repeat them, just as they were written, with as much ease as I can say the Lord's Prayer."[271] After matriculating into high school, William Sr. remembered being "deeply in love with school and study. Very often I reached the schoolhouse before the janitor arrived. From the nickels and dimes which I received for errands and small jobs I would save sufficient money to buy my books."[272] Along the way he earned excellent grades.

After saving a good chunk of money towards his tuition—about 30 dollars—and scoring superbly on qualifying examinations, following "high school Pickens entered" the historically African American "Talladega College in Alabama," completing his bachelor's degree in 1902.[273] In addition to his outstanding academic standing, William Sr. became known as a terrific orator, earning several intercollegiate competitions, as well as invitations to outside speaking engagements, including a "meeting of the American Missionary Association" that was "held in Springfield, Mass., in October" 1900. "On my way to Springfield I met for the first time Dr. Booker T. Washington, who was likewise invited to speak at the annual meeting," Pickens recalled. "And although the incident has probably never recurred to the mind of that honorable gentleman, I remember that when he learned my mission, he shared with me his space in the Pullman car and treated me with such kindly consideration that I was asked by passengers if I was not Mr. Washington's son."[274]

William Sr. next set his sights on Yale University, which seemed to be an outlandishly ambitious goal for a young black student whose forebears had been enslaved and tenant farmers in South Carolina and Arkansas. "The old problem of further education returned," Pickens realized. "I refused a position in our High School at Little Rock because I wanted to go to Yale or Harvard .... Dean Henry P. Wright of Yale, after reading the recommendations of my former teachers, had written that I could enter the junior class,"[275] surely quite a victory for Pickens. In addition to reading the works of "Carlyle and Emerson, Latin and German, in anticipation of work at Yale,"[276] Pickens personally "became acquainted with Paul Laurence Dunbar, the negro poet, who was living in Chicago. He cheered me on and wrote encouraging letters until I had finished at Yale .... There was pathos in Dunbar's constant praise of the fact that I did not touch any kind of strong drink nor any form of tobacco."[277]

Indeed, Pickens ascertained that when he matriculated, "negro students were less than one-half of one percent of the three thousand men at Yale,"[278] where he continued to be recognized as a soaring intellect and orator for which he accepted "a check for fifty dollars with appreciation from the Yale Glee, Banjo and Mandolin Clubs Association." During that time he received "daily twenty-five or more appreciative letters."[279] Among those, "Mrs. Corinne Roosevelt Robinson, sister of the President, had never quite forgotten me since my little summer campaign speech in 1900, and she sent Godspeed and a personal check. One of the most highly appreciated letters came from ex-Pres. Grover Cleveland. A good lady of Newport gave me my first and only diamond pin."[280] Pickens graduated from Yale in 1904 as a member of the prestigious Phi Beta Kappa "and was in the highest ranking group of his class."[281]

Teaching at his undergraduate alma mater, Talladega College, in Alabama, and other African American institutions of higher learning would be next for Pickens, following his graduation from Yale:

> Upon completion of his degree, Pickens began teaching foreign languages and other subjects at Talladega College. He spent ten years there and then went to Wiley University in Texas where he served as head of the departments of Greek and Sociology for one year. In 1915 Pickens accepted the position of Dean of Morgan College in Baltimore. He remained at

Morgan for five years, serving as Vice-President in the last two years .... While pursuing his career as a college professor, Pickens also received the following degrees [or honorary recognitions]: a diploma from the British Esperanto Association, 1906; a Master of Arts degree from Fisk University, 1908; a doctorate in Literature from Selma University, 1915, and an L.L.D. from Wiley University, 1918.[282]

Just after graduating from Yale, Pickens married in 1905 Minnie Cooper McAlpine, a native of Meridian, Mississippi, and a graduate of Tougaloo College, a historically black college in that state. The couple "subsequently had three children," including William Jr., who was William Pickens III's father, as well as Ruby and Harriet,[283] a graduate of Smith College and Columbia University. In fact, Harriet was destined to become a lieutenant as one of the two "first female African American officers in the Navy" in the WAVES during World War II in December 1944. Her compatriot was Ensign Frances Wills.[284] Both were assigned to Hunter College in New York City to help train incoming recruits.[285]

By 1913, Pickens began to proverbially "stretch his wings" intellectually by making "his first of many trips abroad to attend conferences and deliver lectures in England, Scotland, German, Poland, Russia, Switzerland and Austria." He would continue such travel throughout his lifetime, tragically destined to transition from this world to the next while globetrotting on the high seas. As an "inveterate traveler," Pickens would also traverse "through most of ... Central America, the West Indies and Canada." Pickens also became "a well-known contributor to the press and leading periodicals, and was a contributing editor of the Associated Negro Press for twenty-five years."[286]

The aunt of William Pickens III, Harriet Pickens, became, with Frances Wills, the Navy's first African American WAVES. (Wikimedia Commons)

In addition to authoring his autobiography, *The Heir of Slaves* (1911), and then later expanding it in *Bursting Bonds* (1923), Pickens wrote a collection of short stories, *The Vengeance of the Gods* (1922), as well as his acclaimed *The New Negro, His Political, Civil and Mental Status and Related Essays* (1916).[287] That was just before he would join as "director of branches"[288] and greatly expand the NAACP as part of the Niagara Movement of black rights activists led by preeminent black scholar W. E. B. Du Bois. Pickens recalled in *Bursting Bonds*:

> Early in the century William Edward Burghardt Du Bois, of Atlanta University, had formed the "Niagara Movement," by getting together the few liberal-minded Negro men who in that perilous time dared to have thoughts of their own about their own, and who were foolhardy enough to run the risk of the great crime of being called "radicals." I had become a member of this organization, which was the first national movement of colored people with a primary regard for their equal citizenship. The immediate heir and successor of that organization is the one now known as the National Association for the Advancement of Colored People.[289]

As the organization's first field secretary, Pickens was beyond courageous and quite prolific with greatly expanding the organization's chapters;[290] such duties often required him to travel and speak in the hotbeds of unrelenting, and often deadly, racism infested by the likes of such white-supremacist groups as the Ku Klux Klan. He exclaimed during a stump speech in 1919 following World War I that it was necessary "for every man to serve," including African Americans. In fact, "where he is most able to serve is public economy and is to the best interest of the state,"[291] Pickens continued. "This lamentable war that was forced upon us should make that plain to the dullest of us." Obviously incensed about the mostly menial roles assigned to black Americans, Pickens elaborated: "Suppose that when this war broke out … our whole country had been like Mississippi, where a caste system was holding the majority of the population in the triple chains of ignorance, semi-serfdom and poverty. Our nation would be now either the unwilling prey or the golden goose for the Prussian," Pickens declared, referring to some of Europe's then rampaging fascist forces. "The Negro asks American labor in the name of democracy to get rid of its color caste and industrial junkerism."[292]

William Pickens Sr., PhD, worked closely with preeminent scholar W. E. B. Du Bois (above), a leader of the Niagara Movement and NAACP. (Wikimedia Commons)

Although over the years Pickens moved away from participating as an officer in the NAACP—in 1942 he "officially" accepted a position with the United States Department of the Treasury selling war bonds.[293] As America's involvement in World War II intensified, his overall stances regarding black rights and equality, according to some observers, seemed to "synthesize"[294] the most acceptable positions held by fellow blacks about Booker T. Washington and, especially, W. E. B. Du Bois, who had by then also started to distance himself from the NAACP. Interestingly, Pickens was sometimes compared to and mentioned in the same sentence as Du Bois and Washington, perceived by many as two of the most powerful black leaders of "the first half of 20th century,"[295] in addition to Marcus Garvey. Indeed, "Booker T. Washington, W. E. B. Du Bois, and William Pickens show strong desire to burst into community," notes scholar José Endoença Martins in his January 2002 article "New Negroes' Bursting into Community: Booker T. Washington, W. E. B. Du Bois, and William Pickens."[296] According to the accompanying abstract, the article "places Pickens between two great modalities of intellectual involvement with black community: Washington's and Du Bois's, the other New Negroes," as "Pickens makes the synthesis of these two views of intellectual experience in Black America,"[297] combining pragmatism with intellectualism, some observers concluded. That's despite much of the African American intelligentsia, including Du Bois and Pickens, criticizing Washington for being too much of an accommodationist within racist America. "Pickens makes a strong statement of the aggressive humanhood that motivates the New Negro to fight, to live, or die for the right to be regarded as a man,"[298] Martins contends. "Rejecting the status of a useful item defended by Washington, he advises us that no man [or woman] should be reduced to a part of a machinery. The New Negro's human status must be seen as one in progress, pursued with combat and aggressiveness because, as he notes, rights are not given you, you fight for them."[299]

Despite harboring views that could have been interpreted as "militant," via "the request of the Treasury Department of the United States, Pickens took a leave of absence from the NAACP in May 1941 and went to work for the Defense Savings Staff Section."[300] It wasn't long before Pickens was "designated Chief of the Interracial Section, the National Organization Division of the Treasury in 1942."[301] It's then that "he officially severed his employment with the NAACP and became the first Black person affiliated with the Treasury Division in twenty-five years," focusing on selling war bonds to African Americans. "When the war ended, rebuffed by Walter White [then head of the NAACP] in his attempt to return to the"[302] black rights organization, Pickens "continued with the Treasury Department selling to blacks the idea of thrift through government securities."[303] Pickens retired "from the Treasury Department at age 70, in 1951," traveling "extensively throughout the world" while "writing articles for various newspapers,"[304] often about black equality as the budding civil rights era began to sweep in a new cadre of freedom fighters.

During a "Caribbean cruise," the fascinating and exceptionally productive life of William Pickens Sr. would come to a tragic end on Tuesday, April 6, 1954, after he became ill "aboard the SS *Mauretania* off Kingston, Jamaica," reported *The New York Times*.[305] "According to Walter White, executive secretary of the N.A.A.C.P., who received the information, exact cause of death was not immediately determined," the paper reported. "However, it was believed that death was caused by a heart ailment." Pickens was described in the article as a "73-year-old scholar, author and champion of equal rights for Negroes" who "was returning to New York from a Caribbean cruise. He was accompanied by his wife, Mrs. Minnie Pickens."[306] She ultimately gave the approval for her husband to be buried at sea, according to several sources. The couple had been living in the 200 block of West 139th Street, according to the *Times*, with Pickens also leaving behind "a son, William Pickens Jr.; two daughters, Harriet Pickens and Mrs. Ruby Holbrook, and two grandchildren, all of New York."[307]

Yet, William Pickens Sr. and his activist peers had already sown the mighty seeds of liberation. On the very day that Pickens died in 1954, the April 6 edition of the Montgomery, Alabama, newspaper, *The Montgomery Advertiser*, ran a letter by the Reverend Uriah J. Fields that would help to usher in the civil rights movement:[308] "The Negro citizens of Montgomery are fed up with having to stand up on buses when there are empty seats in front," the good reverend wrote. "Especially buses going to and from areas which are predominantly inhabited by Negroes."[309] A young black preacher with a gift for oratory, just like William Pickens Sr., whose ancestors had also been slaves, traveled from Atlanta to lead the charge by way of the courageousness of such heroines as Rosa Parks, who refused to give up her bus seat to a white man. His name was Rev. Dr. Martin Luther King Jr., and he would go on to guide what became known as the Montgomery bus boycott, igniting one of the greatest social revolutions known to humankind.

CHAPTER 10

Honoring the Ancestors and Legacy of the Historic Interracial Relationship

The remains of some of Sag Harbor's earliest African Americans and others rest in the cemetery of the St. David African Methodist Episcopal Zion Church, founded in 1835 during the height of the whaling industry. (Wikimedia Commons/Capt. Jay Ruffins)

About two decades before his untimely death on the SS *Mauretania* in 1954, William Pickens Sr. hopped in his car and "first motored out to Sag Harbor in the 1930s,"[1] likely from his residence in New York City. Back then there was no interstate highway system and gas stations were dozens of miles apart, stretching a trip that today would take a few hours to as many as six hours along narrow roads to Long Island's shore[2] on the "east end" of "Gardiners Bay," situated "on the site of a [bygone] Montauk Indian village" known as Wegwagonock, dating back to at least 1707.[3] Furthermore, even in New

York, African Americans traveling during the early 1900s had to be on the lookout for alternative accommodations or services due to racism and Jim Crow segregation.[4] Upon arriving in the Sag Harbor area, likely by way of dusty meandering roads transecting earth-toned marshland and leading to the bay's serene sandy beaches massaged by cascading waves and squawking seagulls gliding the sapphire heavens' winds, "he got out of his car in his suit and tie clasp, looked around, then got back in" his car. "'It was too rustic, and it wasn't his thing,'" William Pickens III told *The New York Times* in 1996 about his grandfather's first impressions of what became known as part of the "Black Hamptons." "'But his children,'" including William Pickens Jr., as well as his sisters, future naval officer Harriet and Ruby, destined to become a noted teacher, "'reveled in it.'"[5]

Born September 27, 1936, in New York City's Harlem as the Great Depression raged from 1929 to 1941, Pickens Sr.'s grandson, William Pickens III, reminisced about his family being fortunate enough to visit and acquire property on Sag Harbor, a bayside enclave that harbored early Native Americans and African-descended whalers. The first African Americans came due to "the whaling industry," Pickens explained during an interview with journalist Trymaine Lee on MSNBC in 2021.[6] "Whaling was the economic arm of Sag Harbor in the 1830s," said Pickens, who had begun to visit Sag Harbor, Long Island, with his family at age 10 around 1946 during World War II. "You needed to have men who would be willing to go for a year and a half away from America to whale, go out to the Pacific." In fact, sometimes such sailors "had to go around South America,"[7] noted Pickens, who "grew up in Laurelton, Queens and visited Sag Harbor during the summer for decades before finally settling in the historic whaling village fulltime in 2004" with his beloved wife, Patricia, affectionately known as "Pat."[8]

"There was no Panama Canal," Pickens continued. "So when you signed on a ship here, a few Blacks from Africa's Cape Verde Islands, from Harlem, from Brooklyn, a token number became shipmates on these whaling craft,"[9] although some sources indicate the numbers of African-descended sailors on such vessels sometimes were quite significant.[10] "And they would be gone for 18 months. But that was really the first African presence in Sag Harbor."[11]

Pickens, in fact, realized that land opportunities were an exceptionally rare opportunity for people of color—especially after European settlers arrived, too often hoarding prime land for segregated development. Indeed, according to Pickens, two of the earliest black property owners in Sag Harbor were the first African American president of the historically black college in Atlanta that was the Reverend Dr. Martin Luther King's alma mater, Morehouse College,[12] John

Hope (1868–1936), and his wife, Lugenia. "So you're going back to the 19th century," Pickens recalled. In fact, "by 1900 John Hope, the great scholar from Georgia,"[13] had married Lugenia Burns, a distinguished and well-known black rights "social activist."[14] As fate would have it, "his wife went from Savannah, Georgia, to Sag Harbor by boat," Pickens recalled. "She was going to live in New York. But she got off the boat in Sag Harbor and liked it so much that she rented a room and then built a house."[15]

William Pickens III met his wife, Audrey Patricia (née Brannen), on Sag Harbor's beach, marrying her in 1962. (William Pickens III Archives)

The word was amplified among upwardly mobile African Americans that Sag Harbor and nearby areas presented opportunities to vacation, especially for those from the New York metropolitan area such as the Pickenses. At the time, many beaches throughout America were closed to or barely accessible to black folks. Pickens III's Aunt Ruby, he said, had been "friendly with" Lugenia Hope, so that's how his family learned about Sag Harbor. "So, it started very small," Pickens explained. "It wasn't till the '30s that more African Americans came to Sag Harbor." In fact, "there was a school teacher who taught at Brooklyn Technical High School,"[16] not far from where the Pickens family lived in a Brooklyn townhouse. "And he came out and built four or five little cottages for his friends. And he rented them out. And that started more volume of coming to Sag Harbor back in the '30s" as such African Americans avoided taking expensive vacations while the Depression raged.[17] "Sag Harbor afforded you a fishing opportunity," as well as swimming and boating. "And they started coming out by train and boat to check it out," with lot sales accelerating "after World War II."[18]

At Sag Harbor "you [African Americans] could own the bay front," Pickens pointed out, unlike in other nearby areas. "You could actually own property that would guard against intrusions on the beach," he further explained. "That was the fundamental difference. And that's why the beachfront lots went … really fast. Because the men and women recognized, 'Well, here's a glorious opportunity.' We had our own beach. And that was the … difference: beachfront ownership."[19]

Standing with William Pickens III is former Secretary of State Colin Powell who visited Sag Harbor as a child and later, while an adult. (William Pickens III Archives)

According to the 1996 *New York Times* report and interview of Pickens, "over the years, some of the most well-known black Americans have either rented, bought or been houseguests in a handful of enclaves outside the mostly white village of Sag Harbor."[20] Many of the "homes" were described as "modest, on small lots; Azurest, Ninevah and Sag Harbor Hills are the three enclaves on water, and have the most cachet."[21] Notably, "Langston Hughes once read poems[22] on the porch of Mr. Pickens's father, and Colin Powell," the former chairman of the Joint Chiefs of Staff and the United States secretary of state, the first African American to hold such positions, "came to fish as a boy" on Sag Harbor. "Ron Brown, the Secretary of Commerce" for the United States, who was "killed in a plane crash in April [1996], met his wife, Alma, at a party in Sag Harbor Hills in 1959,"[23] reminiscent of how Pickens met his wife, Pat, on Sag Harbor's beach.[24] "After the two were married in 1962, the Browns always returned as guests, occasioning a series of weekend-long parties, with peach blueberry pie."[25]

And there were other affluent African Americans who found the Sag Harbor area to be an irresistible sanctuary. Kenneth Chenault, the former chairman of American Express, owned property "in Azurest; Bruce Llewellyn, Mr. Powell's cousin and one of the nation's wealthiest investors, used to rent in Sag Harbor Hills" before purchasing a home in nearby Bridgehampton. Pickens further told the *Times*: "The new entrepreneurs have a wider play. They can go wherever their money can take them."[26] He continued: "But we gave them the anchor. They stood on our shoulders. Whatever grief and guff society had to offer, we took it."[27]

Yet, Pickens was concerned that in recent years developers increasingly eyed properties on the island as assessments and property values—and associated taxes—had skyrocketed, threatening the historic culture of Sag Harbor. "Well, it's changed a little bit," Pickens admitted during the MSNBC interview.[28] "But I think there's a determination now that the families who can stay here will stay here," he said. "Because to replace this is almost impossible. It was wonderfully accessible for us. But now it's accessible to everybody. And all we can do is guard against the encroachment by staying here and paying our bills, paying our taxes, improving our properties. That's the only way we're gonna survive this."[29]

Surviving and thriving certainly weren't foreign concepts for Bill Pickens. "He attended [from 1954–1958][30] the University of Vermont where he majored in history and political science, and became the first African American student to be elected president of the student body."[31] "He was also elected president of the Honor Society and president of the fraternity Tau Epsilon Phi."[32] In fact, along the way, Pickens helped to eradicate the racist "entertainment" tradition of belittling African Americans in blackface at the college, the so-called "Kake Walk"[33] that was prevalent then on many college campuses and elsewhere. Furthermore, just several years before his passing in September 2021, Pickens "gifted his alma mater with" a "collection of significant and rare books on African American history, literature, civil rights and black life in America, including inscribed volumes passed down from his father and grandfather with handwritten words from Hughes, James Weldon Johnson and others."[34]

After joining the U.S. Air Force in 1958 as a second lieutenant, Pickens was deployed to Japan and began to earnestly learn the Japanese language and otherwise immerse himself deeply in the culture, including martial arts. Meanwhile, Pickens became so fascinated with Japanese dolls that he gathered a collection of "more than 70" eventually shown at Columbia University's C. V. Starr East Asian Library.[35]

Following the service, Pickens pursued a career in business, first as an executive for a range of well-known companies such as Booz Allen Hamilton, Western Electric, Marine Midland Bank, and Philip Morris[36] before launching "his own consulting firm, Bill Pickens Associates, in 1979."[37] Along the way, Pickens "also served on the board of multiple nonprofit organizations, was founding chair of the Paul Robeson Foundation and, following in his grandfather's footsteps," became quite active in the NAACP.[38]

In addition to often advocating for his grandfather, William Pickens Sr., and Robeson, "in 1975, Pickens created the William Pickens Prize, a cash award for the top senior essayist from Yale's Department of African American Studies, in honor of his grandfather, whose portrait hangs in the chairman's office in the university's Arts and Sciences Department."[39] Pickens III, who was a slender, outspoken, and affable man with a contagious grin and laugh, seemed often quite aware of the irony and importance of his progenitors' impressive accomplishments as African Americans. "'It's funny,'" he said during an interview with *The Independent*, one of a group of Dan's Independent

Media papers serving the Sag Harbor, Long Island, vicinity. "'You walk into the university and all you see are pictures of all these white guys on the walls and then you see my grandfather. I'm sure it causes a pause.'"[40]

In fact, it was on May 8, 2009, as much of America was still exhilarated by the 2008 election of the first African American commander in chief, President Barack Obama, when William Pickens III and his grown children, the late William Pickens IV, John Montier, and Pamela, trekked to Philadelphia[41] in temperatures hovering around freezing. They "traveled from New York State for the" Philadelphia Museum of Art's "January 13, 2009, unveiling of the oil paintings, masterfully composed in 1841 and depicting Hiram Charles Montier and wife Elizabeth Brown Montier proudly sitting for a very skilled but relatively unknown Philadelphia-based artist, Franklin R. Street."[42]

Among hordes of onlookers, members of the press, and museum officials, Pamela, who cohosted the unveiling with her brothers and father, reminded the audience that the portraits were passed down over many decades including by her father's family-historian mother "or her grandmother, Emilie Brown Montier [Pickens], born 1901."[43] "The portraits have always been very significant to us," Pamela proudly declared. "Regular people do have regular histories that intersect with the extraordinary,"[44] she added, referencing the election of Obama, who also has mixed-raced ancestors.

William Pickens III and his daughter Pamela Alison Pickens noted that the election of the first African American president Barack Obama, who spoke in March 2010 at the Cheltenham, Pa.-based Arcadia University in the vicinity of land once owned by their ancestor Cremona Morrey, represents great possibilities for equal opportunity and upward mobility for African Americans and others. (Official White House Photo by Pete Souza via Wikimedia Commons)

William Pickens III and his wife, Patricia, pose in front of Hiram and Elizabeth Montier, depicted in rare portraits of affluent African Americans. (William Pickens III Archives)

Pamela's brother, John Montier Pickens, told *The Philadelphia Inquirer* that after the images were discovered under an elder relative's bed, the family "restored them …. The stars lined up. It's extraordinary …. This is truly an American story that needed to be shared, and what better place to share it? This is indeed the ultimate homecoming."[45]

Museum officials seemed to be ecstatic too about the very rare images of affluent, middle-class African Americans who were apparently free and thriving during the early to mid-19th century. Alice Beamesderfer, then interim head of curatorial affairs at the museum, said, "We are thrilled to be able to represent in our American galleries these exceptional paintings that document Philadelphia's early African American community."[46] She further asserted: "The Montier portraits present a wonderful opportunity to learn about Philadelphia's diverse past and specifically about African American life here [in Philadelphia] during the mid-19th century."[47]

Kathleen Foster, then the museum's curator of American art and now The Robert L. McNeil, Jr., Senior Curator of American Art, and Director of the Center for American Art, agreed that the "fascinating story" behind the paintings, as well as the artwork itself, are essential for acknowledging the "intriguing" accomplishments of such African Americans and various challenging social conditions that they faced.[48]

Mark Mitchell, in 2009 working at the museum as assistant curator and manager of the Center for American Art, was well aware of the portraits' historical significance. "The Montier family's connection to one of the first families of Philadelphia makes these portraits all the more significant."[49]

William Pickens III learned that the remains of ancestors not previously buried at the family graveyard in Edge Hill's Guineatown were buried at Eden Cemetery in Collingdale, Pennsylvania, southwest of Philadelphia. (William Pickens III Archives)

Two years following that 2009 showing of the portraits, in 2011—after about two decades "of searching"—Bill Pickens was contacted by a staffer of the primarily African American Eden Cemetery in Collingdale, a suburban community on the outskirts of southwest Philadelphia. "She'd found records showing that at least four of his ancestors were buried at Eden in unmarked plots," including "his great-great-grandparents Elizabeth and Hiram Montier."[50]

However, most of Pickens's dozens of buried ancestors have yet to be found following their supposed reinterment from the family's Guineatown cemetery—variously known as the Montieth Cemetery, Edge Hill Cemetery, the Cemetery for Colored Folks, the Colored Cemetery, or Montier Cemetery—in what is today Cheltenham Township's Glenside community due to a road-widening project in the early 1960s. Nevertheless, Pickens was delighted that Jones had found documentation that Hiram and Elizabeth rested at Eden.[51] The couple lay among such historic notables as the great contralto singer Marian Anderson, who reportedly took music lessons in South Philadelphia and the La Mott community of Cheltenham during the early 1900s, as well as William Still,[52] "the father of the Underground Railroad," who operated a commissary or sutler's post on the grounds of Camp William Penn where federal African American soldiers trained for the Civil War, also in Cheltenham. "He'd come far in his quest to trace his bloodline to the union of a former slave and the son of Philadelphia's first mayor. He'd found birth records, death records, tax records property records, and the first U.S. Census, which listed three of his ancestors, going back eight generations,"[53] according to *The Philadelphia Inquirer*. "He possessed the 1798 indenture—written on deerskin and bearing a bullet hole—that established his family's burial grounds in Glenside."[54]

Upon his arrival at Eden, Pickens and his family were greeted by "Mina Cockroft, Eden's general manager," who had been "waiting for her guests with a map, a plastic marker, and a bouquet of silk flowers. Together they rode together up a hill to the Lebanon section, Lot No. 105."[55] In fact, as "they passed Marian Anderson, Pickens recalled how growing up in Philadelphia, his mother used to play dolls with the great contralto."[56]

Despite not being able to discover the resting spots of his ancestral family matriarch, Cremona Morrey Fry; or her daughter, Cremona Montier; or the latter's husband, John; or, indeed, scores of others buried in Guineatown, Pickens was thankful for the blessing of finding Hiram and Elizabeth Montier. "To find his people, to know they were cared for made Pickens ecstatic. He talked about the importance of closure and the joy of discovery, about knowing who you come from."[57]

Still, Pickens and researchers have searched relentlessly for records that might possibly indicate exactly when and where those buried in Guineatown were moved. Indeed, some observers have speculated that the remains may not have been reinterred after all. Might some of those originally interred in fact still be resting in proximity to a Knights of Columbus facility and residences near the 200 block of Limekiln Pike in Glenside where the original cemetery was reportedly located?[58] Tragically, countless African American cemeteries have been built over or the remains have been otherwise unrecognized or discarded throughout the United States. There is documentation that the Guineatown cemetery was intact during the late 1800s, according to the article, "MONTIETH GRAVEYARD. A Burial Ground for Colored People in Cheltenham," in a Montgomery County-area newspaper, probably *The Norristown Herald*, discovered in a scrapbook of the Montgomery County Historical Society, dated November 20, 1897. The graveyard, the article says, "is in the extreme northwest corner" of the township, "at the eastern confines of the stirring town of Edge Hill, adjoining the grounds of the public school of the place,"[59] probably the "Edge Hill School" that "was built in 1890" featuring "a fine-toned bell" that had been transferred from the nearby Audenried School.[60]

> On December 15, 1890, on land purchased from George D. Heist, the Edge Hill School opened on Limekiln Pike near the old Montier Cemetery. The growth of the local iron ore industry had brought an increase of population in the Edge Hill Village area. In 1901 an addition was made to the original 3 room school. The school closed in 1940 as a result of decreasing enrollment and in 1948 was sold to the Knights of Columbus, who still occupy it.[61]

Many of the children enrolled at the Edge Hill School and living in the area were described as Italian and African American,[62] ethnicities facing intense discrimination during the late 1800s and early 1900s.

The "MONTIETH GRAVEYARD" article even provides information about the size of the Guineatown cemetery: "It is about 40 × 45 feet in space, and on the left hand side of the Limekiln pike leading east of the village"—a road that had been "laid out in 1693, by a provincial council."[63] Although the article identifies a "slave holder" named "John Murray" as someone who provided the land for the cemetery,[64] it is quite possible that the benefactor was Richard Morrey (sometimes spelled Murray), who by the time of his death in 1754 would have been aware of Guineatown's growing African American community. However, it's worth noting that Richard did have a brother, John Murray (or Morrey), who died in 1698.[65] When Richard's father Humphrey Morrey passed away in 1715 and his will probated in 1716,[66] almost two decades after his son John dying in 1698, Guineatown would likely not have been a completely developed community; meanwhile a check of Ancestry.com and FamilySearch census, wills, and other records did not reveal a John Murray living in Cheltenham, despite at least one such individual living in nearby communities. Within the ensuing years, Richard Morrey or his father, Humphrey, arranged for or agreed to the emancipation or self-emancipation of Cremona and her children, according to some sources; meanwhile, other sources indicate that liberation came for Cremona and presumably her children closer to 1746 when Richard and Cremona's marital relationship ended, with Richard soon after marrying Sarah (Allen) Beasley. Richard also in 1746 made arrangements for Cremona to acquire the 198 acres via a complex 500-year "demise" agreement.[67] Robert Lewis, identified as being the first child born to Richard and Cremona Morrey during the early to mid 1730s, eventually acquired and held the official 1798 deed to the cemetery—a document that still is possessed by Pickens family members today.

Also observed were the names of some of the interred "on the grave stones in the well-enclosed yard," including "Caroline and Mary Mullin, also David

HONORING THE ANCESTORS AND LEGACY • 203

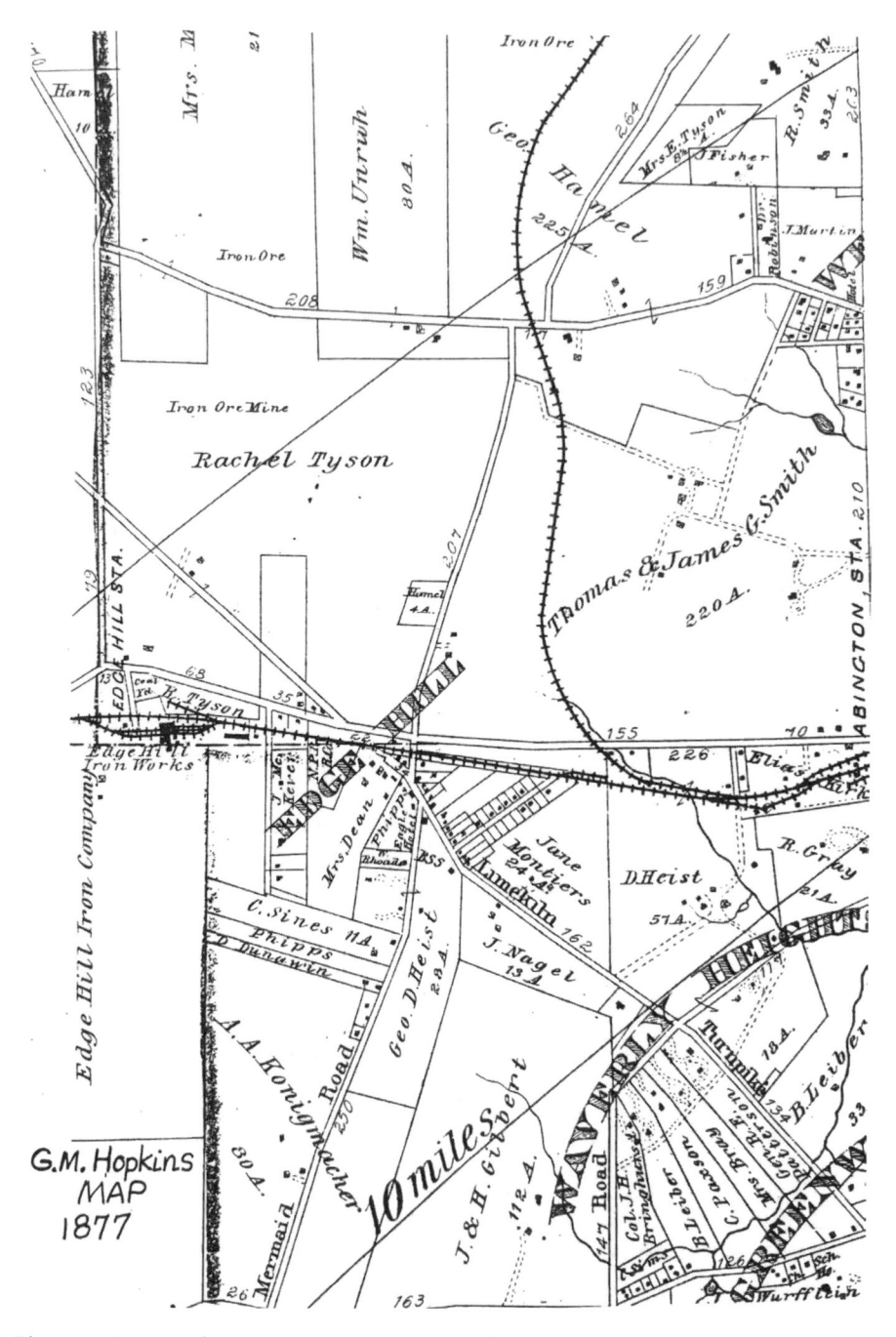

This 1877 G. M. Hopkins map shows the community of Edge Hill including Jane Montier's residence and property where the Guineatown cemetery was located. (Old York Road Historical Society)

204 • THE MONTIERS

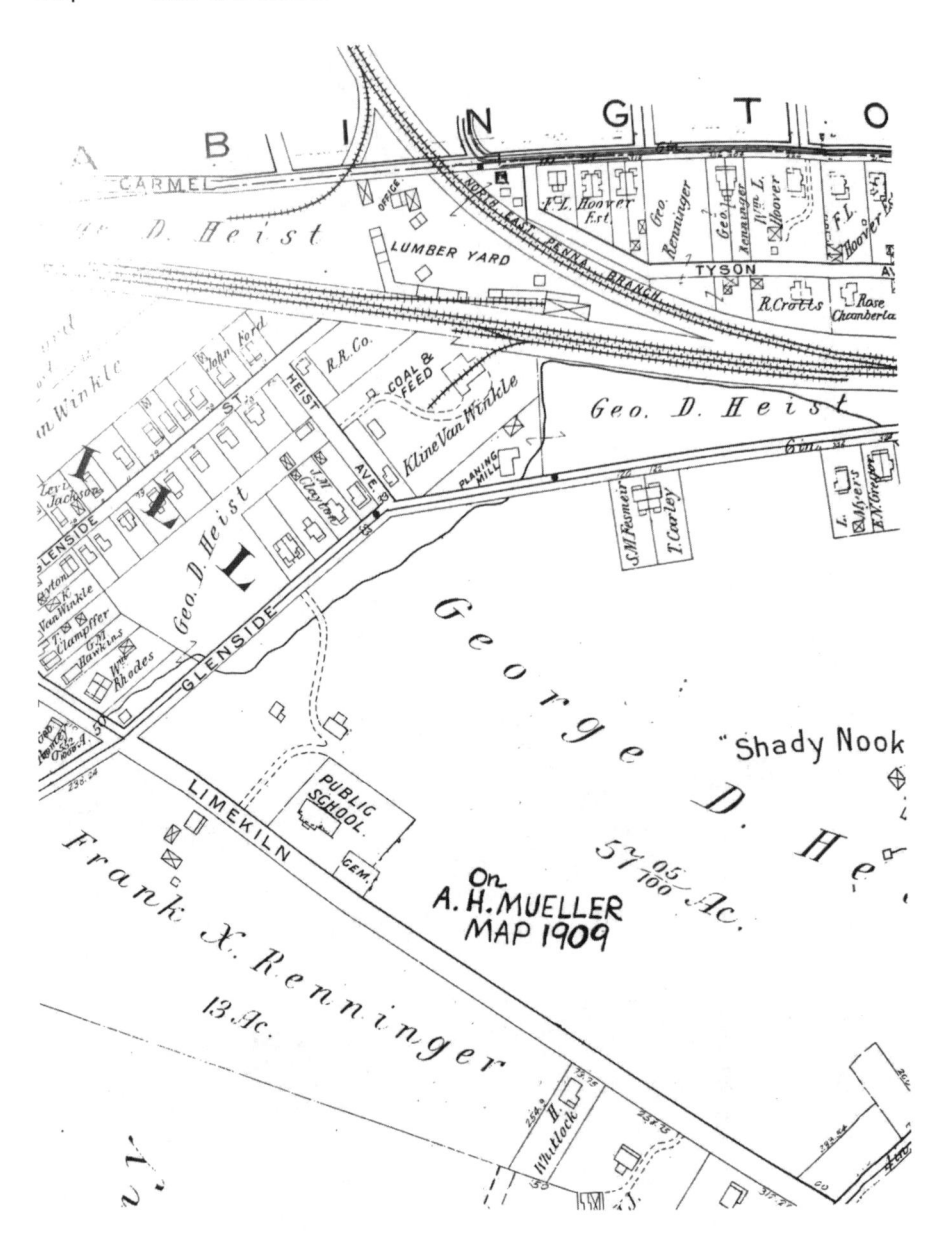

According to this 1909 map composed by A. H. Mueller, the Guineatown cemetery was still in existence, next to the public school along Limekiln Pike. (Old York Road Historical Society)

Stover," as well as "Matilda Hilton, John Knight," and "Jane Montieth," a Morrey-Montier descendant.[68] "Only about 7 grave stones are to be seen in this yard, yet we were told there were about 75 interments," according to the writer of the article, identified as W. E. Corson. "An esteemed, aged and greatly respected citizen of the place, who resided quite near the burial plot, Mr. Joseph Nagle, informed us that body had been put upon body, frequently in the same ground in late, subsequent interments being dug and a second body deposited."[69]

Apparently, the property was overall impressively maintained, according to the writer. "The yard has a good wall and the place is kept in creditable order. Some three or four forest trees of fair size add to the improvement of the place," the newspaper scribe observed. "Colored people principally are buried in this place, though some white people, through intermarrying, found their interment and last abode in this place, with a people 'with a skin not colored like their own.'"[70]

At least one historical text written by an eyewitness indicates that the cemetery, which had eventually become overgrown with "weeds," certainly was accessible in 1917,[71] several decades before Limekiln Pike in the Glenside vicinity was supposedly widened during the early 1960s, according to various reports. Edward B. Phillips, in his essay "The Record of a Hike on the Bethlehem Pike," remembered walking by the cemetery in September 1917 and observing several tombstones, as well as buildings and residents that included African Americans:[72]

> Climbing another hill on the [Limekiln] pike, I came to the Edge Hill public school building, a modern structure, the janitor of which told me that it was attended largely by negro and Italian children. Just as he imparted this information the children came rushing into the lawn-like yard from the school, and I was thus enabled to verify his assertion. I also understood why the place was formerly called Guineatown.
>
> I asked one of the teachers, who was standing on the steps, one or two questions about the locality, but she was unable to answer them, saying they just came up from the city to teach. Local history should be taught in all public schools and by teachers properly informed on the subject.[73]

Phillips, obviously concerned about the tendency to overlook such topics pertaining to African Americans, continued, with quite a revelation, in a section subtitled, "Inspecting Old Tombstones": "Adjoining this school is a small plot of ground enclosed with a tall iron fence," Phillips wrote. "This is the mysterious private burying ground for negroes. Pushing my way through the tall weeds, I found several headstones," including one of Pickens's likely Montier ancestors. "An old broken stone conveyed no information to me. The others were inscribed as follows: 'Jane Montier, 1814–1859'; 'Anna Matilda Hilton, 1839–1888' 'Caroline H. Mullin, 1842–1864.'"[74]

Although Phillips seems to have accurately recorded Jane's 1814 birth year, Ancestry.com records indicate that Jane Montier died at about age 70 in November 1883,[75] not 1859 as Phillips said. Her burial was handled by the Kirk & Nice Funeral Home,[76] noted "as the first funeral home in the United States," founded in 1761[77] and based not far from Jane's Germantown residence in northwest Philadelphia. Indeed, it is worth noting that Kirk & Nice was willing to actually perform burial services for an African American family during a period when most such white-owned enterprises certainly would not have done so due to racism.

Ancestry.com's records indicate that the decedent Anna Matilda Hilton was born about 1840 and died February 9, 1888, when she was already "widowed."[78] During the prior year, Philadelphia's 1887 city directory lists an Anna M. Hilton and her "Spouse," George Hilton, living in the 200 block of Centre Street in Germantown,[79] a community where Jane Montier also resided. Interestingly, Ancestry also notes in another entry that an individual identified as "Anna Matilda Caroline Montier," who was designated the daughter of Solomon and Susannah Montier, was baptized on April 11, 1849, at the First United Methodist Church of Germantown.[80] Consequently, is it possible that Phillips, who strolled through the Guineatown cemetery in 1917, somehow inadvertently combined the names of the third-referenced burial, Caroline H. Mullin, with "Anna Matilda Caroline Montier"? Or, are the two individuals the same person?

Indeed, also interred in the cemetery was 14-year-old Caroline Hoy, born about 1846, identified as ethnically "White" and living in nearby Upper Merion Township, with Peter B. Hoy, age 23, and Margaret Hoy, 22, according to the 1860 United States census via FamilySearch.org.[81] "It is likely that the girl living with the young couple, Peter ... and Margaret (Mullen) Hoy was her sister Caroline, born in 1846," says a notation in an Ancestry.com entry.[82]

Notably, "Jane Montier, a dressmaker who never married and a daughter of Hiram [Montier], became the owner of the family's properties in Cheltenham[83] and Germantown."[84] Her father, Hiram, helped to cofound the New Bethel African Methodist Episcopal Church of Germantown before passing away July 8, 1861, just after the Civil War commenced in April of that year when Confederate forces attacked South Carolina's Fort Sumter. "The Reverend Amos Wilson, pastor of Bethel AME Church, was named administrator of" Jane's estate, ultimately selling her Edge Hill property to George D. Heist in 1886. Jane[85] and her father, Hiram, were buried in Guineatown's cemetery.[86]

Meanwhile, there is online documentation indicating that a "Cemetery for Colored Folks" in Glenside within area code 19038 on Limekiln Pike via City-data.com property valuation records, was assessed in 2009 at "$5,470" that consisted of "Land area" totaling "1,800 square feet" and described as "Paved." There's also a "Sale date" of January 1, 2000, and a description of the parcel as "non-taxable property."[87] The property records website of Montgomery County, Pennsylvania, confirms much of City-Data's information, as well as displays the "Land Use Description" as "EXEMPT CEMETERIES (PRIVATE)" and the "Sale Price" as "$0." The "Grantor" *and* "Grantee" are identified as the "CEMETERY FOR COLORED FOLKS."[88] No cemetery is visible today in that immediate area.

After the "Negros Burial Ground" was discovered in Lower Manhattan during the construction of a government services building, Pickens's concerns about the disposition of his ancestors' remains were published in the August 16, 1992, edition of *The New York Times* in a poignant letter to the editor titled "I Thought of My Family Burial Ground Outside Philadelphia."[89] In fact, teams of archeologists and scientists were summoned to study, document, and preserve part of the New York site, as well as evaluate the DNA of the remains—intriguingly leading to such popular genetic-evaluation services as AfricanAncestry.com, led by Gina Paige and Rick Kittles, a renowned black scientist who worked on the New York site.[90] "As a descendant of an 18th-century African American family in Philadelphia," Pickens wrote in *The New York Times* letter, "I visited the Negros Burial Ground unearthed in Lower Manhattan to pay my respects. Profoundly moved by this discovery, and pleased that a preservation agreement seems to be in the works …, I thought again of my own family burial ground outside of Philadelphia."[91]

"This private burial place, formerly nestled in the rolling hills of historic Glenside, Pa., was established by lawful deed and indenture in September 1798 by three male family stalwarts,"[92] including Robert Lewis.[93] "They decided to do this to assure a decent, dignified burial for all members of the John Montier family 'for a tenure of 500 years,'" wrote Pickens, clearly building his case. "The Montiers were aware that even Quaker libertarians were not disposed to dignified burials for African Americans. (John Montier was born in 1740, and his home, built in 1770, stands today.)"[94] (Note: some sources indicate that the home in question was built in 1772.)

"Indeed, my family may have been aware of the treatment accorded blacks in old New York during the Colonial period," the family patriarch wrote. "Today, I proudly hold the original indenture, written in 18th-century English on a deerskin and witnessed by Quaker neighbors, then duly attested by county justices,"[95] Pickens continued before providing crucial details.

"Alas, the Commonwealth of Pennsylvania, in the late 1950s or early 1960s, embarked on a road-widening project along Lime Kiln Pike, a major Colonial road between Philadelphia and Valley Forge,"[96] where General George Washington's troops, including African Americans, nearly perished during the Revolutionary War, but saved in part by one of Pickens's African-descended Bustill ancestors, Cyrus Bustill, providing bread to the beleaguered troops, according to family tradition and other sources. "Sometime before that, a Roman Catholic church placed a driveway adjacent to and undoubtedly over the very ground under which my family was interred,"[97] circumstances that obviously angered Pickens, as he moved on to making his final points:

> By walking off the measurements from the 1798 deed and reviewing the road-widening map, I unhappily discovered in 1990 that my family burial ground had been unceremoniously plowed under.[98]
>
> I have made inquiries of the Pennsylvania attorney general's office and among nearby cemeteries to learn if my 75 relatives thought to be buried in that ground had been disinterred and reinterred elsewhere. Thus far, the trail is blank.[99]

"The lesson is painfully clear," Pickens concluded his 1992 letter to the *Times*. Pickens would eventually learn, however, about limited reinterments of his kinfolk first laid to rest in cemeteries other than the one in Guineatown. "African Americans in death were as ill treated as in life, private property notwithstanding. To consecrate the Negros Burial Ground in New York is a fitting solution," read an outraged Pickens's 1992 words, and "to desecrate my private family burial ground in Pennsylvania was a blistering sin. The Montier Family Association was formed in 1990 to combat this tyranny and to salute the decency of Colonial black folk."[100]

The letter was signed, "WILLIAM PICKENS 3D President, Montier Family Assn. New York, Aug. 9, 1992."[101]

However, during the WHYY-PBS television program *The Montiers: An American Story*, which aired in 2018 throughout the Philadelphia metropolitan area, Pickens acknowledged: "In 1960 the bodies were either disinterred or buried in a road widening process, which is heartbreaking. I was very angry when I learned that maybe they had just bulldozed my history away." He was happy to learn, however, that some of the remains of family members likely originally buried at other Philadelphia-area cemeteries, including Lebanon Cemetery, established in 1903, were reinterred at Delaware County's Eden Cemetery, both cemeteries primarily reserved for African Americans. "We are finding more of the family reinterred, which is very good," Pickens noted.[102]

Three decades after writing to *The New York Times*, when Pickens would transition to the hereafter at age 85 on September 27, 2021, and join his

WHYY-PBS producer Karen Smyles was among those participating in a panel concerning her production, *The Montiers: An American Story*, and other fascinating elements of the family. Posing here are Samuel Cameron, PhD (Arcadia professor); Karen Smyles; the late William Pickens III; former Arcadia archivist Diane Bockrath; and David Rowland, president of the Old York Road Historical Society. (Arcadia University)

ancestors, the whereabouts of those Guineatown forebears had still not been determined, and that remains the case today. Among the tragically uncounted African Americans are the many buried nationwide in unmarked graves or who were interred in cemeteries that have been either desecrated or paved over for so-called development, including more than a few of Pickens's previously "counted" forebears. "This is about the larger story of Black history, of American history," the chair of the Department of Anthropology at the University of South Florida, Antoinette Jackson, told *The New York Times* in 2022.[103] "These cemeteries, so many of which have been erased, are a fulcrum for our understanding of who we are as a nation. They offer a window into the people of a community."[104]

Details in the *Times* article seem remarkably like the possible fate of the Montier cemetery and its approximately 75 sacred remains, a microcosm of a terrible national macro-phenomenon:

> For decades, burial grounds that held names, stories and history slipped away. Some were unkept or abandoned as members of Black communities died off or some moved away. Some were unprotected and neglected by cities responsible for their care. Others were lost to the environment or to development—completely paved over and now lying beneath highways, stadiums, office buildings, parking lots and subdivisions.

William Pickens III said he was honored that a street, Montier Rd. in Cheltenham Township, bears the surname of his ancestors. (William Pickens III Archives)

But in recent years, cemeteries dating back to the 1800s have been found on property behind churches, under high school and college campuses, deep in wooded lots. These discoveries are just the beginning of a tedious journey.[105]

Over the years, in addition to Bill Pickens, local historical groups in Cheltenham Township, as well as scholars, journalists, and others, have sought absolute proof concerning the fate of Guineatown's cemetery, but with very limited results. The township, Montgomery County, and state organizations, as well as other groups have yielded virtually no data because of the reported scarcity of related records and even the absence of news reports during the early to mid-1960s concerning the supposed reinterments. Burial and census records have failed to provide definitive information.

The search continues: "Reclaiming burial grounds and connecting descendants to their ancestors involves detective work: collecting oral histories from family members and local elders; tracking death certificates; studying property maps and deeds; and combing spotty and unforgiving records," according to the *Times*.[106] "Descendants and volunteer groups, working with archaeologists, often form foundations or associations to gain custody of—or at least access to—land to look for headstones, depressions and any other clues that may help determine the numbers of people interred and the boundaries of a cemetery."[107] Pickens took a few of these steps, but the work remains unfinished, complicated by the fact that the cemetery is no longer visible above ground due to paving and structural or housing developments.

Yamona Pierce, according to the *Times*, like Pickens, started such an association after learning about her revered African American ancestors, "her third great-grandparents, Jane Hamilton and Owen Hood." They "had been sharecroppers in Harris County, Ga.," and ultimately "buried in Pierce Chapel African Cemetery." Upon traveling there from the Washington, DC, area with "her two daughters," Pierce was devastated to learn the burial ground "was littered with trash, furniture and car tires." The experience motivated Pierce to start "a nonprofit, the Hamilton Hood Foundation (named after her relatives)," along the way hooking up "with community organizations" that "raised money through grants and private donations." Subsequently, "50 headstones have been found on the two-acre site."[108]

Closer to Pickens's ancestral Guineatown origins in Pennsylvania, during 2022, "the African American Cultural Heritage Action Fund, an initiative by the National Trust for Historic Preservation, awarded Pennsylvania $50,000 to develop a statewide program to protect and restore African American cemeteries and burial grounds," the *Times* reported.[109] In fact, in 2023 Pennsylvania Hallowed Grounds and Preservation Pennsylvania granted "awards to 13 African American cemeteries to assist in their ongoing preservation efforts as part of an African American Cemetery Stewardship Program," ranging from the African Union Church of South Coventry in Chester County and the Thornbury AME Cemetery of Delaware County to the Zion Hill Cemetery in Lancaster County and Byberry Township's African American Burial Ground in Philadelphia County. "Direct grant assistance is available for projects costing between $3,000–$7,000."[110]

Although the Montier Cemetery today appears to be nonexistent above the ground, it would likely be quite fruitful to investigate the possibility of remains underground with radar or sonar technology to ascertain if the Montiers and others were reinterred elsewhere or are still in the ground, having been paved over sometime before the mid-1900s. "Ground Penetrating Radar [GPR] is a tool that uses electromagnetic waves to image the subsurface," according to the website of Kutztown University professor, Dr. Laura Sherrod, who specializes in geophysics and hydrology. Interestingly, "electromagnetic waves from the antenna" by way of "reflections" or images are analyzed and "recorded by the control unit and used to generate a GPR profile output, similar to seismic survey output."[111] Such technology has been used at the "Bethlehem Cemetery—Mass Grave," resulting from the global 1918 Spanish influenza "outbreak" in Bethlehem, Pennsylvania, to "Mouns Jones archaeological site in Douglassville, PA" that is "believed to be the first permanent settlement in Berks County," Pennsylvania.[112]

Furthermore, the Pennsylvania Historical and Museum Commission notes: "The archeology of grave sites usually becomes necessary in conjunction with new construction in an urban environment. Excavations accidentally unearth human remains that had not been expected."[113] It's an important consideration because "in many cities on the east coast, despite new directives for land planners to understand the past history of a site before digging through the Section 106 process," proper protocols have sometimes not been followed. Indeed, Section 106, which took effect in 1966, probably just after the Limekiln Pike road-widening project, is a regulation that "requires federal agencies to consider the effects on historic properties of projects they carry out, assist, fund, permit, license, or approve throughout the country."[114] In fact, the commission acknowledged that "African American burial grounds in former Potter's Fields or buried churchyards have been uncovered in both New York City and Philadelphia,"[115] including the Big Apple's aforementioned "Negros Burial Ground." That New York gravesite was discovered during the early 1990s, and Philadelphia's First African Baptist Church burial ground at Eighth and Vine Streets was located when workers found remains while excavating to build a subway line near the Delaware River during the mid-1980s.[116]

The Philadelphia site up until 1984 was "the only Black pre-Civil War urban cemetery ever excavated outside the South," according to this author's June 10, 1984, article for the *Philadelphia Inquirer* magazine.[117] The story focused on African American cultural anthropologist and archeologist Janet Collins, who was digging for John Milner Associates, a distinguished archeology firm, at the site that may have included some of her ancestors. Collins, the sister of acclaimed Philly community activist and radio and television journalist, the late E. Steven Collins, back then felt "from the evidence … compiled, that the old cemetery was the burial ground of at least one of her forefathers."[118] She surmised that some of her ancestors may have worshipped at the nearby church on "the land … purchased in the late 1700s by a man named Henry Simmons, a former slave from Virginia, who, having bought his freedom, went on to become a wealthy Philadelphia clothes dealer."[119] Indeed, some of the Montiers or their extended family members or friends may have even been patrons of Simmons's enterprise or First Baptist congregants. "In 1816 Simmons founded the First African Baptist Church on the site, and served as its pastor until his death in 1848. His wife, Martha, sold the property that same year, and the congregation dispersed in about 1850."[120]

Ultimately, the site fell victim to development, eerily similar to the Montier graveyard in Guineatown. "A few years after Simmons' death, the church was razed. Other buildings arose on the site, including a safe factory and some private residences with yards that backed onto the old cemetery."[121] By 1984 Collins and her team had discovered "a few intact portions of the church's stone wall," as well as "60 skeletons and … nearly 2,200 artifacts," some indicating that the African-descended parishioners might have retained and practiced customs from the Motherland, Africa.[122]

The site's project director, England-born Michael Parrington, thought that "a small, blue-edged, pearlware plate" that was "found within the rib area of a child" about "9 years old," as well as a "larger utensil" situated within an older male's remains, could have been part of African burial rites.[123] "The African burial custom represented is the practice of placing utensils last used by the deceased into the grave when the burial is made," according to Parrington. "It's likely that the adult would use a larger utensil, as opposed to the child using a smaller [bowl-like] one."[124]

Further examinations of the skeletal remains indicated that many of those buried at the downtown Philadelphia site suffered from arthritis and fractures, indicative of immensely difficult and heavy hard work. And because of the large number of tooth cavities found—even in children—scientists believe their diets consisted of minimally nutritious food with very high sugar or glucose contents. "Some of the people have all the molars gone on their jaw … rotted or pulled out," noted Stephanie Pinter, a physical anthropologist for the project, adding that the remains, likely via DNA sampling, were to be analyzed by the Smithsonian's acclaimed "bone detective," J. Lawrence Angel. The remains of a woman, in fact, "still had hair on the head, a little bit of the eye material still left in the socket, and it seems that the brain became liquid and then solidified at the base of the skull," Pinter said.[125]

Is it possible to conduct such studies on remains that might be possibly found via ground-penetrating surveillance perhaps buried at the former Guineatown cemetery?

Similar African mortuary discoveries were made during the New York City cemetery dig, renowned as the African Burial Project, in 1991, when hundreds of remains were unearthed within seven acres in Lower Manhattan "near Chambers Street at Broadway" and the site of a government services building being constructed; a mammoth national monument and associated museum dedicated to those African-descended people sits near the intersection today. "In 1995, Rick Kittles, a PhD student from George Washington University, was brought on to the burial-ground project,"[126] a development that would help to ignite a DNA-analysis movement among African Americans, studied and written about by preeminent black scholar and sociology professor Alondra Nelson. "As a biologist, Kittles had had experience using cutting-edge techniques to sequence DNA. It was at the burial site that Kittles refined the methods that would lead to his commercial venture, African Ancestry,"[127] which reportedly identifies the African ancestries and ethnicities of clients—a service that's also offered to varying degrees by the likes of Ancestry.com for broader populations, including African Americans.

If, ultimately, remains are discovered and evaluated from Cheltenham's Guineatown site, what might be the benefits or consequences? Given today's DNA technology analytical tools, hereditary links could be established and documented to modern descendants of those buried there. For example, in addition to her African American heredity, modern descendant Joyce Mosley says that she does have some Native American DNA, likely an indicator that Cremona Morrey had roots to indigenous Americans, a possibility that Mosley says has been researched by Arcadia University.[128] And perhaps, there might too be evidence of African or Native American mortuary practices, as well as ethnic identities passed down to modern descendants. In fact, it would be vital to finally acknowledge that people of African descent were prominently present and foundational to establishing the local community and, more generally, the United States of America. "We don't want to overplay origin stories," Nelson told *Columbia Magazine*, "but it's very significant that the introduction of DNA analysis for probing history should happen at a site that's about slavery, race, and the founding of the nation." Furthermore, "it becomes a moment for us, both as a community in New York City and as a nation, to say: this *happened*," declared the author of the landmark 2016 book, *The Social Life of DNA: Race, Reparations, and Reconciliation after the Genome*. The same possibility applies to the sacred burials in a cemetery once established in Cheltenham's former Guineatown.

EPILOGUE

Carrying the Torch Forward

Pickens family members Pamela; her mother, Patricia; father, William III; and brother, John Montier at the Philadelphia Museum of Art with the portraits of ancestors Hiram and Elizabeth Montier. (William Pickens III Archives)

After Pickens's beloved wife, Patricia, died of cancer in 2015, following "51 years of marriage," he continued retirement in Sag Harbor and often spoke among family treasures and keepsakes about his magnanimous family history, marveling about its deep multi-ethnic origins, as he did in an interview for a 2018 *Dan's Papers*' article,[1] just a few years after Pat's passing: "My ancestors were among the first people to come to the New World," he pointed out. "They sailed from England and arrived in Oyster Bay [New York] in 1670 [although some sources indicate during the early 1680s]. My great grandfather, five times removed," Humphrey Morrey, "was appointed Mayor of [Philadelphia] by William Penn in 1691,"[2] Pickens noted, his mind likely drifting to the courage and legacy of his African-descended, fourth great-grandmother, Cremona [Satterthwaite] Morrey Fry, despite expressing doubts about her Native American roots in recent years.

The late William IV joins his sister, Pamela, and brother, John Montier, at the Philadelphia Museum of Art with the portraits of ancestors Hiram and Elizabeth Montier, some observers noting striking facial feature similarities between Pamela and her ancestor, Elizabeth. William Pickens III often noted that his granddaughter, Breighan (Bree) Camille Pickens Wilson, the daughter of son William IV, is a multi-generational descendant of the Morrey–Montier–Pickens family line. (Philadelphia Museum of Art)

Nonetheless, Cremona's early relationship with the mayor's son, Richard Morrey, gave birth to one of the most distinguished families in the annals of American history. "They lived through the Boston Massacre, the Stamp Act, the Intolerable Act, and the first and second Continental Congresses. They were here for the signing of the Declaration of Independence. They were counted in the first Census conducted by George Washington in 1790,"[3] Pickens boasted, clearly proud that his distinguished ancestors were some of America's very first "counted" citizens.

During his funeral at the First Baptist Church of Bridgehampton, New York on October 10, 2021, Pastor Tisha Dixon-Williams, assured attendees: "Today we celebrate the glorious new life of our loved one, William Pickens," the high-spirited minister said. "But family," she continued, "as a pastor I have to tell you that you sit in a challenging seat today because grief is the part of the fabric of life that stitches humanity together."[4] A Brooklyn native, Dixon-Williams is a scholar associated with the Samuel DeWitt Proctor School of Theology at Virginia Union University and Princeton Theological Seminary and holds a "Doctor of Practical Theology from Wayland Baptist Theological Seminary."[5]

Joyously animated and upbeat, drawing call-and-response declarations such as "Amen!" and "That's right!" from attendees, the preacher continued: "And unfortunately, the only way to avoid grief is to avoid love. But to avoid love reduces the possibility of any real life—authentic life," she noted, stressing that those present should focus on celebrating the life of the buoyant and effervescent Bill Pickens, not dwell on sorrowful mourning.[6] "It is love and life that brings us to this moment today, not death. So here is what our loved one is challenging us with today—to live in such a way that it's worth dying for—a life well lived,"[7] insisted Dixon-Williams, "the first woman to be elected to office in the 99-year history of First Baptist,"[8] then giving even more praise about Pickens's very full life, reflective of many of his esteemed forebears. "And we can all agree today that his life was a life well lived. And so today from this point forward, I don't want you to linger on the question, 'What if I die?' From this day forward, I want you to ask, 'What if I never lived?'"[9]

The Reverend Dr. Suzan Denise Johnson Cook, ambassador-at-large for international religious freedom during the Obama presidency and formerly a top advisor to former Secretary of State Hillary Clinton and ex-president Bill Clinton,[10] displayed a purple African kente cloth, representing royalty. "We are at a royal celebration," insisted Johnson Cook,[11] who also held senior pastorships at New York area churches and served as a professor at the New York Theological Seminary, as well as chaplain of the New York City Police Department.[12] "So today we do a toast symbolically to Bill Pickens. It's to honor one that we love so much. So we're going to *start* with a toast and *end* with an Amen!"[13]

Noted theologian and Harlem native[14] Johnson Cook prayerfully concluded, "We thank you for a man whose life shone so brightly that it opened doors and led [to] paths ...—that we now walk on,"[15] similar to the Montier ancestral pathways that Pickens and the families' Paul Robeson traversed.

Sag Harbor Mayor Jim Larocca, a Vietnam veteran who affectionately shared his title of "mayor" with Pickens, like others in the audience, noted that Pickens had "an instinct in him" that massaged, embraced, and extracted the best from people. "Maybe the first or second time I went up to the house—sitting among all that history—and he asked me and got

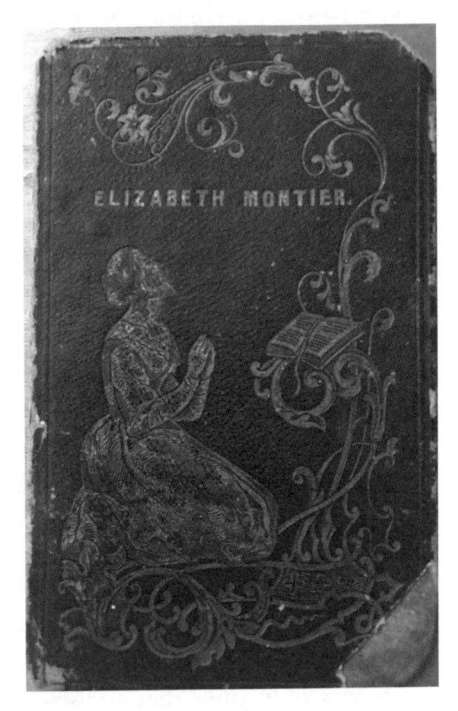

The Pickens family still holds on to the family Bible that belonged to ancestor Elizabeth Montier. (William Pickens III Archives)

218 • THE MONTIERS

William Pickens III proudly displays his family portraits. (William Pickens III Archives)

me talking about experiences I had never talked with anyone else about,"[16] Larocca confessed. "And it was so genuine, so authentic; I'd have to say I fell in love with him. He was *that* person and it was for me a moment that I got some things out that I had never been able to get out." Larocca relished that their "friendship grew and grew," honoring that Pickens "took pride in his country, his place, his family, his community, himself."[17]

Also commending Pickens was Philippine-native Loida Nicolas Lewis, Esq., previously chair and CEO of the "$2 billion multinational food company" TLC Beatrice International that was founded by her late husband, the trailblazing African American lawyer and outstanding entrepreneur Reginald F. Lewis who dynamically led the conglomerate before dying of brain cancer in 1993.[18] She spoke directly to Pickens and his wife, Pat, during her remarks: "You were truly the mayor and first lady of Sag Harbor," said Lewis, with property in the Sag Harbor area, and now serving as chair of the Reginald F. Lewis Foundation.[19] She reminisced that from the "generosity of your heart, Pat and you donated to the Reginald F. Lewis Museum of Maryland African History & Culture a Pickens' family heirloom—no less than the painting by Hale Woodruff dated 1927 of … [Bill Pickens's grandfather] William Pickens Sr." Lewis marveled that Pickens Sr. had been a cofounder of the NAACP and a Yale University honor student, that he "spoke" a half-dozen languages and racked up other distinguished accomplishments.[20]

"It was only then that I discovered your illustrious history," continued Lewis.[21] She took comfort in knowing that Bill and Pat Pickens were once again in heavenly embrace, "where my beloved Reginald is also" in that godly realm—a glorious place where they would all one day jubilantly reunite, predicted Lewis,[22] today an advisory board member of the University of Southern California's Center on Public Diplomacy.[23]

Pat and Bill Pickens's beloved daughter, Pamela, marveled about her father's insatiable thirst for knowledge, as well as his vigor, dynamism, unparalleled optimism, and limitless love of history: "He took to history organically. He studied the history of America and his family and where they would intersect. He was totally into it," she remembered, inspired by his legendary focus on human rights and so much more. "Those were great moments to witness" as "he reveled in the experiences of life," she said, noting how much she relished and loved those fatherly attributes.[24]

Remarkably, Pickens died on his birthday. His "sunrise" was on September 27, 1936, his "sunset" on that exact day 85 years later in 2021. He transitioned that day about the time when daughter Pamela said she noticed something quite uplifting in the heavens, a double rainbow,[25] perhaps symbolic of her parents, Patricia and William Pickens III, joining hands again for eternity among the ingratiating and watchful spirits of their Guineatown ancestors. Curiously, while walking the beach on the other side of the bay and peering into the heavens above the Atlantic Ocean from whence Cremona (Satterthwaite) Morrey Fry's parents and ancestors probably arrived on ships as enslaved Africans from the Motherland, John Montier Pickens, also spotted that double rainbow. He interpreted it too as confirmation from his beloved father, Bill Pickens, that his dad indeed was again in his wife Patricia's embrace[26] among their celebrating forebears.

***

It's not hard to envision Bill Pickens's trail-blazing ancestor, Cremona (Satterthwaite) Morrey Fry, contemplating her extraordinary life and legacy on land that she and her family survived on, as she approached age 60 in 1770 when she too would join the ancestors at the dawn of the American Revolution. Born enslaved about 1710, at least according to most sources, Cremona or "Mooney," as she was sometimes referred to, miraculously survived the travails of slavery to become essentially the founding matriarch of multiple generations of dynamic African Americans who were integral in establishing and pushing forward the so-called "great American experiment".

And her child-producing, interracial marital relationship with Richard Morrey was bodacious for much of the decade the couple pierced the boundaries of America's colonial society. And that's despite circumstantial evidence indicating that the union succumbed to anti-interracial or Eurocentric pressures likely intertwined with related interpersonal stresses, ultimately resulting in their apparent breakup around 1746.

Yet, at some point during the incalculable depth of their union Richard and Cremona were arguably so enraptured with each other that they willingly defied the potentially horrible societal retributions that ranged from fines, banishment, and torturous maiming to imprisonment or lifetime enslavement, a punishment that Cremona and her children certainly could have suffered if prosecuted. And unlike some of his European-descended contemporaries who had a range of relationships with black women, Richard Morrey essentially bequeathed to Cremona almost two hundred acres of land, a profound gesture that is essentially unheard of in the annals of American history—virtually assuring that Cremona and their children would have a significant chance at prospering. Yet, there are some, including modern Montier-Morrey descendants, who contend that Cremona's early free labor as an enslaved black woman should have been compensated in such an immense way—perhaps one of the most powerful and earliest forms of reparations.

The fact that Richard Morrey would execute such a unique transaction, albeit with conditions, as the relationship ended and he was about to marry another woman is quite perplexing on the surface. However, it's not hard to imagine that the severance of their bond, for whatever reasons, must have been quite traumatic for Richard and Cremona, who as a black woman more than likely had to negotiate and navigate elements of coercion within their dynamic relationship and society itself. Yet, Cremona's intelligence, wisdom, and foresight had to be quite convincing and commendable considering her essentially powerless legal position in a rampantly racist and sexist society.

In the end, despite both Cremona and Richard moving on, with "Mooney" even giving birth to at least one son during a new union with her second known partner, the African American John Fry or Frye,[27] tantalizing questions still remain. After having up to five children together from approximately 1736 to 1746, were there still emotional ties between Richard Morrey and Cremona Fry after the essentially common-law marital relationship ceased? Would some element of their supposed "love" for each other still burn as an eternally glowing ember that might never be extinguishable?

The final resting spots of Richard Morrey and Cremona Fry have not been definitively found and are now perhaps lost to the ages—at least for now. Richard was reportedly buried somewhere near his country estate in Cheltenham, in an unidentified secluded grave or perhaps a mausoleum.[28] The elder Cremona is presumed to be resting with early inhabitants of Guineatown in the bygone family cemetery, perhaps with some of her children, such as daughter Cremona Montier, possibly now under a paved parking lot, street, or in the ground of a nearby residential property. Yet, although the present locations of their physical remains are unknown, the essence of the couple's pioneering relationship thrives to some degree in all of us, as we continue to wrestle with concepts of race, social status, and even "love."

"Concerning Shakespeare's Othello," Richard and Cremona's great descendant Paul Robeson once said regarding his trailblazing 1940s role as an African-descended Moor warrior navigating an interracial love affair with his Caucasian partner, Desdemona, within European Venetian society, "it is an interesting point that the great dramatist as far back as 1600 posed the question of the acceptance by a society of one of alien culture and race."[29] Not long before his own 1976 death in Philadelphia as the nation celebrated its bicentennial, Robeson was persecuted beyond human endurance and given dozens of electroshock treatments, seemingly intent on destroying his magnificent mind of ingenious black activism and pride while advocating for the unity of all humankind. "And therefore this is a play which is of great interest to us moderns today as we face the whole problem of relations of peoples between different races and cultures,"[30] Robeson concluded, later finding some solace and peace during his final days at his sister's home in Philadelphia—never forgetting the unparalleled sacrifices of his enslaved African brethren as he spent his last days so close to where the family's essence would take hold and flourish through the ages. Indeed, those were likely some of the very profound considerations of Richard and Cremona as they, perhaps, reminisced from time to time about the emotionally charged swirling winds of their consequentially momentous interracial union.

Endnotes

Preface

1. "Richard Morrey's Negroes Claim to 198 Acres of Land in Cheltenham leased to them by Richard Murrey for 500 years," in *Haverford College Quaker & Special Collections*, encompasses "Morrey, Humphrey Documents [N.D.] including draft of codicil to Will, lease of 198 acres to Richard (son of Humphrey) Morrey's 'Negro.'" The documents can be found within the "Morrey, Humphrey land indenture—1712" file included in the MC 1182 *Dorothy Merriman Schall Collection*—Box 12, accessed November 30, 2023.
2. "Descriptions of Eighteenth-Century PHILADELPHIA before the Revolution," *National Humanities Center*, 2023, accessed December 17, 2023, https://nationalhumanitiescenter.org/pds/becomingamer/growth/text2/philadelphiadescriptions.pdf. Dr. Alexander Hamilton, who was not related to the Founding Father with the same name, wrote in a September 19, 1744, diary entry: "At my seeing of the city of Philadelphia, I conceived a quite different notion of both city and inhabitants from that which I had before from the account or description of others."
3. Ibid. Titan Leeds, the Philadelphia publisher of *The Genuine Leeds Almanac for the Year of Christian Account 1730*, wrote in his "A Memorial to William Penn" about Philadelphia becoming "the Athens of Mankind," declaring: "Shall Liberal Arts to such Perfection bring, Europe shall mourn her ancient Fame declin'd, And Philadelphia be the Athens of Mankind."
4. "Tacony," Delaware River City Corp., 2015, accessed December 15, 2023, https://drcc-phila.org/portfolio-items/tacony.
5. "Why the long name?" Tookany/Tacony-Frankford Watershed—TTF Watershed, 2023, accessed Dec. 15, 2023, https://ttfwatershed.org/who-we-are/faqs.
6. Donald Scott Sr., *Remembering Cheltenham Township*, American Chronicles (Charleston, SC: The History Press, 2009), 32.
7. Theodore W. Bean, ed., *History of Montgomery County, Pennsylvania* (Philadelphia: Everts & Peck, 1884), 40.
8. Ibid., 678.
9. Scott Sr., *Remembering Cheltenham Township*, 32.
10. Rev. S. F. Hotchkin, *The York Road, Old and New* (Philadelphia: Binder & Kelly, Publishers, 1892), 122.
11. Scott Sr., *Remembering Cheltenham Township*, 97.
12. Ibid., 65.
13. Ibid., 52–53.
14. Ibid., 62.
15. Donald Scott Sr., *Camp William Penn, 1863–1865: America's First Federal African American Soldiers' Fight for Freedom* (Atglen, PA: Schiffer Publishing, 2012, 2021), 24.
16. Ibid.
17. Ibid., 34.

224 • THE MONTIERS

18 "Montier, Francis—2d US Colored Cavalry," Fold3 by Ancestry.com, NARA M1817. Compiled military service records of volunteer Union soldiers in the 1st through 6th U.S. Colored Cavalry and the 5th Massachusetts Cavalry (Colored), 2023, accessed September 8, 2023, https://www.fold3.com/image/261443257/montier-francis-21-page-1-us-civil-war-service-records-cmrs-union-colored-troops-1st–6th-cavalry-186.
19 Joyce Mosley, *Gram's Gift*, (Bloomington, IN: AuthorHouse, 2020), 25.
20 "Cyrus B. Miller … 24th U.S. Colored Infantry," U.S., Colored Troops Military Service Records, 1863–1865, Ancestry.com, 2007, accessed September 8, 2023, https://www.ancestry.com/imageviewer/collections/1107/images/miusa1861m_08847700182.
21 Scott Sr., *Camp William Penn*, 535–536. An unsigned correspondence, likely written by a soldier in the 24th USCT, was published in the April 15, 1865, edition of African Methodist Church's *Christian Recorder* newspaper, the day Lincoln was assassinated, describing aspects of Harriet Tubman's April 6, 1865, presentation to the 24th USCT at Camp William Penn.
22 "William Robeson in the U.S., Colored Troops Military Service Records, 1863–1865," Ancestry.com, 2023, accessed November 4, 2023, https://www.ancestry.com/discoveryui-content/view/223553.
23 Mosley, *Gram's Gift*, 22.
24 Ibid., 25–26. The Morrey–Bustill–Montier family historian and author Joyce Mosley writes that her ancestor, Cyrus Bustill Miller, was an antislavery activist and Underground Railroad operative. He likely associated with William Still, "the father of the Underground Railroad," especially during secret meetings at Lebanon Cemetery, reserved for African Americans. Several of Mosley's other activist ancestors rest in graves at Eden Cemetery in Collingdale, Pennsylvania, among the remains of Philadelphia's assassinated black 19th-century leader Octavius Valentine Catto, William Still, and the great contralto singer Marian Anderson.
25 Mosley, *Gram's Gift*, 14–15.
26 Anna Bustill Smith's typed document, "THE BUSTILL FAMILY," with what appears to be her handwritten signature, indicates: "On May 1, 1782, Cyrus Bustill was named Contractor for baking of all the flour used at the Port of Burlington, New Jersey. This was a patriotic contribution to the struggle of the Continental Forces for which he baked the bread for four months, and accepted no pay. General George Washington gave him a silver dollar as a souvenier [sic]." Smith's typed document was found at the University of Pennsylvania's University Archives within the Nathan Francis Mossell Papers (Box 1, Folder 50, UPT 50-M913) by this author on Thursday, December 21, 2023.
27 Reginald H. Pitts, "Robert Lewis of Guineatown, and 'The Colored Cemetery [sic] in Glenside,'" *Old York Road Historical Society Bulletin* LI (1991): 43.
28 "Owner: CEMETERY FOR COLORED FOLKS," *City-data.com*, 2023, accessed December 3, 2023, https://www.city-data.com/montgomery-county-pa-properties/L/Limekiln-Pike-14.html.
29 Charlette Caldwell, "MONTIER FAMILY HOMESTEAD," *SAH Archipedia*, 2023, accessed October 19, 2023, https://sah-archipedia.org/buildings/PA-03-091-0001.
30 Reginald H. Pitts, "The Montier Family of Guineatown," *Old York Road Historical Society Bulletin* LIII (1993): 23.
31 Caldwell, "MONTIER FAMILY HOMESTEAD."
32 Donald Scott, "The Montiers: An American Family's Triumphant Odyssey," Afrigeneas.org, August 31, 2004, accessed June 28, 2024, https://www.afrigeneas.org/library/montier_article.html.
33 Scott, "Triumphant Odyssey."
34 Daniel N. Rolph, "Black History Month: Inter-Racial Marriages and Relationships in Colonial Pennsylvania," *Historical Society of Pennsylvania's Hidden Histories*, February 4, 2011, accessed November 24, 2023, http://frontierhistory.blogspot.com/2011/02/.

35 Pitts, "The Montier Family," 23. The article notes: "Sometime after 1735, he [Richard Morrey] began an affair with the young slave girl that produced five children: Robert, born c. 1735, Caesar, c. 1737, Elizabeth, c. 1739, Rachel, c. 1742 and the youngest of them, Cremona Montier, born about 1745," the year before Richard would bequeath 198 acres to Cremona and shortly thereafter begin another relationship that resulted in marriage.

36 Scott, "Triumphant Odyssey." It's important to note that either before or during Richard's relationship with Cremona, depending on the source, he "had been married to a woman named Ann according to the will of their son Thomas Morrey," a marriage that I confirmed in USGenWeb's site of reproduced will abstracts in Book E: 1726–1736: Philadelphia County.

37 Ibid.

38 A. Leon Higginbotham Jr., *In the Matter of Color: Race & The American Legal Process: The Colonial Period*, (New York: Oxford University Press, 1980), 274.

Chapter 1

1 Reginald H. Pitts, "'Richard Morrey, Gent.,' of Cheltenham Township; and His 'Negro Woman Mooney,'" *Bulletin of the Historical Society of Montgomery County Pennsylvania* XXXI, no. 4 (Spring 1999): 261.

2 Dominique R. Wilson, "Sexual Exploitation Of Black Women From The Years 1619–2020," *Journal of Race, Gender, and Ethnicity* 10 (Spring 2021): 122–129, accessed August 4, 2023, https://digitalcommons.tourolaw.edu/cgi/viewcontent.cgi?article=1079&context=jrge.

3 Kimberly V. Jones, *"Favorite of Heaven": The Impact of Skin Color on Atlantic Ethnic Africans in the Eighteenth Century* (master's thesis, Eastern Illinois University—Touro College Jacob D. Fuchsberg Law Center, 2016), 121–122, accessed May 26, 2023, https://thekeep.eiu.edu/cgi/viewcontent.cgi?article=3499&context=theses.

4 Kate Tuttle, "Hemings, Sally (b. 1773, Bermuda Hundred, Va.; d. 1836), African American slave who may have been the mistress of Thomas Jefferson," in *AFRICANA: The Encyclopedia of African and African American Experience*, eds. Kwame Anthony Appiah and Henry Louis Gates Jr. (New York: Basic Civitas Books, 1999), 949.

5 Annette Gordon-Reed, *The Hemingses of Monticello: An American Family* (New York: W.W. Norton & Company, 2008), 271.

6 Gwendolyn DuBois Shaw, "The Freedom to Marry for All: Painting Interracial Families during the Era of the Civil War," in *The Civil War in Art and Memory*, ed. Kirk Savage (New Haven, CT: Yale University Press, 2016), 5–14. In addition to Shaw's profound artistic analysis of the Montier portraits, etc., Lucia Olubunmi R. Momoh, the Constance E. Clayton Curatorial Fellow at the Philadelphia Museum of Art, also provides intriguing perspectives, especially concerning Elizabeth Brown Montier's portrait (painted 1841 by Franklin R. Street) in *The Philadelphia Show*'s 2023 journal, pg. 92, within her article, "The Proof is in the Portrait: A Close Look at an Antebellum Portrait of a Free Black Woman Painted in Philadelphia": "Elizabeth's portrait reveals both the social standing and ambitions of a young bride-to-be. Dressed in the latest fashion, she sits upright while resting her arm on the scroll end of a carved wooden seat that is placed before rich emerald and scarlet draperies …. Framed by full arched brows, her large brown eyes engage us. Her gaze, a potential window into her soul, leads me to wonder, 'Just who *was* Elizabeth Brown Montier?'"

7 Shaw, "Freedom to Marry for All," 8.

8 Ibid.

9 Pitts, "'Richard Morrey, Gent.,'" 268.

10 Ibid.

11 Ibid., 269.
12 Ibid.
13 Melinda Elder and Susan Stuart, "Were The Gillows Of Lancaster Slave Traders?", *Contrebis* Vol. 39 (2021), accessed May 27, 2023, https://lahs.archaeologyuk.org/Contrebis/elderstuartgillow.pdf.
14 Pitts, "'Richard Morrey, Gent.,'" 261.
15 Ibid., 261.
16 Jean R. Soderlund, "Black Women in Colonial Pennsylvania," in *African Americans in Pennsylvania: Shifting Historical Perspectives*, eds. Joe William Trotter Jr. and Eric Ledell Smith (University Park, PA, and Harrisburg, PA: The Pennsylvania State University Press and The Pennsylvania Historical and Museum Commission, 1997), 76.
17 Ibid., 76.
18 Ibid., 82.
19 Lisa Clayton Robinson, "Jacobs, Harriet Ann (b. 1813?, Edenton, N.C.; d. March 7, 1897, Washington, D.C.), African American writer known especially for her autobiography, which is the most significant African American slave narrative by a woman," in *AFRICANA: The Encyclopedia of African and African American Experience*, eds. Kwame Anthony Appiah and Henry Louis Gates Jr. (New York: Basic Civitas Books, 1999), 949.
20 S.W.L., "Why the world has so many Guineas," *The Economist*, September 12, 2017, accessed May 29, 2023, https://www.economist.com/the-economist-explains/2017/09/12/why-the-world-has-so-many-guineas.
21 Martin Bauml Duberman, *Paul Robeson* (New York: Alfred A. Knopf, 1989), 5.
22 Stephen M. Magu, *Towards Pan-Africanism: Africa's Cooperation Through Regional Economic Communities (RECs), Ubuntu and Communitarianism* (Singapore: Springer Nature Singapore, 2023), 70, accessed June 30, 2024, https://www.google.com/books/edition/Towards_Pan_Africanism.
23 S.W.L., "Why the world has so many Guineas."
24 Soderlund, "Black Women in Colonial Pennsylvania," 74.
25 Pitts, "'Richard Morrey, Gent.,'" 265.
26 Jack H. Schick, "Slavery in Pennsylvania," *Friends Journal*, September 1, 2012, accessed March 18, 2023, https://www.friendsjournal. org/slavery-in-pennsylvania/.
27 Pitts, "'Richard Morrey, Gent.,'" 265–266.
28 Cheltenham Township, "Cheltenham Township History," 2023, accessed March 9, 2023, https://www.cheltenhamtownship.org/pview.aspx?id=2894&catid=70#gsc.tab=0.
29 Gary B. Nash, "Slaves and Slave Owners in Colonial Philadelphia," in *African Americans in Pennsylvania: Shifting Historical Perspectives*, eds. Joe William Trotter Jr. and Eric Ledell Smith (University Park, PA, and Harrisburg, PA: The Pennsylvania State University Press and The Pennsylvania Historical and Museum Commission, 1997), 44.
30 Ibid.
31 Nash, "Slaves and Slave Owners," 46.
32 Ibid., 55.
33 Ibid., 44.
34 Darold D. Wax, "Africans on the Delaware: The Pennsylvania Slave Trade, 1759–1765," *Pennsylvania History: A Journal of Mid-Atlantic Studies* 50, no. 1 (1983): 38–49, accessed March 18, 2023, http://www.jstor.org/stable/27772875.
35 Preservation Society of Charleston, "Gadsden's Wharf: 340 CONCORD STREET," 2023, accessed June 2, 2023, https://www.preservationsociety.org/locations/gadsdens-wharf/.
36 Pitts, "'Richard Morrey, Gent.,'" 267.
37 Ibid., 266–267.

ENDNOTES • 227

38 "Barbarities in the West Indias," National Museums—Liverpool—International Slavery Museum, 2004, accessed June 2, 2023, https://www.liverpoolmuseums.org.uk/artifact/barbarities-west-indias.
39 Maalik Stansbury, "Barbados Slave Codes," St. Mary's University, October 19, 2016, accessed June 2, 2023, https://stmuscholars.org/barbados-slave-codes/.
40 Selena T. Rodgers, "Next Wave of Post Traumatic Slave Syndrome Survivors: Black Women Resisters in Academia," *Advances in Social Work* 21 No. 2/3 (Summer 2021): 438–459, accessed June 30, 2024, https://journals.iupui.edu/index.php/advancesin socialwork/article/view/24159/23856. Regarding this article's subheading "Post Traumatic Slave Syndrome Theory," Rodgers notes that "Joy Degruy (2005) coined the term 'PTSS theory,' which she describes as 'the manifestations of an institutionalized legacy of traumas ... reflected in many behaviors and beliefs passed down to subsequent generations.'"
41 Pitts, "'Richard Morrey, Gent.,'" 270.
42 Marcus Rediker, "The 'Quaker Comet' Was the Greatest Abolitionist You've Never Heard Of," *Smithsonian*, September 2017, accessed August 7, 2023, https://www.smithsonianmag.com/history/quaker-comet-greatest-abolitionist-never-heard-180964401/.
43 Benjamin Lay, *All slave-keepers that keep the innocent in bondage, apostates*, *University of Michigan—Evans Early American Imprint* (Printer Benjamin Franklin, 1837), 33, accessed August 7, 2023, https://quod.lib.umich.edu/e/evans/N03401.0001.001/1:3?rgn=div1;view=fulltext.
44 Ibid., 35.
45 Ibid., 44.
46 Giulia Bonazza, "Slavery in Europe during the Atlantic Slave Trade," Oxfordre.com, September 15, 2022, accessed March 5, 2023, https://oxfordre.com/africanhistory/display/10.1093/acrefore/9780190277734.001.0001/acrefore-9780190277.
47 "Germantown Quaker Petition Against Slavery," National Park Service—Guidebook to The American Civil Rights Experience, updated April 5, 2016, accessed June 30, 2024, https://www.nps.gov/articles/quakerpetition.htm.
48 Mosley, *Gram's Gift*, 5, 7, 10.
49 Dan Graves, "#404: George Fox and the Quakers," Christian History Institute, 2023, accessed June 14, 2023, https://christianhistoryinstitute.org/study/module/george-fox.
50 Arthur O. Roberts, "George Fox and the Quaker (Friends) Movement," Georgefox.edu, 2023, accessed June 14, 2023, https://www.georgefox.edu/about/history/quakers.html.
51 "William Penn—1644–1718," Quakers in the World, February 26, 2022, accessed June 14, 2023, https://www.quakersintheworld.org/quakers-in-action/3/William-Penn.
52 J. William Frost, "George Fox's Ambiguous Antislavery Legacy," Brynmawr.edu, 1994, accessed June 14, 2023, https://brycchancarey.com/slavery/quakersandslavery.htm.
53 Thomas J. Sugrue, "The Peopling and Depeopling of Early Pennsylvania: Indians and Colonists, 1680–1720," *The Pennsylvania Magazine of History and Biography* CXVI, no. 1 (January 1992): 3–30, accessed June 30, 2024, https://journals.psu.edu/pmhb/article/view/44737/44458.
54 Nash, "Slaves and Slave Owners," 44.
55 James Wolfinger, "African American Migration," The Encyclopedia of Greater Philadelphia, 2023, accessed June 4, 2023, https://philadelphiaencyclopedia.org/essays/african-american-migration/.
56 Ibid.
57 Michelle Craig McDonald, "Coffeehouses," The Encyclopedia of Greater Philadelphia, 2023, accessed June 4, 2023, https://philadelphiaencyclopedia.org/essays/coffeehouses/.
58 George Washington, *The Writings of George Washington, Vol. XI (1785–1790)*, 1891, 2023, accessed June 4, 2023, https://oll.libertyfund.org/title/ford-the-writings-of-george-washington-vol-xi-1785-1790.

59 Carl G. Karsch, "City Tavern: A Feast of Elegance," Carpenters' Hall, 2023, accessed June 5, 2023, https://www.carpentershall.org/city-tavern-a-feast-of-elegance.
60 "Benjamin Lay (1681–1759) of Colchester, London, Barbadoes, Philadelphia," *The Journal of the Friends' Historical Society* Vol. 33 (1936):16, 2024, accessed June 30, 2024, https://sas-space.sas.ac.uk/6777/1/Vol.%2033%20-%201936.pdf.
61 Rev. S. F. Hotchkin, M.A., "BENJAMIN LAY," in *The York Road, Old and New* (Philadelphia, PA: Binder & Kelly, Publishers, 1892), March 25, 2011, accessed December 9, 2023, https://ia800200.us.archive.org/23/items/cu31924010448706/cu31924010448706.pdf.
62 A June 6, 2023, email sent to this author from the local Cheltenham-based historian and author Dr. Thomas Wieckowski, an officer in the Old York Road Historical Society, indicates that Benjamin Lay's second cave dwelling may have been situated in what is today the "Hollywood section" of Abington Township, "between Manor [College] and Alverthorpe [Park]," part of an estate originally owned by Lessing J. Rosenwald, former chair of the retail giant Sears, Roebuck & Co. Rosenwald's philanthropy during the early 20th century helped to establish hundreds of schools for African American children throughout the South.
63 Kristin E. Holmes, "Cast out by the Quakers, Abington's abolitionist dwarf finally has his day," *The Philadelphia Inquirer*, April 19, 2018, accessed August 6, 2023, https://www.inquirer.com/philly/news/quakers-benjamin-lay-dwarf-abolitionist-slavery-abington-friends-meeting-20180419.html.
64 "London Coffee House Historical Marker," ExplorePAhistory.com, 2024, accessed June 6, 2023, https://explorepahistory.com/hmarker.php?markerId=1-A-21. The state historical marker reads: "LONDON COFFEE HOUSE—Scene of political and commercial activity in the colonial period, the London Coffee House opened here in 1754. It served as a place to inspect black slaves recently arrived from Africa and to bid for their purchase at public auction." The associated article continues: "Slavery was a feature of everyday life in colonial Pennsylvania. In the 1760s, more than 4,400 enslaved Africans and African Americans lived in the colony. Nearly one of every six white households in Philadelphia had at least one slave. Slavery had first come to the colony in 1684 when the Isabella, out of Bristol, England, docked in Philadelphia with 150 enslaved Africans. A year later William Penn himself had at least three slaves at Pennsbury, his manor estate just north of Philadelphia."
65 "A Slave Ship," Lest We Forget Museum of Slavery, December 12, 2013, accessed June 6, 2023, https://lwfsm.com/index.php/2013/12/12/a-slave-ship/.
66 "Benjamin Franklin," Penn & Slavery Project—University of Pennsylvania, 2023, accessed June 6, 2023, https://pennandslaveryproject.org/exhibits/show/slaveownership/earlytrustees/benfrank.
67 "Advertisements from the Pennsylvania Gazette," Historical Society of Pennsylvania, *Preserving American Freedom: The Evolution of American Liberties in Fifty Documents*, 2023, accessed June 10, 2023, http://digitalhistory.hsp.org/preserving-american-freedom.
68 Ibid.
69 Ibid.
70 "To be lett, by SAMUEL MORRIS," *The Pennsylvania Gazette*, June 6, 1751, accessed March 9, 2023, https://www.newspapers.com/article/the-pennsylvania-gazette/15665696/.
71 "RUN away on the 20th Inst, from Joseph James of Cohansey," *Pennsylvania Gazette*, July 6, 1738, accessed March 9, 2023, https://www.newspapers.com/article/the-pennsylvania-gazette-run-away-lazaru/126158913/.
72 Theodore W. Bean, ed., *History of Montgomery County, Pennsylvania* (Philadelphia: Everts & Peck, 1884), 303.
73 "To be SOLD by the said Thomas Howard, a couple of likely Negro Girls, one Bermudas born, the other Antigua," *Pennsylvania Gazette*, June 29, 1738, accessed June 12, 2023, https://www.newspapers.com/article/the-pennsylvania-gazette-to-be-sold-by-t/126160037/.

74 Constance Garcia-Barrio, "Colonial women of color shaped history and paved the way for others," *Grid* 114 (November 2018), accessed June 30, 2024, https://gridphilly.com/blog-home/2019/1/14/colonial-women-of-color-shaped-history-and-paved-the-way-for-others/.
75 "Alice, d. 1802," The Library Company of Philadelphia, 2023, accessed June 12, 2023, https://digital.librarycompany.org/islandora/object/digitool%3A69944.
76 Charles L. Blockson, *African Americans in Pennsylvania: Above Ground and Underground* (Harrisburg, PA: RB Books, 2001), 37–38.
77 Ibid., 38.
78 "Thomas Forten," Geni.com, April 29, 2022, accessed June 12, 2023, https://www.geni.com/people/Thomas-Forten/6000000001900730093.
79 "James Forten," Geni.com, April 28, 2022, accessed June 12, 2023, https://www.geni.com/people/James-Forten/6000000010914443256.
80 Julie Winch, "'You know I Am a Man of Business': James Forten and the Factor of Race in Philadelphia's Antebellum Business Community," Papers Presented at a Conference on "The Future of Business History" Hagley Museum and Library, special issue, *Business and Economic History* 26, no. 1 (Fall 1997): 213–228, accessed June 30, 2024, https://www.jstor.org/stable/23703308.
81 Rayford W. Logan, "FORTEN, JAMES [SR.] (1766–1842)," in *Dictionary of American Negro Biography*, eds. Rayford W. Logan and Michael R. Winston (New York and London: W.W. Norton & Company, 1982), 234–235.
82 "COLORED INDEPENDENTS. DISTURBERS AT THEIR MEETING. A Gang, Led by a Notorious Henchman of Convict Mouat, Creates Disorder by Attempting to Counteract Enthusiasm Among a Large Gathering of Stewart Men," *The Philadelphia Times*, September 5, 1882, accessed August 25, 2023, https://www.newspapers.com/image/52199204/?terms=Montier&match=1.
83 "Hiram Mauntier," 1820 United States Census, Cheltenham, Montgomery, Pennsylvania, USA, digital image s.v. *Ancestry.com*, 2023, accessed August 25, 2023, https://www.ancestry.com/discoveryui-content/view/857410:7734. The article emphasizes: "In some Northern cities, for brief periods of time, black property owners voted. A very small number of free blacks owned slaves. The slaves that most free blacks purchased were relatives whom they later manumitted."
84 "The African American Odyssey: A Quest for Full Citizenship—Free Blacks in the Antebellum Period," Library of Congress, 2023, accessed June 12, 2023, https://www.loc.gov/exhibits/african-american-odyssey/free-blacks-in-the-antebellum-period.html.
85 James Gigantino, "Slavery and the Slave Trade," The Encyclopedia of Greater Philadelphia, 2023, accessed June 13, 2023, https://philadelphiaencyclopedia.org/essays/slavery-and-the-slave-trade/.
86 Gigantino, "Slavery and the Slave Trade."
87 Edward Lawler Jr., "The President's House in Philadelphia: A Brief History," Independence Hall Association, 2023, accessed June 13, 2023, https://www.ushistory.org/presidentshouse/history/briefhistory.php.
88 Soderlund, "Black Women in Colonial Pennsylvania," 74.
89 Ibid.
90 Pitts, "'Richard Morrey, Gent.,'" 272. Pitts remarks: "As Richard noted in the [1746] deed [granting her indirectly almost 200 acres of land], Cremona" had become "a free woman, having 'for twenty-pounds' bought her freedom, 'prior to this deed.' For the lack of a certification of manumission—a document expressly stating that the bearer was a free man or woman—the deed itself would suffice."
91 Cheltenham Township, "Cheltenham Township History," 2023, accessed August 4, 2023, https://www.cheltenhamtownship.org/pview.aspx?id=2894#gsc.tab=0.
92 Pitts, "'Richard Morrey, Gent.,'" 261.

93   Gigantino, "Slavery and the Slave Trade."
94   Bean, *History of Montgomery County, Pennsylvania*, 303.
95   Scott Sr., *Remembering Cheltenham Township*, 32.
96   Walter Licht, et al., "The Original People and Their Land: The Lenape, Pre-History to the 18th Century," West Philadelphia Collaborative History, 2023, accessed June 13, 2023, https://collaborativehistory.gse.upenn.edu/stories/original-people-and-their-land-lenape-pre-history-18th-century.
97   Ibid.
98   Schick, "Slavery in Pennsylvania."
99   Ibid.
100 Ibid.
101 Licht, et al., "The Original People and Their Land."
102 Ibid.
103 Schick, "Slavery in Pennsylvania."
104 "Cremona SATTERTHWAITE," Ancestry.com, 2023, accessed June 13, 2023, https://www.ancestry.com/genealogy/records/cremona-satterthwaite-24-215vbr2.
105 According to the Morrey–Bustill–Montier family historian and author Joyce Mosley, Caesar Morrey lived in the Burlington, New Jersey, area during the mid-18th century about the same time as Cyrus Bustill, who would marry Caesar's sister, Elizabeth Morrey, a daughter of Cremona and Richard Morrey. Mosley wonders if Cyrus and Elizabeth met via her brother, Caesar. Joyce Mosley and John Montier Pickens, Zoom interview of November 3, 2023, recorded with permission from the interviewees by author Donald Scott Sr., MP4. Length 02:56:20, video 1234272029.
106 "Cremona Morrey (Satterthwaite)," Geni.com, May 1, 2022, accessed June 13, 2023, https://www.geni.com/people/Cremona-Morrey/6000000062270380925.
107 Daniel DiPrinzio, "March 21–24: Arcadia Celebrates Life of Legendary Cremona Morrey with Art Exhibition, Documentary Screening, and Panel Discussion with the Montier Family," Arcadia University, March 15, 2022, accessed December 30, 2023, https://www.arcadia.edu/news/march-21-24-arcadia-celebrates-life-of-legendary-cremona-morrey-with-art-exhibition-documentary-screening-and-panel-discussion-with-the-montier-family/. A prior panel discussion at the college featured panelists Diane Bockrath (Arcadia archivist), William Pickens III (Montier family descendant), Sam Cameron (Arcadia), and David Rowland (Old York Road Historical Society).
108 M. M. Schofield, "The Letter Book Of Benjamin Satterthwaite Of Lancaster, 1737–1744," The Historic Society of Lancashire & Cheshire vol. 113 (1961), 142, accessed March 4, 2023, https://www.hslc.org.uk/journal/vol-113-1961/attachment/113-6-schofield/.
109 "Benjamin Satterthwaite (1718–1792)," Art UK—Lancashire County Museum Service, 2023, accessed June 15, 2023, https://artuk.org/discover/artworks/benjamin-satterthwaite-17181792-151761.
110 Schofield, "The Letter Book Of Benjamin Satterthwaite," 142.
111 F. S. Stickney, ed., *Fenner Bryan Satterthwaite, Together With The Obituary Proceedngs Of The Washington Bar, Etc.* (Norfolk, VA: Virginia Steam Print, 1887), 9, accessed March 4, 2023, https://www.forgottenbooks.com/en/download/BiographicSketchesofFennerBryanSatterthwaite1887_10072152.pdf.
112 Stickney, *Fenner Bryan Satterthwaite*, 10.
113 Ibid., 19.
114 Ibid., 29–33.
115 "Fenner Bryan Satterthwaite Papers, 1857–1913 [Description]," North Carolina Digital Collections, 2024, accessed May 26, 2024, https://digital.ncdcr.gov/Documents/Detail/fenner-bryan-satterthwaite-papers-1857-1913/726080.
116 "Benjamin Franklin," Penn & Slavery Project.

117 Ibid.
118 "By virtue of a write to me directed, will be exposed to sale by way of public vendue," *Pennsylvania Gazette*, June 7, 1753, accessed May 26, 2023, https://www.newspapers.com/image/39392590/?terms=%22William%20Satterthwaite%22&match=1.
119 "Satterthwaite family papers, 1735–1924 MC.950.157—Finding aid prepared by Kara Flynn," Haverford College Quaker & Special Collections, April 1, 2016, accessed May 26, 2023, https://library.haverford.edu/finding-aids/files/950-157.pdf.
120 Carl LaVO, "LaVO: A tale of fractured love on Lumberville's Coppernose Hill," *Phillyburbs.com*, April 18, 2016, accessed May 26, 2023, https://www.phillyburbs.com/story/lifestyle/columns/2016/04/18/lavo-tale-fractured-love-on/17828056007/.
121 Ibid.
122 Ibid.
123 Cynthia Feathers and Susan Feathers, "Franklin and the Iroquois Foundations of the Constitution," *The Pennsylvania Gazette*, January 1, 2007, https://thepenngazette.com/franklin-and-the-iroquois-foundations-of-the-constitution/. The "Iroquois Confederacy Of Nations—Hearing Before The Select Committee On Indian Affairs—United States Senate," convened on December 2, 1987, in Washington, DC, noted in a "concurrent resolution": "To acknowledge the contribution of the Iroquois Confederacy of Nations to the development of the United States Constitution and to reaffirm the continuing government-to-government relationship between Indian tribes and the United States established in the Constitution." The document further notes: "Whereas the original framers of the Constitution, including most notably, George Washington and Benjamin Franklin, are known to have greatly admired the concepts, principles and governmental practices of the Six Nations of the Iroquois Confederacy," acknowledging that "the confederation of the original Thirteen Colonies into one republic was explicitly modeled upon the Iroquois Confederacy as were many of the democratic principles which were incorporated into the Constitution itself."
124 Blockson, *African Americans In Pennsylvania*, 32.
125 Jubilee Marshall, "Race, Death, and Public Health in Early Philadelphia, 1750–1793," *Pennsylvania History: Journal of MidAtlantic Studies* 87, no. 2 (Spring 2020): 364–389, accessed June 25, 2023, https://www.jstor.org/stable/10.5325/pennhistory.87.2.0364.
126 Richard S. Newman, *Freedom's Prophet: Bishop Richard Allen, the AME Church, and the Black Founding Fathers* (New York and London: New York University Press, 2008), 60–61.
127 Phillis Wheatley, "To the Right Honourable WILLIAM, Earl of DARTMOUTH, His Majesty's Principal Secretary of State for North America, &cc.," in *Poems on Various Subjects, Religious and Moral* (Denver, CO: W. H. Lawrence & Co., 1886–1887). The Gilder Lehrman Institute of American History notes: "Born in Africa, Phillis Wheatley was captured and sold into slavery as a child. She was purchased by John Wheatley of Boston in 1761. The Wheatleys soon recognized Phillis's intelligence and taught her to read and write. She became well known locally [and later throughout Europe and the United States] for her poetry. Through the Wheatley family, Phillis came into contact with many prominent figures." In her poem, "Wheatley then declares that her love of freedom comes from being a slave and describes being kidnapped from her parents, comparing the colonies' relationship with England to a slave's relationship with a slave holder."

Chapter 2

1 David Cressy, *England on Edge: Crisis and Revolution 1640–1642* (New York: Oxford University Press, 2006), xi.

232 • THE MONTIERS

2 Jane H. Ohlmeyer, "English Civil Wars ... Also known as: Great Rebellion, Wars of the Three Kingdoms," Britannica.com, 2023, accessed June 24, 2023, https://www.britannica.com/event/English-Civil-Wars.
3 "Quakers in Britain—Our history: A radical church born during radical times," Quaker.org.uk, 2018, accessed June 24, 2023, https://www.quaker.org.uk/about-quakers/our-history.
4 Ibid.
5 "Humphrey Morrey and His Wife Ann, Wealthy Quakers," Takingthelongerview.org, May 8, 2020, accessed July 29, 2023, https://takingthelongerview.org/?s=Humphrey+Morrey+.
6 Cheshire, England, Parish Registers, 1538–1909, Audlem, Cheshire, England, digital image s.v. "Humphray [sic] Morrey," 2023, accessed May 2, 2024, *Ancestry.com*.
7 England, Select Births and Christenings, 1538–1975, All Saints, Newcastle-Upon-Tyne, Northumberland, England, digital image s.v. "William Morrey," 2023, accessed June 25, 2023, Ancestry.com.
8 Cheshire, England, Parish Registers, 1538–1909, Malpas, Cheshire, England, digital image s.v. "William Morrey," 2023, accessed June 25, 2023, *Ancestry.com*.
9 Cheshire, England, Parish Registers, 1538–1909, Wybunbury, Cheshire, England, digital image s.v. "William Morrey," 2023, accessed June 25, 2023, *Ancestry.com*.
10 "Morrey History, Family Crest & Coats of Arms," HouseofNames.com, 2023, accessed June 25, 2023, https://www.houseofnames.com/morrey-family-crest.
11 Pitts, "'Richard Morrey, Gent.,'" 262.
12 Carter G. Woodson, "Anthony Benezet," *The Journal of Negro History* II, no. 1 (January 1917), accessed June 30, 2024, https://www.gutenberg.org/files/20752/20752-h/20752-h.htm.
13 Ibid., 43–44.
14 "Black Founders: The Free Black Community in the Early Republic," Library Company of Philadelphia, 2011, accessed June 30, 2023, https://www.librarycompany.org/blackfounders/section5.htm.
15 "Humphrey Morrey and His Wife Ann," Takingthelongerview.org.
16 "Richard Morrey and His Two Wives," Takingthelongerview.org, May 8, 2020, accessed March 27, 2023, https://takingthelongerview.org/index.php/2020/05/08/richard-morrey-and-his-two-wives/.
17 Sue Long, who reported that she is descended from Matilda, the daughter of Richard Morrey and his first wife, Ann (with the possible surname or maiden name of Turner), provided this author with family history data that correlates with other sources in an email dated June 11, 2013, focusing initially on Richard's father Humphrey and first wife, also named Ann. Long also noted that Richard was quite savvy regarding business and legal affairs: "In his will Humphrey (the elder) left his estate to the male heirs of his sons. This caused a serious problem for Richard after his cousin Humphrey (the younger) died before him, and Richard's son Thomas died unmarried (leaving an interesting will and inventory with scientific toys like microscopes). Richard did have a daughter Matilda (who had children) and the children with Cremona, but they were not eligible to inherit. So Richard had to break the entail, in a very interesting legal maneuver spelled out in several long deeds." Furthermore, within "another deed he [Richard] conveyed property to her [his first wife Ann], fulfilling a promise that he made to her before they were married that she would have some property under her control and in her own name. ... We know that she left a will, from a mention in the Abington Meeting minutes of a legacy left to the meeting." Long said, however, that evidence indicating that Richard probated the will had not been found by her at the time she sent the 2013 email to this author.
18 Humphrey Morrey in *Appletons' Cyclopedia of American Biography, 1600–1889*, eds. James Grant Wilson and John Fiske (New York: D. Appleton and Company, 1888), 408, digital image s.v. 2023, Ancestry.com.

19 *Encyclopedia of Philadelphia*, "MORREY (or MURRAY), HUMPHREY—(c. 1641–1715)," ed. Joseph Jackson (Harrisburg, PA: National Historical Association, 1931), 899, digital image s.v. 2023, Ancestry.com.
20 "Humphrey Morrey and His Wife Ann," Takingthelongerview.org.
21 Benjamin F. Thompson, *History of Long Island from its Discovery and Settlement to the Present Time* (New York: Robert H. Dodd, 1918), 304–305.
22 Ibid.
23 Quaker Arrivals at Philadelphia 1682–1750, Philadelphia, Pa., digital image s.v. "Certificates of Removal Received at Philadelphia Meetings, 1682–1750," 2024, accessed July 23, 2024, Ancestry.com.
24 This John Jay was not the Founding Father and first chief justice of United States Supreme Court born in 1745.
25 Thompson, *History of Long Island*.
26 Ibid.
27 Gregory B. Keen, *The Descendants of Jöran Kyn of New Sweden* (Philadelphia, PA: The Swedish Colonial Society, 1913), 22, accessed June 28, 2023, https://www.forgottenbooks.com/en/download/TheDescendantsofJoranKynofNewSweden10609319.pdf.
28 Pitts, "'Richard Morrey, Gent.,'" 263.
29 "John Murrey in the U.S., Quaker Meeting Records, 1681–1935," Ancestry.com via Haverford College [database online], 2023, accessed December 17, 2023, https://www.ancestry.com/discoveryui-content/view/1100215860:2189.
30 "John Morrey: North America, Family Histories, 1500–2000," in *A brief pedigree of Merritt Lum Budd, Jr, born November 16, 1916*, 2023, accessed December 17, 2023, https://www.ancestry.com/discoveryui-content/view/1257837:61157.
31 David Ross, ed., "St. Bartholomew-the-Great," Britain Express.com, 2023, accessed August 30, 2023, https://www.britainexpress.com/attractions.htm?attraction=1586.
32 "Humphrey Morrey and His Wife Ann," Takingthelongerview.org.
33 Ibid.
34 Ibid.
35 Sarah Anne Barbour-Mercer, "Prosecution and Process: Crime and the Criminal Law in Late Seventeenth-Century Yorkshire" (PhD diss., University of York, 1988), 218–219, accessed June 30, 2024, https://etheses.whiterose.ac.uk/14157/1/234919.pdf.
36 Ibid.
37 Matthew Green, "Lost in the Great Fire: which London buildings disappeared in the 1666 blaze?," *The Guardian*, August 20, 2016, accessed June 30, 2024, https://www.theguardian.com/cities/2016/aug/30/great-fire-of-london-1666-350th-anniversary-which-buildings-disappeared.
38 Gottlieb Mittelberger, "Gottlieb Mittelberger's Journey to Pennsylvania in the Year 1750 and Return to Germany in the Year 1754," *Voices of a People's History of the United States, 10th Anniversary Edition*, eds. Howard Zinn and Anthony Arnove (New York: Seven Stories Press, 2014), 73.
39 Ibid.
40 Pitts, "'Richard Morrey, Gent.,'" 262.
41 Josiah Granville Leach, "Colonial Mayors of Philadelphia: Humphrey Morrey, First Mayor, 1691–1692," *The Pennsylvania Magazine of History and Biography* (1894), 423, accessed July 29, 2023, https://books.google.com/books/about/The_Pennsylvania_Magazine_of_Historyand.html?id=OMcbAAAAMAAJ.
42 Ibid.

234 • THE MONTIERS

43   Josh Levy, "Trading on the Waterfront in Early America: The Manuscript Division Acquires Business Records of Two Quaker Merchants," Library of Congress blog, April 14, 2022, accessed June 28, 2024, https://blogs.loc.gov/manuscripts/2022/04/trading-on-the-waterfront-in-early-america-the-manuscript-division-acquires-business-records-of-two-quaker-merchants/.
44   Leach, "Colonial Mayors of Philadelphia: Humphrey Morrey, First Mayor, 1691–1692," 426.
45   Ibid.
46   Ibid.
47   Ibid.
48   Pitts, "'Richard Morrey, Gent.,'" 268.
49   "Morrey, Humphrey with Edward Shippen Accounts, 1726–34," Haverford College Quaker & Special Collections, MC 1182 Dorothy Merriman Schall Collection, Box 4.
50   Craig W. Horle, et al., eds., *Lawmaking and Legislators in Pennsylvania, Vol. 1, 1682–1709* (Philadelphia: University of Pennsylvania Press, 1991), 554.
51   Alvin Rabushka, "The Colonial Roots of American Taxation, 1607–1700: The low-tax beginnings of American prosperity," Hoover Institution, August 1, 2002, 77–78, accessed June 27, 2023, https://www.hoover.org/research/colonial-roots-american-taxation-1607-1700.
52   Ibid.
53   Ibid.
54   Ibid.
55   Peter B. Kotowski, "The Best Poor Man's Country?: William Penn, Quakers and Unfree Labor in Atlantic Pennsylvania," (PhD diss., Loyola University Chicago, 2016), accessed June 27, 2023, https://ecommons.luc.edu/luc_diss/2138.
56   Pitts, "'Richard Morrey, Gent.,'" 266.
57   Ibid.
58   Ibid., 262.
59   Lynn van Rooijen-McCullough, "William Frampton In Philadelphia," *Mixed Genes*, accessed June 25, 2023, https://mixedgenes.eu/william-frampton-in-philadelphia/. The writer references Darold D. Wax's April 1962 article, "Quaker Merchants and the Slave Trade in Colonial Pennsylvania," that appears in *The Pennsylvania Magazine of History and Biography*, starting on page 143, regarding Frampton selling African slaves.
60   Pitts, "'Richard Morrey, Gent.,'" 265–266.
61   Jack H. Schick, "Slavery in Pennsylvania," *Friends Journal*, September 1, 2012, accessed August 3, 2023, https://www.friendsjournal.org/slavery-in-pennsylvania/.
62   Willis P. Hazard, *Annals of Philadelphia and Pennsylvania in the Olden Time: or, Memoirs, Anecdotes, and Incidents of Philadelphia and Its Inhabitants from the Days of the Founders* (Philadelphia, PA: J. M. Stoddart & Co., 1877), accessed August 3, 2023, https://www.forgottenbooks.com/en/download/AnnalsofPhiladelphiaandPennsylvaniaintheOldenTime1879_10222713.pdf.
63   Hannah Benner Roach, "The Planting of Philadelphia: A Seventeenth-Century Real Estate Development, II," *The Pennsylvania Magazine of History and Biography* (1968), 148–149, accessed June 25, 2023, https://journals.psu.edu/pmhb/article/view/42376.
64   Ibid., 171–172.
65   Willis Shirk, "Old Rights Warrant to First Purchaser Humphrey Morrey," *Pennsylvania Heritage, Our Documentary Heritage* (Spring 2007), accessed June 25, 2023, http://paheritage.wpengine.com/article/old-rights-warrant-first-purchaser-humphrey-morrey-1683/.
66   "LOCAL HISTORY SKETCH. Interesting Local Matter Collected by 'E. M.,'" *The Ambler Gazette*, October 27, 1910, 3. Provided by local Cheltenham-area historian and writer David Harrower on February 16, 2017, indicating that in the Edge Hill area of Cheltenham, Humphrey Morrey early

ENDNOTES • 235

on owned a "large tract of 250 acres," likely during the late 1600s. However, he greatly expanded his land acquisitions before his death.

67 Leach, "Colonial Mayors of Philadelphia: Humphrey Morrey, First Mayor, 1691–1692," 424–425.
68 George Allen, "The Rittenhouse Paper Mill and Its Founders," *Germantown Crier* 4, no. 1 (March and June, 1952), 15, accessed June 29, 2023, https://historic germantownpa.org/wp-content/uploads/2020/11/GC-The-Rittenhouse-Paper-Mill-and-Its-Founders.pdf.
69 Jewels Tauzin, "William Bradford: 'Father of American Printing,'" *Trinity Church—Wall Street*, August 20, 2021, accessed June 29, 2023, https://trinitywallstreet.org/stories-news/william-bradford-father-american-printing.
70 "John Peter Zenger—American printer," *Britannica*, January 1, 2023, accessed June 29, 2023, https://www.britannica.com/biography/John-Peter-Zenger.
71 Tauzin, "William Bradford: 'Father of American Printing.'"
72 "John Murrey in the U.S., Quaker Meeting Records, 1681–1935," Ancestry.com via Haverford College [database online], accessed December 17, 2023, https://www.ancestry.com/discoveryui-content/view/1100215860:2189.
73 "Matilda (Morrey) Flannigan (abt. 1680—abt. 1750)," *WikiTree*, July 19, 2019, https://www.wikitree.com/wiki/Morrey-38.
74 Pitts, "'Richard Morrey, Gent.,'" 263.
75 Ibid., 266.
76 Ibid.
77 Ibid.
78 Ibid., 267.
79 Ibid.
80 Ibid.
81 "Richard Morrey and His Two Wives," Takingthelongerview.org.
82 Leach, "Colonial Mayors of Philadelphia: Humphrey Morrey, First Mayor, 1691–1692," 424–425.
83 Ibid.
84 "Richard Morrey and His Two Wives," Takingthelongerview.org.
85 "Chapter Four" in the following detailed book about the history of the Harmer family states that William Harmer emigrated from England "to Pennsylvania sometime between 1684 and 1695," settling in what is today, Cheltenham Township. According to a quoted passage within the book from Genealogical Society Library (PA M 4c Vol. 2, 282), Harmer "received a grant of one thousand acres of land from William Penn, on a portion of which the borough of Jenkintown and vicinity is located." The Guineatown–Edge Hill area of Glenside in Cheltenham was sometimes referred to as Harmer Hill. Please see: *A History of the Harmer Family* (Salt Lake City, UT: Harmer Family Genealogical Society, 1959), 30, accessed July 23, 2024, https://ia800709.us.archive.org/19/items/historyofharmerf00unse/historyofharmerf00unse.pdf.
86 Pitts, "'Richard Morrey, Gent.,'" 264.
87 "Anthony Kimble and Matilda Morrey," Takingthelongerview.org, May 8, 2020, accessed June 30, 2024, http://takingthelongerview.org/index.php/2020/05/08/anthony-kimble-and-matilda-morrey/.
88 Sue Long reports that she is a descendant of Richard and Ann [Turner] Morrey [likely via their daughter Matilda], according to a November 18, 2002 post on Ancestry.com that can be accessed at http://boards.ancestry.com/surnames.morrey/5.6.8.11/mb.ashx: "I am descended from Matilda Morrey, granddaughter of Humphrey and daughter of Richard and Ann. Matilda married Anthony Kimble and lived in Bucks County, Pennsylvania, on land inherited from her wealthy family." Long notes that Richard's father, Humphrey Morrey, who became the first mayor of Philadelphia (circa 1691), "married twice, to Ann --, in England, and in 1693 to Sarah Baynton, sister of Peter

Baynton." Long continued: "Richard married … in 1746, Sarah Beasley. The Morrey family had connections to the wealthy Budd family. There are some interesting stories about these families, including a relation to Paul Robeson, through Richard's mistress Cremona, whom he acknowledged in his will."

89 Frenise A. Logan, "The British East India Company and African Slavery in Benkulen, Sumatra, 1687–1792," *The Journal of Negro History* 41, no. 4 (October 1956): 339, accessed July 1, 2023, https://www.journals.uchicago.edu/doi/epdf/10.2307/2715359.

90 Takingthelongerview.org.

91 Ibid.

92 "Joseph Turner: 1701–1783—Penn Connection—Founder and trustee 1749–1779," Penn Libraries University Archives & Records Center, 2023, accessed July 2, 2023, https://archives.upenn.edu/exhibits/penn-people/biography/joseph-turner/.

93 "William Allen: 1704–1780—Penn Connection—Founder and trustee 1749–1780," Penn Libraries University Archives & Records Center, 2023, accessed July 2, 2023, https://archives.upenn.edu/exhibits/penn-people/biography/william-allen/.

94 Ibid.

95 "Richard Morrey and His Two Wives," Takingthelongerview.org.

96 Ibid.

97 Ibid.

98 Ibid.

99 "Richard Morrey, Miscellaneous, Ann Morrey, Abington Monthly Meeting …," Ancestry.com, *U.S., Quaker Meeting Records, 1681–1935* [database online], 2023, accessed December 20, 2023, https://www.ancestry.com/discoveryui-content/view/599451011:2189: Before her death before or about 1746, Richard Morrey's wife Ann was given permission by her husband, according to this entry in Abington Monthly Meeting (AMM) records, that also provided "five pounds" legacy payment(s) to the AMM.

100 "Richard Morrey and His Two Wives," Takingthelongerview.org.

101 Ibid.

102 Ibid. It's interesting to note that according to ushistory.org, the prominent Philadelphian Benjamin Franklin's son, Francis (Franky) Folger Franklin died in 1736 "at age 4 of smallpox," according to "The Electric Ben Franklin: Benjamin Franklin Timeline: 1706–1741," at https://www.ushistory.org/franklin/info/timeline.htm. Franklin apparently wrote in his diary, according to Virginia S. Hart for the website journey.salem.edu, "In 1736 I lost one of my sons, a fine boy of four years old, by the small-pox, taken in the common way. I long regretted bitterly, and still regret that I had not given it to him by inoculation," circumstances that may have negatively impacted Franklin's relationship with his wife, Debra (Read), according to some scholars. "This I mention for the sake of parents who omit that operation, on the supposition that they would never forgive themselves if a child died under it." Meanwhile, FindaGrave.com says Franklin's brother James Franklin died in Rhode Island in 1735 during an outbreak of diphtheria or "throat distemper," as described by several sources. Furthermore, Suzanne M. Shultz notes in a varsitytutors.com article, "Epidemics in Colonial Philadelphia 1699–1799 and The Risk of Dying," that 114 people died in Boston during a scarlet fever outbreak in 1635–1636, based on the data of "William Douglass, a colonial Boston physician."

103 E. Digby Baltzell, *Philadelphia Gentlemen: The Making of a National Upper Class* (Papamoa Press, 1958, 2018), 16.

104 Reginald H. Pitts, "'Richard Morrey, Gent.," 263.

105 Ibid.

106 Horle et al., *Lawmaking and Legislators in Pennsylvania*, 554.
107 Pitts, "'Richard Morrey, Gent.,'" 263.
108 Ibid., 262.
109 J. Franklin Jameson, ed., *Original Narratives of Early American History—Narratives of Early Pennsylvania, West New Jersey and Delaware: 1630–1707* (New York: Charles Scribner's Sons, 1912), 127–128, accessed June 30, 2024, https://tile.loc.gov/storage-services/public/gdcmassbookdig/narrativesofearl03myer/narrativesofearl03myer_djvu.txt.
110 Ibid., 127.
111 Ibid.
112 "Humphrey Morrey and His Wife Ann," Takingthelongerview.org.
113 Ibid.
114 "Richard Morrey and His Two Wives," Takingthelongerview.org.
115 Pitts, "'Richard Morrey, Gent.,'" 264.
116 "Humphrey Morrey and His Wife Ann," Takingthelongerview.org.
117 Pitts, "'Richard Morrey, Gent.,'" 263.
118 "Richard Morrey in the Philadelphia County, Pennsylvania, U.S., Will Index, 1682–1819," Ancestry.com, accessed July 30, 2023, https://www.ancestry.com/discoveryui-content/view/.83649:4695?tid=&pid=&queryId=3866fb6ca622e58f0e5da44be7560c5e&_phsrc=GdY1853&_phstart=successSource.
119 Ibid.
120 Ibid.
121 Ibid.
122 Mark E. Reinberger and Elizabeth McLean, *The Philadelphia Country House: Architecture and Landscape in Colonial America* (Baltimore, MD: Johns Hopkins University Press, 2015), 113.
123 Ibid., 187.
124 Ibid. Regarding Samuel Morris having an enslaved worker identified as James Nettles, the authors cite Dorothy B. Templeton's *The Historical Narrative Research Report: Hope Lodge; Historic Structures Report* (Philadelphia, PA: Martin J. Rosenblum & Associates, 1984), 33. Meanwhile, a Samuel Morris, in the March 5, 1751 edition of Benjamin Franklin's *Pennsylvania Gazette*, evidently paid for the advertisement offering the sale of African Americans to be published.
125 Ibid.
126 Baltzell, *Philadelphia Gentlemen*, 16.
127 Ibid., 126.
128 "Anthony Kimble and Matilda Morrey," Takingthelongerview.org.
129 "Humphrey Morrey and His Wife Ann," Takingthelongerview.org.
130 Pitts, "'Richard Morrey, Gent.,'" 264.
131 "The Budd Family, Address of Col. Enos Goble Budd, Delivered at Budd's Lake, Morris County, New Jersey, August 14th, 1878 at the First Re-Union" (New York: Press of F. W. Sonneborn, 1881), 8–9, accessed July 28, 2023, https//www.seekingmyroots.com/members/files/G000703.pdf.
132 Soderlund, "Black Women in Colonial Pennsylvania," 73.
133 Baltzell, *Philadelphia Gentlemen*, 128.
134 Reinberger and McLean, *The Philadelphia Country House*, 47.

Chapter 3

1   Although some documents indicate that Cremona Morrey may have made arrangements to purchase her own freedom from Richard Morrey for 20 pounds, other sources say that she and her

children were liberated by either Richard Morrey or his father, Humphrey Morrey, the first mayor of Philadelphia. The Morrey–Bustill–Montier family historian and author Joyce Mosley says that Cremona had been emancipated by Richard after his father's 1715 death and that her "children were free because she was a free woman." Descendant John Montier Pickens added that Cremona and/or her children likely became free sometime between 1715 to 1732. "The [emancipation] papers were actually given to the [liberated] person," Mosley said, so such surviving records are scarce. Liberated blacks had to keep such documents in their possession in case they were "stopped on the street" by someone or so-called authorities trying to determine if they were enslaved or not: Joyce Mosley and John Montier Pickens, Zoom interview of November 3, 2023, recorded with permission by author Donald Scott Sr., MP4. Length 02:56:20, video 1234272029.

2   "LOCAL HISTORY SKETCH. Interesting Local Matter Collected by 'E. M.,'" *The Ambler Gazette*, August 23, 1906, 2. David Harrower sent a February 16, 2017, message to the author with the referenced article attached to the email, indicating: "At the north end of Edge Hill village are two very old stone houses on the west side of the Mermaid road, and of the deep railroad cut, here bridged over. Not much is known about their early history, or the people they have sheltered in the past. These, however, stand on what was the original Richard Morey plantation of 198 acres, and which at his death, before the Revolution, was divided and given to his freed slaves. One of them was Cremona Morey, afterwards wife of John Fry, a free negro. This was in 1748. About 1772 a tract here came into possession of Caspar Martin from Isaac Knight, a trustee for the emancipated slaves of the Morey family," a possible indication that the Morreys liberated such enslaved workers as Cremona or "Mooney."

A similar article, "LOCAL HISTORY SKETCH. Interesting Local Matter Collected by 'E. M.,'" was published in *The Ambler Gazette* on page 2 of the June 11, 1903, edition. Provided by Harrower on February 16, 2017, it indicates that much of Edge Hill consisted of the 198 acres that was essentially passed to Cremona Morrey via Richard Morrey: "Originally, this, like all others about Edge Hill, was part of the 198 acres owned by Richard Morrey, in Colonial times. It came into possession of Casper Martin, a tract comprising 81 acres before the beginning of the Revolution. There is no deed on record to Martin, but probably the grantor to him was Isaac Knight, as trustee for the emancipated slaves of the Morrey family."

An additional article, also titled "LOCAL HISTORY SKETCH. Interesting Local Matter Collected by 'E. M.,'" was published on page 7 of the January 5, 1911, edition of *The Ambler Gazette*. Harrower provided it to the author on February 16, 2017, noting: The following data was found via "the Norristown records" that "goes back to 1772. It was part of 198 acres, which John Fry, in that year sold to Isaac Knight, who was the holder during the Revolutionary period and for 27 years. In 1789 he detached a lot of 11 acres to Caesar Morrey, who paid 61 pounds for the lot, there being no house. It bordered the Limekiln road. The next year Morrey, sold to Isaiah Hubbs, the holder for six years. In 1796 Hubbs sold to Abner Bradfield," the article notes. "The old-time history of the tract, of which these lots are a small fragment goes back to Humphrey Morrey Sr., who had 700 acres covering all Edge Hill. In 1715 his will granted the same to his grandson, Humphrey Morrey Jr. … The latter died about 1732. His will ordered sale, and it was bought by Edward Shippen, Jr. In 1762 Edward Shippen sold this, the north portion, of 117 acres to George Reiter, for 300 pounds."

3   Gordon-Reed, *The Hemingses of Monticello*, 353–354.
4   Ibid.
5   "Slavery and the Making of America—The Slave Experience: Men, Women, and Gender," WNET-PBS, 2004, accessed June 30, 2024, https://www.thirteen.org/wnet/slavery/experience/gender/history2.html.

6   "Richard Morrey and His Two Wives," Takingthelongerview.org.
7   Ibid.
8   Pitts, "The Montier Family of Guineatown," 23.
9   Ibid.
10 Ibid.
11 Pitts, "'Richard Morrey, Gent.,'" 270.
12 "Richard Morrey and His Two Wives," Takingthelongerview.org.
13 Leach, "Colonial Mayors of Philadelphia," 427.
14 "Anthony Kimble and Matilda Morrey," Takingthelongerview.org.
15 Pitts, "'Richard Morrey, Gent.,'" 269.
16 Ibid.
17 "On Slaveholders' Sexual Abuse of Slaves: Selections from 19th- & 20th-century Slave Narratives," National Humanities Center Resource Toolbox—The Making of African American Identity: Vol. 1, 1500–1865, 2007, accessed July 8, 2023, https://nationalhumanitiescenter.org/pds/maai/enslavement/text6/masterslavesexualabuse.pdf.
18 Allison Lange, "Women's Rights in the Early Republic," National Women's History Museum, 2015, https://www.crusadeforthevote.org/early-republic.
19 "On Slaveholders' Sexual Abuse of Slaves."
20 "Richard Morrey and His Two Wives," Takingthelongerview.org. The writer notes various transaction of Richard Morrey and his first wife, Ann (Turner) Morrey, as well as considers the possibility that Thomas Turner, a resident of London, might be her father.
21 Ibid. The writer notes: "Ann Morrey died some time between 1735 and 1746. Administration on her estate was granted to her husband Richard …. In June 1746 Richard married Sarah Allen, a widow at Trinity Church Oxford [in the Philadelphia vicinity] …. Sarah's background is unclear, although much has been speculated about her. Her brother was John Beasley; he served as the executor of Richard's estate …. When she married Richard, she was the widow of an Allen."
22 Benjamin Quarles, "PURVIS, ROBERT, SR.," in *Dictionary of American Negro Biography*, eds. Rayford W. Logan and Michael R. Winston (New York: W. W. Norton & Company, 1982), 508–510.
23 "COLORED INDEPENDENTS. DISTURBERS AT THEIR MEETING. A Gang, Led by a Notorious Henchman of Convict Mouat, Creates Disorder by Attempting to Counteract Enthusiasm Among a Large Gathering of Stewart Men," *The Philadelphia Times*, September 5, 1882, 4. Hiram Montier, a descendant of Cremona Morrey Fry, is listed at a gathering of African-American Republicans at Liberty Hall, including such well-known anti-slavery abolitionists as Robert Purvis and William Still, renowned as the "father of the Underground Railroad," according to *The New York Times*.
24 The online Society of the First African Families of English America biography, "Meet the Author: Joyce Mosley," published by SOFAFEA.org, notes that she "assumed the role of family historian over twenty years ago. Her family is among the first families to reside in Pennsylvania and New Jersey. She can trace her family history to the 1600's to the first mayor of Philadelphia, Humphrey Morrey, and to Cyrus Bustill." The article further notes: "Bustill was born enslaved, purchased his freedom, and baked bread for George Washington's troop[s] at Valley Forge. Her family history began before the Revolutionary War," later featuring kinfolk who "were active in the Underground Railroad, enlisted in the United States Colored Troops, and trained at Camp William Penn." The passage also points out that "the Morrey/Bustill family is one of the founding families of Cheltenham Township, just outside Philadelphia. They are also among the founding families of several African American churches in Philadelphia and surrounding neighborhoods, including the historic African Episcopal Church of St. Thomas, founded in 1792 as the first black Episcopal Church in the USA."

Furthermore, "Joyce is a member of the National Society of the Daughters of the American Revolution (DAR), the Colonial Daughters of the 17th Century, The Society of Founding Families of New Jersey and Pennsylvania, the African American Genealogy Group, and the Sons and Daughters of the United States Middle Passage." The passage concludes by noting that Mosley's "lineage has been accepted by the Society of the First African Families of English America and by the National Society Daughters of the American Revolution," as well as recognize by the Association for the Study of African American Life and History.

25   Soderlund, "Black Women in Colonial Pennsylvania," 74.
26   Ibid.
27   Rolph, "Black History Month: Inter-Racial Marriages."
28   Ibid.
29   Ibid.
30   Higginbotham Jr., *In the Matter of Color*, 274.
31   Edward Raymond Turner, *The Negro in Pennsylvania: Slavery-Servitude-Freedom: 1639–1861*, (Washington, DC: The American Historical Association, 1911), 29–30.
32   Higginbotham Jr., *In the Matter of Color*, 285–286.
33   "RUN away, on Sunday Night last, from David Lindsay, of Northampton, Bucks county, a Negro man, named Dove," *The Pennsylvania Gazette*, July 21, 1748, accessed June 30, 2024, https://www.newspapers.com/image/39394847.
34   "To be SOLD, A Strong able Negroe wench, and her son," *The Pennsylvania Gazette*, November 16, 1752, accessed June 30, 2024, https://www.newspapers.com/image/39389554.
35   Ibid., 286. Edward Raymond Turner, in *The Negro in Pennsylvania: Slavery-Servitude-Freedom: 1639–1861*, writes that Benjamin Franklin was accused of having a black "paramour" in a footnote on page 31, as well as bibliography entry, page 293, both referencing "'*What is Sauce for a Goose is also Sauce for a Gander* … An Epitaph on a certain great man. Written by a departed spirit, etc. Phila., 1764—Franklin said to have had a negro paramour.'—R.B."
36   "Thomas Jefferson and Robert Hemings in Philadelphia," National Park Service, July 5, 2021, accessed July 21, 2023, https://www.nps.gov/articles/independence-jeffersonphiladelphia.htm.
37   Fawn M. Brodie, "HEMINGS, SALLY (1773–1835)," in *Dictionary of American Negro Biography*, eds. Rayford W. Logan and Michael R. Winston (New York: W. W. Norton & Company, 1982), 305.
38   Ibid.
39   Ibid.
40   Sherri Burr, "Aaron Burr Jr. and John Pierre Burr: A Founding Father and his Abolitionist Son," University of New Mexico School of Law, 2020, accessed August 3, 2023, https://digitalrepository.unm.edu/law_facultyscholarship/794.
41   Ibid.
42   Ibid.
43   Ibid.
44   Ibid.
45   "Alexander Hamilton and Aaron Burr's Duel," PBS.org, 2023, accessed August 3, 2023, https://www.pbs.org/wgbh/americanexperience/features/duel-alexander-hamilton-and-aaron-burrs-duel/.
46   Sherri Burr, "Aaron Burr Jr. and John Pierre Burr."
47   Ibid.
48   Ibid.
49   Ibid.
50   Mosley and John Montier Pickens, Zoom interview of November 3, 2023, recorded with interviewees' permission by author Donald Scott Sr., MP4. Length 02:56:20, video 1234272029.

51 Ibid.
52 Margaret Hope Bacon, *But ONE Race: The Life of Robert Purvis* (Albany, NY: State University of New York Press, 2007), 1–2.
53 Ibid.
54 Ibid., 2–3.
55 Quarles, "PURVIS, ROBERT, SR.," 508.
56 Bacon, *But ONE Race*, 2.
57 Ibid., 2.
58 Ibid.
59 Ibid., 5.
60 Ibid.
61 Ibid., 3.
62 Ibid., 9.
63 Quarles, "PURVIS, ROBERT, SR.," 509.
64 "Purvis, Robert," Encyclopedia.com, May 9, 2018, accessed March 8, 2023, https://www.encyclopedia.com/history/historians-and-chronicles/historians-miscellaneous-biographies/robert-purvis.
65 "COLORED INDEPENDENTS. DISTURBERS AT THEIR MEETING," 4.
66 Bacon, *But ONE Race*, 14.
67 Ibid.
68 Ibid.
69 The Morrey–Bustill–Montier family historian and author Joyce Mosley says Grace Bustill and other blacks practicing Quakerism were often not allowed to officially join Quaker congregations, including the Arch Street Meeting House where a segregated "Negro Bench" was institutionalized. "Grace and her daughter Sarah kept going; they suffered the humility … of having to sit on the 'Negro Bench'—and in fact their white friends weren't even allowed to sit with them." Mosley and John Montier Pickens, Zoom interview of November 3, 2023, recorded with permission by author Donald Scott Sr., MP4. Length 02:56:20, video 1234272029.
70 Ibid.
71 Julie Winch, *A Gentleman of Color: The Life of James Forten* (New York: Oxford University Press, 2002), 165.
72 The Morrey–Bustill–Montier family historian and author Joyce Mosley recognizes that Cremona Morrey chose to take on Richard's surname Morrey, or a variation of it, "Murray," but still believes the relationship may have been conditional. "After the 10 years he married somebody else," Mosley said. "So, it may have been, you know, that was her compensation for the 10 years was to give her the land." Co-descendant John Montier Pickens pondered if the relationship was "transactional," considering Richard's privileged background and wealthy upbringing, etc. Meanwhile, Mosley questioned whether the couple's possible first child, Robert Lewis, was intentionally given the surname "Lewis" because they tried to keep the relationship and "their child" undercover. "By the second child I think they had established their relationship and by that time I'm trying to research if Ann [Richard's first wife] had moved out—by the second child." As one researcher wondered, another intriguing question to consider is whether Cremona had an earlier relationship with someone with the surname of Lewis that resulted in the birth of her first child?: Joyce Mosley and John Montier Pickens, Zoom interview of November 3, 2023, recorded with permission by author Donald Scott Sr., MP4. Length 02:56:20, video 1234272029.
73 Ibid.
74 Joyce Mosley further notes: "Cremona was smart enough to be able to be the woman of the house. I'm sure she was smart enough to want something for her and her children," quite likely liberation

242 • THE MONTIERS

and means to survive: Joyce Mosley and John Montier Pickens, Zoom interview of November 3, 2023.
75 Jeff Thibodeau, *Be Your Best! A Roadmap to Living a Healthy, Balanced and Fulfilling Life* (Dog Ear Publishing, LLC, 2007), 12.
76 Higginbotham Jr., *In the Matter of Color*, 274.
77 Ibid.
78 Ibid.
79 Ibid.
80 Ibid., 282.
81 Ibid., 274–275.
82 Ibid., 289.
83 Ibid., 309.
84 Soderlund, "Black Women in Colonial Pennsylvania," 74.
85 "On Slaveholders' Sexual Abuse of Slaves."
86 Pitts, "'Richard Morrey, Gent.,'" 271.
87 Pitts, "The Montier Family of Guineatown," 23.
88 W. E. Burghardt Du Bois, *The Philadelphia Negro: A Social Study* (Philadelphia: University of Pennsylvania, 1899), 13.
89 Du Bois, *The Philadelphia Negro*, 15.
90 Ibid., 414.
91 Ibid.
92 Ibid. 236.
93 Ibid., 236–237.
94 Ibid., 237.
95 Ibid.
96 The March 17, 1775, edition of *The Virginia Gazette* noted that "ON Wednesday last a Negro man, belonging to Mr. Adam Baker, in Cheltenham township, was found hanging on a tree, by some women who were passing along the road. He hung himself, it is supposed, thinking he would go back to his own country, having given that as a reason for a former attempt, when, the rope breaking, prevented his intention." The article was accessed January 2, 2017, via Accessible Archives Inc.
97 Erin Blakemore, "How two centuries of slave revolts shaped American history," NationalGeographic.com, November 8, 2019, accessed July 10, 2023, https://www.nationalgeographic.com/history/article/two-centuries-slave-rebellions-shaped-american-history.
98 Ibid.

Chapter 4

1 Karen Smyles, producer, *The Montiers: An American Story*, PBS-WHYY (Philadelphia), March 15, 2018, accessed September 19, 2023, https://www.pbs.org/video/the-montiers-an-american-story-t7lf1a/.
2 "Richard Morrey and His Two Wives," Takingthelongerview.org.
3 Joyce Mosley and John Montier Pickens, Zoom interview of November 3, 2023, recorded with permission by author Donald Scott Sr., MP4. Length 02:56:20, video 1234272029.
4 Ibid.
5 Mosley says that Cremona would have been in an "awkward position" while she possibly lived under the same roof with Ann and her husband, Richard Morrey. Mosley explains: "She [Cremona] worked in his house. She was part of his staff." Co-descendant John Montier Pickens asserted that "she [Cremona] was property," at least before her liberation, a circumstance that was likely ripe

for coercion. Mosley further considered the scenario of whether Richard was "promiscuous" while having minimal "respect" for his wife Ann. Zoom interview of November 3, 2023.

6   Ibid.
7   Catherine Hezser, "Master-Slave Relationships," in *Jewish Slavery in Antiquity* (Oxford: Oxford University Press, 2005), 149–178, accessed June 30, 2024, https://doi.org/10.1093/acprof:oso/9780199280865.003.0008.
8   Farah Stockman, "'She was Part of This Family': Jefferson Descendants Reflect on Sally Hemings Exhibit," *The New York Times*, June 16, 2018, accessed December 11, 2023, https://www.nytimes.com/2018/06/16/us/jefferson-sally-hemings-descendants.html?referringSource=articleShare.
9   Ibid.
10 "The Declaration House Through Time," Independence National Historical Park, 2024, accessed June 30, 2024, https://www.nps.gov/articles/000/independence-dechousehistory.htm.
11 Stockman, "'She was Part of This Family.'"
12 The Morrey–Bustill–Montier family historian and author Joyce Mosley says her seventh great-grandfather was Humphrey Morrey, the first mayor of Philadelphia, circa 1691: Joyce Mosley and John Montier Pickens, Zoom interview of November 3, 2023, recorded with permission by author Donald Scott Sr., MP4. Length 02:56:20, video 1234272029.
13 Ibid.
14 Stockman, "'She was Part of This Family.'"
15 Lisa Clayton Robinson, "Jacobs, Harriet Ann (b. 1813?, Edenton, N.C.; d. March 7, 1897, Washington, D.C.), African American writer known especially for her autobiography, which is the most significant African American slave narrative by a woman," *AFRICANA: The Encyclopedia of African and African American Experience*, eds. Kwame Anthony Appiah and Henry Louis Gates Jr. (New York: Basic Civitas Books, 1999), 949.
16 Harriet A. Jacobs, *Incidents in the Life of a Slave Girl. Written by Herself*, ed. Lydia Maria Francis Child (Documenting the American South, University of North Carolina at Chapel Hill, 1860–1861, 2003), 45, accessed August 4, 2023, https://docsouth.unc.edu/fpn/jacobs/jacobs.html.
17 Solomon Northup, (*Twelve Years a Slave: Narrative of Solomon Northup, a Citizen of New-York, Kidnapped in Washington City in 1841, and Rescued in 1853*, ed. Natalia Smith (London: Sampson Low, Son & Company, 1853), 186, accessed June 30, 2024, https://docsouth.unc.edu/fpn/northup/northup.html.
18 Robinson, "Jacobs, Harriet Ann."
19 Northup, *Twelve Years a Slave*, 189.
20 Ibid.
21 Ibid.
22 Ibid.
23 "James Thomson Callender," Monticello and the University of Virginia in Charlottesville, 2023, accessed July 26, 2023, https://www.monticello.org/research-education/thomas-jefferson-encyclopedia/james-callender.
24 Pitts, "The Montier Family of Guineatown," 23.
25 Scott Sr., *Remembering Cheltenham Township*, 34.
26 Pitts, "Robert Lewis of Guineatown," 43.
27 Vestry member and historical co-chair Ginny McCracken of Trinity Church, Oxford, sent this author an email dated March 3, 2018, concerning Caesar [Murray] Penrose's approximately 50-year service as sexton of Trinity. There's some indication that Caesar was at some earlier point either enslaved, an apprentice, or indentured in New Jersey, likely by the Penroses, before becoming a member of Trinity. McCracken reported that his previously visible gravestone, according to church records,

said: "'In Memory of Caesar Penrose,* Sexton of this Church more than half a century. Good and faithful servant, well done. Enter thou into the joy of thy Lord.' *Colored. Died in 1831.'" On Wednesday, December 20, 2023, this author found the above epitaph also at The Library Company of Philadelphia on page 56 of the *Historical Sketch Of The Parish Of Trinity Church, Oxford, Philadelphia* (published 1857 by Lindsay & Blakiston), which was read during services on Sunday, August 2, 1857, by the Reverend Edward Y. Buchanan, rector. Reverend Buchanan's brother, James Buchanan, served as president of the United States.

28 Ibid.
29 Ibid.
30 Ibid.
31 Frances D. Pingeon, "Blacks in the Revolutionary Era," *New Jersey Historical Commission*, 1976, 7, accessed November 24, 2023, https://dspace.njstatelib.org/xmlui/bitstream/handle/10929/18644/h6731975e_v14.pdf?sequence=4&isAllowed=y.
32 Ibid.
33 Ibid.
34 Higginbotham Jr., *In the Matter of Color*, 274.
35 "Philadelphia," History.com, 2024, accessed July 17, 2023, https://www.history.com/topics/us-states/philadelphia-pennsylvania.
36 Soderlund, "Black Women in Colonial Pennsylvania," 82.
37 Nash, "Slaves and Slave Owners," 45.
38 Pitts, "Robert Lewis of Guineatown," 43–44.
39 "Reynier Tyson," Ancestry.com, 2023, accessed July 17, 2023, https://www.ancestry.com/genealogy/records/reynier-tyson-24-2jkxkpf.
40 Ibid.
41 "Reynier Tyson," FindaGrave.com, accessed July 17, 2023, https://www.findagrave.com/memorial/189806767/reynier-tyson.
42 "1688 Petition Against Slavery," Germantown Mennonite Historic Trust The Historic 1770 Germantown Mennonite Meetinghouse, 2023, accessed July 17, 2023, http://www.meetinghouse.info/about-us.html.
43 Ibid.
44 Edwin C. Jellett, "Gardens and Gardeners of Germantown—FORMATIVE PERIOD: 1683–1740," *Germantown History* (Germantown, PA: The Site and Relic Society of Germantown, 1915), 264.
45 John W. Jordan, ed., "TYSON FAMILY," in *Colonial and Revolutionary Families of Pennsylvania: Genealogical and Personal Memoirs*, 395–399, 2024, accessed June 30, 2024, Ancestry.com, https://www.ancestry.com/imageviewer/collections/23613/images/dvm_GenMono005730-00214-1?ssrc=&backlabel=Return&pId=407.
46 Pitts, "Robert Lewis of Guineatown," 46.
47 Ibid.
48 Ibid.
49 "Richard Morrey and His Two Wives," Takingthelongerview.org
50 Pitts, "'Richard Morrey, Gent.,'" 283.
51 The Morrey–Bustill–Montier family historian and author Joyce Mosley said she found documentation at Howard University's Moorland-Spingarn Collection (two requisition forms that she provided to the Daughters of the American Revolution) indicating that Cyrus Bustill baked bread for George Washington's Revolutionary Army. He then delivered the bread to Valley Forge, Mosley said: Joyce Mosley and John Montier Pickens, Zoom interview of November 3, 2023, recorded with permission by author Donald Scott Sr., MP4. Length 02:56:20, video 1234272029.

52 "Richard Morrey and His Two Wives," Takingthelongerview.org.
53 Ibid.
54 Ibid.
55 Pitts, "'Richard Morrey, Gent.,'" 283.
56 The duplicated biographical article, "Nathan Francis Mossell, M.D.: 1856–1946," originally published in the March 1954 edition of the *Journal of the National Medical Association* (Vol. 46, No. 3), briefly discusses the establishment of South New Jersey's Gouldtown. The document was found at the University of Pennsylvania's University Archives within the Nathan Francis Mossell Papers (Box 1, Folder 7 UPT 50-M913), 129, by this author on Thursday, December 21, 2023.
57 Pitts, "The Montier Family of Guineatown," 23.
58 Pitts, "Robert Lewis of Guineatown," 48.

Chapter 5

1 The Morrey–Bustill–Montier family historian and author Joyce Mosley acknowledges Richard Morrey was much older compared to the younger Cremona when their relationship started. His birth in 1675 and Cremona's in about 1710 would have made him about 35 years older than Cremona. When the relationship likely commenced in about 1736, he and Cremona would have been approximately 61 and 26 years old, respectively. So, did the age disparity contribute to Cremona's possible feelings of being coerced during the relationship, in addition to her initially being an enslaved worker and then employee of Richard? Meanwhile, descendant John Montier Pickens said he believed the relationship "was more hidden," especially considering the early 18th-century remoteness of Richard's estates in Northern Liberties and Cheltenham, where Cremona likely worked as a servant: Joyce Mosley and John Montier Pickens, Zoom interview of November 3, 2023, recorded with permission by author Donald Scott Sr., MP4. Length 02:56:20, video 1234272029.
2 Daina Ramey Berry, "How Sally Hemings and Other Enslaved People Secured Precious Pockets of Freedom," History.com, March 14, 2019, accessed August 4, 2023, https://www.history.com/news/slavery-negotiations-freedom-concubines-thomas-jefferson-sally-hemings.
3 Pitts, "'Richard Morrey, Gent.,'" 272. As reported, the information regarding Cremona's reported self-purchase for the nominal amount of "twenty pounds" came from the "Deed of Bargain and Sale, Richard Morrey to His Negro Woman Mooney otherwise known as Cremona Morrey," Philadelphia County Deed Book G-7:539-543, dated January 6, 1746.
4 An examination by this author of the original "Bargain & Sale for 500 years, Richard Morrey to His Negro Woman Cremona Morrey," at the Philadelphia City Archives, furthermore revealed the following: "The Receipt whereof he the said Richard Morrey doth hereby acknowledge and there of doth acquit & forever discharge the said Cremona Morrey her Heirs Executors Administrators & assigns & every [one] of them by these presents hath **demised** bargained & sold and by these Presents doth **demise** bargain and sell unto the said Cremona Morrey All that Messuage & Tract of land thereunto belonging situate in Cheltenham Township aforesaid Beginning at a Maple Tree marked for a Corner in the line of Isaac Tysons land … To have and to hold the said messuage Plantation Tract of land and Premises hereby demised or mentioned to be demised with the appurtenances unto the said Mooney or Cremona Morrey's her Executors Administrators." The document further stipulates for the annual rental cost of "one Pepper Corn" the "said Negro Mooney her Executors Administrators & assigns & every [one] of them shall or lawfully may at all times here after during the said Term hereby granted freely quietly & peaceably have hold and enjoy the said Plantation Tract of land & Premises hereby demised or mentioned to be demised with the appurtenance & receive and take all and singular the Rents & issues & Profits thereof without … Trouble or Mollestation

of him the said Richard Morrey his Heirs or assigns or of any other Person or Persons whatsoever lawfully Claiming or to Claim by from or under him them or any of them. In witness whereof the said Richard Morrey hath hereunto set his Hand & Seal the twenty second Day of January in the year of Our Lord One thousand seven hundred & fortyfive/6—1745/6—Richard Morrey—Sealed & Delivered in the Presence of us—Paul Isaac Voto—C. Brokden."

Underneath the above deed, an additional notation indicates: "The Thirty first day of May 1746 Before me William Allen Esq. One of the Justices, Etc., Came the within named Richard Morrey & acknowledged the within written Deed ... to be his Act & Desired the same may be recorded as his Deed—Witness my Hand & Seal the day & year abovesaid—Will Allen (seal)—Recorded the 4th September 1747." This deed was found in the Philadelphia County Deed Book G-7:539-543, dated January 6, 1746, and most recently accessed at the Philadelphia City Archives by the author on Tuesday, December 12, 2023.

The above language seems to indicate that Cremona paid the sum of 20 pounds to Richard Morrey, possibly, for her liberation as an enslaved worker about the same time that the 500-year lease arrangement was made with language that appears to protect Cremona and her heirs from encroachers or adversaries intent on taking her land via supposed legal, illegal, or other means. Simultaneously, according to a range of sources, such "demised" deeds, indicative of the repeated use of the word "demise" or "demised" (also known as "mortgages by demise"), were worded so that the so-called mortgagee or that person's heirs could pay a nominal annual rental or lease fee (in this case "one pepper corn"), often by way of a trustee. The 500-year term may have been largely symbolic in some cases, especially considering that under certain conditions, ownership could return to the mortgagor or that person's heirs. Despite the above language seemingly providing Cremona with impressive protections, indications are that Cremona's land was eventually acquired by a range of parties, including some of her heirs, as well as the heirs of her second husband, John Fry or Frye, and some of Richard's European-descended heirs. There were also subsequent acquisitions of substantial acreage by neighbors and others of land that was originally owned by Cremona. The complicated arrangement consisting of Cremona possibly paying Richard 20 pounds for her liberation and utilizing a male trustee for the supposed long-term lease agreement might be because Cremona was originally an enslaved African-descended woman dealing with a range of laws designed to thwart land ownership and other rights for women and blacks. It would have been virtually impossible or inconceivable for Cremona to own land as an enslaved black woman, under any pretense.

5   Berry, "How Sally Hemings and other Enslaved People."
6   Pitts, "'Richard Morrey, Gent.,'" 272.
7   "Cheltenham Township History," Cheltenhamtownship.org, 2024, accessed August 4, 2023, https://www.cheltenhamtownship.org/pview.aspx?id=2894#gsc.tab=0.
8   Pitts, "Robert Lewis of Guineatown," 43.
9   Pitts, "'Richard Morrey, Gent.,'" 272.
10 "January 1745/6 Lease from Richard Morrey to Negro Mooney alias Cremona for 198 Acres of Land," in Haverford College Quaker & Special Collections, within "Negro Mooney Title to the Land she holds in Cheltenham." The documents can be found within "Humphrey Morrey Legacies/Legatees of Morrey Estate" file included in the MC 1182 Dorothy Merriman Schall Collection—Box 4, accessed November 30, 2023.
11 Ibid.
12 Ibid.
13 Ibid.
14 An announcement in the February 26, 1754, edition of Benjamin Franklin's *Pennsylvania Gazette* proclaimed that "ALL persons indebted to the estate of Richard Morrey," who was recently "deceased,

ENDNOTES • 247

are desired to pay: And those who have any demands against the said estate, are desired to bring in their accounts, that they may be adjusted and settled, by JOHN BASELER, executor." Directly beneath that announcement, a related ad stipulated: "N.B. To be sold at publick vendue, on Saturday, the 2d of March next, at the late dwelling house of the said Morrey, near Bedminster, in the Northern Liberties, sundry sorts of houshold [sic] goods, viz. Chairs, tables, beds, desk, looking glasses, pictures, kitchen furniture, &c. The sale to begin at nine o'clock in the morning, where attendance will be given." The article was accessed January 2, 2017, via Accessible Archives Inc.

15 "Richard Morrey's Negroes Claim to 198 Acres of Land in Cheltenham leased to them by Richard Murrey for 500 years," in Haverford College Quaker & Special Collections, encompasses "Morrey, Humphrey Documents [N.D.] including draft of codicil to Will, lease of 198 acres to Richard (son of Humphrey) Morrey's 'Negro.'" The documents can be found within "Morrey, Humphrey land indenture—1712" file included in the MC 1182 Dorothy Merriman Schall Collection—Box 12, accessed November 30, 2023.

16 "N.B. Certain two Negroes, viz, Money [sic] and Fry, claim 45 acres …," *The Pennsylvania Gazette*, July 23, 1767.

17 Ibid.

18 Pitts, "'Richard Morrey, Gent.,'" 270–271.

19 An announcement in the August 20, 1747, edition of Benjamin Franklin's *Pennsylvania Gazette* in part focuses on "Leonard Morrey, late of Cheltenham," indicating that he died not long after his cousin, Richard Morrey, with legal representatives threatening lawsuits against estate debtors: "And all persons indebted to Leonard Morrey, late of Cheltenham, Philadelphia county, are hereby noticed, that if they do not pay their respective debts very shortly, they will be sued, without further loss of time, by his attornies [sic], George Okill, and Robert Greenway." The article was accessed January 2, 2017, via Accessible Archives Inc.

20 Pitts, "'Richard Morrey, Gent.,'" 271.

21 Leonard Morrey's attorneys were still trying to sell his New Jersey properties in late 1749, up to a couple of years after Leonard's death, according a September 14, 1749, announcement that appeared in Benjamin Franklin's *Pennsylvania Gazette*: "A Certain messuage, plantation, and tract of land, containing two hundred acres, situate in the township of Waterford, in the county of Gloucester, in West New Jersey, now in the tenure of Samuel Tue, about 3 miles from Philadelphia, and fronting the river Delaware, will be sold at publick vendue, on Thursday, the 5th day of October next, at the Ferry house of Daniel Cooper, the title is good. The sale to begin at 3 o'clock in the afternoon, by George Okill, and Robert Greenway, attornies [sic] of Leonard Morrey." The article was accessed January 2, 2017, via Accessible Archives Inc.

22 "Richard Morrey and His Two Wives," Takingthelongerview.org.

23 Pitts, "'Richard Morrey, Gent.,'" 271.

24 "Richard Morrey's Negroes Claim to 198 Acres of Land in Cheltenham leased to them by Richard Murrey for 500 years," in Haverford College Quaker & Special Collections.

25 Pitts, "'Richard Morrey, Gent.,'" 72.

26 "Richard Morrey and His Two Wives," Takingthelongerview.org.

27 Ibid.

28 Ibid.

29 Ibid.

30 Ibid.

31 "Deed—Richard Morrey & Wife to Israel Pemberton," Philadelphia City Archives, microfilm, Deed H:345, 1–261, Reel 22, accessed Tuesday, December 12, 2023.

32 Ibid.

248 • THE MONTIERS

33 Ibid.
34 Pitts, "'Richard Morrey, Gent.,'" 271.
35 "Richard Morrey and His Two Wives," Takingthelongerview.org.
36 Ibid.

Chapter 6

1 "Geography & Travel: Cheltenham England, United Kingdom," Britannica.com, accessed August 17, 2023, https://www.britannica.com/place/Cheltenham-England.
2 Scott Sr., *Remembering Cheltenham Township*, 15. In the 1945 *Old York Road Historical Society Bulletin* article "Preserving the Heritage of Cheltenham Township," historian Ralph Morgan notes that, "prior to the coming of [the state's founder] William Penn in 1682, Cheltenham Township was the hunting ground of the Lenni Lenape Indians, whose headquarters were on a bluff, overlooking the Neshaminy, near Newtown, Pennsylvania," in Bucks County (adjacent to Montgomery County, which contains Cheltenham).
3 Ibid., 25.
4 Pitts, "'Richard Morrey, Gent.,'"
5 Sue Long, "Morrey portion [Post]" Ancestry.com, "Surnames: Morrey, Kimble, Baynton, Budd, Beasley," posted November 18, 2022, https://www.ancestry.com/boards/surnames.morrey/5.6.8.: Long notes that she is a descendant of Richard's first wife, Ann, as well as acknowledges that he later married Sarah Beasley in 1746.
6 Ginny McCracken, a vestry member and historian at Philadelphia's Trinity Church Oxford, revealed records in the church archives during this author's visit on Tuesday, March 6, 2018, indicating that Richard Morrey and Sarah Allen were married at the church. "It is recorded in our record books that a Richard Morrey married Sarah Allen, of Philadelphia, on June 2nd, 1746," she confirmed in an email to the author, dated March 12, 2018.
7 Pitts, "'Richard Morrey, Gent.'"
8 Pitts, "The Montier Family of Guineatown," 24.
9 "Richard Morrey and His Two Wives," Takingthelongerview.org.
10 Pitts, "'Richard Morrey, Gent.,'" 276.
11 "Albert Fry, Philadelphia City Death Certificates, 1803–1915," FamilySearch.org, February 18, 2021, accessed August 17, 2023, https://www.familysearch.org/ark:/61903/1:1:VKZF-K6X.
12 Donald Scott Sr., "Lecture inspires, leads to discovery," *The Reporter*, June 30, 2011, accessed August 17, 2023, https://www.thereporteronline.com/2011/06/30/a-place-in-history-187/.
13 Search.org.
14 "Gen. Samuel Miles, Mayor of Philadelphia," Geni.com, 2023, accessed August 17, 2023, https://www.geni.com/people/Gen-Samuel-Miles-Mayor-of-Philadelphia/60000 00003222437591.
15 Pitts, "The Montier Family of Guineatown," 24.
16 Ibid., 24.
17 "John Fry Et al [sic] to Isaac Knight," Philadelphia City Archives, Philadelphia County Deed Book D-21:501, dated January 23, 1772, accessed by this author on Tuesday, December 12, 2023.
18 Ibid.
19 Ibid.
20 Pitts, "'Richard Morrey, Gent.,'" 276–277.
21 Scott Sr., *Remembering Cheltenham Township*, 28.
22 "Wall House History," Cheltenhamtownship.org (MunicipalOne.com), 2023, accessed August 17, 2023, https://www.cheltenhamtownship.org/pview.aspx?id=3595#gsc.tab=0.

23 An original handwritten deed recorded on September 20, 1790, involving "Isaac Knight to Robert Lewis" was found at the University of Pennsylvania's University Archives within the Nathan Francis Mossell Papers (Box 1, Folder 50, UPT 50-M913) by this author on Thursday, December 21, 2023. The text, on pages 87–88, in part says: "Reciting Indenture from John Fry and others to Isaac Knight dated Jan. 22, 1772 and Recorded in Philad. In Deed Book No. 21 Page 501& for a Messuage and tract of 198 acres of land in Cheltenham Township … for and during all residue of 500 years … never the less for the use the said John Fry during his natural life and from and after his decease in trust to make Sale of said premises and distribute the monies equally between the Said Six children … of Cremona Morray …" The document further stipulates that "Isaac Knight and others to be to the advantage and benefit of said heirs to said estate to make … Several divisions of about 69 acres of said land and make thereof together with all the residuary part of said 198 acres and distribute the monies as … said [within the] trust deed mentioned."

24 Pitts, "'Richard Morrey, Gent.,'" 277.
25 "John Fry Et al [*sic*] to Isaac Knight," Philadelphia City Archives.
26 Pitts, "The Montier Family of Guineatown," 24.
27 Pitts, "'Richard Morrey, Gent.,'" 279.
28 Ibid., 279–281.
29 Pitts, "Robert Lewis of Guineatown," 45.
30 Pitts, "'Richard Morrey, Gent.,'" 279.
31 Ibid., 279–281.
32 An original handwritten copy of a deed refers to Robert Lewis's will and an agreement involving land transactions (including the Montier family "burying ground") concerning Robert Lewis's sons "David Lewis and Amos Lewis to Hiram Montier," recorded on May 14, 1822: "Reciting the … Deed from Isaac Knight to Robt Lewis … Deed Book 5, 302." The document was found at the University of Pennsylvania's University Archives within the Nathan Francis Mossell Papers (Box 1, Folder 50, UPT 50-M913) by this author on Thursday, December 21, 2023. The text, on pages 90–91, in part says: "And the … Will of Robt Lewis dividing among other things a Messuage and Lot of 17 acres of land … unto said David Lewis and Amos Lewis as Trustees in common and to their heirs and assigns …" The document also refers to "a burying ground as expressed in a certain Indenture made by Robt-Lewis and Jane his Wife dated Sept 15, 1798 to have and to hold unto the said Hiram Montier his heirs and assigns to the only proper use and [on] behalf of the said Hiram Montier his heirs and assigns for ever [*sic*]."
33 Pitts, "Richard Morrey, Gent.,'" 279–281.
34 Ian Webster, "$100 in 1789 is worth $3,473.76 today," Officialdata.org, accessed August 17, 2023, https://www.officialdata.org/us/inflation/1789.
35 Nikole Hannah-Jones, "DEMOCRACY," in *The 1619 Project: A New Origin Story*, eds. Hannah-Jones et al. (New York: The New York Times Company-Random House LLC, 2021), 19.

Chapter 7

1 "Cremona Montier," Geni.com, April 28, 2022, accessed June 30, 2024, https://www.geni.com/people/CremonaMontier/6000000062269643555.
2 Nash, "Slaves and Slave Owners in Colonial Philadelphia," 47.
3 Anne Moore Mueller, "John Woolman," 2023, accessed August 24, 2023, https://web.tricolib.brynmawr.edu/speccoll/quakersandslavery/commentary/people/woolman.pdf.
4 "Anthony Benezet," Pennsylvania Center for the Book, 2023, accessed August 24, 2023, https://pabook.libraries.psu.edu/literary-cultural-heritage-map-pa/bios/Benezet__Anthony.

5 Scott Sr., *Remembering Cheltenham Township*, 34.
6 Pitts, "Robert Lewis of Guineatown," 46, 48.
7 Pitts, "The Montier Family of Guineatown," 23.
8 Mark Picard, *Dictionary of French Family Names in North America: Onomastics and Genealogy* (Cambridge, UK: Cambridge Scholars Publishing, 2020), 252.
9 "Denis Bernard ... Also Known As: 'Denis Bernard Du Montier,'" Geni.com, 2023, accessed August 24, 2023, https://www.geni.com/people/Denis-Bernard/6000000009082789647.
10 Patrick Hanks, "MOUNTEER," FamilySearch.org Dictionary of American Family Names, 2023, accessed August 24, 2023, https://www.familysearch.org/en/surname?surname=MOUNTEER.
11 "Monteith Family History," Ancestry.com, 2023, accessed August 24, 2023, https://www.ancestry.com/name-origin?surname=monteith.
12 Charles Augustus Hanna, *The Wilderness Trail: Or, The Ventures and Adventures of the Pennsylvania Traders on the Allegheny Path, Vol. 1* (New York: G. P. Putnam's Sons—The Knickerbocker Press, 1911), 246.
13 Ibid.
14 "John Montier [Montour] c. 1744–1830," FamilySearch.org, 2024, accessed June 30, 2024, https://www.familysearch.org/tree/person/details/K2JD-G5S.
15 Pitts, "Robert Lewis of Guineatown," 48.
16 Sandy Smith, "Just Listed: The Montier Homestead in Glenside," *Philadelphia Magazine*, October 8, 2019, https://www.phillymag.com/property/2019/10/08/house-for-sale-glenside-montier-homestead/. It's worth noting that a Morrey–Bustill–Montier family descendant, Joyce Mosley, says the Montier home was constructed in 1772 by Hiram Montier, according to pg. 8 in her 2020 AuthorHouse book, *Gram's Gift*. Other sources indicate that Hiram expanded the residence that was said to have been originally built by Cremona, Jr., and her husband, John Montier.
17 "Storied colonial home bears an African American legacy," Myauctionfinds.com, accessed August 20, 2023, https://myauctionfinds.com/2019/11/14/storied-colonial-home-bears-an-african-american-legacy/.
18 "About this home—This Georgian Colonial has a rich & deep history," Redfin.com, accessed August 20, 2023, https://www.redfin.com/PA/Glenside/312-Limekiln-Pike-19038/home/38286953.
19 "… Montier Property [-] More Info Request," Letter of September 30, 2021, from the Pennsylvania State Historic Preservation Office-Pennsylvania Historical and Museum Commission, Commonwealth Keystone Building, 400 North Street, 2nd Floor, Harrisburg, PA 17120.
20 Scott Sr., *Remembering Cheltenham Township*, 41.
21 Ibid., 40.
22 Ibid.
23 Ibid., 40–41.
24 Ibid., 41.
25 Ibid.
26 Ibid.
27 Reinberger and McLean, *The Philadelphia Country House*, 113.
28 Ibid.
29 Ibid.
30 Blockson, *African Americans In Pennsylvania*, 74.
31 Gary Shattuck, "George Washington's 'Baker Master,'" *Journal of the American Revolution*, May 27, 2015, accessed August 21, 2023, https://allthingsliberty.com/2015/05/george-washingtons-baker-master/.
32 Pitts, "'Richard Morrey, Gent.,'" 284.
33 Ibid., 282.
34 Ibid., 281.

35 Anna Bustill Smith, "The Bustill Family," *Journal of Negro History* 10, no. 4 (October 1925): 638, accessed August 3, 2023, https://www.journals.uchicago.edu/doi/10.2307/2714143.
36 Pitts, "'Richard Morrey, Gent.,'" 282.
37 Anna Bustill Smith's typed document, "THE BUSTILL FAMILY," with what appears to be her handwritten signature, indicates: "Samuel Bustill, spoken of by Benjamin Franklin in his autobiography, was an eminent New Jersey lawyer and lived in Allentown, a few miles from Burlington [New Jersey]." Smith's typed document was found at the University of Pennsylvania's University Archives within the Nathan Francis Mossell Papers (Box 1, Folder 50, UPT 50-M913) by this author on Thursday, December 21, 2023.
38 Pitts, "'Richard Morrey, Gent.,'" 284.
39 Charles Rosenberg, "Bustill, Cyrus," *Oxford African American Studies Center*, February 28, 2013, accessed June 30, 2024, https://oxfordaasc.com.
40 Pitts, "'Richard Morrey, Gent.,'" 284.
41 Ibid.
42 Ibid.
43 Ibid.
44 John Pickens Montier noted that his descendants and family lines are "well documented." He said: "We have the [1798 land and cemetery] indenture," and "the [family] Bible." He added: "We're well documented Americans." Joyce Mosley and John Montier Pickens, Zoom interview of November 3, 2023, recorded with permission by author Donald Scott Sr., MP4. Length 02:56:20, video 1234272029.
45 Smith, "The Bustill Family," 638.
46 Ibid., 639.
47 Ibid.
48 "Patriots of Color at Valley Forge," Valley Forge National Historical Park, 2023, accessed August 21, 2023, https://www.nps.gov/vafo/learn/historyculture/patriotsofcoloratvalleyforge.htm.
49 Ibid.
50 Ibid.
51 Ibid.
52 Ibid.
53 Benjamin Quarles, *The Negro in the American Revolution* (Chapel Hill: The University of North Carolina Press, 1961, 1996), 135.
54 Ibid., 75.
55 Scott Sr., *Camp William Penn*, 8–9.
56 Quarles, *The Negro in the American Revolution*, 92.
57 Ibid., 92–93.
58 Ibid., 93.
59 Ibid.
60 Ibid.
61 Ibid.
62 Pitts, "'Richard Morrey, Gent.,'" 284. Elizabeth Bustill's advanced age of 84 for a mixed-race African American who died in 1827 was extraordinary. Even by the "turn of the twentieth century, a newborn white American could expect to live for around 48 years. That was 15 years longer than a newborn African American could expect," according to economist.com. Stanford Medicine Ethnogeriatrics reports: "The combination of lower living standards, greater exposure, heavier labor, and poorer medical care gave slaves a higher mortality rate than whites." The National Library of Medicine notes, even after slavery: "In 1920, the life expectancy of African American men was 47.6 years, compared to 59.1 for White males." It's likely that most of Elizabeth's children died of natural causes;

252 • THE MONTIERS

however, since such death-certificate (and often birth) records for 18th-century and 19th-century African Americans were and are very scarce, it's difficult to ascertain specific causes of death, etc.
63   Pitts, "The Montier Family of Guineatown," 25.
64   Ibid.
65   Ibid.
66   Ibid.
67   Ibid.
68   Winch, *A Gentleman of Color*, 116.
69   Pitts, "'Richard Morrey, Gent.,'" 282.
70   Winch, *A Gentleman of Color*.
71   Ibid.
72   Larry R. Gerlach, "ROBESON, PAUL," in *African American Lives*, eds. Henry Louis Gates Jr. and Evelyn Brooks Higginbotham (New York: Oxford University Press, 2004), 714–717.
73   Valerie Russ, "Philadelphia's Paul Robeson House is hosting a weeklong celebration of Robeson's 125th birthday, culminating with Sweet Honey in the Rock," *The Philadelphia Inquirer*, April 5, 2023, accessed June 30, 2024, https://www.inquirer.com/news/paul-robeson-house-museum-celebrating-125th-birthday-week-activities-20230405.html.

Chapter 8

1   Blockson, *African Americans In Pennsylvania*, 103.
2   Carter G. Woodson and Anna Bustill Smith, "A COMMUNICATION," *Journal of Negro History* 10, no. 4 (October 1925): 645–647, accessed June 28, 2024, https://www.journals.uchicago.edu/doi/pdf/10.2307/2714144.
3   Anna Bustill Smith's typed document, "THE BUSTILL FAMILY," with what appears to be her handwritten signature, indicates: Cyrus and Elizabeth Morrey Bustill's son "David Bustill was the father of nine children: James Mapps, Charles Hicks, Elizabeth Douglass, Joseph Cassey (my grandfather), Sarah Haynes, Maria Louise, Hester Stewart, Mary Williams and Rebecca Atlee." The text then focuses on the couple's son, Joseph Cassey Bustill, who became "an Orthodox Quaker" and "was born in Philadelphia, Pennsylvania, on September 30, 1822. He was the father of Anna Bustill Smith [the author of this family-history document] and a grandson of Cyrus Bustill." Smith further notes: "Joseph Bustill married Sarah Humphrey in Gettysburg, Pennsylvania," who "was the daughter of Chippewa Indians, born in the Chippewa village, two miles below Niagara Falls, New York." Remarkably, "Joseph Bustill was the youngest member of the Underground Railroad Company," Smith writes, "and one of the few deemed worthy of membership at the age of 18." Smith's typed document was found at the University of Pennsylvania's University Archives within the Nathan Francis Mossell Papers (Box 1, Folder 50, UPT 50-M913) by this author on Thursday, December 21, 2023.
4   Woodson and Smith, "A COMMUNICATION."
5   Pitts, "'Richard Morrey, Gent.,'" 282.
6   "Morrey portion: Re: Humphrey Morrey," Ancestry.com, 2023, accessed November 24, 2023. Norman Miller indicated in an April 24, 2012 post on Ancestry.com that he is "a descendant of Cyrus Bustill who married Elizabeth Morrey, the daughter of Richard and Cremona," adding that "Cyrus and Elizabeth owned parcels of land in Glenside, Pa.," where Guineatown was said to have been located.
7   *Mark Twain's Scrap Book* (New York: Daniel Slote & Company, Pennsylvania County Histories) features the Frankford, Pennsylvania, *Herald* newspaper article dated January 27, 1900, accessed

December 8, 2023, https://ia803107.us.archive.org/15/items/pennsylvaniacoun79unse/pennsylvaniacoun79unse.pdf.

8 Ibid.
9 VERITAS, "OUR BAND MEETS AT 16 BUSTLETON PIKE: A Powerful Long Time Ago This Was the Oldest House in Our Midst," *The North American*, June 6, 1904, is located in the Campbell Collection in the "Bridesburg, etc." folder: The article, found at the Historical Society of Pennsylvania on November 21, 2023, indicates: "Almost 200 years ago Mr. Cyrus Bustil [sic] was living in our midst when he started to keep company with Miss Sattawalwee who was Mr. Sattawalwee's pretty daughter who was an Indian. Soon after they married and started to live at No. 16 where they had 6 children. This was the start of Bustleton." The article further notes: "Mr. Sattawalwee was [an] Indian chief of the Delaware Indians and lived down on the Pennypack and used to come up to No. 16 every year or so to see the little Bustils. He died sometime after leaving a number of grand children who grew up in later years to be men and women except a few who died before."
10 Ibid.
11 Ibid.
12 Anna Bustill Smith's typed document, "THE BUSTILL FAMILY," with what appears to be her handwritten signature, indicates: Cyrus Bustill's "mother was an African woman stolen from her native land when young, and sold into slavery, and he, according to the laws and customs of slavery, was born a slave." Smith's typed document was found at the University of Pennsylvania's University Archives within the Nathan Francis Mossell Papers (Box 1, Folder 50, UPT 50-M913) by this author on Thursday, December 21, 2023.
13 Rosenberg, "Bustill, Cyrus." In this abstract, Cyrus Bustill is identified as a "baker, community leader, cautious abolitionist, and patriarch of a talented African American family well known into the nineteenth and twentieth centuries," who "was born in Burlington, New Jersey. His narrative records that he belonged to 'the Estate of Samuel Bustill of the City of Burlington, but he Dying when I was Young I was Sold to John Allen of the Same City.'" The abstract continues: "The name of Bustill's mother is recorded only as Parthenia; Samuel Bustill, an English-born lawyer who died in 1742, was his father as well as his owner." The passage notes "Lloyd Louis Brown's detailed history of the Bustill family in *The Young Paul Robeson: On My Journey Now* (1997)."
14 *Mark Twain's Scrap Book*.
15 "#8 Cyrus Bustill: The Man Who Knew His Worth," Quaker Stories, February 28, 2019, accessed December 8, 2023, https://quakerstories.org/2019/02/28/cyrus-bustill-the-man-who-knew-his-worth/.
16 Euell A. Nielsen, "First African Presbyterian Church, Philadelphia, Pennsylvania," Blackpast.org, February 24, 2015, accessed December 8, 2023, https://www.blackpast.org/african-american-history/first-african-presbyterian-church-philadelphia-pennsylvania-1807/.
17 Smith, "The Bustill Family," 638–644.
18 *Images Of America: Cheltenham Township* (Charleston, SC: Arcadia Publishing, 2001), 122. It's quite likely that patrons and possibly workers at the Eagle Hotel, constructed in 1710 in Cheltenham's Edge Hill area and where food and spirits were likely sold, hailed from nearby Guineatown. Such establishments often served as stagecoach stations, eateries (that served alcoholic spirits), community meeting places, and voting centers. The caption under a late 19th-century or early 20th-century image of workers and patrons (a couple of them possibly African Americans), says: "The Eagle Hotel was built in 1710 and stood on the northwest corner of Limekiln Pike and Willow Grove Avenue. The hotel was a major stopping place on the Limekiln Pike, which existed in a very primitive form as early as 1693, and was established as a toll road in 1840. Today the building is the Edge Hill Tavern."
19 Pitts, "'Richard Morrey, Gent.,'" 281.

254 • THE MONTIERS

20 Timothy H. Horning, "Horace Mather Lippincott Papers," University of Pennsylvania Archives and Records Center, September 2013, https://archives.upenn.edu/collections/finding-aid/upt50l765/. A brief biography about Lippincott says he "was born on April 20, 1877 in Philadelphia" as "the only child of Philadelphia lumber merchant Robert C. Lippincott and Cynthia Shoemaker Mather Lippincott." He was a graduate of Germantown Academy in 1892, as well as the University of Pennsylvania in 1897. Lippincott would later serve as head of the General Alumni Society, as well as editor of the *Pennsylvania Gazette*, an alumni magazine bearing the name of Penn cofounder Benjamin Franklin's colonial-era newspaper. "He was also the author of several books, articles, and pamphlets, including (but not limited to): *The Colonial Homes of Philadelphia and its Neighborhood* (1912), *A Portraiture of the People Called Quakers* (1915), *George Washington and the University of Pennsylvania* (1916), *Early Philadelphia, Its People, Life, and Progress* (1917), *The University of Pennsylvania, Franklin's College* (1919), and *An Account of the People Called Quakers in Germantown, Philadelphia* (1923)." Married to Sarah Styer Jenkins in 1914, the couple had a son, architect Horace Mather Lippincott Jr. The elder "Lippincott died on January 12, 1967, aged 89."
21 Pitts, "'Richard Morrey, Gent.'"
22 "London Coffee House Historical Marker," ExplorePAhistory.com, 2023, accessed June 6, 2023, https://explorepahistory.com/hmarker.php?markerId=1-A-21.
23 Ibid.
24 Edward B. Phillips, "The Record Of A Hike On The Bethlehem Pike," in *Historical Sketches: A Collection of Papers Prepared for the Historical Society of Montgomery County, Pennsylvania* (1920), 226, accessed June 29, 2024, https://archive.org/details/historicalsketch06hist.
25 Scott Sr., *Remembering Cheltenham Township*, 37–38.
26 Pitts, "'Richard Morrey, Gent,'" 282.
27 "Community Revitalization in New Cassel, New York," The National Center for Suburban Studies at Hofstra University, December 2008, accessed June 18, 2023, https://www.hofstra.edu/pdf/academics/css/ncss_newcassel_monograph022409.pdf.
28 Jason Romisher, "Lawnside, New Jersey," The Encyclopedia of Greater Philadelphia, 2023, accessed August 24, 2023, https://philadelphiaencyclopedia.org/essays/lawnside-new-jersey/.
29 Pitts, "'Richard Morrey, Gent.,'" 282.
30 Scott Sr., *Remembering Cheltenham Township*, 29.
31 Ibid.
32 Ibid.
33 Ibid., 37–38.
34 Pitts, "Robert Lewis of Guineatown," 48.
35 "Marvina Bower," "United States Census, 1850," database with images, FamilySearch, 2023, accessed August 29, 2023, https://www.familysearch.org/ark:/61903/1:1:M4Cw-SLD.
36 "Harper Hill," "United States Census, 1850," database with images, FamilySearch, 2023, accessed August 29, 2023, https://www.familysearch.org/ark:/61903/1:1:M4CW-SLD.
37 Pitts, "'Richard Morrey, Gent.,'" 282.
38 An original handwritten copy of the "Will of Robt Lewis Dated 15th of Sept 1798 … Registered 27th of June 1799 … In Will Book No. 2, page 113," was found at the University of Pennsylvania's University Archives within the Nathan Francis Mossell Papers (Box 1, Folder 50, UPT 50-M913) by this author on Thursday, December 21, 2023. The text, on pages 89–90, in part says: "I also will and order that my dear Wife Jane Lewis shall be directly supported out of My Real Estate while she remains my Widow …. I give and bequeath unto my two Sons David Lewis and Amos Lewis my messuage and tract on a piece of land wherein, on I now dwell situate in Cheltenham aforesaid … to be equally divided between them." Other financial legacies were also declared that involved Lewis's heirs and "the Sum of 120 pounds."

39 Pitts, "Robert Lewis of Guineatown," 46.
40 Pitts, "The Montier Family of Guineatown," 25.
41 Ibid.
42 Samuel Emlen Jr., "a prominent and wealthy Quaker merchant from Philadelphia," married Susanna Dillwyn in 1795, a couple of years before their "historic manor house," West Hill, "was built between May 1797 and July 1799" in Burlington Township, New Jersey. The couple moved to their new residence in July 1799. It's possible that Robert Lewis also worked at the Burlington mansion, likely permitted by Susanna to read books that he seemed to crave. Tragically, in "December, 1813, Susanna discovered a tumor in her left breast, irregularly shaped, about the size of a partridge egg. Terrorized of surgery, she optioned for other procedures," that were unsuccessful. However, she agreed to having surgery that seemed to prolong her life. Five years after undergoing a mastectomy "without" anesthesia in 1814, Susanna died in 1819, "making her one of the earliest breast cancer survivors in" the country: See "About West Hill—Information on Susanna and Samuel Emlen," West Hill, 2015, http://www.westhillnj.org/about.html.
43 Pitts, "The Montier Family of Guineatown," 25.
44 Much of what is known about William Allinson comes from his 270-page journal that "spans more than a decade of his adult life, and includes mature reflections on both personal and spiritual matters." In addition to writing about antislavery initiatives and Native American rights, his friendships with "important Quaker figures"— including "Jesse Kersey, George Dillwyn, Martha Routh, Ann Mifflin, Isaac Bonsall, and Elias Hicks"—are examined. See information about the "William Allinson journal, 1802–1814," and Allinson's biography at: "Allinson, William, 1766–1841," William L. Clements Library, The University of Michigan, accessed December 25, 2023, https://findingaids.lib.umich.edu/catalog/umich-wcl-M-2865.1all.
45 Pitts, "The Montier Family of Guineatown," 25.
46 Samuel Emlen Jr.'s wife Susanna Dillwyn was exceptionally close to her father, William Dillwyn of London: "Although Susanna lived almost her entire life apart from her father, their letters are frequent and deal primarily with family matters and kin. However, there is frequent comment concerning such topics as yellow fever; abolitionism and slavery; Native Americans; breast cancer." More information about her correspondence can be found via "Dillwyn and Emlen family correspondence, (1770–1818 (inclusive)," kept at the Library Company of Philadelphia. This information, "Emlen, Susanna Dillwyn, 1769–1819," was found via the Philadelphia Area Archives, 2023, accessed December 25, 2023, https://findingaids.library.upenn.edu/records.
47 Pitts, "The Montier Family of Guineatown," 25–26.
48 Ibid., 26.
49 Ibid.
50 Ibid.
51 Ibid.
52 Pitts, "The Montier Family of Guineatown," 26. A Robert Montier is identified by historian-author Gary Nash as "probably one of the former St. Domingue slaves [on what is today the modern island of the Dominican Republic and Haiti]," who "became one of [Philadelphia's] most successful bottlers of beer by 1806." Although it's not likely that the Robert Montier who worked for the Emlens was enslaved on Saint-Domingue, his father John Montier may have lived on the island according to a range of sources. See Gary B. Nash's *Forging Freedom: The Formation of Philadelphia's Black Community: 1720–1840* (Cambridge, MA: Harvard University Press, 1988), 152.
53 Pitts, "The Montier Family of Guineatown," 26.
54 Ibid.
55 Ibid.
56 Ibid.

57 "Robert Montier," Pennsylvania, U.S., Wills and Probate Records, 1683-1993, 2023, Ancestry.com, accessed November 30, 2023, https://www.ancestry.com/discoveryui-content/view/3618933:8803.
58 Pitts, "The Montier Family of Guineatown," 27.
59 Ibid.
60 Ibid. The given name of Robert Montier's wife is identified as "Susan" Lewis in the Reginald Pitts article, "The Montier Family of Guineatown," 27. A "Susan Montier" (born in 1806) is listed as a daughter of Robert Lewis Montier Sr. (1775–1815) and Rachel Lewis (1774–1840), according to a FamilySearch.org family tree at familysearch.org/tree/person/details/L25N-WXD, "Robert Lewis Montier Sr.: 1775–1815," possibly making Robert Montier and Susan Lewis cousins. Meanwhile, another FamilySearch.org article, "Hiram Charles Montier: 1780–1861," at familysearch.org/tree/person/details/GQ61-984 indicates that Hiram Charles Montier was married to "Susannah Lewis," born 1783 to Robert Lewis Sr. and his wife Jane, possibly making Susannah and Hiram cousins.
61 "Hiram Mauntier," 1820 United States Census, Cheltenham, Montgomery, Pennsylvania, USA, digital image s.v. *Ancestry.com*, 2023, accessed August 25, 2023, https://www.ancestry.com/discoveryui-content/view/857410:7734.
62 "The African American Odyssey: A Quest for Full Citizenship—Free Blacks in the Antebellum Period," Library of Congress, 2024, accessed August 25, 2023, https://www.loc.gov/exhibits/african-american-odyssey/free-blacks-in-the-antebellum-period.html. The article notes: "In some Northern cities, for brief periods of time, black property owners voted. A very small number of free blacks owned slaves. The slaves that most free blacks purchased were relatives whom they later manumitted."
63 Pitts, "The Montier Family of Guineatown," 27.
64 Ibid., 30.
65 According to Steven Hahn's 2003 award-winning Harvard University Press book *A Nation Under Our Feet: Black Political Struggles in the Rural South from Slavery to the Great Migration*, African Americans galvanized to counter the devastating effects of the 1850 Fugitive Slave Act: "Subscribing to antislavery newspapers, joining black abolition societies, collaborating on autobiographical accounts of their enslavement and escape, attending conventions that pressed for black civil and political rights, and organizing to resist enforcement of the Fugitive Slave Law, a good many of the runaways became schooled in modern politics."
66 Pitts, "The Montier Family of Guineatown," 30.
67 Ibid., 28.
68 Ibid.
69 "War of 1812—African American Stories," National Park Service, 2014, accessed August 25, 2023, https://www.nps.gov/subjects/warof1812/african-american-story.htm.
70 Pitts, "The Montier Family of Guineatown," 28.
71 Ibid. It is possible that the married couple Solomon Montier and Elizabeth Lewis Montier were cousins according to a FamilyTree genealogy chart at: https://www.familysearch.org/tree/person/details/G4XP-QPS. An Elizabeth Lewis is listed as a daughter of Robert and Jane Lewis.
72 Ibid.
73 Ibid.
74 Ibid.
75 Phillips, "The Record Of A Hike On The Bethlehem Pike," 225.
76 Ibid.
77 Pitts, "The Montier Family of Guineatown," 28.
78 An original handwritten deed recorded July 28, 1790, involving "Isaac Knight to Cremona Montier, Wife of John Montier" was found at the University of Pennsylvania's University Archives within the Nathan Francis Mossell Papers (Box 1, Folder 50, UPT 50-M913) by this author on Thursday,

December 21, 2023. The text, on pages 91–92, in part says: "Cremona Montier died the 31st of July 1825. Jos Montier was appointed Administrator of her Estate Aug 15, 1825 (Bond Book 3-53) on the same day filed inventory showing personal property valued at $15.50. No settlement was filed in Register's Office." The text continues: "The Petition of Jos Montier Administrator of Cremona Montier Dec'd was presented setting forth that the said Cremona Montier died intestate July 31, 1825, leaving three sons Joseph, Solomon & Hiram and the issue of a deceased child to wit." The land, "containing 20 acres more or less," appears to have been seized because "her personal estate is insufficient for the payment [of] her debts and to educate and support said minors etc," identified as "Robt & John Montier." Furthermore, the document declares: "And praying the Court to Grant him an order to make sale of the premises for that purpose." However, the property was ultimately kept in the family. Before the end of the year, "Said administrator made report that he sold the said premises to Hiram Montier and Solomon Montier for $800."

79   Ibid.
80   Ibid.
81   Handwritten Montgomery County Orphans Court documentation in "Docket No. 5, Page 161," noted during the "Nov. Term, 1826," that remarkably "Joseph Montier Administrator filed his settlement showing a [balance] due the [Cremona Montier] estate of" almost $400. The document was found at the University of Pennsylvania's University Archives within the Nathan Francis Mossell Papers (Box 1, Folder 50, UPT 50-M913), on page 94, by this author on Thursday, December 21, 2023.
82   Scott, "The Montiers: An American Family's Triumphant Odyssey."
83   Ibid.
84   Ibid.
85   Donald Scott Sr., "Rare portraits reflect black family's legacy," Afrigeneas.com, February 15, 2009, accessed June 28, 2024, https://www.afrigeneas.org/library/portraits_article.html.
86   Pitts, "The Montier Family of Guineatown," 29.
87   Scott Sr., "Rare portraits reflect black family's legacy."
88   Pitts, "The Montier Family of Guineatown," 29.
89   "Will of Joseph Montier," Ancestry.com. Pennsylvania, U.S., Wills and Probate Records, 1683–1993 for Solomon Montier, Wills, Vol 008–009, 1838–1855, 2023, accessed August 26, 2023, https://www.ancestry.com/discoveryui-content/view/3618941:8802.
90   Ibid.
91   An original handwritten deed (in "Deed Book No. 126, Page 254") recorded August 10, 1861, involving "Solomon Montier & Susannah or Hannah his wife" selling land to David Heist was found at the University of Pennsylvania's University Archives within the Nathan Francis Mossell Papers (Box 1, Folder 50, UPT 50-M913) by this author on Thursday, December 21, 2023. The text, on pages 99–100, in part says: "In consideration of $700 granting … to David Heist his heirs executors administrators" for a "messuage and tract of land" originally belonging to "Hiram Montier Dec'd" in Cheltenham Township. The amount of land is indecipherable due to a torn page. Meanwhile, in a transaction recorded in "Deed Book No. 94, Page 1," on May 19, 1854, the couple sold to the Pennsylvania Railroad "a triangular piece of land" in the amount of $56.25. The information was found in the above-referenced "Box 1, Folder 50" at the University Archives on Thursday, December 21, 2023.
92   Pitts, "The Montier Family of Guineatown," 30.
93   Scott Sr., *Remembering Cheltenham Township*, 37–38.
94   Ibid., 39.
95   Ibid., 37–38.
96   Ibid., 38.

97 Ibid., 39.
98 Ibid., 38.
99 Ibid.
100 Ibid., 37–38.
101 Reginald H. Pitts, "Moses Highgate, Miller of Cheltenham Township," *Old York Road Historical Society Bulletin* XLIX (1989): 20.
102 The 1820 United States Federal Census indicates that Moses Highgate was living within a household of 10 "Total Free Colored Persons" in "Cheltenham, Montgomery [County], Pennsylvania." At least six of the residents were children "Under 14" years, including four males and two females. Two residents, a male and female, were between 14 and 25 years old. Presumably, Moses and his wife (the two remaining adults) were categorized between the ages of 26 to "45 and over": "Moses Highgate in the 1820 United States Federal Census," Ancestry.com [database online], Census Place: Cheltenham, Montgomery [County], Pennsylvania; Page 244; NARA Roll: M33_100: Image 586, 2023, accessed December 24, 2023, https://www.ancestry.com/discoveryui-content/view/857467:7734.
103 The names of Moses's son Amos and wife Mary (Miller) Highgate appear on the March 2, 1910, Pennsylvania death certificate of their son, Ezekiel Potts Highgate, born February 18, 1810, who essentially died of "Extreme old age," living for about a century. At the time of his death, Ezekiel (probably misidentified as "white") had been a "farmer" who was "widowed" and living in Licking Township, Clarion County, Pennsylvania: Ancestry.com and Pennsylvania Historical and Museum Commission; Harrisburg, PA, USA; Pennsylvania (State). Death Certificates, 1906–1968; Certificate Number Range: 021801-025800, 2023, accessed December 24, 2023, https://www.ancestry.com/discoveryui-content/view/269955:5164.
104 Pitts, "Moses Highgate, Miller of Cheltenham Township," 20.
105 Ibid.
106 Ibid.
107 Ibid.
108 Ibid.
109 Ibid.
110 African Americans could be abducted without due process during periods when draconian laws, including the Fugitive Slave Act of 1850, federally empowered virtually any citizen to accuse blacks of being fugitives from enslavement. In fact, according to the Morrey–Bustill–Montier family historian and author, Joyce Mosely, her ancestor Rachel Bustill's husband, Jeremiah Bowser, was almost abducted: "If it wasn't for the fact that some Quakers vouched … that he was a resident of Philadelphia … the slave catchers had already made arrangements to take him South": Joyce Mosley and John Montier Pickens, Zoom interview of November 3, 2023, recorded with permission by author Donald Scott Sr., MP4. Length 02:56:20, video 1234272029.
111 Pitts, "Moses Highgate, Miller of Cheltenham Township," 20.
112 According to an 1855 Philadelphia death certificate, a William Highgate died at age 48 in Philadelphia; that William Highgate is featured in an attached family tree with his wife identified as Mary Highgate. See "Wiliam Highgate," "Pennsylvania, Philadelphia City Death Certificates, 1803–1915," FamilySearch, accessed December 24, 2023, https://www.family search.org/ark:/61903/1:1:JKQ9-X25.
113 Pitts, "Moses Highgate, Miller of Cheltenham Township," 20.
114 Mary A. Highgate, born 1793 as a yellow fever epidemic raged in the Philadelphia area killing many thousands of people, lived to be 91 years old, passing away as a widow in March 1884. She was buried at Lebanon Cemetery in Philadelphia on March 27, 1884. Mary had been residing in the 200 block of Currant Alley in Philadelphia's Ward 8. Her occupation was described as "Lady," perhaps an indication of her impressive wealth: See "Mary A. Highgate," "Pennsylvania, Philadelphia

ENDNOTES • 259

City Death Certificates, 1803–1915," FamilySearch, 2023, accessed December 24, 2023, https://www.family search.org/ark:/61903/1:1:JXLR-W4F.

115   Pitts, "Moses Highgate, Miller of Cheltenham Township," 21.
116   "The Relative Worth of $35,000 in 1880," MeasuringWorth.com, 2023, accessed August 28, 2023, https://www.measuringworth.com/dollarvaluetoday/?amount=-35000&from=1880.
117   Pitts, "Moses Highgate, Miller of Cheltenham Township," 20.
118   Ibid., 21.
119   The 1830 United States Federal Census indicates that Moses Highgate was living within a household of six "Free Colored Persons" in "Cheltenham, Montgomery [County], Pennsylvania." At least three of the residents were female children "Under 10" years, as well as two "Females" aged "10 thru 23": "Moses Highgate in the 1830 United States Federal Census," Ancestry.com [database online], Census Place: Cheltenham, Montgomery [County], Pennsylvania; NARA microfilm publication M19, 201 rolls, 2010, accessed December 24, 2023, https://www.ancestry.com/discoveryui-content/view/2083801:8058.
120   Pitts, "Moses Highgate, Miller of Cheltenham Township," 21.
121   Scott Sr., *Remembering Cheltenham Township*, 39.
122   Pitts, "Moses Highgate, Miller of Cheltenham Township," 21.
123   Ibid., 22.
124   Scott Sr., *Remembering Cheltenham Township*, 39.
125   Ibid., 38.
126   Quaker records confirm that Moses Highgate died "abt 1842" via information from the Abington Monthly Meeting: "Moses Highgate in the U.S., Quaker Meeting Records, 1681–1935," Ancestry.com [database online], 2023, accessed December 24, 2023, https://www.ancestry.com/discoveryui-content/view/2275865:2189.
127   Scott Sr., *Remembering Cheltenham Township*, 39.
128   Following his death on July 27, 1842, Moses Highgate was buried at the Abington Friends Cemetery in Jenkintown, Pennsylvania, indicating that he was likely a practicing African American Quaker: "Moses Highgate in the U.S., Find a Grave Index, 1600s-Current," 2023, Ancestry.com, accessed December 24, 2023, https://www.findagrave.com/memorial/191306601/moses-highgate.
129   Pitts, "Moses Highgate, Miller of Cheltenham Township," 20.
130   Ibid.
131   Ibid.
132   "Mary Elizabeth Irvin," "Pennsylvania, Philadelphia City Death Certificates, 1803–1915," database with images, FamilySearch, 2023, accessed August 29, 2023, https://familysearch.org/ark:/61903/1:1:J61T-DV3.
133   "Our Story," Kirk & Nice, Inc., Kirkandniceinc.com, 2023, accessed August 29, 2023, https://www.kirkandniceinc.com/our-story.
134   Ibid.
135   Pitts, "Moses Highgate, Miller of Cheltenham Township," 20.
136   Ibid., 20–21.
137   "Paul Robeson quotes on art and protest," PBS-American Masters, March 30, 2022, accessed June 30, 2024, https://www.pbs.org/wnet/americanmasters/paul-robeson-quotes-on-art-and-protest/21208/.

Chapter 9

1   Shaw, "The Freedom to Marry for All," 7–8.

2   Patrick Grubbs, "Riots (1830s and 1840s)," The Encyclopedia of Greater Philadelphia, 2023, accessed September 2, 2023, https://philadelphiaencyclopedia.org/essays/riots-1830s-and-1840s/.
3   Shaw, "The Freedom to Marry for All," 8.
4   Grubbs, "Riots (1830s and 1840s)."
5   Shaw, "Freedom to Marry for All," 7–14.
6   The Paul Robeson Foundation's executive director is Susan Robeson, the granddaughter of Paul Robeson, as noted by the Morrey–Bustill–Montier family historian and author Joyce Mosley. Susan Robeson is a well-known television and documentary film producer, as well as an author of books about her grandfather, based in the metropolitan New York City vicinity: Joyce Mosley and John Montier Pickens, Zoom interview of November 3, 2023, recorded with permission by author Donald Scott Sr., MP4. Length 02:56:20, video 1234272029.
7   Scott, "Triumphant Odyssey."
8   Shaw, "Freedom to Marry for All," 8.
9   "A SLAVE SECRETED," *Philadelphia Public Ledger*, June 18, 1841, 4.
10 "Today in History—September 3 ... Frederick Douglass," The Library of Congress, December 17, 2020, accessed June 30, 2024, https://www.loc.gov/item/today-in-history/september-03.
11 Scott Mingus, "How Pennsylvania became a safe haven for Harriet Tubman after she escaped slavery in Maryland," *The York Daily Record*, December 11, 2019, accessed June 20, 2024, https://www.ydr.com/in-depth/news/2019/10/29/harriett-tubman-underground-railroad-path-slavery-escape-pa/3863408002/.
12 Asiaku Berhanu, "William Still: An African American Abolitionist ... Lucretia Mott (1793–1880)," Temple University Libraries, 2023, accessed September 5, 2023, http://stillfamily.library.temple.edu/exhibits/show/william-still/people-and-places/mott--lucretia.
13 Donald Scott, "Camp William Penn's Black Soldiers in Blue," Historynet.com, September 23, 1999, accessed September 5, 2023, https://www.historynet.com/camp-william-penns-black-soldiers-in-blue-november-99-americas-civil-war-feature/.
14 Ibid.
15 Ibid.
16 Scott Sr., *Camp William Penn*, 33.
17 Scott, "Camp William Penn's Black Soldiers in Blue."
18 Grubbs, "Riots (1830s and 1840s)."
19 Ibid.
20 Ibid.
21 Shaw, "The Freedom to Marry for All," 8.
22 Robert Stein, "The Free Men of Colour and the Revolution in Saint Domingue, 1789–1792," *Histoire Sociale* XIV, no. 27 (May 1981): 7–10, accessed September 5, 2023, https://hssh.journals.yorku.ca/index.php/hssh/article/download/37971/34432/44375.
23 Pitts, "The Montier Family of Guineatown," 23.
24 "World Directory of Minorities and Indigenous Peoples—Haiti," Minority Rights Group International, 2007, accessed June 30, 2024, https://www.refworld.org/docid/4954ce1ac.html.
25 "HAITI: A Brief History of a Complex Nation," The University of Kansas Institute of Haitian Studies, 2023, accessed September 4, 2023, https://haitianstudies.ku.edu/haiti-brief-history-complex-nation.
26 Samuel Momodu, "Tacky's War (1760–1761)," Blackpast.org, December 3, 2021, accessed June 30, 2024, https://www.blackpast.org/global-african-history/tackys-war-1760-1761/.
27 Shaw, "The Freedom to Marry for All," 8.
28 Ibid.
29 Ibid.

30   Du Bois, *The Philadelphia Negro*, 173.
31   Ibid., 172.
32   Ibid.
33   Ibid., 173.
34   Theodore Hershberg, "Free Blacks in Antebellum Philadelphia: A Study of Ex-Slaves, Freeborn, and Socioeconomic Decline," in *African Americans in Pennsylvania: Shifting Historical Perspectives*, eds. Joe William Trotter Jr. and Eric Ledell Smith (University Park, PA and Harrisburg, PA, The Pennsylvania State University Press and The Pennsylvania Historical and Museum Commission, 1997), 127.
35   Ibid.
36   Du Bois, *The Philadelphia Negro*, 175.
37   Hershberg, "Free Blacks in Antebellum Philadelphia," 127.
38   Ibid., 131.
39   Du Bois, *The Philadelphia Negro*, 177.
40   Ibid., 178.
41   Hershberg, "Free Blacks in Antebellum Philadelphia," 137.
42   Ibid.
43   Alex Bush, "1816: the Year Without a Summer," *Massachusetts Historical Society*, April 7, 2020, accessed June 30, 2024, https://www.masshist.org/beehiveblog/2016/11/1815-the-year-without-a-summer/.
44   "Agricultural: At a special meeting of 'The Philadelphia Society for promoting agriculture," *Massachusetts Historical Society*, 2023, accessed September 4, 2023, http://balthazaar.masshist.org/cgi-bin/Pwebrecon.cgi?DB=local&BBID=199779.
45   "1820 United States Federal Census for Thomas Street … Philadelphia Upper Delaware Ward," Ancestry.com, 2023, accessed September 7, 2023, https://www.ancestry.com/discoveryui-content/view/908552:7734.
46   "U.S., City Directories, 1822–1995 for Thomas Street—Philadelphia, Pennsylvania, City Directory, 1864," Ancestry.com, 2023, accessed September 7, 2023, https://www.ancestry.com/discoveryui-content/view/1190009575:2469.
47   "Thomas Street—Population Schedules of the Seventh Census of the United States 1850: Philadelphia, Census Records 1850," FamilySearch.org, 2023, accessed September 6, 2023, https://www.familysearch.org/ark:/61903/3:1:S3HY-63B7-FH3.
48   Michael Sean Munger, "1816: 'The Mighty Operations Of Nature': An Environmental History Of The Year Without Summer" (Thesis, University of Oregon, 2012), 75, 2023, accessed September 6, 2023, https://scholarsbank.uoregon.edu/xmlui/bitstream/handle/1794/12417/Munger_oregon_0171N_10408.pdf.
49   Aaron O'Neill, "Child mortality in the United States 1800–2020," Statista.com, June 21, 2022, accessed June 30, 2024, https://www.statista.com/statistics/1041693/united-states-all-time-child-mortality-rate.
50   "William George Klett—Death—Pennsylvania, Philadelphia City Death Certificates, 1803–1915," database with images, FamilySearch, February 18, 2021, accessed September 5, 2023, https://familysearch.org/ark:/61903/1:1:JXRF-FMR.
51   "Bishop—Death—Pennsylvania, Philadelphia City Death Certificates, 1803–1915," database with images, FamilySearch, February 18, 2021, accessed September 5, 2023, https://www.familysearch.org/ark:/61903/1:1:JXR6-RZX.
52   "William Mcmutry—Death—Pennsylvania, Philadelphia City Death Certificates, 1803–1915," database with images, FamilySearch, February 18, 2021, accessed September 5, 2023, https://www.familysearch.org/ark:/61903/1:1:JXR6-SMQ.

53 Anita Jacobsen, ed., *Jacobsen's Biographical Index of American Artists*, Vol 1, Book IV (Carrollton, TX: A.J. Publications, 2002), 3126, accessed September 5, 2023, https://archive.org/details/jacobsensbiograp0001unse_h1d9.

54 Peter Faulk, ed., *Who was Who in American Art, 1564–1975: 400 Years of Artists in America* (Madison, CT: Sound View Press, 1999), 3202, accessed September 5, 2023, https://archive.org/details/whowaswhoinameri0003unse/page/n3/mode/2up.

55 Jamey Gigliotti, "Revolutionary Artists, Revolutionary Institution," Pennsylvania Center for the Book, 2023, accessed September 7, 2023, https://pabook.libraries.psu.edu/literary-cultural-heritage-map-pa/feature-articles/revolutionary-artists-revolutionary-institution.

56 "Pennsylvania Academy of Fine Arts Historical Marker," ExplorePAhistory.com, 2023, accessed September 7, 2023, https://explorepahistory.com/hmarker.php?markerId=1-A-19D.

57 Shauna L. Hayes, "Thomas Sully," Pennsylvania Center for the Book, 2007, accessed September 7, 2023, https://pabook.libraries.psu.edu/literary-cultural-heritage-map-pa/bios/Sully__Thomas.

58 Ibid.

59 "Franklin R. Street in the Pennsylvania and New Jersey, U.S., Church and Town Records, 1669–2013," Ancestry.com, 2023, accessed September 4, 2023, https://www.ancestry.com/iscoveryui-content/view/5428038:2451.

60 "Historic St. George's United Methodist Church," The United Methodist Church General Commission on Archives and History, N.D., accessed September 4, 2023, http://www.gcah.org/research/travelers-guide/historic-st.-georges-united-methodist-church.

61 Ibid.

62 "The Reverend Absalom Jones, 1746–1818," The Archives of the Episcopal Church, 2017, accessed September 4, 2023, https://episcopalarchives.org/church-awakens/exhibits/show/leadership/clergy/jones.

63 Rebecca Bayeck, "Robert Douglass Jr., 19th Century African American Artist," Schomburg Center for Research in Black Culture, May 22, 2020, accessed September 4, 2023, https://www.nypl.org/blog/2020/05/22/robert-douglass-jr-african-american-artist.

64 Winch, *A Gentleman of Color*, 116.

65 According to the Morrey–Bustill–Montier family historian and author Joyce Mosley, the distinguished teacher and abolitionist Sarah Mapps Douglass, married her cousin, the Reverend William Douglass of the African Episcopal Church of St. Thomas, who was a widower with nine children. Mosley described the marriage as acrimonious, a description that is confirmed in other sources: Joyce Mosley and John Montier Pickens, Zoom interview of November 3, 2023, recorded with permission by author Donald Scott Sr., MP4. Length 02:56:20, video 1234272029.

66 Bayeck, "Robert Douglass Jr., 19th Century African American Artist."

67 Ibid.

68 "Franklin R. Street (1816–1882)—Find a Grave Memorial," FindaGrave.com, May 16, 2014, accessed September 4, 2023, https://www.findagrave.com/memorial/129875078/franklin-r-street.

69 "F. R. Street—Death—Pennsylvania, Philadelphia City Death Certificates, 1803–1915," FamilySearch.org, April 6, 2021, accessed September 4, 2023, https://www.familysearch.org/ark:/61903/1:1:JK3Q-VY1.

70 "Thomas Street, 'Pennsylvania, Philadelphia City Death Certificates, 1803–1915,'" FamilySearch.org, 2023, accessed September 20, 2023, https://familysearch.org/ark:/61903/1:1:JD1H-TJK.

71 "Thomas Street," FindaGrave.com, 2023, accessed September 20, 2023, https://www.findagrave.com/memorial/240369785/thomas-street.

72 "U.S., City Directories, 1822–1995 for Thomas Street—Philadelphia, Pennsylvania, City Directory, 1861," Ancestry.com, 2023, accessed September 4, 2023, https://www.ancestry.com/discoveryui-content/view/1189944948:2469.

ENDNOTES • 263

73 "Deborah Street in the U.S., Find a Grave Index, 1600s-Current," Ancestry.com, 2023, accessed September 4, 2023, https://www.ancestry.com/discoveryui-content/view/222675611:60525.
74 "Deborah Street in the Pennsylvania and New Jersey, U.S., Church and Town Records, 1669–2013," Ancestry.com, 2023, accessed September 4, 2023, https://www.ancestry.com/discoveryui-content/view/2022373085:2451.
75 "Francis Street—Philadelphia City Death Certificates, 1803–1915," FamilySearch.org, 2023, accessed September 8, 2023, https://www.familysearch.org/ark:/61903/1:1:JFN4-J68.
76 "Jane Street in the Philadelphia, Pennsylvania, U.S., Death Certificates Index, 1803–1915," Ancestry.com, 2023, accessed September 8, 2023, https://www.ancestry.com/discoveryui-content/view/1355586:2535.
77 "U.S., City Directories, 1822–1995 for Jane Street—Philadelphia, Pennsylvania, City Directory, 1886," Ancestry.com, 2023, accessed September 8, 2023, https://www.ancestry.com/discoveryui-content/view/172953307:2469.
78 "Jane E. *Simler* Street," FindaGrave.com, 2023, accessed September 8, 2023, https://www.findagrave.com/memorial/129875019/jane-e-street.
79 "Jane Street in the Philadelphia, Pennsylvania," Ancestry.com.
80 The Morrey–Bustill–Montier family historian and author Joyce Mosley says a 19th-century African American diarist, Emilie Frances Davis (who married into the Bustill family), provides exceptional details concerning everyday life for blacks during the Civil War in Philadelphia and other outstanding historical information. Her narratives, *Emilie Davis's Civil War: The Diaries of a Free Black Woman in Philadelphia, 1863–1865*, includes information about Mosley's Bustill ancestors and other prominent African Americans. In fact, according to the diary that was edited and republished in 2014 by Judith Giesberg via The Pennsylvania State University, Davis married George Bustill White following the war on December 13, 1866. George was "a son of Jacob C. White," a very well-known entrepreneur and black activist. George "was also the brother of Jacob Jr. (Jake), who cofounded the Pythians, a black baseball team [with the celebrated black scholar and activist Octavius Valentine Catto]." The diaries also include her wide-ranging interactions with prominent black Philadelphians, as well as viewing President Abraham Lincoln's body at Independence Hall on Saturday, April 22, 1865, following his assassination about a week earlier on April 15, 1865. "Emilie declared it 'a sight worth seeing.'": Joyce Mosley and John Montier Pickens, Zoom interview of November 3, 2023, recorded with permission by author Donald Scott Sr., MP4. Length 02:56:20, video 1234272029.
81 "Montier, Solomon—Case Files of Approved Pension Applications of Civil War and Later Navy Veterans, compiled ca. 1861–1910," Fold3 by Ancestry.com, 2023, accessed September 10, 2023, https://www.fold3.com/image/67603065/montier-solomon-39436-page-41-us-navy-survivors-certificates-1861-1910.
82 "Solomon Montier in the 1850 United States Federal Census," Ancestry.com, 2023, accessed September 17, 2023, https://www.ancestry.com/discoveryui-content/view/5076753:8054.
83 "William Montier in the Geneanet Community Trees Index," Ancestry.com, 2023, accessed September 17, 2023, https://www.ancestry.com/discoveryui-content/view/6947396318:62476.
84 "Montier, Solomon—Case Files of Approved Pension Applications of Civil War and Later Navy Veterans, compiled ca. 1861–1910," 2023, accessed September 24, 2023, Fold3 by Ancestry.com.
85 "NavSource Online: 'Old Navy' Ship Photo Archive—USS Princeton (II)," Navsource.org, September 13, 2019, accessed September 24, 2023, https://www.navsource.org/archives/09/86/86608.htm.
86 "Ratings Focus: Landsmen," Civilwarbluejackets.com, 2023, accessed September 24, 2023, https://civilwarbluejackets.com/2023/01/24/ratings-focus-landsmen.
87 Ibid.
88 Ibid.

89 Ibid.
90 "[Solomon Montier] Pennsylvania, U.S., Veterans Burial Cards, 1777–2012," Ancestry.com, 2023, accessed September 17, 2023, https://www.ancestry.com/discoveryui-content/view /236086:1967.
91 "Montier, Solomon—Case Files of Approved Pension Applications of Civil War and Later Navy Veterans, compiled ca. 1861–1910," 2023, accessed September 24, 2023, Fold3 by Ancestry.com.
92 "NavSource Online: 'Old Navy' Ship Photo Archive—USS Princeton (II)," Navsource.org.
93 "United States Naval Enlistment Rendezvous, 1855–1891," database with images, FamilySearch.org, May 22, 2014, accessed September 24, 2023, https://familysearch.org/ark:/61903/3:1:939N-89FV-5.
94 Ibid.
95 Ibid.
96 Ancestry.com, 2023, accessed September 14, 2023, https://www.ancestry.com/discoveryui-content/view/42009:9748.
97 AmericanCivilWar.com, 2023, accessed September 14, 2023, https://americancivilwar.com/tcwn/civil_war/Navy_Ships/USS_Aroostook.html.
98 "Francis Montier in the Web: US, African American Civil War Sailor Index, 1861–1865," Ancestry.com, 2023, accessed September 14, 2023, http://www.nps.gov/civilwar/search-sailors-detail.htm?sailorId=MON0024.
99 "USS Aroostook: Civil War Union Naval Ship," AmericanCivilWar.com.
100 "Montier, Robert—2d US Colored Cavalry," Fold3 by Ancestry.com, NARA M1817. Compiled military service records of volunteer Union soldiers in the 1st through 6th U.S. Colored Cavalry and the 5th Massachusetts Cavalry (Colored), 2023, accessed September 20, 2023, https://www.fold3.com/memorial/638102369/robert-montier.
101 Scott, "Camp William Penn's Black Soldiers in Blue."
102 "Montier, Robert—2d US Colored Cavalry," Fold3 by Ancestry.com.
103 Ibid.
104 "Montier, Robert—2d US Colored Cavalry," Fold3 by Ancestry.com.
105 "Montier, Francis—2d US Colored Cavalry," Fold3 by Ancestry.com, NARA M1817. Compiled military service records of volunteer Union soldiers in the 1st through 6th U.S. Colored Cavalry and the 5th Massachusetts Cavalry (Colored), 2023, accessed September 9, 2023, https://www.fold3.com/image/261443257/montier-francis-21-page-1-us-civil-war-service-records-cmrs-union-colored-troops-1st-6th-cavalry-186.
106 "United States Colored Troops 2nd Regiment Cavalry," National Park Service, February 26, 2015, accessed September 9, 2023, https://www.nps.gov/rich/learn/historyculture/2nduscc.htm.
107 Ibid.
108 Ibid.
109 Ibid.
110 Ibid.
111 Scott Sr., *Camp William Penn*, 608–610. In fact, the following passage on page 351 in the hardback version of the Camp William Penn book says: "One of the Camp William Penn soldiers to join the Buffalo Soldiers was Benjamin F. Davis, born in West Chester, Pennsylvania in 1849 and a veteran of the 32nd USCT. Davis joined the Cavalry in 1867, serving a couple of enlistments in the 10th Cavalry and then five years as a sergeant major in the 9th Cavalry. He then rose to become post quartermaster sergeant in 1885, and apparently was married the next year in 1886 at the home of a friend, Sergeant John H. Ferguson of the 9th Cavalry. He retired on April 23, 1895, following almost 20 years as a 'regimental sergeant major and post quartermaster sergeant,'" eventually settling in Washington, DC. Other soldiers and officers from Camp William Penn also became Buffalo Soldiers.
112 "Montier, Robert—2d US Colored Cavalry," Fold3 by Ancestry.com.

ENDNOTES • 265

113 "Montier, Francis—2d US Colored Cavalry," Fold3 by Ancestry.com.
114 Smyles and Murray, *The Montiers: An American Story*.
115 "Menoken, James H.—1-32-USCT 5-1063," Fold3 by Ancestry-Pennsylvania Historical & Museum Commission, US, Pennsylvania Veterans Card Files, 1775–1916, 2023, accessed October 17, 2023, https://www.fold3.com/image/712282309/menoken-james-h-page-1-us-pennsylvania-veterans-card-files-1775-1916.
116 Smyles and Murray, *The Montiers: An American Story*.
117 Scott Sr., *Camp William Penn*, 307–308.
118 Ibid., 8–24.
119 Ibid., 233–241.
120 Mosley, *Gram's Gift*, 25–26.
121 "Cyrus B. Miller ... 24th U.S. Colored Infantry," U.S., Colored Troops Military Service Records, 1863–1865 [database online], Ancestry.com, 2023, accessed December 13, 2023, https://www.ancestry.com/imageviewer/collections/1107/images/miusa1861m_08847700183.
122 Ibid.
123 Scott Sr., *Camp William Penn*, 108.
124 Ibid.
125 Ibid.
126 Amanda B. Moniz, "Making money and doing good: The story of an African American power couple from the 1800s," National Museum of American History, February 9, 2018, https://americanhistory.si.edu/blog/bowser. Moniz notes: "The [Bowser] couple's associational activity included working to advance the welfare of African Americans. As a member of the Ladies' Union Association of Philadelphia, a charity established by free African American women during the Civil War, Lizzie played a leading role in raising money to care for black soldiers and then freed people ... David's philanthropy also included leading an effort to aid African American victims denied assistance from white-led relief efforts during a yellow fever outbreak in New Orleans."
127 Donald Scott Sr., *Camp William Penn*.
128 "David Bustill Bowser in the U.S., Find a Grave Index, 1600s-Current," Ancestry.com, 2023, accessed September 17, 2023, https://www.ancestry.com/discoveryui-content/view/40196640:60525.
129 Scott Sr., *Camp William Penn*, 184.
130 Ibid., 42–43.
131 "John Brown's Raid," Harpers Ferry National Historical Park, June 9, 2022, accessed September 17, 2023, https://www.nps.gov/articles/john-browns-raid.htm.
132 "William Robeson in the U.S., Colored Troops Military Service Records, 1863–1865," Ancestry.com, 2023, accessed September 17, 2023, https://www.ancestry.com/discoveryui-content/view/223553.
133 Duberman, *Paul Robeson*, 4.
134 "William Robason in the 1860 U.S. Federal Census—Slave Schedules," Ancestry.com, 2023, accessed September 2, 2023, https://www.ancestry.com/discoveryui-content/view/93297571:7668.
135 "William Robeson in the U.S., Colored Troops Military Service Records, 1863–1865," Ancestry.com, 2023, accessed September 2, 2023, https://www.ancestry.com/discoveryui-content/view/223553:1107.
136 Ibid.
137 Scott Sr., *Camp William Penn*, 276.
138 Ibid.
139 Ibid.
140 Ibid.
141 Ibid., 275.

142 "Crowd at Lincoln's second inauguration, March 4, 1865," Library of Congress–Prints & Photographs Online Catalog, 2023, accessed September 19, 2023, http://hdl.loc.gov/loc.pnp/ppmsc.02927.
143 Scott Sr., *Camp William Penn*, 278.
144 Ibid.
145 Ibid., 280.
146 Ibid.
147 Ibid.
148 Ibid.
149 Scott Sr., *Camp William Penn*, 275.
150 Ibid., 282.
151 "… 22nd Regiment U.S. Colored Troops: A Tribute [t]o The United States Colored Troops Who Fought [f]or Our Freedom," The Historical Marker Database, June 8, 2021, accessed September 19, 2023, https://www.hmdb.org/m.asp?m=174937.
152 Scott Sr., *Camp William Penn*, 283.
153 Duberman, *Paul Robeson*, 4.
154 Ibid., 4–5.
155 Ibid., 5.
156 The brochure, "Souvenir Program of the Testimonial in Honor of Dr. Nathan F. Mossell—Founder of Douglass Hospital," indicates that "PAUL ROBESON" appeared "in Person" and sang various "Selections." The program also featured civil rights activist "ARTHUR HUFF FAUSET" as the "Principal Speaker" focusing on the "Topic: 'Pioneering.'" The event was held on Sunday, February 4, 1940, at the McDowell Community Church located in the heart of Philadelphia's African American community, 21st Street and Columbia Avenue. Furthermore, the brochure included a brief biography concerning Dr. Mossell, credited with founding the first African American hospital in the Philadelphia metro area, including that he "was born on July 27, 1856, at Hamilton, . Canada, the son of a brick manufacturer, Aaron Mossell and his wife Eliza Bowers Mossell." The text adds that Mossell "was the first Negro graduate from the Medical School of the University of Pennsylvania and his life has been an inspiration similar to that of the great American Frederick Douglass for whom the hospital is named. Dr. Mossell stands out today as a leader, builder, thinker and No. 1 citizen." Paul Robeson was the son of the formerly enslaved Civil War soldier William Drew Robeson; his mother, Maria Louisa Bustill Robeson, was descended from Cyrus Bustill and Elizabeth Morrey, a daughter of Cremona and Richard Morrey. The document was found at the University of Pennsylvania's University Archives within the Nathan Francis Mossell Papers (Box 1, Folder 1, UPT 50-M913) by this author on Thursday, December 21, 2023.
157 Duberman, *Paul Robeson*, 5.
158 David Staniunas, "A Reckoning in Princeton," Presbyterian Historical Society, February 18, 2016, accessed September 19, 2023, https://www.history.pcusa.org/blog/2016/02/reckoning-princeton.
159 Ibid.
160 Ibid.
161 Ibid.
162 Ibid.
163 Duberman, *Paul Robeson*, 5.
164 Ibid., 5–6.
165 "The Presidents of Princeton University: Woodrow Wilson—1902–10," The Trustees of Princeton University, 2019, accessed September 19, 2023, https://pr.princeton.edu/pub/presidents/wilson/.
166 Ibid.
167 Duberman, *Paul Robeson*, 6.

168 Ibid.
169 Ibid.
170 Herb Boyd, "Rev. William Drew Robeson, patriarch of a distinguished family," *New York Amsterdam News*, April 15, 2021, accessed September 22, 2023, https://amsterdamnews.com/news/2021/04/15/rev-william-drew-robeson-patriarch-distinguished-f/.
171 Ibid.
172 Duberman, *Paul Robeson*, 5.
173 Anna Bustill Smith's typed document, "THE BUSTILL FAMILY," with what appears to be her handwritten signature, indicates: "William Drew Robeson [Jr.] graduated from Trenton High School, Trenton, New Jersey and from Lincoln University, Pennsylvania in 1902. He studied medicine at the University of Pennsylvania, but the death of his mother interrupted, and he later graduated from the College of Physicians and Surgeons, Boston, Massachusetts. He interned at Freedmans [sic] Hospital [in] Washington, D.C., and was Resident Physician at the time of his death, November 20, 1925." Smith's typed document was found at the University of Pennsylvania's University Archives within the Nathan Francis Mossell Papers (Box 1, Folder 50, UPT 50-M913) by this author on Thursday, December 21, 2023.
174 Duberman, *Paul Robeson*, 5.
175 Ibid.
176 Paul Robeson with Lloyd L. Brown, *Here I Stand* (Boston: Beacon Press, 1958), 7.
177 Duberman, *Paul Robeson*, 8.
178 Joseph Illick, "African Americans: Childhood in Slavery, Childlike in Freedom … and Paul Robeson as Child and Parent," in *Paul Robeson: Essays on His Life and Legacy*, eds. Joseph Dorinson and William Pencak (Jefferson, NC: McFarland & Company, Inc., 2004), 24. The author writes that Robeson profoundly loved his father, William Drew Robeson: "But far more than anyone else, it was his father, the ex-slave, who shaped his early life. 'The glory of my boyhood years was my father,' he recalled in the opening line of his autobiography. 'I loved him like no one in all the world.'"
179 Robeson and Brown, *Here I Stand*, 7.
180 Boyd, "Rev. William Drew Robeson, patriarch of a distinguished family."
181 Duberman, *Paul Robeson*, 8.
182 Ibid.
183 Rodger Streitmatter, *Raising Her Voice: African American Women Journalists Who Changed History* (Lexington: The University Press of Kentucky, 1994), 39, accessed September 21, 2023, https://web.archive.org/web/20200507034049id_/https://uknowledge.uky.edu/cgi/viewcontent.cgi?article=1006&context=upk_african_american_studies.
184 Ibid.
185 "Charles H. Bustill … Pennsylvania Marriages, 1709–1940," 2023, FamilySearch.org, accessed September 21, 2023, https://www.familysearch.org/ark:/61903/1:1:Q2WN-6S9V.
186 Charles Rosenberg, "Bustill, Charles Hicks," Oxford African American Studies Center, February 28, 2013, accessed September 21, 2023, https://oxfordaasc.com/browse?t=AASC_Occupations%3A1153&t0=AASC_Eras%3A3.
187 Robeson and Brown, *Here I Stand*, 6–7.
188 Ibid.
189 Ibid.
190 Ibid.
191 Scott Sr., "The Montiers: An American Family's Triumphant Odyssey."
192 The actual second-annual 1912 Bustill family reunion invitation was found at the University of Pennsylvania's University Archives within the Nathan Francis Mossell Papers (Box 1, Folder 51,

UPT 50-M913) by this author on Thursday, December 21, 2023. It was sent to many guests, including Paul Robeson and his family: "You are invited to attend the Second Annual Re-union of the descendants of the Bustill Family Monday, June the seventeenth, nineteen hundred and twelve from nine a.m. to seven-thirty p.m. at Maple Grove, Philadelphia, Pa.—Exercises at one-thirty o'clock sharp—This invitation admits two."

193 The program brochure for the "12th ANNUAL REUNION of THE DESCENDANTS of CYRUS BUSTILL," dated June 26, 1923, was found at the University of Pennsylvania's University Archives within the Nathan Francis Mossell Papers (Box 1, Folder 51, UPT 50-M913) by this author on Thursday, December 21, 2023, that was distributed to guests at Maple Grove in the Philadelphia vicinity. The parts of the program included "I. Opening hymn ... 'America!' II. Invocation ... Dr. Freeman. III. Family History ... Mrs. [Gertrude Emily Hicks Bustill] Mossell. IV. Address ... Rev. Garrett. V. Neerology ... Maple Pierce. VI. Address ... Rev. Imes. ... VII. Closing Hymn ... 'God be with you 'till we meet again.'"

194 Anna Bustill Smith's typed document, "THE BUSTILL FAMILY," with what appears to be her handwritten signature, indicates on page 5: "Gertrude Bustill married Dr. Nathan F. Mossell, the first Negro medical graduate of the University of Pennsylvania, and founder of the first Negro hospital (Douglass) and training school for nurses in Philadelphia, Pennsylvania ... For many many years she wrote for the leading dailies of the city, including the 'Philadelphia Press', 'Times', 'Inquirer', and 'North American'. She also wrote for many Negro weeklies and monthly magazines, including the 'New York Age', 'The Christian Recorder', 'The Boston Advocate', 'The Women's Era', and others'." Smith's typed document was found at the University of Pennsylvania's University Archives within the Nathan Francis Mossell Papers (Box 1, Folder 50, UPT 50-M913) by this author on Thursday, December 21, 2023.

195 Robeson and Brown, *Here I Stand*, 7.

196 According to Gertrude Bustill Mossell's original typed "OBITUARY," likely composed by family historian Anna Bustill Smith, she was a prolific fundraiser for her husband, Dr. Nathan Francis Mossell establishing the Douglass Hospital, the first such institution for African Americans in the Philadelphia region. "Mrs. Mossell raised $40,000 for the Frederick Douglas [sic] Hospital," notes "the 25th anniversary report of the hospital." In addition to the obituary focusing on Gertrude Mossell's accomplishments as a fundraiser for other organizations and stellar journalism career, it notes that bygone loved ones and survivors included several notable members of her immediate and extended family. The famous black activist and scholar Paul Robeson and his preacher brother, Benjamin, were much respected members of the family, as was Sadie T. Alexander, the first black woman to graduate from the University of Pennsylvania's law school. Her father, Aaron A. Mossell, was the first African American to graduate from that institution. Furthermore, the African Methodist Episcopal Church bishop, Benjamin Tucker Tanner, was her maternal grandfather, whose son was the famous black painter Henry O. Tanner. Sadie Alexander's husband was Raymond Pace Alexander, the first black graduate of the University of Pennsylvania's Wharton School of Business. The 1948 "OBITUARY" was found at the University of Pennsylvania's University Archives within the Nathan Francis Mossell Papers (Box 1, Folder 45, UPT 50-M913) by this author on Thursday, December 21, 2023.

197 Duberman, *Paul Robeson*, 8.

198 Ibid.

199 "Colorism." Merriam-Webster.com, 2023, accessed September 21, 2023, https://www.merriam-webster.com/dictionary/colorism.

200 Duberman, *Paul Robeson*, 8.

201 Ibid., 6–8.

202 Ibid., 9.
203 Ibid.
204 Ibid.
205 Ibid.
206 Ibid.
207 Ibid., 9–10.
208 Ibid., 10.
209 Ibid., 11.
210 Ibid.
211 Ibid.
212 Gerlach, "ROBESON, PAUL," *African American Lives*, 714–715.
213 Ibid., 715.
214 "The African American Odyssey: A Quest for Full Citizenship—World War 1 and Postwar Society," Library of Congress, 2023, accessed September 23, 2023, https://www.loc.gov/exhibits/african-american-odyssey/world-war-i-and-postwar-society.html.
215 Gerlach, "ROBESON, PAUL," *African American Lives*, 715.
216 "Landmark Legislation: The Fourteenth Amendment," United States Senate, 2023, accessed September 24, 2023, https://www.senate.gov/about/origins-foundations/senate-and-constitution/14th-amendment.htm.
217 Gerlach, "ROBESON, PAUL," *African American Lives*, 715.
218 Scott Sr., "Rare portraits reflect black family's legacy."
219 "Educator and Civic Leader: William Pickens," Yale University, 2023, accessed September 24, 2023, https://afamstudies.yale.edu/academics/undergraduate-major/william-pickens-prize/educator-and-civic-leader-william-pickens.
220 Gerlach, "ROBESON, PAUL," *African American Lives*, 715.
221 Emma G. Fitzsimmons, "Paul Robeson Jr., Activist and Author, Dies at 86," *The New York Times*, April 27, 2014, B8, https://www.nytimes.com/2014/04/28/arts/activist-and-author-paul-robeson-jr-dies-at-86.html.
222 Gerlach, "ROBESON, PAUL," *African American Lives*, 715.
223 Ibid.
224 Ibid.
225 Ibid.
226 Ibid.
227 Ibid.
228 Ibid.
229 Ibid.
230 Duberman, *Paul Robeson*, 65.
231 Ibid., 65–66.
232 Ibid., 66.
233 Gerlach, "ROBESON, PAUL," *African American Lives*, 715.
234 Ibid.
235 Ibid.
236 Ibid.
237 Ibid.
238 Ibid., 715–716.
239 Ibid., 716.

240 Evan J. Molinari, "My Soul, My Integrity, My Freedom: Paul Robeson, Jackie Robinson, and their Competing Perspectives within the Struggle for Black Equality During the Second Red Scare" (Thesis, Bates College, 2016), 157, accessed November 24, 2023, https://scarab.bates.edu/honorstheses/157/.
241 Gerlach, "ROBESON, PAUL," *African American Lives*, 716.
242 Ibid.
243 Ibid.
244 Ibid.
245 Ibid.
246 Ibid.
247 Ibid., 717.
248 Philip S. Foner, *Paul Robeson Speaks: Writings, Speeches, Interviews 1918–1974* (New York: Citadel Press, 1978), 28.
249 Duberman, *Paul Robeson*, 34.
250 Ibid., 17.
251 An interesting account involving the Browns, etc., "The Flanagan-Allen-Brown-Montier-Martin Families of Pa," posted by way of Genealogy.com that was updated on October 10, 2013, by William Barcelona Blythe of Lindenwold, New Jersey, notes: "The family research begins with Bridget Flanagan, born in County Cork, Ireland in 1821 to Mary Flanagan, born in 1799. Bridget became pregnant at a young age while being single, and moved to England with her mother, where she met and married an East Indian from Calcutta, India who adopted the English name of Francis Allen and together they had nine children that we know of at this time. Agnes Anastasia Allen was one of three children born in England, in July 1841. The family migrated to America August 24, 1848, arriving in Philadelphia, Pa., where they settled in the vicinity of West Philadelphia Ward #4, Philadelphia, Pa. Bridget & Frank Allen had nine (9) children in all, three (3) ... born in England and six (6) was born in Philadelphia. Agnes met and married William D. Brown and they settled in Philadelphia with Agnes's sister Mary Allen residing with them, the marriage produced two daughters, Evelyn Gertrude Brown and Laura Emma Brown, the later met and married Jerome Watson Montier, son of Hiram Charles Montier and Elizabeth Brown Montier and the marriage produced four children, Maude Anastasia Montier, Edna E. Montier, Helen Marie Montier, and a son named Hiram Jerome Montier ....," accessed December 10, 2023, https://www.genealogy.com/ftm/b/l/y/William-B-Blythe-Clementon/index.html.
252 Trymaine Lee, Interview with William Pickens III, "Summer in the Black Hamptons: a refuge of freedom and joy," MSNBC.com, 2021, accessed December 10, 2023, https://www.msnbc.com/podcast/into-america/summer-black-hamptons-refuge-freedom-joy-n1298436.
253 Ibid.
254 John Montier Pickens, the grandson of Emilie Brown Pickens, says his grandmother was instrumental in cofounding and expanding the African American cultural and social organization Jack and Jill of America. Online sources indicate that she served as the second president of the group from 1948 to 1950. Many of the early members or organizers of Jack and Jill had attended Emilie Brown Pickens's tea parties, according to John. The family was also heavily involved with the YMCA, he added: Joyce Mosley and John Montier Pickens, Zoom interview of November 3, 2023, recorded with permission by author Donald Scott Sr., MP4. Length 02:56:20, video 1234272029.
255 Ibid.
256 Oliver Peterson, "Sag Harbor SANS Advocate William Pickens III Dies at 85," Danspapers.com, October 1, 2021, accessed December 21, 2023, https://www.danspapers.com/2021/10/sag-harbor-william-pickens-obit/.

257 William Pickens Sr., *The Heir of Slaves: An Autobiography, Documenting the American South-University of North Carolina at Chapel Hill*, 1911 and 1997, 3, accessed September 27, 2023, https://docsouth.unc.edu/fpn/pickens/pickens.html.
258 "William Pickens," FindaGrave.com, August 2, 2022, accessed December 21, 2023, https://www.findagrave.com/memorial/242241756/william-pickens.
259 Ibid.
260 Pickens Sr., *The Heir of Slaves: An Autobiography*, 5.
261 Ibid., 5.
262 Ibid., 5–6.
263 Ibid., 6.
264 Ibid.
265 Ibid.
266 Ibid., 6–7.
267 Ibid., 7.
268 Ibid.
269 Ibid., 7–8.
270 Ibid., 8.
271 Ibid., 40.
272 Ibid., 41.
273 "William Pickens papers (Additions) 1909–1950," The New York Public Library Archives & Manuscripts, Schomburg Center for Research in Black Culture, 2023, accessed September 28, 2023, https://archives.nypl.org/scm/20751.
274 Pickens Sr., *The Heir of Slaves: An Autobiography*, 109.
275 Ibid., 112.
276 Ibid., 114.
277 Ibid., 115–116.
278 Ibid., 125.
279 Ibid.
280 Ibid., 125–126.
281 "William Pickens papers (Additions) 1909–1950."
282 Ibid.
283 Ibid.
284 Sarah Concepcion, "America250: Navy Veteran Harriet Pickens," VA News, 2023, accessed September 28, 2023, https://news.va.gov/98241/america250-navy-veteran-harriet-pickens/.
285 Laurie King, "WAVES Trailblazers: Lt. j.g. Harriet Ida Pickens and Ensign Frances Wills, the first African American WAVES officers," The Mariners' Museum and Park, June 9, 2021, accessed September 28, 2023, https://www.marinersmuseum.org/2021/06/waves-trailblazers-lt-j-g-harriet-ida-pickens-and-ensign-frances-wills-the-first-african-american-waves-officers/.
286 "William Pickens papers (Additions) 1909–1950."
287 Ibid.
288 "(1919) William Pickens, 'The Kind of Democracy the Negro Expects," BlackPast.org, January 28, 2007, accessed September 28, 2023, https://www.blackpast.org/african-american-history/1919-william-pickens-kind-democracy-negro-expects/.
289 William Pickens, *Bursting Bonds* (Boston: The Jordan & More Press, 1923), 151.
290 "Educator and Civic Leader: William Pickens," Yale University, 2023.
291 "(1919) William Pickens, 'The Kind of Democracy the Negro Expects,'" BlackPast.org.
292 Ibid.

272 • THE MONTIERS

293 "William Pickens papers (Additions) 1909–1950."
294 José Endoença Martins, "New Negroes' Bursting into Community: Booker T. Washington, W. E. B. Du Bois, and William Pickens," Researchgate.net, January 2002, accessed June 30, 2024, https://www.researchgate.net/publication/289528306.
295 Ibid.
296 Ibid.
297 Ibid.
298 Ibid.
299 Ibid.
300 "William Pickens papers (Additions) 1909–1950."
301 Ibid.
302 Ibid.
303 Ibid.
304 Ibid.
305 "WILLIAM PICKENS, NEGRO LEADER, 73—Former Field Secretary of N.A.A.C.P. Dies on Cruise—Retired Treasury Aide," *The New York Times*, April 7, 1954, 31, accessed June 30, 2024, https://timesmachine.nytimes.com/timesmachine/1954/04/07/92563297.html?pageNumber=31.
306 Ibid.
307 Ibid.
308 Daron Shultziner, "The Social-Psychological Origins of the Montgomery Bus Boycott: Social interaction and Humiliation in the Emergence of Social Movements," UCLA.edu, July 10, 2013, accessed June 30, 2024, https://www.sscnet.ucla.edu/polisci/faculty/chwe/ps269/shultziner.pdf
309 Ibid.

Chapter 10

1 Elisabeth Bumiller, "It's a Summer Thing; For Like-Minded New Yorkers, a Season of Separation," *The New York Times*, May 26, 1996, 27, accessed September 27, 2023, https://www.nytimes.com/1996/05/26/nyregion/it-s-a-summer-thing-for-like-minded-new-yorkers-a-season-of-separation.html.
2 William Pickens III, interview with Trymaine Lee, "Black Joy in the Summertime" transcript, MSNBC, June 11, 2021, accessed September 27, 2023, https://www.msnbc.com/podcast/transcript-summer-black-hamptons-refuge-freedom-joy-n1270563.
3 "Geography & Travel: Sag Harbor, New York— United States," *Encyclopaedia Britannica*, December 9, 2013, accessed October 6, 2023, https://www.britannica.com/place/Sag-Harbor.
4 Erika Wood, "NY's Jim Crow laws—back in the day, and what remains today," Brennan Center for Justice, March 1, 2010, accessed October 6, 2023, https://www.brennancenter.org/our-work/analysis-opinion/nys-jim-crow-laws-back-day-and-what-remains-today.
5 Bumiller, "It's a Summer Thing."
6 William Pickens III, interview with Trymaine Lee, "Black Joy in the Summertime" transcript, MSNBC.
7 Ibid.
8 Peterson, "Sag Harbor SANS Advocate William Pickens III Dies at 85."
9 William Pickens III, interview with Trymaine Lee.
10 "An Open Opportunity: African American Whalers Found Freedom At Sea," *Long Island Weekly*, February 21, 2023, accessed October 13, 2023, https://longislandweekly.com/an-open-opportunity-african-american-whalers-found-freedom-at-sea/.

11. Ibid.
12. Leroy Davis, "John Hope: 1868–1936," New Georgia Encyclopedia, revised July 21, 2020, accessed October 4, 2023, https://www.georgiaencyclopedia.org/articles/education/john-hope-1868-1936/.
13. William Pickens III, interview with Trymaine Lee, "Black Joy in the Summertime" transcript, *MSNBC*.
14. Leroy Davis, "John Hope: 1868–1936."
15. William Pickens III, interview with Trymaine Lee.
16. Ibid.
17. Ibid.
18. Ibid.
19. Ibid.
20. Bumiller, "It's a Summer Thing."
21. Ibid.
22. The Morrey-Montier descendant John Montier Pickens confirmed that the great African American author-poet Langston Hughes read poems at the Pickenses' residence(s) circa 1927–1931: Joyce Mosley and John Montier Pickens, Zoom interview of November 3, 2023, recorded with permission by author Donald Scott Sr., MP4. Length 02:56:20, video 1234272029. It's also notable that the acclaimed African American writer, Colson Whitehead, who became familiar with such literary giants as Hughes and others of the Harlem Renaissance while growing up, reflected on his own summer sojourns to Sag Harbor in the celebrated 2009 novel *Sag Harbor*, focusing on the primary character (Benji) maturing as a young African American from an affluent family.
23. Bumiller, "It's a Summer Thing."
24. John Montier Pickens noted that his father William Pickens III first met his wife (John's mother Audrey Patricia née Brannen) on the beach at Sag Harbor: Joyce Mosley and John Montier Pickens, Zoom interview of November 3, 2023.
25. Ibid.
26. Ibid.
27. Ibid.
28. William Pickens III, *MSNBC* interview with Trymaine Lee.
29. Ibid.
30. "Celebrating Diverse Voices at UVM: Ten Black Experiences," The University of Vermont—Division of Diversity, Equity & Inclusion, accessed October 6, 2023, https://www.uvm.edu/diversity/celebrating-diverse-voices-uvm-ten-black-experiences.
31. Peterson, "Sag Harbor SANS Advocate William Pickens III Dies at 85."
32. Ibid.
33. "Celebrating Diverse Voices at UVM: Ten Black Experiences."
34. Peterson, "Sag Harbor SANS Advocate William Pickens III Dies at 85."
35. Ibid.
36. Ibid.
37. Ibid.
38. Ibid.
39. Ibid.
40. Ibid.
41. Scott Sr., "Rare portraits reflect black family's legacy."
42. Ibid.
43. Ibid.
44. Ibid.

45   Ibid.
46   Ibid.
47   Ibid.
48   Ibid.
49   Ibid.
50   Daniel Rubin, "Daniel Rubin: A bit of detective work leads back to his ancestors," *The Philadelphia Inquirer*, June 23, 2011, accessed November 6, 2023, https://www.inquirer.com/philly/news/local/20110623_Daniel_Rubin__A_bit_of_detective_work_leads_back_to_his_ancestors.html.
51   Ibid.
52   Ibid.
53   Ibid.
54   Ibid.
55   Ibid.
56   Ibid.
57   Ibid.
58   Scott Sr., "The Montiers: An American Family's Triumphant Odyssey."
59   "MONTEITH GRAVEYARD: A Burial Ground for Colored People in Cheltenham," published November 20, 1897, likely in the *Norristown Times Herald*, was sent via email on February 14, 2014, by Cheltenham-area writer-historian David Harrower. He discovered the article in the archives of the Historical Society of Montgomery County within a scrapbook.
60   Alexander W. Scott, "HISTORY and DEVELOPMENT of the SCHOOL DISTRICT of CHELTENHAM TOWNSHIP," 6, Classcreator.com, accessed November 14, 2023, https://www.classcreator.com/000/7/5/5/35557/.pdf.
61   Ibid., 16.
62   Scott Sr., *Remembering Cheltenham Township*, 40.
63   "MONTEITH GRAVEYARD: A Burial Ground for Colored People in Cheltenham," emailed to author February 14, 2017 by writer-author David Harrower.
64   A January 2017 transcribed version of "MONTEITH GRAVEYARD: A Burial Ground for Colored People in Cheltenham" was emailed by the local writer, historian, and officer of the Cheltenham Township Historical Commission and Old York Road Historical Society, Dr. Thomas Wieckowski, to this author on March 4, 2018.
65   "John Murrey in the U.S., Quaker Meeting Records, 1681–1935," Ancestry.com via Haverford College [database online], 2023, accessed December 17, 2023, https://www.ancestry.com/discoveryui-content/view/1100215860:2189.
66   "Humphrey Murrey in the U.S., Quaker Meeting Records, 1681–1935," Ancestry.com [database online], 2023, accessed July 29, 2023, https://www.ancestry.com/discoveryui-content/view/99882172:2189. Humphrey's death year was recorded by the "Philadelphia Yearly Meeting" as being "abt 1716." His death was reportedly in September 1715 and his will was probated in 1716.
67   "Bargain & Sale for 500 years, Richard Morrey to His Negro Woman Cremona Morrey," Philadelphia City Archives, Philadelphia County Deed Book G-7:539-543, dated January 6, 1746, accessed by this author on Tuesday, December 12, 2023.
68   W. E. Corson, "MONTIETH GRAVEYARD: A Burial Ground for Colored People in Cheltenham," emailed to author on February 14, 2017, by David Harrower.
69   W. E. Corson, "MONTIETH GRAVEYARD: A Burial Ground for Colored People in Cheltenham," transcribed in January 2017 by Dr. Thomas Wieckowski.
70   Ibid.

71 Phillips, "The Record Of A Hike On The Bethlehem Pike," 216, 1920.
72 Ibid.
73 Ibid., 224.
74 Ibid., 224–225.
75 "Jane Montiers in the Philadelphia, Pennsylvania, U.S., Death Certificates Index, 1803–1915," Ancestry.com, 2023, accessed October 13, 2023, https://www.ancestry.com/discoveryui-content/view/2210002:2535. It's worth noting that a map, "G.M. Hopkins MAP 1877," indicates that the family plot or cemetery in Guineatown was located "on Jane Montier's land" along the "Limekiln Turnpike" adjacent to the estate of "D. Heist," as depicted on pg. 47 of Reginald H. Pitts' 1991 *Old York Road Historical Society Bulletin* article, "Robert Lewis of Guineatown, and 'The Colored Cemetary [sic] in Glenside."
76 "Jane Mountier in the Pennsylvania and New Jersey, U.S., Church and Town Records, 1669–2013," Ancestry.com, 2023, accessed October 13, 2023, https://www.ancestry.com/discoveryui-content/view/2022665656:2451.
77 "Our Story," Kirk & Nice, Inc., 2023, accessed October 13, 2023, https://www.kirkandniceinc.com/our-story.
78 "Anna Matilda Hilton in the Philadelphia, Pennsylvania, U.S., Death Certificates Index, 1803–1915," Ancestry.com, 2023, accessed October 13, 2023, https://www.ancestry.com/discoveryui-content/view/2298419:2535.
79 "Anna M. Hilton in the U.S., City Directories, 1822–1995," Ancestry.com, 2023, accessed October 13, 2023, https://ancestry.com/discoveryui-content/view/145350811:2469.
80 "Anna Matilda Caroline Montier in the Pennsylvania and New Jersey, U.S., Church and Town Records, 1669–2013," Ancestry.com, 2023, accessed October 13, 2023, https://www.ancestry.com/discoveryui-content/view/2020190867:2451.
81 "Caroline Hoy … United States Census, 1860," FamilySearch.org, 2023, accessed October 13, 2023, https://www.familysearch.org/ark:/61903/1:1:MX58-BJJ.
82 "Add an update for Caroline Hoy," Ancestry.com (meg2116), 2012 and 2023, accessed October 13, 2023, https://www.ancestry.com/discoveryui-content/view/4142645:7667.
83 An original handwritten deed recorded May 23, 1862, pertaining to Cremona Morrey Jr.'s executors' Joseph Ottinger and Charles Montier passing to Jane Montier significant land and the Montier homestead was found at the University of Pennsylvania's University Archives within the Nathan Francis Mossell Papers (Box 1, Folder 50, UPT 50-M913) by this author on Thursday, December 21, 2023. The text, on pages 96–97, in part indicates that Jane Montier was to receive "two adjoining tracts of land with the Stone Mansion House, Barn and other out buildings thereon erected situate in Cheltenham Township."
84 Scott Sr., "The Montiers: An American Family's Triumphant Odyssey."
85 "Jane Montier in the New Jersey, U.S., Wills and Probate Records, 1739–1991," Ancestry.com, 2023, accessed December 20, 2023, https://www.ancestry.com/discoveryui-content/view/1981559:8796. Jane Montier's barber nephew, George Congo (born 1833), chose her to be an "Executrix" of his will, and beneficiary, declaring "all the Legacy left me by my Grand father Hiram Montier which is the Real Estate in Cheltenham Montgomery County to have and to hold for her own especial Benefit." The document stipulates "Jane Montier" as "the Executrix therein named on the Twenty Sixth day of February 1867." In fact, a George Congo served in Company A of the 22nd United States Colored Troops (USCT), one of 11 federal African American regiments to train at Camp William Penn in what is today Cheltenham Township, according to Ancestry.com's "U.S., Colored Troops Military Service Records, 1863–1865." His military documents identify him as previously being a farmer when he enlisted at age 17 on January 8, 1864, for three years, standing about 5

feet 5 inches with a "yellow" complexion, "hazel" eyes, and "black" hair. Although Congo had been living in the Trenton, New Jersey, area—a state where many members of the 22nd USCT were born—George Congo (the soldier) was born in Bucks County, Pennsylvania, according to the records. He was mustered out of service in Brownsville, Texas, on October 16, 1865, as a sergeant in Company A. Does George's surname, Congo, indicate that that line of the family came from Africa's Congo region?

86 Scott Sr., "The Montiers: An American Family's Triumphant Odyssey." It's worth noting that Ena Lindner Swain's 2017 book, *The Evolution of Abolitionism in Germantown and Its Environs*, also explores on pg. 202 (via Google Books) the Montier family's important involvement in establishing an African Methodist Episcopal Church in Philadelphia's Germantown area: "The Montiers, Hiram, Charles and George Henry, were instrumental in purchasing the grounds for New Bethel A.M.E. Church of Germantown, Centre Street. On April 18, 1857, [William] Lewis conveyed the lot to Charles and Hiram Montier, acting as trustees of New Bethel A.M.E. Church of Germantown, for $300.00. In 1858, the founders met at the home of Amando Monticelo and Ann Hilton. In 1859, they met in a stone building at Morton and Rittenhouse Streets. Five years after its founding, on October 9, 1862, William Lewis and Charles Montier sold the church building and lot to the congregation for $1.00."

87 "Owner: CEMETERY FOR COLORED FOLKS," City-data.com, 2023, accessed October 12, 2023, https://www.city-data.com/montgomery-county-pa-properties/L/Limekiln-Pike-14.html.

88 "CEMETERY FOR COLORED FOLKS—LIMEKILN PIKE," Montcopa.org, 2023, accessed October 12, 2023, https://propertyrecords.montcopa.org.

89 William Pickens III, "I Thought of My Family Burial Ground Outside of Philadelphia," Letter to the Editor, *The New York Times*, August 16, 1992, accessed August 20, 2023, https://www.nytimes.com/1992/08/16/opinion/l-i-thought-of-my-family-burial-ground-outside-philadelphia-052792.html.

90 Lydialyle Gibson, "Long way home: Chicago geneticist Rick Kittles stirs controversy and hope with a DNA database designed to help African Americans unearth their roots," *University of Chicago Magazine* 100, no. 3 (January/February 2008), accessed June 30, 2024, https://magazine.uchicago.edu/0812/features/kittles.shtml.

91 Pickens III, "I Thought of My Family Burial Ground Outside of Philadelphia."
92 Ibid.
93 "1790 United States Federal Census for Robert Lewis," Ancestry.com. The National Archives in Washington, DC: First Census of the United States, 1790. Cheltenham, Montgomery, Pennsylvania; [database on-ine], accessed July 16, 2023, https://www.ancestry.com/discoveryui-content/view/324568:5058. Robert Lewis is listed in 1790 (during that "First Census of the United States") as essentially the head of household in a family of 13 "Free Persons." Living nearby, some presumably in what was considered to be Guineatown, where Lewis and his family almost certainly lived, included the families of John Montier, Margaret Fry, and Cuffee Gardner.
94 Pickens III, "I Thought of My Family Burial Ground Outside of Philadelphia."
95 Ibid.
96 Ibid.
97 Ibid.
98 Ibid.
99 Ibid.
100 Ibid.
101 Ibid.

102 Smyles and Murray, *The Montiers: An American Story*.
103 Audra D. S. Burch, "Nearly 'Erased by History': African Americans Search for Lost Graves," *The New York Times*, October 15, 2022 (Updated October 17, 2022), accessed October 21, 2023, https://www.nytimes.com/2022/10/15/us/nearly-erased-by-history-african-americans-search-for-lost-graves.html.
104 Ibid.
105 Ibid.
106 Ibid.
107 Ibid.
108 Ibid.
109 Ibid.
110 "Pennsylvania Hallowed Grounds has partnered with Preservation Pennsylvania," PreservationPennsylvania.org, 2018-2024, accessed October 21, 2023, https://www.preservationpa.org/special-projects/african-american-cemetery-project/.
111 "Ground Penetrating Radar," Kutztown University, 2023, accessed October 21, 2023, https://faculty.kutztown.edu/sherrod/Equipment/GPR.aspx.
112 Laura Sherrod, "Mouns Jones House," Kutztown University, 2022, accessed October 21, 2023, https://faculty.kutztown.edu/sherrod/Projects/MounsJones.aspx.
113 "Archaeology of Grave Sites—Cemetery Preservation and Recordation," Pennsylvania Historical and Museum Commission, August 26, 2015, accessed October 21, 2023, http://www.phmc.state.pa.us/portal/communities/cemetery-preservation/documentation/archaeology.html.
114 Ibid.
115 Ibid.
116 Donald Scott, "Unearthing the Bones of Her Ancestors," *The Philadelphia Inquirer*, June 10, 1984, 29, accessed June 22, 2024, https://www.newspapers.com/image/176323817/.
117 Ibid.
118 Ibid.
119 Ibid.
120 Ibid.
121 Ibid.
122 Ibid.
123 Ibid.
124 Ibid.
125 Ibid.
126 Paul Hond, "The Double-Edged Helix," *Columbia Magazine*, Winter 2015–16, accessed June 30, 2024, https://magazine.columbia.edu/article/double-edged-helix.
127 Ibid.
128 The Morrey–Bustill–Montier family historian and author Joyce Mosley said: "My research shows that 'Mooney'—Cremona [Morrey]—was Native American—[as well as] some of the research that Arcadia [University] did in fact," concerning Cremona's Native American ancestry. Mosley also said that some recent research indicates that one of Cremona's Native American progenitors, quite possibly her father, "signed the [1683] treaty at [Penn] Treaty Park with William Penn," Pennsylvania's founder: Joyce Mosley and John Montier Pickens, Zoom interview of November 3, 2023, recorded 1 p.m. (with interviewees' permission) by author-interviewer Donald Scott Sr., MP4. Length 02:56:20, video 1234272029.

Epilogue

1. Valerie Bando-Meinken, "A Walk Down Memory Lane with William Pickens III," *Dan's Papers*, June 26, 2018, accessed October 29, 2023, https://www.danspapers.com/2018/06/a-walk-down-memory-lane-with-william-pickens-iii/.
2. Ibid.
3. Ibid.
4. "William Pickens III Memorial Service," First Baptist Church of Bridgehampton, streamed live on October 9, 2021, YouTube video, 1:53:43, https://www.youtube.com/live/pon373ssZfE?si=2BetItfKVZUC0ReQ.
5. "Rev. Tisha Dixon-Williams—Pastor, Author, and Innovator," Whosthatladymin.com, 2020, accessed October 20, 2023, https://www.whosthatladymin.com/pastor-tisha-dixon-williams-bio.
6. "William Pickens III Memorial Service."
7. Ibid.
8. "Rev. Tisha Dixon-Williams—Pastor, Author, and Innovator."
9. "William Pickens III Memorial Service."
10. Joshua Du Bois, "Dr. Suzan Johnson Cook Sworn-In as New Ambassador-at-Large for International Religious Freedom," National Archives, June 3, 2011, accessed October 20, 2023, https://obamawhitehouse.archives.gov/blog/2011/06/03/dr-suzan-johnson-cook-sworn-new-ambassador-large-international-religious-freedom.
11. "William Pickens III Memorial Service."
12. Carlton McLellan, "SUZAN DENISE JOHNSON COOKE (1957-)," Blackpast.org, November 23, 2015, accessed October 20, 2023, https://www.blackpast.org/african-american-history/cook-suzan-denise-johnson-1957/.
13. "William Pickens III Memorial Service."
14. McLellan, "SUZAN DENISE JOHNSON COOKE (1957-)."
15. "William Pickens III Memorial Service."
16. Ibid.
17. Ibid.
18. "LOIDA LEWIS," University of Southern California Center on Public Diplomacy, 2023, accessed October 20, 2023, https://uscpublicdiplomacy.org/users/loida_lewis.
19. Ibid.
20. "William Pickens III Memorial Service."
21. Ibid.
22. Ibid.
23. "LOIDA LEWIS."
24. "William Pickens III Memorial Service."
25. Ibid.
26. Joyce Mosley and John Montier Pickens, Zoom interview of November 3, 2023, recorded with permission from the interviewees by author Donald Scott Sr., MP4. Length 02:56:20, video 1234272029.
27. Pitts, "'Richard Morrey, Gent.,'" 277.
28. A January 2017 transcribed version of the article, "MONTIETH GRAVEYARD: A Burial Ground for Colored People in Cheltenham," was emailed by a local historian to this author on March 4, 2018. The article indicates that a "John Murray," more than likely misidentified and in reality Cremona's longtime marital partner Richard Morrey (sometimes spelled Murray)—Richard did have a brother, John, who died as a young man—was buried about a mile from Edge Hill. "The singular place where this man of a century and a half ago, was put, at his direction, is on the left

hand side of the railroad, leading east, in Cheltenham township, quite near the Springfield Township line. This hole, or vault in some sense, which at one time was neatly arched, is up on the bank, well enough away from the cut of the railroad not to be interfered with by it. It is in an angle of fences that enclose fields and the spacious lawn of Mr. Clay Kemble, whose handsome residence and appurtenances are at the summit of a slope at the foot of which, but outside, and as we have stated, on a receptacle for old tin cans, fruit vessels, from the dwellings around."

29   Foner, *Paul Robeson Speaks*, 146. In a September 1943 letter to the editor (of PM magazine), Robeson complained about inaccuracies in an "article on Sunday, Sept 12" based on an interview "printed as released by the United Press." Robeson's letter provides perspectives regarding his role as Othello and related issues of race, "love, jealousy, pride and honor."

30   Ibid.

Index

abolitionism, 15, 21–22, 30, 45, 49, 68, 72–76, 88, 100, 123, 132, 143, 148, 153, 155–56, 161, 166–67
activism, 2, 10, 21–23, 49, 79, 102, 118, 128, 132–34, 151, 154, 161, 167–71, 182, 184, 189–91, 195, 212, 221
African Episcopal Church of St. Thomas, 21, 32, 75, 79, 137, 160
Allen, Richard, 21, 32, 37, 79, 110–11, 117, 135, 160, 202
Allen, Sarah *see* Beasley, Sarah
American Revolution, 2, 23, 32, 75, 97, 123–24, 128, 132, 140, 219
antislavery, 2, 15, 22–23, 30, 37, 45, 49, 56, 68, 74–76, 92, 100, 132–34, 143, 148, 153, 154, 156, 161, 166–67, 171
Arcadia University, 2, 27–28, 198, 209, 214
Army
    3rd Pennsylvania Artillery, 131
    United States Colored Troops (USCT), 164–65, 168
        2nd United States Colored Cavalry, 164–65
        6th United States Colored Troops, 131
        8th United States Colored Troops, 155
        22nd United States Colored Troops, 167
        24th United States Colored Troops, 165–66
        32nd United States Colored Troops, 166
        43rd United States Colored Troops, 131–32
        45th United States Colored Troops, 168–70

Barbados, 6, 13–15, 20–21, 29, 39, 45, 61
Beasley, Sarah, 67, 81, 85, 92, 110, 116, 202
Benezet, Anthony, 36–37, 49, 123
Bowser, David Bustill, 2, 133–34, 155, 166–69
Burlington, 2, 136, 141–43
Burr, Aaron, 68, 72–76, 80
Burr, John Pierre, 72–75
Bustill, Cyrus, 2, 79, 102, 128–34, 136–37, 139, 141–42, 161, 166, 171, 208
Bustill, Maria Louisa, 10, 134, 168–69, 171–76
Bustill Jr., Samuel, 2, 129, 137
Bustill Smith, Anna, 3, 130, 136

Camp William Penn, 2, 75, 131–34, 154–55, 164–70, 201
Caribbean, 1, 13–14, 16, 28, 50, 94, 101, 123–24, 134, 156, 191 *see also* Barbados
Catto, Octavius Valentine, 170
census, 22, 117, 140–41, 144–45, 148–49, 157–59, 168, 201–2, 206, 210, 216
Center for American Art, 199

Cheltenham Township, 1–3, 10–11, 42, 99, 106, 109, 115–16, 125, 133, 135, 138–39, 150, 200, 210 *see also* Guineatown, Limekiln Pike
Cherokee, 27, 185
Civil War
    American, 2, 3, 30, 75, 77, 131–32, 134, 138, 145, 147, 149, 154, 162–67, 169–70, 178, 201, 206, 212
    English, 35
colonialism, 12, 18, 20–24, 29, 42, 46, 55, 58, 66, 69, 71, 83, 85, 88, 97, 100, 125, 129, 131, 156, 159, 180, 182, 207–8, 219
communism, 182
Constitution, the, 17, 31, 96, 121, 155

Declaration of Independence, 71, 74, 93, 120, 216
Delaware Valley, 5, 10, 12, 129, 160
Du Bois, W. E. B., 2, 85–87, 136, 148, 157, 175, 179, 181, 189–90 *see also Philadelphia Negro, The*
Dunmore War, 125

Eagle Hotel, 135, 137–38
Edge Hill, 2, 3, 17, 33, 109, 113, 117, 120–21, 125, 127, 135–38, 142, 144–47, 150, 200–6
Emlen, Samuel, 142–43
Emlen, Susannah, 143
Emmons, Mary, 68, 72–73, 75, 80

fascism, 180–81, 189
Forten, James, 21, 79, 132, 134
Forten, Thomas, 21
Founding Fathers, 32, 45, 63, 137, 148
Fox, George, 16, 35, 38 39, 43
Frampton, William, 10, 38–39, 42, 46–47
Franklin, Benjamin, 15, 17–21, 25, 30, 32, 45, 53, 70–71, 88, 97, 108, 111, 159

Free African Society (FAS), 21, 32, 79, 128, 132, 137, 171 *see also* Allen, Richard, Jones, Absalom
Fry, Albert, 117
Fugitive Slave Act, 145, 149

Germantown, 14–15, 49, 66, 100, 118, 142, 145, 149, 151, 206
Great Fire of London, 37, 41
Guineatown, 3, 17, 33, 75, 79, 97, 101–2, 117–18, 120–21, 124–25, 127–29, 134, 135–51, 154, 167, 175, 200–14, 219–20

Haiti, 72–74, 103, 124, 156 *see also* Saint-Domingue
Hamilton, Alexander, 72–74
Hemings, Sally, 5–6, 63, 65, 68, 72–73, 80–81, 91, 93–96, 105–7
Hope Lodge, 19, 59, 128
House of Representatives, 30, 73, 182
Hughes, Langston, 184, 196–97
Huguenot ancestry, 36–37, 124

India, 53, 72–73
Iroquois, 31

Jacobs, Harriet, 9, 94
Jefferson, Thomas, 5–6, 45, 63, 68–76, 80–81, 91–97, 106, 148
Jim Crow laws, 171–72, 194
Jones, Absalom, 21, 32, 79, 132, 137, 160

King Jr., Martin Luther, 191, 194
Korean War, 130
Ku Klux Klan, 189

Lay, Benjamin, 14–18, 45, 49, 148
Leech, Tobias, 11, 25, 97, 99, 115–16, 119
Lenape, 1, 5, 7, 8, 16, 19, 25–27, 31, 44, 103, 116, 137
Lenni Lenape *see* Lenape

Limekiln Pike, 2–3, 52, 110, 121, 123, 125, 137, 139, 144–45, 148, 150, 201–2, 204–6, 212
Lincoln, Abraham, 164, 166, 169–71
London Coffee House, 13, 18, 32, 55, 137
Long Island, 38–39, 42, 138, 184, 193–94, 198

Methodist, 71, 77, 206
    Episcopal Church, 3, 21, 32, 37, 79, 160, 177, 193, 206
Mississippi, 186, 188–89
Montgomery bus boycott, 191
Montgomery County, 1, 7, 20, 25, 27, 109, 117, 125, 131, 135, 146, 150, 201, 207, 210
Montier, Hiram Charles, 3, 6, 22–23, 68, 79, 103, 125, 144–47, 153–54, 160–81, 183–91, 198–201, 206, 215–16
Montier, John, 1, 3, 22, 94, 103, 118, 120–21, 123–25, 127, 129, 131, 133, 142, 144–46, 156, 198–99, 207, 215–16, 219
Montier, Robert, 143–44, 164
Montier, Solomon, 102, 118, 146–47, 151, 163–64
Mooney *see* Morrey, Cremona
Morrey, Cremona, 1–4, 5–10, 12–33, 36, 37, 44, 47, 50–61, 63–77, 79, 161, 168–69, 80–89, 91–101, 103, 105–10, 115–21, 123, 125, 127–28, 130–31, 134–36, 139, 141–44, 146, 168–69, 198, 201–2, 214–15, 219–21
Morrey, Elizabeth, 2, 128, 134, 136–37, 139, 161
Morrey, Humphrey, 1, 10, 11, 27, 35–40, 42–52, 55–60, 83, 93, 108–10, 119, 202, 215
Morrey, Matilda, 49
Morrey, Richard, 1, 2, 49–61, 63–72, 75, 79–80, 81–84, 92–93, 96, 97, 99, 103, 105–9, 111–13, 115–19, 128, 136–39, 161, 202, 215, 219–20
Mossell, Dr. Nathan Francis, 2–3, 103, 171–72, 175–76
Mother Bethel African Methodist Episcopal, 21, 32, 79, 160
Mott, Lucretia, 68, 75, 79, 133, 148, 154, 167
murder, 10, 14, 41, 60, 74, 82, 83
Murray, Caesar, 7, 27, 97–102, 120, 124, 129, 133, 138, 142–43

National Association for the Advancement of Colored People (NAACP), 2, 118, 136, 148, 175, 181–82, 184–85, 189–90, 197, 218
Naval vessel
    USS *Aroostook*, 164
    USS *Juniata*, 164
    USS *Princeton*, 163
    USS *Sassacus*, 163
    USS *State of Georgia*, 163
Native American, 1, 2, 5–7, 19–27, 43–44, 87, 124, 134, 165, 185, 194, 214–15
Negro Mooney, 1, 50, 58, 79, 108 *see also* Morrey, Cremona
New York, 2–3, 10, 35–42, 43–59, 61, 77, 88, 93, 95, 148–49, 164, 175, 184, 188, 191–98, 201, 207–8, 212–17
Northup, Solomon, 95 *see also Twelve Years a Slave*

Obama, Barack, 198, 217
Othello, 179–80, 182, 221
Oyster Bay, 10, 38, 39, 42, 215

Parks, Rosa, 191 *see also* Montgomery bus boycott
Pemberton, Israel, 8, 60, 111–12
Pennsylvania Gazette, 18–20, 25, 30, 70, 88, 108–9, 112

Penn, William, 2, 8, 10–11, 16, 20–21, 26–27, 35, 39, 43–48, 52, 58–60, 75, 102, 110, 131–37, 148, 154–55, 161, 164–70, 201
Philadelphia Museum of Art, 3, 103, 154, 198, 215–16
Philadelphia Negro, The, 85, 157 see also Du Bois, W. E. B.
Pickens III, Dr. William, 3, 27, 56, 91, 93, 103, 109, 148, 153–54, 175, 184, 188, 194–200, 209–10, 215–19
Powell, Colin, 196
Presbyterian Church, 49, 79, 137, 142, 171–76
Princeton, 2, 134, 138, 171–76, 216
  University, 173
Purvis, Robert, 22, 68, 76–81, 133, 167
Purvis, William, 68, 78, 80–81

Quaker, 1, 8, 23–26, 29–31, 35–49, 51–61, 66, 69, 79, 92, 99, 100–2, 108, 110–13, 116, 118–19, 123, 127–29, 132, 133, 142–43, 148, 150, 154, 159, 171, 174–75, 207

racism, 5, 64, 66, 86, 89, 92, 94, 100, 102, 120–21, 130, 155, 161, 163, 171 73, 178, 181–83, 189, 194, 197, 206, 220
rape, 10, 82 83, 85, 93, 96 see also sexual abuse
Revolutionary War, 17, 21, 23, 72, 75, 79, 103, 117, 120, 125, 127–29, 131–33, 208
Robeson, Paul Leroy, 3, 10, 22, 79, 102, 118, 134, 146, 163, 168–84, 197, 217, 221
Robeson, William Drew, 10, 168, 170–78, 183
Russia, 180–81, 188 see also Soviet Union

Sag Harbor, 184, 193–96, 198, 215, 217–18

Saint-Domingue, 156
Satterthwaites, 1, 5, 7, 9, 23, 25–31, 68, 79, 94, 106, 215, 219
sexual abuse, 94 see also rape
Shaw, George Bernard, 181
shoemaker, 98, 100–2, 124, 127, 139, 144–46
slaveholder, 5, 6, 10, 12, 15–17, 22, 23, 25, 29, 45, 59–60, 70, 78, 88, 92, 116, 128
Smithsonian, The, 15, 213
Society of Friends see Quaker
South Carolina, 9, 12, 13, 15, 29, 68, 76–78, 88, 131, 166, 185–87, 206
Soviet Union, 181–83 see also Russia
Street, Franklin R., 3, 146, 153–54, 158, 161–63, 198
Sully, Thomas, 160–61, 166

Tacony Creek, 115, 119, 139
Tubman, Harriet, 154–55, 164, 166
Twelve Years a Slave, 95 see also Northup, Solomon
Tyson, Reynier, 100, 124

Underground Railroad, 22, 68, 74–75, 79, 148, 154, 169, 171, 175, 200
Upper Dublin, 138, 141, 145–46

Washington, Booker T., 179, 187, 190
Washington, George, 17, 21, 23, 45, 75, 79, 96, 121, 125, 128, 130, 142, 148, 160–61, 208, 213, 216
WAVES, 188
West Indies, 9, 12, 14, 29, 188
Wheatley, Phillis, 33
Wilson, Woodrow, 173
women of color, 20, 75, 76, 80
Woodson, Carter G., 3, 36, 130, 136
Woolman, John, 45, 49, 123
World War I, 178, 189
World War II, 188, 190, 194–95